RECLAIMING POPULAR DOCUMENTARY

RECLAIMING POPULAR DOCUMENTARY

Edited by
Christie Milliken and Steve F. Anderson

INDIANA UNIVERSITY PRESS

This book is a publication of

Indiana University Press
Office of Scholarly Publishing
Herman B Wells Library 350
1320 East 10th Street
Bloomington, Indiana 47405 USA

iupress.org

© 2021 by Indiana University Press

All rights reserved

No part of this book may be reproduced or utilized in any form or by any means, electronic or mechanical, including photocopying and recording, or by any information storage and retrieval system, without permission in writing from the publisher. The paper used in this publication meets the minimum requirements of the American National Standard for Information Sciences—Permanence of Paper for Printed Library Materials, ANSI Z39.48-1992.

Manufactured in the United States of America

First printing 2021

Library of Congress Cataloging-in-Publication Data

Names: Milliken, Christie, editor. | Anderson, Steve F., editor.
Title: Reclaiming popular documentary / edited by Christie Milliken and Steve F. Anderson.
Description: Bloomington : Indiana University Press, [2021] | Includes bibliographical references and index.
Identifiers: LCCN 2020057344 (print) | LCCN 2020057345 (ebook) | ISBN 9780253056870 (hardback) | ISBN 9780253056887 (paperback) | ISBN 9780253056894 (ebook)
Subjects: LCSH: Documentary films—History and criticism. | Motion picture audiences.
Classification: LCC PN1995.9.D6 R373 2021 (print) | LCC PN1995.9.D6 (ebook) | DDC 070.18—dc23
LC record available at https://lccn.loc.gov/2020057344
LC ebook record available at https://lccn.loc.gov/2020057345

Dedicated to Jonathan Kahana

CONTENTS

Acknowledgments ix

1. Pop Docs: The Work of Popular Documentary in the Age of Alternate Facts / *Christie Milliken and Steve F. Anderson* 1

   Part I. Popular Documentary Today 13

2. Reclaiming the Popular for Public Interest Documentary / *Ezra Winton* 15

3. Public Television's Role in the US Documentary Ecology / *Patricia Aufderheide* 36

   Part II. Documentary Ecologies 55

4. On (Not) Falling from the Sky: Fly-Over Global Documentary as Capitalist Body Genre / *Zoë Druick* 57

5. Accelerating Deceleration: Slow Violence and Time-Lapse Cinematography / *Devon Coutts* 75

6. From Elegy to Kitsch: Spectacles of Epistephilia in *Food, Inc.* and Early Food Documentaries / *Sabiha Ahmad Khan* 91

   Part III. Short Forms and Web Practices 113

7. Errol Morris, the *New York Times*, Docmedia, and Op-Docs as Pop Docs / *Anthony Kinik* 117

8. Popular Music and Short-Form Nonfiction: Is the Web a Forum for Documentary Innovation? / *Michael Brendan Baker* 139

9. From the Essay Film to the Video Essay: Between the Critical and the Popular / *Allison de Fren* 157

Part IV. Auteurs, Politics, and Popularity   179

10. Errol Morris and the Ends of Irony / *Jonathan Kahana*   181

11. Vérité: Lauren Greenfield and the Challenge of Feminist Documentary / *Shilyh Warren*   200

12. *Citizenfour* and the Antirepresentational Turn: Aesthetics of Failure in the Information Age / *S. Topiary Landberg*   220

Part V. Documentary Genres   239

13. Of Kids and Sharks: Victims, Heroes, and the Politics of Melodrama in Popular Documentary / *Christie Milliken*   241

14. Strategies of the Popular Music Documentary's Recovery Mode / *Landon Palmer*   259

15. Assembling *Nanking*: Archival Filmmaking in the Popular Historical Documentary / *Dylan Nelson*   277

Part VI. Engaging Audiences   299

16. Virality Is Virility: Viral Media, Popularity, and Violence / *Alexandra Juhasz*   303

17. Populism, Participation, and Perpetual Incompletion: Performing an Urban History Commons / *Rick Prelinger*   324

18. The Armchair Juror: Audience Engagement in True Crime Documentaries / *George S. Larke-Walsh*   340

19. New (Old) Ontologies of Documentary / *Steve F. Anderson*   356

Index   371

ACKNOWLEDGMENTS

We would like to acknowledge the many individuals who have supported this project since its inception, especially our acquiring editors at Indiana University Press, Allison Chaplin and Janice Frisch. The manuscript benefited greatly from the press's meticulous review process, which included extremely insightful, generous, specific—and, of course, anonymous—feedback from reviewers to whom we will never be able to adequately express our respect and appreciation.

This volume is deeply inspired by and indebted to many years of association with the Visible Evidence community, with whom many of the ideas and topics included in the book were incubated, tested, and refined. Within this community, special gratitude is due to our longtime mentor and colleague Michael Renov, who set both of us on the path toward documentary studies many years ago at the University of Southern California and who continues to create pathways for generations to come. We are additionally grateful to our contributors for their patience and responsiveness at every stage of this process, and the even greater patience of our family members—especially Jay, Jack, Leo, Charlie, Emily, Holly, Quiller, and Ginger—without whose support none of this is even imaginable.

This volume is dedicated to the memory of Jonathan Kahana, whose untimely death as this volume achieved its final form represents an incalculable loss for the field as well as the many people who knew and loved him.

RECLAIMING POPULAR DOCUMENTARY

1

POP DOCS

The Work of Popular Documentary in the Age of Alternate Facts

Christie Milliken and Steve F. Anderson

Isolation and indifference are the enemy. With regimes of knowledge increasingly fragmented and politicized for short-term gain, the stakes of documentary media and collective discourses of truth are higher—and more difficult to negotiate—than ever. This volume aims to carve a space between the well-trodden domains of documentary studies and popular culture, arguing that it is at this conjunction that we find some of the most vital forms of engagement with the most pressing issues of our time. Through a series of individual investigations, *Reclaiming Popular Documentary* articulates a concerted sense of the interconnection between viewing subjects and the topics of documentary investigation that resonate most broadly. Whether we focus on popular entertainment genres, specific films or auteurs, or changing modes of exhibition and viewing, the stakes that loom large in all directions are nothing less than the functioning of democracy, the decency with which humans treat each other, and the ultimate survival of the planet. Of course, we do not suppose that documentary media offer the best or only platform to engage such issues, but we insist on the value of unflinching critique that targets the products of popular culture as well as the industries, infrastructures, and predispositions that produce them. Popular documentary is uniquely suited to oppose the drift toward isolation and indifference by bringing people together and inducing them to care about issues of consequence. By reclaiming the intersection of documentary and the popular, we hope to reinvigorate awareness of the capacity for documentary media to play a key role in mobilizing the power of collective intelligence, cultural awareness, and social action.

The renewal of documentary in recent decades has taken place in the context of significant social, environmental, technological, and geopolitical changes. In a time of proliferating voices, documentary functions as a global commodity, its distribution enabled by the rise of digital networks and social media, the increase in specialized cable programming, and the expansion of genres and festivals designed to appeal to broad publics. At the same time—and with notable exceptions—collective critical attention to "popular" documentary has remained relatively underdeveloped in the burgeoning field of documentary studies.[1] Indeed, among the many subfields of cinema and media studies, documentary studies has often seemed remarkably willing not only to *neglect* works that may be considered popular but actually to *malign* them compared with works that are more commonly privileged but less often seen. There are, of course, exceptions: a veritable subgenre of documentary publishing has accrued around a handful of—mostly white Western, male—auteurs such as Michael Moore, Werner Herzog, Errol Morris, Morgan Spurlock, and a few others. Several monographs on documentary published over the past decades devote chapters to specific films or subgenres that would be categorized as "mainstream," particularly recent work on environmental documentary, music, biography, and sports docs or even notorious festival or box office successes.[2] Any perusal of major film studies conference programs—including the pathbreaking, documentary-focused Visible Evidence—from past decades certainly confirms attention to popular documentaries on a case-by-case basis. But never before has a single volume assembled a deliberative, critical engagement with issues specific to popular documentary. Even the Visible Evidence book series published by University of Minnesota Press, an innovative collection of twenty-eight volumes dedicated to the study of documentary that ran from 1997 to 2014, produced no single volume that offers sustained engagement with the complex interstices of documentary studies and the popular.

Over a decade ago, Ruby Rich argued that "documentary studies has tended toward a kind of isolation: from other directions in cultural studies, from international perspectives on its own traditions, and from alternative methods for assessing standards of truth telling and representational veracity within documentary traditions . . . the coherence of documentary studies as practiced most normatively is sometimes bought at the expense of imaginative possibility."[3] While media studies, film studies, and cultural studies have widely expanded their objects of analysis, documentary scholars have tended to focus on traditional forms, embracing new critical models, to be sure, but ultimately sustaining the divide between "high" and "low" in terms of documentary practices, platforms, and publics. To some extent, this lacuna must relate to the lack of coordinated attention to popular appeal, spectatorial pleasure, and reception in documentary film scholarship. Yet despite the florescence of many popular subjects, forms, and practices, documentary studies has remained surprisingly inattentive to the role of documentary in popular culture.

Reclaiming Popular Documentary explores how the recent explosion of popular documentary troubles or enlivens existing theories and critical methodologies for understanding its role within a dense and rapidly changing landscape of popular media. This collection deliberately casts a wide net over a predominantly twenty-first-century time frame in order to represent and theorize popular documentary as a dynamic and varied subfield. It presents essays by both leading and emerging theorists as well as historians and makers who reflect critically on technological innovations, new articulations of old modes, documentary film festivals, changing distribution platforms and practices, privileged and underrepresented auteurs, and the redomaining of established genres, modes, and practices.

At earlier moments in the evolution of the field, the very notion of "popular documentary" might have seemed like an oxymoron, slipping into the large fissures separating documentary studies' sober discourse and postmodernism's playful recuperation of pop culture. With that said, we acknowledge that the history of documentary film is characterized by periods of intense productivity and florescence followed by moments of relative languish. Documentary has enjoyed many periods of popularity, with its emergence and consolidation around the feature-length format (perhaps most famously via the popular anthropological documentaries of Robert Flaherty); Soviet agitprop and European avant-gardist experimentation in the 1920s; its institutionalization and consolidation in Great Britain, the United States, and Canada in the 1940s; and particularly the vast apparatuses of investment and expansion during World War II in the service of the war propaganda, battle records, training, and indoctrination films. Direct cinema and cinema vérité as they emerged in the 1960s and 1970s constitute another period of intense productivity and formal innovation, with particular subgenres such a biodocs, music docs, identity politics documentaries, and natural history, historical, and movement documentaries continually in production and circulation. Our focus is on the ongoing period of productivity that began without abatement in the late 1980s and the amplification of scholarly attention to documentary that coincides with this proliferation, facilitated by the blockbuster successes in that decade and beyond with films such as Errol Morris's *The Thin Blue Line* (1988) and Michael Moore's *Roger and Me* (1989).

Reclaiming Popular Documentary builds on the momentum already well underway among documentary scholars to theorize an expanding range of nonfiction media genres and tactics: docudrama/dramadocs, reenactment, animation, documentary games, and virtual reality, to name only a few.[4] This anthology takes the discussion a step further by sharpening our understandings of documentary as a particularly vital form of media culture, preserving both a rigorous commitment to the "documentary contract" as well as concessions to fiction-based tendencies and the pleasures of the popular.[5] While questions of access to truth and the trustworthiness of media continue to be overshadowed by superficial debates over "fake news" and "alternate facts," *Reclaiming Popular Documentary* offers an insistent reminder that discourses of truth have never been reducible to a simple binary. The analytical tools and methods developed over many decades by scholars of documentary media bring much-needed historical and critical perspectives to the complex evolution of authority in fields from politics to journalism. By assuming popular media as a forum for serious analysis of social issues, this book asserts the relevance of documentary as a central component of today's media landscape.

In the context of cinema and media studies, documentary continues to be a particularly vibrant area of study, as evidenced by the publication of numerous documentary-related volumes in the last ten years. Yet a survey of this field reveals that "popular documentary" has been embraced within neither the realm of popular culture nor that of documentary. The voluminous (more than six-hundred-page) *A Companion to Popular Culture* (2016) from Wiley Blackwell, for example, includes only a single chapter devoted to documentary; and while popular forms (especially reality television and nature programming) are routinely referenced in documentary-oriented volumes, no previous book has explicitly articulated the concerns and stakes of documentary in terms of popular media.[6] We believe popular documentary occupies a position of adjacency and resonance with several particularly dynamic areas of documentary publishing and that the time is ripe for defining and claiming popular documentary as a significant area of intersectional scholarship.

Given the expansive terrain that the term *popular documentary* implies, this collection makes no claims to be exhaustive. In a sense, these essays cumulatively illuminate the multifaceted connotations of *popular* outlined by Raymond Williams in *Keywords* as variously "widespread," "well-liked by many people," "inferior kinds of work," work made with a sense of calculation to "win favor with the people," and/or "culture actually made by the people for themselves."[7] Our contributors were invited to establish their own take on what popular documentary means and to develop their arguments in relation to a common series of questions motivating the anthology as a whole and shaping its coherence. Accepting as axiomatic the ongoing resurgence of documentary, we ask what kinds of knowledge, theory, and practice are made possible by framing documentary *as popular*? What is the relationship between documentary and entertainment and between popular documentary and advocacy? Can popular documentary be productively reconceived in relation to genre, modes, or rhetorical forms? Assuming the popular is defined in contrast to other categories (either implicitly or explicitly), what might those other categories be? Can terms like *highbrow, lowbrow,* and even *middlebrow* be productively applied to documentary?

By positing the *popular* as a *productively* ambiguous term, our contributors engage a wide variety of texts and contexts: some films by well-established auteurs (such as Laura Poitras and Errol Morris), others by filmmakers who have had award-winning commercial and festival success but who generally remain off the academic radar, and still others that are collaborative and community-based projects, as well as more recent web-based, televised, or immersive projects. This anthology tactically integrates the voices of makers and scholar-makers along with more traditional historians and theorists of documentary. In keeping with our commitment to blurring the lines between popular and scholarly discourse, we find that creators bring a unique awareness of documentary's evolving role within popular culture. We are additionally interested in complicating the convention of asking makers simply to reflect on the process by which their work is created. Dylan Nelson's reflection on the role of archival footage in her historical documentary *Nanking*, for example, expands into a broad and theoretically grounded reflection on the complicated role of entertainment, narrative, and referentiality in the use of archival footage. Likewise, Rick Prelinger's account of his construction and staging of a series of film "events" engages issues of spectatorship, community, and liveness in particular spaces and times. Documentary filmmaker and scholar Allison de Fren focuses not on her own acclaimed work as a video essayist but on the historical and economic contexts in which videographic scholarship continues to blur the lines between textual analysis, essayistic video, and fan remixes. And in her contribution to this volume, longtime documentary filmmaker and scholar Alexandra Juhasz turns her attention not to motion picture media but to the cultural economy of the internet and the role and limitations of social media for spreading information and sustaining cultural debates. In combination, we view these perspectives as offering a crucial counterpoint to more traditional studies of documentary theory and history.

A subgenre of popular documentary that raises provocative ambiguities is that of the digital documentary, a permeably bounded category that includes web-docs and mobile and interactive documentaries, or "i-docs," as well as transmedia documentaries, documentary games, and various experiments with nonfiction in the domains of virtual and augmented reality. Here too, the definitional status of the *popular* remains fluid in relation to these emerging documentary forms. Simply because a work is distributed online and therefore has the potential to reach a global audience does not necessarily locate it within the realm of the popular. As Steve F. Anderson notes, the still emerging form of VR documentary, for example, is insistently promoted as a site of popular intervention in social and environmental issues, even though its total viewership achieves barely a fraction of daily reality TV broadcasts. While the recent generation of immersive documentary remains rooted in anachronistic conceptions of unitary and compliant modes of viewer experience, Anderson asks us to remember the lessons of history with regard to individual viewer agency and the potentials of resistant reading. What is at stake in this book's framing in terms of the popular is therefore insufficiently described in terms of the sheer numbers or geographic diversity of a given work's audience. Rather, the works selected for this volume orbit asynchronously around what we might tentatively call a "popularity-function," that is, works that engage discursively—whether intentionally or not, successfully or not—with issues that have broad, human consequence beyond the frame or beyond a given work's status as media object, sociopolitical advocacy, artistic expression, or commercial enterprise.

Mindful of the degree to which popularity can denigrate some documentaries and documentary forms, our framing of the popular in *Reclaiming Popular Documentary* remains attentive to the perennial frictions between art, advocacy, and entertainment. To that end, two contributors (Michael Brendan Baker and Landon Palmer) address one of the most popular and enduring subgenres, the music documentary, considering the myriad ways in which this evolving category has provided fertile ground for shaping star images, offering audiovisual records of live music events, promoting the anniversaries of classic albums and events, and contributing to narratives of popular and forgotten musicians, genres, and histories. While Baker asks what the implications of digital platforms have meant for short-form music docs and their proliferation, Palmer considers the recent resurgence of "recovery" docs—those that strive to rehabilitate forgotten or undervalued talent, often with the paradoxical goal of interrogating and reinforcing well-worn canons.

Veteran documentary historian and theorist Patricia Aufderheide focuses on the seminal role played by public television in the growth—and popularity—of American documentary from the late 1960s onward, arguing for its pioneering impact on the creation of historical mini-series, science series, the personal essay genre, and long-form investigative documentary. Public broadcasting, she argues, also continues to play a crucial role for independent documentarians who prize an authorial voice (Ken Burns and Fred Wiseman being notable examples), since the proliferating "factual programming" marketplace tends to demand conformity to a more branded form of nonfiction product. As Aufderheide contends: "Public TV's role in funding and showcasing social issue, point-of-view documentary has had everything to do with documentary filmmakers taking coordinated, political action [writ large]."

Jonathan Kahana turns to the work of Errol Morris, observing a tropological shift across his so-called War Trilogy from irony to the excuse. Reading both utterances as negative speech acts, or "counterperformative speech acts," Kahana considers the *unpopularity* of *The Unknown Known* and *Standard Operating Procedure*, in terms of this rhetorical shift (in marked contrast to the enormous critical and commercial success of *The Fog of War*). What Kahana finds in the "self-enclosed discursive economy" of the former/disgraced Abu Graib soldiers Morris interviews in *Standard Operating Procedure* is less the performance of a confession—or gesture to truth—than "self-exculpating excuses" with no measure of external reference to truth at all. This tension between sympathetic treatment of interviewees and their troubled and troubling encounter with bureaucratic state speech leads Kahana to a sharp rebuke of Morris's rhetorical turn. Another chapter on the work of Errol Morris similarly tackles his less popular, or *popularly written about*, work for the *New York Times* Op-Docs series. Anthony Kinik explores convergences between the newspaper and documentary, using Morris's contribution to the series and his writing for the Opinionator column, to argue for the transformative role of this new subgenre of online documentary circulating under the umbrella of establishment news journalism.

Another vital and hugely popular subgenre—the ecodocumentary—is elaborated in chapters by Devon Coutts, Zoë Druick, and Sabiha Ahmad Khan, who explore formal trends (time-lapse and aerial photography) as well as representational strategies (infographics) in their engagements with films about disappearing glaciers, bleaching coral, global panoramas, industrial food production, and agribusiness. These chapters engage the ethics and politics of environmentalism alongside formal/aesthetic trends across many key films—for example, *Chasing Coral*, *Chasing Ice*, *Planet Earth*, and

Food, Inc.—of the past two decades. Concurrent with the proliferation of ecodocumentary, the rise of critical festival studies and the place of dedicated documentary film festivals offers a crucial, emerging area of scrutiny. Ezra Winton's contribution to the collection offers a much-needed consideration of documentary festival studies that addresses the politics of programming, curation funding, profitability, and entertainment in relation to Toronto's annual Hot Docs Festival. Like others in this volume, Winton brings deliberative skepticism to his assessment of the popular. Tracking the rapid growth and emerging success of Hot Docs, Winton invites consideration of what "popular" documentary means, how commercialization and audience attendance become part of the festival's calculus, and how its gatekeepers operate in a festival context.

Conspicuously underdeveloped in the contemporary documentary publishing landscape is sustained attention to the intersections between specific fiction and nonfiction genres, such as melodrama and suspense or crime thrillers, and studies explicitly motivated by issues such as contemporary feminist politics. Shilyh Warren, for example, simultaneously explores the slick reality TV aesthetics informing the work of feminist auteur Lauren Greenfield and recovers and interrogates a specific feminist vérité tradition that informs that filmmaker's undertheorized body of work. Another genre that circulates alongside reality TV, the crime thriller, specifically the true crime serial—has led to the hugely popular criminal justice and *in*justice forms. George S. Larke-Walsh and S. Topiary Landberg consider the tactics of fictive and representational strategies in their exploration of crimes and criminality in *Making a Murderer* and *Citizenfour*, respectively. Landberg reads an anti-representational turn across a range of popular post 9/11 documentaries, concentrating specifically on Laura Poitras's portrait of Edward Snowden, noting its vacillation between observational tactics and strategies of the documentary thriller, foregrounding cover-ups, obfuscation, and representational failure. Similarly, Christie Milliken stakes a claim for reading documentary in relation to melodrama, arguing that although the relationship between melodrama and documentary is certainly acknowledged in popular *criticism* of many mainstream documentaries, the older, pejorative connotation of the mode—long since banished from the study of *fiction* and melodrama—can fruitfully animate our theoretical engagement with documentary studies proper. Milliken asks that if we accept—as many film scholars have argued—that melodrama is "a system for making sense of experience,"[8] how can we continue to ignore its pervasiveness as a mode in documentary itself?

Reclaiming Popular Documentary is divided into six sections, each of which maps a specific area of practice or theoretical concern within popular documentary, staging implicit debates among authors and providing diverse perspectives on each area of investigation. Each section includes a brief introduction that situates the work of each chapter in relation to the section's theme. The volume offers a contemporary survey that is also mindful of the past, defining and analyzing the most urgent, neglected or emergent issues in today's contested discourses of truth. The eclectic mix of essays reflects our goal for this collection: to offer energizing ways of thinking about the popular in relation to documentary and documentary in relation to the popular. We seek a critical frame to position documentary scholarship and its favored objects of study in productive tension with issues of advocacy, entertainment, and broad social consequence. Bringing long-standing issues of nonfiction expression into dialogue with varied conceptions of the popular, we hope to forge critical pathways that both illuminate neglected issues from the past and position the field to engage emerging forms of documentary in the future.

In a moment when documentary's claims to truth and authenticity are most doggedly challenged, this volume insists that what is at stake in contemporary discourses of truth and their contestation is neither abstract nor academic. Instead of counterposing a well-worn and overly simplified dichotomy between truth and fiction, these essays help reframe *the popular* in documentary by better understanding "how documentary uses the strategies of fictional construction to get at truths."[9] Our goal is to collect material that students, scholars, and interested documentary viewers may already be familiar with, or at least have access to, especially with the rising popularity of streaming sites and the archive of popular documentary material it provides. We hope that this diverse collection will engage students and scholars interested in the politics, aesthetics, and ethics of popular culture grounded in a mode that aligns—however tortuously—with claims to the real and from there to better understand our world, the ways we represent it, and our ability to change it.

Notes

1. Some recent titles include: Benson and Snee, *Michael Moore and the Rhetoric of Documentary*; Bernstein, *Michael Moore*; Middleton, *Documentary's Awkward Turn*; Ames, *Ferocious Reality*; Ricciardelli, *American Documentary Filmmaking in the Digital Age*; Rothman, *Three Documentary Filmmakers*; and the more journalistic McCreadie, *Documentary Superstars*.

2. A very small sample would include Duvall, *Environmental Documentary*; Smaill, *Documentary*; Chris's *Watching Wildlife*; and Hogarth, *Realer Than Reel*. Just one example of a

documentary film that has sustained substantial (critical) popularity across multiple platforms and disciplines (including environmental, anthropological, ethnographic, geopolitical, and globalization studies) would be Hubert Sauper's *Darwin's Nightmare* (2004).

3. Rich, "Documentary Disciplines," 108–113.

4. Some of the most provocative essays to offer insightful overviews of the state of documentary practice and its emergence "into the spotlight" over the past few decades include: Rich, "Documentary Disciplines"; Arthur "Extreme Makeover"; L. Williams, "Mirrors without Memories"; and Aufderheide, "Changing Documentary Marketplace."

5. In several of his insightful overviews, Paul Arthur remarks on the "polemical dialogues both with previous nonfictions and styles and with reigning codes of dominant cinema in commercial documentary fare." Here he is certainly talking about "popular documentary" without invoking the term. See Arthur, "Jargons of Authenticity," 109. In "Extreme Makeover," Arthur asks, tellingly, "whether audiences respond to documentaries because of comforting similarities or because of discernible differences from other commercial modes?" (23).

6. One of the most prolific subgenres of popular documentary, the sports documentary, is the subject of numerous journal articles as well as the edited anthology Ingle and Sutera, *Genre and Gender in Sports Documentaries*. Here again, the emphasis may be on a popular sport or star athlete(s), but it is generally not a critical engagement with these texts in relation to the popular. Keith Beattie offers an illuminating chapter on popular surfing films in *Documentary Display*.

7. R. Williams, *Keywords*, 236–237.

8. Brooks, *Melodramatic Imagination*, xvii.

9. L. Williams, "Mirrors without Memories," 20.

References

Ames, Eric. *Ferocious Reality: Documentary According to Werner Herzog*. Minneapolis: University of Minnesota Press, 2012.

Arthur, Paul. "Extreme Makeover: The Changing Face of Documentary." *Cineaste* 30, no. 3 (Summer 2005): 18–23.

———. "Jargons of Authenticity (Three American Moments)." In *Theorizing Documentary*, edited by Michael Renov, 108–134. New York: Routledge, 1993.

Aufderheide, Patricia. "The Changing Documentary Marketplace." *Cineaste* 30, no. 3 (Summer 2005): 24–28.

Beattie, Keith. "Nonfiction Surf Film and Video: Sick, Filthy and Delirious." In *Documentary Display: Reviewing Nonfiction Film and Video*, 108–128. New York: Wallflower/Columbia University Press, 2008.

Benson, Thomas, and Brian Snee, eds. *Michael Moore and the Rhetoric of Documentary*. Carbondale: Southern Illinois University Press, 2015.

Bernstein, Matthew, ed. *Michael Moore: Filmmaker, Newsmaker, Cultural Icon*. Ann Arbor: University of Michigan Press, 2010.

Brooks, Peter. *The Melodramatic Imagination: Balzac, Henry James, Melodrama, and the Mode of Excess*. New Haven: Yale University Press, 1995.

Burns, Gary, ed. *A Companion to Popular Culture*. New York: Wiley Blackwell, 2016.

Chris, Cynthia. *Watching Wildlife*. Minneapolis: University of Minnesota Press, 2006.

Duvall, John. *The Environmental Documentary: Cinema Activism in the Twenty-First Century*. New York: Bloomsbury Academic, 2017.

Hogarth, David. *Realer Than Reel: Global Directions in Documentary.* Austin: University of Texas Press, 2006.
Ingle, Zachary, and David M. Sutera, eds. *Genre and Gender in Sports Documentaries: Critical Essays.* Lanham, MD: Scarecrow Press, 2013.
McCreadie, Marsha. *Documentary Superstars: How Today's Filmmakers Are Reinventing the Form.* New York: Allworth, 2009.
Middleton, Jason. *Documentary's Awkward Turn: Cringe Comedy and Media Spectatorship.* New York: Routledge, 2015.
Renov, Michael. *The Subject of Documentary.* Minneapolis: University of Minnesota Press, 2004.
Ricciardelli, Lucia. *American Documentary Filmmaking in the Digital Age.* New York: Routledge, 2018.
Rich, B. Ruby. "Documentary Disciplines: An Introduction." *Cinema Journal* 46, no. 1 (Fall 2006): 108–115.
Rothman, William, ed. *Three Documentary Filmmakers: Errol Morris, Ross McElwee, Jean Rouch.* Albany: SUNY Press, 2009.
Smaill, Belinda. *The Documentary: Politics, Emotion, Culture.* New York: Palgrave MacMillan, 2010.
Williams, Linda. "Mirrors without Memories: Truth, History, and the New Documentary." *Film Quarterly* 46, no. 3 (Spring 1993): 9–21.
Williams, Raymond. *Keywords: A Vocabulary of Culture and Society.* Oxford: Oxford University Press (1985).

CHRISTIE MILLIKEN is Associate Professor in the Department of Communication, Popular Culture, and Film at Brock University. She is author of journal articles and book chapters on sex education film and video, 1960s cinema, and AIDS video activism.

STEVE F. ANDERSON is Professor of Digital Media in the UCLA School of Theater, Film, and Television and in the Department of Design Media Arts. He is author of *Technologies of History: Visual Media and the Eccentricity of the Past* and of *Technologies of Vision: The War between Data and Images.*

PART I.
POPULAR DOCUMENTARY TODAY

We begin with two chapters offering an overview of the state of popular documentary today. While documentary has found its way into numerous corners of the media landscape, the contemporary exhibition contexts of public television and popular festivals reveal distinct aspects of these two poles of popular documentary consumption. In both chapters, a central tension exists between the costs and benefits of pursuing radical or alternative modes of documentary versus embracing varying degrees of popular acceptance. In juxtaposition, these two chapters provide both historical context and a critical paradigm that resonate throughout the remainder of the book.

Taking the hugely successful Toronto Hot Docs Film Festival as his case study, Ezra Winton chronicles the rapid growth, professionalization, and commercial orientation that have transformed the community and progressive-oriented documentary politics that inspired the festival's early iterations. Winton considers the stakes of commercialization and success from a "critical festival studies" perspective, using Morgan Spurlock's film *POM Wonderful: The Greatest Movie Ever Sold* (2011) to argue against the mainstreaming of documentary and documentary film festivals. By advocating for a reclamation of "the popular" in the public interest documentary against the neoliberal "private interest documentary auteurism" seen in so many mainstream "premiere" films, Winton considers what is sacrificed in the age of the festival, arguing for a slow, deliberative, decelerated festival experience.

In her overview of documentary exhibition and the politics of public broadcasting, Patricia Aufderheide explores the critical role of PBS and especially ITVS in shaping the contemporary documentary landscape. Chronicling the influence of the 1960s mainstream, journalistic mode of televisual public affairs documentary, counterposed with an organized documentary community whose members have fought to have their work included on the network, Aufderheide sees a resulting formal and topical expansion of expression. She considers the rise of specific documentary styles and mini-genres that resulted from the embattled politics of public broadcasting, concluding that the small, marginal space created on public TV for independent documentary has both permitted a widening of expression in the public sphere while also forcing documentary filmmakers to make work accessible to broad, national television audiences.

2

RECLAIMING THE POPULAR FOR PUBLIC INTEREST DOCUMENTARY

Ezra Winton

As documentary festivals advance agendas apace with the steady commercial enclosure of the cultural and social commons, and as film festival scholarship has a tendency to describe and revere large commercial festivals, I am compelled to consider the ways in which documentary can continue to be a promising site of cultural participation, radical intervention, and public interest. With that in mind, this chapter contributes to what I have called "critical festival studies," a designation for emerging scholarship that in part critically tracks how major festivals like Toronto's Hot Docs Canadian International Documentary Festival govern documentary's deviation from its established edifying "populist" commitment.[1] My intention is to engender a broader conversation about what it means to reclaim or rehabilitate populist programming in the service of public interest. By that, I refer to films that are made and curated with social and collective values placed above private, commercial values. In order to enter that discussion, I contend, we must first carefully look at the shifting terrain of *the popular* in film and the ways in which festivals—Hot Docs in particular—are calibrating and impelling their programming with commercial fare meant to attract. In particular, the festival leverages flashy productions to open the annual event, which function as *keystone films* that infuse the entire genre and production milieu of documentary with their pervasive form. An archetypal example of this kind of keystone film is Morgan Spurlock's *POM Wonderful Presents: The Greatest Movie Ever Sold* (2011), which I examine in detail before moving on to a brief discussion of the connectivity between popularity and speed. What follows is motivated by the possibility of reclaiming the popular for public interest documentary, and to that end, I conclude by tying commercial enclosure concerns in documentary to the need for *decelerated* festivals.

Gauging the Popular Form

The Economist, a mainstream publication that doesn't leap to mind when thinking about film culture, once gauged the verve of documentary, declaring the following: "Once marginalised as the dull work of worthy film-makers, documentaries are increasingly appealing to the mainstream."[2] What exactly are the forces that have aided documentary's ascension to the mainstream? At what point does one pronounce a media artifact or an artwork appealingly "popular" and what exactly does that descriptor say about, in this case, a documentary film? Is a documentary popular if it has a score higher than ninety on Metacritic or Rotten Tomatoes or if it is acquired by Netflix, which (infamously) does not share its viewing metrics? Is a doc popular when it wins prestigious awards like the Palme d'Or at Cannes or an Oscar in Hollywood (or is it popular if it is merely forwarded or nominated)? Is popularity measured in audience numbers, and if so, is there a difference between YouTube plays, in-flight views, and tickets sold at brick-and-mortar cinemas? Or, like the creation of the cinematic canon itself, is a film popular when cultural gatekeepers and those with sumptuous symbolic capital prop it up, manifesting its notoriety by the very nature of the lofty curatorial company it keeps?

Etymologically speaking, *popular* pertains to a certain affirmative relationship with "the people," as in the word's Latin root *populus* (people), which telegraphs to the late Middle English usage, "prevalent among the general public," up to its description of art and entertainment in the early nineteenth century—"favoured by people generally"—a popular documentary then would be one admired and liked by "the people." Who exactly these people are and why they like the documentary in question are of course major keys to unlocking the puzzle of audience appreciation. I could point out that most of my family has never heard of the majority of the documentaries that have played festivals or even won awards. Nor, for that matter, have millions upon millions of other folks across the globe.

This fact of diminished visibility and knowability for documentary in the larger mainstream mediascape became strikingly evident to me several years ago in Toronto during the Hot Docs documentary film festival. I was debating with one of the festival's top stewards about corporate sponsorship (Coca-Cola had been invited to represent the environmental film section) and had worked myself into quite a tizzy, due in part to the cultural bubble effect: I experienced the Hot Docs festival as one of the most important cultural events of the year, unintentionally inflating its significance, perhaps. During the parley, the festival's manager looked at me and then gestured to the crowded Toronto sidewalk, which was full of hustling and bustling pedestrians, and said,

"How many of these people do you think have even *heard* of Hot Docs, much less care about these ethical questions we're debating?" It was a sobering point that still serves to remind me of documentary's status in the "attention economy," where according to Richard A. Lanham, the myriad "stuff and fluff" that commands our attention tends toward the dramatic and fantastic rather than the austere and pedantic, the unsexy qualities long associated with documentary.[3] So it would seem that "popularity" is also about the shape of the wedge (as in who is doing the appreciating), not just the portion of the pie. Yet in our current neoliberal, individual-fetishizing capitalist ordering system for culture, counting is crucial and numbers are king, a calculating fact of the tyranny of accumulation, whether via the accretion of festival audience numbers or pecuniary denominations earned on a production's commercial returns. Still, defining "ordinary people" (such as those walking along on that busy Toronto street), as Raymond Williams once pointed out, is as vexing as defining "culture."[4]

Much the way a "loss leader" discount item attracts customers to big-box stores where shoppers will then spend money on other items that reward the seller with marked-up profits rather than discounted losses, opening festival films at Hot Docs, which is the largest documentary festival in North America, draw in customers with their own kind of bargain: the experience of a documentary that is entertaining and upbeat and that, despite the genre's reputation for disruption, certainly won't disrupt a nice night out (with discomforting politics or aesthetic complexity). The opening-night film form, which constitutes a kind of popular documentary for its commercial ambitions or relations, may not appear worth any worry should it remain an exception to the rule, whereby the rest of a festival's programming resembled something differentiated from opening night. But forty-nine-dollar, front-aisle microwaves beget discount stores that eventually dot the landscape. As an archetypal "leader," this type of film—a kind of keystone film discussed later—is increasingly shaping festivals' programs, and this trend is evident at Hot Docs.[5] It is this kind of populism—a cultural populist mass appeal kind of popularity that communication studies scholar Jim McGuigan has probed in his books *Cultural Populism* (1992) and *Cool Capitalism* (2009), to which I now briefly turn.

On Cultural Populism and Hot Docs

Populism is regularly positioned as the antithesis to elitism—a term signifying a framing of politics and culture that is considered more exclusive and intellectual and therefore historically and contemporarily more refined and dignified, although this is, as McGuigan asserts, shifting as academia increasingly engages seriously with popular and mass commercial culture.[6] McGuigan describes "cultural populism" in his book by the same name as an "intellectual assumption" concerning the "symbolic experiences and practices of ordinary people," and as such it is a framing mechanism for discussions concerning art and culture.[7] As he goes on to say, once again unpacking and deconstructing "ordinary people" is altogether another endeavor, and the term proves slippery with regards to a solid shared understanding and concise definition.

Cultural populism as an intellectual pursuit finds its roots in cultural studies and the theoretical orientation that positions audiences who consume popular media as active agents in the construction of meaning. Cultural theorists like Raymond Williams and Stuart Hall helped justify the study of popular media—such as daytime soaps on television—as well as their associated audiences. Hall's encoding-decoding thesis suggested mainstream and popular media could have multiple readings, or meanings, depending on the viewer and their attendant relations (to economy, culture, history, race, gender, etc.). Stuart Hall and Tony Jefferson's theory of "resistance through rituals" was applied to readers of romance novels, watchers of horror film, and listeners of pop music, all with the understanding that popular media is a worthy subject to take seriously in the academy, which had hitherto regarded those who consume/experience it as sheepish masses.[8] This work provided a theoretical companion to socialism, feminism, antiracism, and prolabor movements and politics, yet it is also useful in validations of contemporary capitalist culture. McGuigan clarifies, "Cultural populism in cultural analysis certainly came from the Left, initially neo-Marxist socialism, followed by feminism and anti-racist multiculturalism. Yet, the positions it took in the 1980s and since have unwittingly been homologous with neo-liberalism."[9]

A focus on consumption, consumer sovereignty, and the privileging of choice have, McGuigan argues, led cultural studies down a path that is positioning the theoretical work of cultural populism neatly within the confines of a neoliberal economic and political order.[10] He continues, "In fact, consumption became the cardinal term of a one-dimensional form of cultural-populist analysis. The audience/consumer was not only active. This remarkable individual was virtually *the* source of meaning-making in cultural exchange, in effect, much more powerful than the agents of authorship and production."[11]

A tangible corollary to this theoretical prognosis is the staging of commercial film festivals like Hot Docs. Canada's preeminent showcase for nonfiction film maintains a steadfast focus on audience numbers as an indicator of success, illustrated by its lead line in each year's postfestival communiqué, such as the 2010 release: "The 17th edition of Hot Docs, North America's leading documentary festival, conference and market, took place April 29–May 9, 2010, and shattered audience rush screening records, delivered more guest filmmakers and subjects, and reaffirmed Hot Docs' place as one of Toronto's leading cultural events and one of the world's leading forums for the documentary industry."[12]

The festival foregrounds rush lines, likening sold-out screenings to success, as measured by popularity. The next paragraph of the release leads with "Total audience numbers increased over 10 per cent to reach 136,000."[13] This emphasis on audience growth fits tidily with neoliberal thinking on economic growth and suggests the audience member is a quantitative measure of success, in addition to the qualitative disposition (of taste) that would lead them to a festival like Hot Docs. While the reverence of steady growth is emphasized at Hot Docs and other large festivals, the qualitative experience created at festival screening spaces also lends itself to neoliberal consumer orientation: namely, abbreviated Q&As (which rarely exceed fifteen minutes) and a paucity of film-subject-related civil society and activist groups present at screenings. Hot Docs managers maintain that longer discussions and the inclusion of stakeholder groups (tabling, speaking, flyering) would negatively slow down the festival.[14] Efficiency (which is a cause and effect of the growth model, itself linked to popularity reckoning) trumps engagement. This is one linkage between commercial values and populist programming. Over the course of a quarter of a century, the festival has occupied a central role shaping documentary cinema and culture and has, as its tag line (seen on its website) suggests, led the charge on curating films that are both "outspoken" and "outstanding." It is to Hot Docs programming I now turn, specifically to an archetypal popular, opening-night doc that epitomizes what I call the "private interest documentary."

Social Change You Can Bank On: *POM Wonderful* as (Popular) Private Interest Documentary

The devilish dance between entertainment and social change has in recent years reached a fevered pitch at many documentary-focused festivals across the minority world,[15] where it would seem there is some support for TV guru Evan Shapiro's claims when he, speaking of the new "social action entertainment" channel Pivot, declared, "Remember, it's entertainment that inspires social change. . . . It's not social change that's entertaining."[16] Here in Canada, opening films have continued to provoke audiences to ask (directly or rhetorically) the institutional caretakers of documentary questions concerning the equation between entertainment and community values, representational ethics and the public interest. In recent years Montreal's *Rencontres internationales du documentaire de Montréal* opened with the obviously racy and woefully sexist *Crazy Horse* (dir. Frederick Wiseman, 2011), and the 2017 opening film *24 Davids* (dir. Céline Baril, 2017) elicited several walkouts by audience members offended by the film's ethical dimensions.[17] Hot Docs, for its part, has fairly consistently opened with films that express the commercial-populist opener subgenre: mass-appeal entertainment values that come with either liberal or denuded politics. The fact that the vast majority of the Toronto festival's openers have been American (home of Hollywood), that many feature celebrity, and that nearly all have a flare for narrative drama and gratification reinforcement means singling out any one film ultimately works for the exercise of highlighting this specialized festival category.[18] Festival openers share popular doc qualities of mass appeal over complex critical engagement, and accordingly, 2011 opener *POM Wonderful Presents: The Greatest Movie Ever Sold* (*PWPTGMES*) is a documentary with private interests at heart—indeed a "docbuster" by Spurlock's estimation,[19] that has provided impressive commercial spoils for the director.

POM Wonderful is a 2011 documentary exposé on advertising and marketing, so it is fitting that the film opens with upbeat bubbly music and handheld panorama shots of advertising-saturated Times Square in New York City. Seconds in, Spurlock's signature buoyant and folksy voice initiates what is near nonstop narration with the following quip: "Everywhere you look these days it seems someone is trying to sell you something." This scripted observation amounts to a likely unintentionally ironic foreshadowing in the sense that Spurlock is also trying to sell the audience something: his film, his film's arguments, his film's sponsors' brands, and the Spurlock brand itself.[20]

The director then notes that "we" are inundated with advertising and quips, "What's a poor multimillion-dollar multinational corporation to do?" With his well-honed tongue-in-cheek style, Spurlock thus positions himself as a populist—with "the people." In this way, the American director-producer addresses *and* conjures the common good folk. His brand of folksy populism relies on a dichotomy of those pulling the strings—the corporate elite—and everyone else, at least at the outset. Notably, he sets this polarity up early in the film, positioning himself as a fellow traveler and guide—someone who has confronted corporations in previous filmic endeavors, thus having established the sense of trust and solidarity that has helped build his demagogic brand. From the outset, *PWPTGMES* hints at a kind of political activism, a wink, wink, nudge, nudge declaration of the vast inequity between the corporate elite and average citizens, which works to position the film as a "bastion of free speech"[21] combatting the powers that be while positioning Spurlock as both an interlocutor between private and public interest worlds and a sympathetic ally to those who, as he simply puts it, are always being sold something. The director, then, would seem to fit into the socially conscious category of filmmakers that Patricia Aufderheide describes as "interlocutors with the public—that is, viewers in their role as democratic citizens and active members of their own society. They associate knowledge with the act of getting involved with political change and monitoring corruption."[22] With Spurlock's previous social-issue documentary *Super Size Me* (2004) as calling card, his appearance as host of *PWPTGMES* certainly fits the bill as a trusted interlocutor fighting for and/or with the public, or "the people."

Not So Radical

Soon after the sarcastic comment about poor corporations Spurlock enthusiastically narrates, "If I'm going to make a docbuster it seems these companies are a good place to start."[23] A quick montage of brand logos segues into the filmmaker's inaugural meeting with industry elite—the two men behind the marketing and production company RadicalMedia. In keeping with a veneer of public interest activism, Spurlock remains on "our side" by taking us behind the scenes (the camera follows him entering these spaces, bringing the audience along), into the belly of the beast of the marketing world, beginning with this highly profitable company. With top-selling clients in Hollywood and assets across the media spectrum, RadicalMedia has made a huge mark in the cultural industries since launching in 1993 (incidentally the first year of the Hot Docs festival).

Thus, Spurlock's radical idea to make a documentary entirely funded by corporate sponsorship that includes in-film product placement is set in motion as he sits down in a brightly lit boardroom with RadicalMedia's founders, who, as fellow privileged men are wont to do, eagerly offer up expert advice on his project. From the jocular exchange that follows (the executives *love* Spurlock's idea to fill a documentary with sponsorship adverts), we do not learn that RadicalMedia is responsible for bullying and censoring media activists—in 2011, the marketing giant threatened organizers of a UK media activism forum with a lawsuit because they had used "Radical Media" in the conference's name.[24] The company has indeed trademarked the term and has aggressively policed infractions. The exclusion of these facts, an intriguing side story that could reveal the ugly, antipublic interest back end of the glossy populist marketing world, demonstrates Spurlock's motivations as an entertainer who is interested in producing commercially oriented products (docbusters) for consumption rather than as a progressive activist interested in animating social change concerning the negative effects of marketing and advertising. Indeed, Spurlock has built a wildly successful career by trading on documentary's public interest and social justice status while producing media and cinema that upholds, and in this case even protects and sanctifies, commercial culture and status quo sociopolitical systems.[25]

Buying In Values

In *PWPTGMES* Spurlock cultivates a false sense of public interest: the film claims to empower audiences with intimate/critical knowledge of the marketing world but offers only puckish narration that accompanies fast-paced montages of business meetings, Spurlock hamming with sponsorship products, and micro-interviews with a smattering of critical voices. The promise of empowerment is even acknowledged by RadicalMedia executive Robert Friedman when he says, on hearing the pitch for Spurlock's film, "When you first hear it, it is the ultimate respect for an audience." This is due to, according to subjects in the film, the level of brash honesty (regarding the corporate sponsorship of the film) the documentary seeks to showcase. Spurlock then responds, "We want it to be the *Iron Man* of documentaries,"[26] to which Friedman replies, "I *love* that you're selling out!" Later in the film another executive amends the earlier refrain and supplies the film with its tagline: "He's not selling out, he's buying in." The message resounds clearly: embracing commercialism doesn't contradict values associated with documentary's commitment to the public interest and social justice, and Spurlock's experiment is somehow different from selling out.[27]

As a filmmaker who makes popular documentaries (according to a number of methodological evaluations, including box office figures) and who indicated very clearly *PWPTGMES* was to be a popular, bankable documentary, or docbuster, Spurlock has championed business or commercial values over community or public interest values. Social values bound up in notions of cooperation, collective dependency, mutual aid, and equity are at odds with and under threat from commercial values espoused in the film—principally those of privatization, individualism, and commodification. Max Haiven refers to a "commodification of social values," where the market continues to claim the commons as commodity and where "these struggles to protect, reclaim and expand the sphere of autonomous values, to insist that capital has no business ruling over the spheres of life, are fundamentally radical in the sense that they strike at the 'root' of capital's modus operandi." This tension around values is bound up in the kinds of ideals a populist documentary filmmaker like Spurlock (and the institutions that champion him) espouse and those that are under threat of a commercial imperative.[28] Nicholas Garnham has identified this struggle over values in his masterful work *Capitalism and Communication*, in which he introduces a chapter titled "The Media and the Public Sphere":

> Our inherited structures of public communication, those institutions within which we construct, distribute and consume symbolic forms, are undergoing profound change. This change is characterized by a reinforcement of the market and the progressive destruction of public service as the preferred mode for the allocation of cultural resources; by a focus on the TV set as the locus for an increasingly privatized, domestic mode of communication; by the creation of a two-tier market divided between the information rich and the information poor, provided with increasingly homogenized entertainment services on a mass scale; lastly, by a shift from largely national to largely international markets in the informational and cultural spheres.[29]

At the end of the 1980s, when Garnham was writing *Capitalism and Communication*, traditional television was still "the primary exhibition venue for documentaries," even after a decade of austerity measures that constricted public broadcasting in Canada and set the public institution on the commercial path to format drama, bargain-basement syndicated series, and so-called reality TV.[30] It was in part a reaction to the calcified codes and conventions of documentary television that spurred the founders of Hot Docs to launch the festival a few years after Garnham's book was published.[31] While the centrality of broadcasting has waned for documentary,[32] one could simply swap "film festivals" for "TV set" in Garnham's analysis. Garnham was focused on dominant institutions of public communication, and I would argue that since the 1990s, a decade that ushered in the global expansion of niche film festivals like those focused on documentary, emphasis has shifted or expanded. Filmmakers increasingly turn to festivals as alternative platforms outside of the corporate entertainment regimes that spurn diversity, localism, politics, and public interest values. My concern is that the community/public values and registers of diversity heralded by "alternative" public communication institutions like Hot Docs are also "increasingly privatized" and risk producing "homogenized entertainment services" should private interest documentary become the populist champion of the festival set. This is, for me and for scholars like Haiven, a problem of values. Where Haiven argues that capitalism "is the ultimate system for assigning value to the world's wealth," he also outlines methods to struggle against the enclosure of the commons where communities return to their roles of arbiters and articulators of value allocation.[33] For members of the documentary community committed to public interest values, Spurlock's brand of nonfiction festival fare poses a concern, especially when elevated to the lofty heights of opening night.

Branded Documentary

As a documentary version of "branded entertainment"[34]—that is to say, brands are incorporated into the entertainment vehicle, often via visual placement (like a car or a soda) or in dialogue[35]—Spurlock's film presents the idea of corporate sponsorship as though it were a natural progression for documentary, as the filmmaker is shown "buying in" by joining forces with the very industry that is ostensibly on the critical chopping block. He wants the audience to buy in as well, selling the idea of wholesale complicity as a gratifying experiment in which the audience can partake, guided by the familiar and trusted director himself. As such, *PWPTGMES* promises to be a *different* consumptive experience (documentary as commercial entertainment with an empowerment twist), similar to the promise of differentiation at commercial festivals, where diversity (cultural, artistic, political, mediated) is still reducible to consumption. The notion of differentiation and novelty the film touts is not opposed to the forces of capital but is rather an extension of market logic into the realm of documentary cinema at the very level of production.

The film's hastily assembled content is mostly made up of abrupt interviews with marketing and Hollywood industry men and the odd critical point made by easy left targets Noam Chomsky and Ralph Nader,[36] intercut with footage of Spurlock shaking corporate gilded fists and enjoying the use of sponsorship products like Mini Cooper cars, clothing lines, food, and men's health and grooming products (the latter of which would lead Spurlock to direct a men's grooming celebrity vehicle called *Mansome*). Technically speaking, the film is poorly made: abysmal handheld camera work, inconsistent sound, choppy, frenetic editing, and a lack of a coherent, compelling narrative make for a substandard and unremarkable film, were it not for the novelty of its financial structure. This failure of technical acuity and compelling storytelling may explain why *PWPTGMES* never fulfilled Spurlock's promise of drawing $10 million at the box office, which if it had was to result in $1 million in sponsorship money from the POM Wonderful juice company.[37] It is likely for this reason the film has later been retitled *The Greatest Movie Ever Sold*, sans corporate pomegranate juice reference. Still, with a production budget of $1.5 million (mostly raised from corporate sponsors) and relatively high production value insert adverts for sponsors, where Spurlock breaks the main exposé thread of the film four times with thirty-second in-film commercials for gold sponsors Jet Blue, POM Wonderful, Mane 'n Tail, and Hyatt Hotels, *PWPTGMES* retains the hallmark ambitions of a popular, private interest documentary, or docbuster.[38]

Private Saves Public

The commodification of publicly subsidized services and media is normalized throughout *PWPTGMES*; if there is no money to make documentaries (from traditional sources like foundations, government programs, and broadcasters), then it is only reasonable to turn to the marketplace of advertising and embrace what Mark Fisher identifies as "capitalist realism"[39]—that is to say, there is no alternative to the ordering metasystem, of which commodification and marketing are functioning parts, and so we must succumb to what Garrett Hardin calls "the tragedy of the commons," where "every new enclosure of the commons involves the infringement of somebody's personal liberty."[40] To reclaim the popular documentary for public interest, we must identify and resist the enclosures on documentary culture, where not only films but also documentary institutions such as festivals serve private interests.[41]

Spurlock, who has told audiences "independent film has truly become the last bastion of free speech,"[42] is a filmmaker who trades on documentary's democratic, public interest, and educative qualities. Yet the business-savvy filmmaker appears—at least with his most recent projects—to have objectives other than democracy and freedom of expression in mind. Ostensibly, *PWPTGMES* is a behind-the-scenes film about the world of marketing, advertising, corporate branding, and sponsorship that promises to empower audiences with knowledge of the dark arts of corporate persuasion. Spurlock has claimed as much to the Hot Docs opening-night audience in 2011, pronouncing that those who watch the documentary will "learn more about advertising and marketing than they ever imagined" and that the film will "change the way you look at advertising, TV, and films." Where Spurlock's *Super Size Me* confronted the wholesome veneer of marketing and outright false claims made by food industry giant McDonald's, *PWPTGMES* is a film about working *with* similarly large and profit-motivated enterprises, not against them. Where *Super Size Me* elicited a damage-control campaign on the part of McDonald's as it attempted to counter the negative message in a popular documentary that convincingly showed the devastating health consequences of consuming the fast-food chain's products for one month, *PWPTGMES* extols the virtues of the multiple corporate partnerships between documentary production and brands featured in its frames.[43]

Fig. 2.1 The Morgan Spurlock action figure, released for Comic-Con (2012), represents an extreme expression of Spurlock's self-referential, commodified approach to documentary filmmaking as branded entertainment.

PWPTGMES is, using Spurlock's own assessment, a docbuster that has enjoyed circulation on the festival circuit and has gone on to achieve a respectable documentary box office success, with figures of $638,476 domestically,[44] as well as other commercial dividends including a distribution deal with Sony Classics and Netflix, sponsorship extensions and cross-platform sales through the film's "co-producing" brands like JetBlue Airlines (which promoted and played the film on flights) and POM Wonderful Juice.[45] *Deadline* reported that Spurlock went on to use his interactions with the brands featured in *PWPTGMES* to start a new company, Warpaint, "a commercial production company that will serve as a home for innovative directors who are looking to expand their craft into more diverse and lucrative opportunities."[46] Spurlock himself states, "After working directly with brands and advertising agencies in the placement exposé *The Greatest Movie Ever Sold*, as well as directing multiple commercial spots for other production companies, I saw an opportunity to create a much more director-driven entity,"[47] highlighting the point that, as an experiment in documentary commercial popularity, the project aims to reach well beyond the documentary itself. Spurlock's brand of private interest documentary auteurism conflates artistic freedom and commercial enterprise: for him, "buying in" isn't just good for business; it also nourishes artistic integrity.

Spurlock's commercial efforts have been heralded as innovative and positive, with his brand of combining entertainment with "social action" considered a winning combination in the festival world (as opening-night film no less) as well as in industry literature. Popular culture and cinema trade magazine *Realscreen* placed Spurlock fifth in its "Trailblazers 2012" list, where the account of the director's documentary trailblazing is peppered with the spoils of private interests: "Morgan Spurlock's diverse portfolio of creative ventures continues to expand year-on-year, and among the highlights for 2012 were the launch of a feature doc and web series with Yahoo!;[48] the launch of commercial production company Warpaint; a UK-based talk show; and even his own limited-edition action figure."[49] After outlining other deals with CNN and an upcoming 3D music video and documentary, the article concludes that "you would be hard pressed to find a filmmaker who has better capitalized on their initial success."[50] Further to that, Spurlock has a philanthropic side: *Realscreen* not only goes on to list Spurlock's achievements but also frames them in the context of advocacy for documentary ("a consistent champion") as well as the unique occasion of the filmmaker's project of "branded content" with a documentary film festival (DOC NYC). Lastly, in a nod to promotional convergence, *Realscreen* reports that Spurlock has joined the board of a *Realscreen* flagship initiative.

Doing Good, Staying Safe

While such configurations risk contaminating programming, where "[sponsors] can in turn, however, use their funding to pressure or influence the programme according to their own needs and wishes,"[51] Hot Docs organizers deny any such crossover between the business and art sides of the festival.[52] However, for a doc festival seeking mainstream status via popular mass appeal content (that trades on documentary's populist associations), *PWPTGMES* functions as the perfect consumer-oriented "doing good" opening film. Sean Farnel, at the time the head programmer of Hot Docs, admits that despite an aversion to formally and politically "safe" films, programming *PWPTGMES* was a safe decision:

> *POM Wonderful* was a good opening-night film at Hot Docs for a number of reasons. Its director is the closest we have to a star in documentary culture, and this presented us with one of the few opportunities we have had to do what fiction festivals do all the time. I like the film as entertainment; because it is a business story a lot in the audience will like it; I knew it wasn't dangerous. Chris [McDonald] and Brett [Hendrie] were nervous it would offend people. There are too many layers of irony to offend. It was a good opening-night film, but as a political film it's pretty soft. But the film is clever: there are a few moments of

self-awareness around consumerism and media and advertising but nothing in the film that will change people's lives.[53]

Here *PWPTGMES* has all the components of a docbuster: celebrity and fame, entertaining content, previously programmed at other festivals (enrollment eminence), and populist affinity (mostly by way of Spurlock). Farnel has said that these qualities have come to be the key ingredients for an opener because opening night is meant to be an overwhelmingly positive experience and "nobody wants anyone leaving depressed."

Conclusions: Keystone Films and Festival Deceleration

In their sober and crucial book on the dysfunctional hustle culture of academia, Maggie Berg and Barbara K. Seeber argue that "approaching our professional practice from a perspective influenced by the Slow movement has the potential to disrupt the corporate ethos of speed."[54] If commercial festivals are mandated to serve the public, they would do well to heed this advice. Documentary has carved out a place of publicness—either with the public's interest in mind or else not delineated by commercial interests—and requires complementary spaces of publicness to be appreciated and achieve its potential impact. The notion of publicness connects back to the roots of documentary as an educative alternative to commercial entertainment, as Zoë Druick maintains: "Indeed, the encouragement of citizen formation through the use of film in classrooms as an alternative to Hollywood fare was part of the self-conscious efforts that helped to usher in the documentary film as a form widely studied and used by educators."[55] Publicness is, then, connected to cultural citizenship, itself linked to the notion that the "freedom to participate in culture is contingent on both freedom from prohibition and freedom to act via political, economic, and media capacities."[56]

Yet public interest and popularity do not always arrive at the same point, which is why, in order to reclaim popular documentary, we must look to public interest documentary filmmaking and institutions that support such efforts. Commercial entertainment is, like capitalism itself, characterized by rapidity and a lack of self-awareness and introspection. The diminishing average shot length in Hollywood is one obvious indicator of how fast things are moving (from approximately twelve seconds in 1930 to two and a half in 2018), but also disconcerting are the ways in which documentary making and culture (including reception) has become systemically inculcated into an uncritical embracement of acceleration and volume: the pressure for higher audience figures each year, the hustle and bustle of wrangling spectators out of screening spaces before they have even had a chance to reflect, the persistence of "parachute filmmaking" (where filmmakers figuratively parachute into a community, capture the story, and then leave) and supersonic production-curation cycles (*Bee Nation* was pitched at Hot Docs in 2016 and opened the festival in 2017), and the quickness of programmers to alight on film fare that has received eminent enrollment by playing well-known, larger festivals like Cannes and Sundance, among many other registers and markers of haste. Slowing down may, as Berg and Seeber suggest, have the potential to disrupt populist private interest documentary making and programming.

I describe *POM Wonderful* and opening-night Hot Docs titles as keystone films because cultural managers and documentary elite have placed significant emphasis on them as central artifacts that lock the festival together. If opening films like *PWPTGMES* were so exceptional that they bore little resemblance to the rest of the documentary program architecture, there would undoubtedly be little cause for concern. But each year I attend Hot Docs I see more *POM Wonderful*s and fewer public interest or radical activist documentaries.

And as is commonly known, when you remove the keystone, the whole artifice tumbles.

Notes

1. See Damiens, "Festivals, Uncut," for a recent example of critical festival scholarship.
2. F. S., "The Shocking Truth."
3. Lanham, *Economics of Attention*, 10–11.
4. Williams, *Keywords*.
5. See Winton, "Good for the Heart and Soul."
6. Students can now take university courses on Drew Barrymore and earn degrees in entertainment studies.
7. McGuigan, *Cultural Populism*, 4.
8. Hall and Jefferson, *Resistance through Rituals*.
9. Ibid., 9.
10. Ibid., 9–14.
11. Ibid., 9.
12. Hot Docs, "*Hot Docs Annual Report*," 2.
13. Ibid.
14. Winton, "Good for the Heart and Soul," 231–233.
15. See a concise and useful explanation of this term in Shallwani, "The Term 'Majority World.'"
16. Benzine, "Pivot's Shapiro."
17. The walkouts have since morphed into a lengthy email discussion with several Montreal-based documentary filmmakers, programmers, and players.
18. See the appendix to this chapter for notes on Hot Docs opening films from 2000 to 2017 (prior editions had mixed opening events).

19. Spurlock purportedly coined this neologism—a term combining *documentary* and *blockbuster*—to signal a nonfiction film that achieves relative blockbuster status (see Friedman, "Word of the Week").

20. After the opening night Hot Docs screening and Q&A with Spurlock, POM Wonderful uniformed workers handed out free juice samples as the audience left the venue. One attendee was overheard describing it as a "marketing coup."

21. The full quote, from the jacket description for Chanan's *Politics of Documentary*, is as follows: "When the film-maker Morgan Spurlock told an American festival audience 'we live in a world where independent documentary film has truly become the last bastion of free speech' he won a round of applause from the packed house."

22. Aufderheide, "Mainstream Documentary," 21.

23. This is a reference to the top-four marketing corporations that according to the film control over 75 percent of US marketing.

24. Masnick, "Company Trademarks 'Radical Media.'"

25. While I was completing this chapter, news broke of Spurlock's confession of sexual misconduct. In his mea culpa essay, the director maintains his confident tone while admitting "I am part of the problem"; see Spurlock, "Part of the Problem."

26. The *Iron Man* franchise, produced by Paramount Pictures, is well known for bringing in massive capital returns through the twin marketing scheme of film promotion and in-film product placement—a branded entertainment approach earning it kudos from the advertising and marketing world and calls for boycotting from critics. See Rose, "Iron Man."

27. Spurlock has never been a public interest filmmaker committed to advancing a social justice agenda and, therefore, has no footing from which to sell out or slip and disappoint.

28. Haiven, *Crises of Imagination*, 49.

29. Garnham, *Capitalism and Communication*, 104–105.

30. Urquhart, "Film and Television," 22.

31. Winton, "Good for the Heart and Soul," 73–75.

32. A trajectory well documented by the Documentary Organization of Canada.

33. Haiven, *Crises of Imagination*, 2, 4.

34. See Sayre, *Entertainment Marketing*; Lehu, *Branded Entertainment*.

35. *Variety*'s "The Best Branded Entertainment of 2014" list provides examples of entertainment vehicles that "balanced" storytelling with crass marketing (see Graser, "Best Branded Entertainment").

36. In one "branded entertainment" sequence, consumer advocate and anticorporate crusader Nader is subtly mocked when Spurlock gifts him a new pair of shoes from one of the film's corporate sponsors while extolling the virtues of the company's products for the camera.

37. The insider-industry aspect of the film is indeed of interest to those working in the documentary milieu, as it offers a new method for funding and making docs in an era of damaging austerity measures, arts cutbacks, and channel closing for the genre.

38. Three of the four adverts can be viewed online; see POM Wonderful, "Exclusive Commercial"; Franklin, "Hyatt Commercial"; and Franklin, "JetBlue Commercial."

39. See Fisher, *Capitalist Realism*.

40. Hardin, "Tragedy of the Commons," 1248.

41. One example of documentary-serving private interests is the short film *Carbon for Water* (dir. Evan Abramson and Carmen Elsa Lopez Abramson, 2011)—an infomercial for a German company that produces water filtration equipment for sale in rural Africa, which was selected for Canada's preeminent environmental film festival Planet in Focus, among others.

42. Quoted from the book jacket for Chanan, *Politics of Documentary*.

43. *Super Size Me* has earned over $20 million worldwide and was made for $65,000 (see Franklin, "JetBlue Commercial"). The documentary also won and was nominated for an impressive raft of prizes (IMBd, "Super Size Me: Awards").

44. Box Office Mojo, "Greatest Movie Ever Sold." This figure doesn't come close to Spurlock's objective of earning $10 million, but *PWPTGMES* represents a docbuster-in-the-making, as it paved the way for Spurlock's future endeavors, including directing the 2013 boy band hagiography *One Direction: This Is Us*, which has earned nearly $70 million at time of writing (Box Office Mojo, "One Direction: This Is Us").

45. POM Wonderful promoted the film on its product packaging and in television commercials. Figures for the extended cross-platform and multiple product revenues are unavailable.

46. Fleming, "Commercials Company Warpaint." Following his admission of sexual misconduct Spurlock resigned as the head of the company in December 2017 (Morrison, "Morgan Spurlock to Leave").

47. Marshall, "Morgan Spurlock and Friends."

48. Both the film and series are called *Mansome*, concern men's grooming habits, and are hosted by two celebrity actors from Hollywood.

49. Realscreen, "Realscreen Presents: Trailblazers 2012, pt. 2."

50. Ibid.

51. Grassilli, "Human Rights Film Festivals," 42.

52. McDonald and Hendrie speak in interviews of the existence of a "Chinese Wall" between programming and sponsorship, which, according to Investopedia, is a term "used in the business world" to describe "a virtual barrier intended to block the exchange of information between departments if it might result in business activities that are ethically or legally questionable"; Kenton, "Chinese Wall."

53. Sean Farnel, interview by Ezra Winton, 2013.

54. Berg and Seeber, *Slow Professor*, 11.

55. Druick's study *Projecting Canada* looks at international and national liberal institutions and their constitutive effects on documentary as an educational form and, therefore, highlights the public nature of documentary from its early years as an instrument of governments and international relations.

56. Miller, *Reluctant Capitalists*, 73.

References

Aufderheide, Patricia. "Mainstream Documentary since 1999." In *The Wiley-Blackwell History of American Film*, vol. 4, edited by Cynthia Lucia, Roy Grundmann, and Art Simon, 1–24. New York: Blackwell, 2012.

Benzine, Adam. "Pivot's Shapiro: 'We Are a General Entertainment Network.'" *Realscreen*, March 28, 2013. http://realscreen.com/2013/03/28/pivots-shapiro-we-are-a-general-entertainment-network/.

Berg, Maggie, and Barbara K. Seeber. *The Slow Professor: Challenging the Culture of Speed in the Academy*. Toronto: University of Toronto Press, 2016.

Box Office Mojo. "The Greatest Movie Ever Sold." Accessed March 4, 2018. http://boxofficemojo.com/movies/?id=greatestmovieeversold.htm.

———. "One Direction: This Is Us." Accessed March 4, 2018. http://www.boxofficemojo.com/movies/?id=onedirection.htm.

Abramson, Evan, and Carmen Elsa Lopez Abramson (dirs.). *Carbon for Water*. YouTube video, September 3, 2014, 23:31. https://www.youtube.com/watch?v=Dj21IANhHDQ. Originally aired 2011.
Chanan, Michael. *The Politics of Documentary*. London: British Film Institute, 2007.
Damiens, Antoine. "Festivals, Uncut: Queer/Ing Festival Studies, Curating Queerness." PhD diss., Concordia University, 2017.
Druick, Zoë. *Projecting Canada: Government Policy and Documentary Film at the National Film Board*. Montreal: McGill–Queen's University Press, 2007.
Fisher, Mark. *Capitalist Realism: Is There No Alternative?* New York: Zero Books, 2009.
Fleming, Mike, Jr. "Morgan Spurlock and Keith Calder Launch Commercials Company Warpaint." *Deadline*, May 7, 2012. http://deadline.com/2012/05/morgan-spurlock-and-keith-calder-launch-commercials-company-warpaint-267673/.
Franklin, Abdul K. "Greatest Movie Ever Sold Hyatt Commercial." Vimeo video, March 24, 2011, 00:30. https://vimeo.com/21455577.
———. "JetBlue Commercial 'Greatest Airline Ever Sold.'" Vimeo video, March 24, 2011, 00:32. https://vimeo.com/21455606.
Friedman, Nancy. "Word of the Week: Doc-Buster." *Fritinancy: Names, Brands, Writing, and the Language of Commerce* (blog), August 25, 2011. http://nancyfriedman.typepad.com/away_with_words/2011/04/word-of-the-week-doc-buster.html.
F. S. [pseud.]. "The Shocking Truth." *Economist*, August 27, 2013. https://www.economist.com/blogs/prospero/2013/08/rise-documentary-film.
Garnham, Nicholas. 1990. *Capitalism and Communication: Global Culture and the Economics of Information*. London: Sage, 2009.
Graser, Marc. "The Best Branded Entertainment of 2014." *Variety*, December 22, 2014. http://variety.com/2014/biz/news/the-best-branded-entertainment-of-2014-1201373904/.
Grassilli, Mariagiulia. "Human Rights Film Festivals: Global/Local Networks for Advocacy." In *Film Festival Yearbook 4: Film Festivals and Activism*, edited by Dina Iordanova and Leshu Torchin, 31–47. St. Andrews, UK: St Andrews Film Studies, 2012.
Haiven, Max. *Crises of Imagination, Crises of Power: Capitalism, Creativity and the Commons*. Black Point: Fernwood Publishing, 2014.
Hall, Stuart, and Tony Jefferson, eds. *Resistance through Rituals: Youth Subcultures in Post-war Britain*. Working Papers in Cultural Studies no. 7/8. Birmingham, UK: Centre for Contemporary Cultural Studies, University of Birmingham, 1975.
Hardin, Garrett. "The Tragedy of the Commons." *Science*, n.s., 162, no. 3859 (1968): 1243–1248.
Hot Docs. *Hot Docs Annual Report 2010*. Hot Docs, 2010.
———. "Welcome to Hot Docs." Accessed April 2, 2018. https://www.hotdocs.ca.
IMBd. "Super Size Me: Awards." Accessed April 10, 2018. http://www.imdb.com/title/tt0390521/awards.
Kenton, Will. "Chinese Wall." *Investopedia*, July 3, 2020. https://www.investopedia.com/terms/c/chinesewall.asp.
Lanham, Richard A. *The Economics of Attention*. Chicago: University of Chicago Press, 2006.
Lehu, Jean-Marc. *Branded Entertainment: Product Placement and Brand Strategy in the Entertainment Business*. London: Kogan Page, 2007.
Marshall, Bob. "Morgan Spurlock and Friends Launch Commercial Production Company." *AgencySpy*, May 7, 2012. https://www.adweek.com/agencyspy/morgan-spurlock-and-friends-launch-commercial-production-company/33777/.
Masnick, Mike. "Marketing Company Trademarks 'Radical Media' Threatens to Sue Real Activist." *Techdirt*, May 3, 2011. http://www.techdirt.com/articles/20110501/00523214103/marketing-company-trademarks-radical-media-threatens-to-sue-real-activists.shtml.

McGuigan, Jim. *Cultural Populism*. London: Routledge, 1992.
———. *Cool Capitalism*. London: Pluto Press, 2009.
Miller, Laura J. *Reluctant Capitalists: Bookselling and the Culture of Consumption*. Chicago: University of Chicago Press, 2006.
Morrison, Matt. "Morgan Spurlock to Leave Production Company after Admitting Sexual Misconduct." Screenrant, December 17, 2017. https://screenrant.com/morgan-spurlock-production-company-sexual-misconduct/.
Nichols, Bill. *Introduction to Documentary*. 2nd ed. Bloomington: Indiana University Press, 2010.
POM Wonderful. "Exclusive Commercial from POM Wonderful Presents: The Greatest Movie Ever Sold." Vimeo video, April 7, 2011, 00:30. https://vimeo.com/22103356.
Realscreen. "Realscreen Presents: Trailblazers 2012, pt. 2." January 25, 2013. http://realscreen.com/2013/01/25/realscreen-presents-trailblazers-2012-pt-2/.
Robbins, Papagena, and Viviane Saglier. "Interview with Ezra Winton, Director of Programming at Cinema Politica." *Synoptique* 3, no. 2 (2015). https://synoptiqueblog.files.wordpress.com/2018/07/5-papagena-robbins-viviane-saglier-interview-with-ezra-winton-director-of-programming-at-cinema-politica.pdf.
Rose, Steve. "Iron Man: Product Placement Galore." *Guardian*, May 5, 2008. http://www.theguardian.com/film/filmblog/2008/may/05/ironman.
Sayre, Shay. *Entertainment Marketing and Communication: Selling Branded Performance, People, and Places*. Upper Saddle River, NJ: Prentice Hall, 2007.
Shallwani, Sadaf. "Why I Use the Term 'Majority World' Instead of 'Developing Countries' or 'Third World.'" *Sadaf Shallwani—Early Childhood Development Research* (blog), August 4, 2015. https://sadafshallwani.net/2015/08/04/majority-world.
Spurlock, Morgan. "I Am Part of the Problem." TwitLonger. December 14, 2017. http://www.twitlonger.com/show/n_1sqc244.
———, (dir.). *POM Wonderful Presents: The Greatest Movie Ever Sold*. Festival viewing. 2011.
Urquhart, Peter. "Film and Television: A Success?" In *CulturalIndustries.ca: Making Sense of Canadian Media in the Digital Age*, edited by Ira Wagman and Peter Urquhart, 17–32. Toronto: Lorimer, 2012.
Waugh, Thomas, ed. *Show Us Life: Toward a History and Aesthetics of the Committed Documentary*. Metuchen, NJ: Scarecrow Press, 1986.
Williams, Raymond. *Keywords: A Vocabulary of Culture and Society*. London: Croom Helm, 1976.
Winton, Ezra. "Good for the Heart and Soul, Good for Business: The Cultural Politics of Documentary at the Hot Docs Film Festival." PhD thesis, Carleton University, 2013.
Zimmermann, Patricia. *States of Emergency: Documentaries, Wars, Democracies*. Minneapolis: University of Minnesota Press, 2000.

EZRA WINTON is Assistant Professor of Communication Studies at Concordia University. He is coeditor of *Documentary Film Festivals* and *Challenge for Change: Activist Documentary at the National Film Board of Canada*. He is currently finishing his monograph, *Buying In to Doing Good: Curatorial Ethics and Documentary Politics at the Hot Docs Film Festival*.

Appendix

Table A.1 Opening films at Hot Docs, from 2000 to 2017

Film	Director	Year	Country	Topic	Synopsis	Politics	Celebrity Status	Sundance?
Bee Nation	Lana Slezic	2017	Canada	Indigenous	Cree children compete in a spelling bee, with no critical angle on the colonial context.	liberal	N/A	N/A
League of Exotic Dancers	Rama Rau	2016	Canada	entertainment/age	Portrait of aging burlesque dancers.	liberal	Subject—minor (dancers)	N/A
Tig	Kristina Goolsby and Ashley York	2015	USA	entertainment/health	An American comedian overcomes personal issues, including health problems.	liberal	Subject—minor (Tig Notaro)	Premiere
The Internet's Own Boy	Brian Knappenberger	2014	USA	surveillance/social media	Profile of information access activist in the United States.	liberal	Subject—minor (Aaron Swartz)	Premiere
The Manor	Shawney Cohen and Mike Galey	2013	Canada	entertainment/sex	Behind-the-scenes at an Ontario strip bar.	none	N/A	N/A
Ai Weiwei: Never Sorry	Alison Klayman	2012	USA	art/activism/China	Profile of Chinese political artist Ai Weiwei.	liberal	Subject—major (Ai Weiwei)	Award winner
POM Wonderful	Morgan Spurlock	2011	USA	advertising	Behind the scenes of US marketing and advertising	liberal	Director—major	Premiere
Babies	Thomas Balmès	2010	France	family/universalism	Observational documentary about babies around the world.	liberal	N/A	N/A
Act of God	Jennifer Baichwal	2009	Canada	weather/free will	The phenomenon of people hit by lightning from around the world.	none	N/A	N/A

Title	Director	Year	Country	Topic/Genre	Description	Political leaning	Subject—minor	Premiere
Anvil: The Story of Anvil	Sacha Gervasi	2008	USA	entertainment/music	A Canadian heavy metal band is thrust out of obscurity for this biopic.	none	Subject—minor (Anvil)	Premiere
In the Shadow of the Moon	David Sington	2007	UK	space travel	NASA's program to put the first man on the moon.	liberal	Subject—major (Neil Armstrong)	Premiere, award winner
The Railroad All Stars	Chema Rodriguez	2006	Spain	sex work/activism/sports	Sex workers in Guatemala play soccer to raise awareness about sexual violence.	liberal	N/A	N/A
Murderball	H. Airub and Dana A. Shapiro	2005	USA	disability/sports	Portrait of the US quad rugby team, which is made up of paraplegic men.	none	N/A	Award winner
The Ritchie Boys	Christian Bauer	2004	Canada/Germany	war/Jewish history	German men enlist in the US World War II effort to fight the Nazis.	liberal	N/A	N/A
My Flesh and Blood	Jonathan Karsh	2003	USA	family/mental health	American woman adopts children with disabilities.	progressive	N/A	Award winner
I Used to Be a Filmmaker (short)	Jay Rosenblatt	2003	USA	family	Fatherhood.	none	N/A	N/A
Blue Vinyl	Judith Helfand and Daniel B. Gold	2002	USA	environment/health/activism	Filmmaker looks at health/environmental risks associated with plastic.	progressive	N/A	Award winner
Startup.com		2001	USA	tech/business	The "internet revolution" and risks faced by new startup businesses.	liberal	N/A	Premiere
Heimspiel	Pepe Danquart	2000	Germany	sports/history	German hockey and politics.	liberal	N/A	N/A
The Worst Jewish Football Team in the World	Gary Ogin	2000	USA	sports/Jewish history	Jewish football team.	none	N/A	N/A

3

PUBLIC TELEVISION'S ROLE IN THE US DOCUMENTARY ECOLOGY

Patricia Aufderheide

Public Television and Documentaries

Public TV has been a mainstay for US documentary makers and an impetus for the growth of the popularity of documentaries.[1] When today's public TV was created by the Public Broadcasting Act of 1967, independent documentary makers were almost entirely excluded from network and local commercial broadcast TV. Time- and place-shifting technologies such as the VCR, DVD, and DVR were yet to come. Before hawking their work to educational institutions, they might, if lucky, get a local theatrical release in independently owned local theaters. For Oscar consideration, they had to show theatrically in both Los Angeles and New York, and this doubled the cost of what almost inevitably was already a money-losing proposition (albeit with publicity value). Public television, their avenue to both local and national televisual audiences, seemed to many documentarians a rare opportunity. They formed a vocal and influential constituency in early public TV programming.

At a time when the broadcast networks had effectively abandoned the "white paper" documentary form and the era of cable reality TV had yet to be born, public TV made documentaries accessible to the 98 percent of US homes reached by local stations' signals (still today more than commercial broadcast). Public TV pioneered entire forms in US television, such as the historical miniseries, the science series, the personal essay documentary genre, and the long-form investigative documentary. Public TV documentary celebrity Ken Burns's work has become so popular and well-known that it has spurred a wave of stylistic imitation (zooming in on and slow panning over still photos) popularly known as "the Ken Burns effect," available as such on FinalCutPro, Apple TV, and iPhoto.

In 2018, Public Broadcasting Service (PBS) showcased two hundred hours of new documentary film, which was seen by 92 million people, according to Nielsen ratings—a fact that makes PBS the undisputed center in American media for documentary. Ratings for PBS documentaries compare favorably with other outlets featuring documentaries. For instance, the science series *NOVA*'s 2018 ratings, at 1.81, outstripped the first quarter 2019 ratings of Discovery (1.07) and the Science channel (0.45). CNN's (Cable News Network) overall prime-time ratings for the first quarter of 2019, at 1.01, matched *FRONTLINE*'s average of 1.00 between 2016 and 2018. Two public TV series that anthologize widely disparate work by independent filmmakers, *Independent Lens* and *POV*, tend to rate lower, at about 0.50, but are also disproportionately responsible for high-profile hits. Independent Television Service (ITVS)–funded films alone, as the ITVS website celebrates, have won forty-three Emmy and thirty-nine Peabody awards. Public TV winners (from both viewership and awards perspectives) in the late 2010s by independent filmmakers, in theaters, on cable, and streaming as well as broadcast television, include *I Am Not Your Negro* (also an Academy Award nominee), *Won't You Be My Neighbor?*, and *Minding the Gap*.[2]

Approaching the third decade of the twenty-first century, documentarians could channel work in the "factual programming" or "unscripted" marketplace (to use two industry phrases) to a variety of basic and premium cable outlets, including Discovery Channel, History Channel, A&E, Court TV, CNN, ESPN (Entertainment and Sports Programming Network), Showtime, and HBO (Home Box Office). They could look for funding from major online video-on-demand venues, such as Hulu, Netflix, and Amazon. They could showcase or even be commissioned to make their work online on YouTube channels, Vimeo, or other streaming services; through traditional news sources such as the *New York Times*'s film and television unit, the *Washington Post*'s videos, or NBC's (National Broadcasting Company) news video service Left Field; or through born-digital news sources such as BuzzFeed and Vice. The production house Field of Vision and the Center for Investigative Reporting both collaborated with commercial and noncommercial venues alike to showcase investigative audiovisual journalism.[3]

But the private dream of every documentarian continued to be theatrical distribution (now made easier with social media and support services). And broadcasting and cablecasting continued to loom large. In

2017, a majority (59 percent) of Americans accessed audiovisual material via broadcast or cable television (the great majority at the scheduled time), even though millennials were increasingly turning from broadcasting to streaming.[4]

And so public broadcasting continued to be important to independent documentary filmmakers. For documentarians who prized authorial voice, it was especially important, because basic cable's commercial imperatives included a tight adherence to brand identity. Premium cable offered only a handful of slots per year. In a national 2016 survey, a third of US documentarians said that a main or contributing source of revenue for their works came from public broadcasters. It was the main source of revenue of 15 percent, making public television the most important single main source of funding for independent documentarians. Distribution on public television, which has a 98 percent reach (larger than commercial TV) in the United States, was also crucial legitimation and branding for future sales, particularly to educational institutions. Educational sales have long provided anchoring revenue for US filmmakers.[5]

Documentarians have also been key to defining public TV in the public eye since 1967, although they have also sometimes been its greatest headache. Indeed, they threatened the future of public TV at its birth. Public broadcasting was structured from the start to be politically vulnerable, since it had no endowment and core services for the stations depended on a federal allocation so small it forced all participants to raise money elsewhere as well. Lawmakers also banned the federally created agency the Corporation for Public Broadcasting from interconnection or creating a network. The resulting decentralized ecology of stations and their support services, such as the programming supplier PBS, is enormously complex.[6]

Public broadcasting's first public affairs documentaries proved an acid test. The liberal-tilted productions of the Ford Foundation–funded production group National Educational Television (NET) were an indicator, for conservative congressmen who voted against the Public Broadcasting Act of 1967, of the threat a public broadcasting service posed. After NET's *Banks and the Poor*, about redlining, aired nationally, focusing on one of President Nixon's important campaign funders, Nixon told the Office of Management and Budget to find out how to defund public TV. When that turned out to be impossible, Nixon declared that public TV should feature culture and the arts, not public affairs. Ever since, public affairs have been part of its public image but also embattled within the decentralized set of services that make up US-style public TV.[7]

Public TV's In-House Genres

In the 1980s, when commercial networks dropped funding for documentaries after Federal Communications Commission requirements for license renewal were drastically simplified, public television plunged into high-profile, strongly branded documentary series produced through stations. Documentary series such as *NOVA* (1974–), *FRONTLINE* (1983–), and *American Experience* (1988–) have evolved a successful strategy, addressing the unspoken but the ever-present threat of politically motivated attacks on public broadcasting. They variously walk a careful line between investigative, potentially controversial material and "safely splendid" (in the words of Erik Barnouw) storytelling.[8]

Their storytelling, often within a journalistic mode that merges traditions established in the 1960s on network television's public affairs documentary series and on BBC (British Broadcasting Corporation) nature and public affairs documentaries, has become a durable, somewhat flexible format. It usually features some combination of a trusted narrator (often a white man speaking in standard English); an essay format; evidential footage; authoritative experts; a victim; *vox populi*; experiential footage that implicitly establishes the rigor, daring, access, and entrepreneurial spirit of the reporter; and a resolution that permits a sense of closure for the viewer. This format, which draws on British BBC and US commercial traditions from the 1960s for public affairs, has also influenced a generation of producers for commercial series on cable, and it remains a durable indicator of quality.

Public TV has also cultivated its own in-house documentarists, also signaling quality, art, and viewer comfort while still promising unique insights into real life. Ken Burns and Frederick Wiseman have both chosen to anchor their work in public TV distribution through PBS; both the filmmakers and PBS have built brands from the collaboration.

Ken Burns may have become the most important purveyor of history for a generation of Americans, in spite of his consistent claim that he is a "storyteller" and not a historian. His multihour works feature well-known topics, including the Civil War, baseball, jazz, the national parks, and the Vietnam War. They share a common theme of national unity out of dissension, as discovered in the personal voices and experiences of individuals who embody a social construct. They feature opposing voices and often implicitly posit a kind of equivalence; for instance, in the Vietnam War series, the two driving oppositions are democracy versus communism and prowar groups versus antiwar ones.

Both reviewers and publicists often construe the viewing of a Ken Burns series as an act of civic engagement. Historical and cultural critics have often noted, on the other hand, that the construction of a "both sides" narrative and the message of the success of the historical process in achieving national unity may misrepresent history and lead viewers to believe that the issues raised are resolved.[9]

Frederick Wiseman, by contrast, has become public TV's talisman for a guarantee of ambitious artistic excellence. His work is less beloved than admired. He produces observational works set in institutions. His earlier work, on a mental asylum, the military, a hospital, and a high school, for example, provided an idiosyncratic, sometimes cynical critique of administrative power in managing human systems; his later work, on ballet, a university, a museum, and a library, for example, tends to celebrate administrative expertise in managing big human systems. His style registers for viewers a serious, and often very long, observational approach to big topics. Although his second long-form work, *Titicut Follies* (1967), about an asylum for mentally ill patients, was both controversial and arguably precipitated change, his later work increasingly examines high-culture institutions and engenders reflection but not necessarily action.[10]

Public TV's leading programmers—executive producers at producing stations, PBS and sometimes, in partnership with others, CPB (Corporation for Public Broadcasting)—have also worked with independent producers to innovate the documentary miniseries in the United States.[11] Public station WGBH in Boston produced, in 1983, the probing thirteen-part series *Vietnam: A Television History*, working with an international set of production houses to tell a story that, unprecedentedly on US television, featured the nationalist and anti-imperialist aspirations of the Vietnamese. The success of the series, despite protests by pro–South Vietnam Vietnamese exiles at some stations, led PBS to seek out other miniseries. The independent production house Blackside, headed by Henry Hampton, raised money widely on the basis of interest, which eventually resulted in broadcasting nationally, of both miniseries on the civil rights movement, *Eyes on the Prize* (1987) and *Eyes on the Prize II* (1990).[12]

The miniseries became an aspired-to model for others seeking to bring underheard stories into American history and has resulted, among others, in the four-part series *The Question of Equality* (1995), the six-part series *Latino Americans* (2013), and the five-part series *Asian Americans* (2020). All the series were coproduced, with independent producers, by public TV's Independent Television Service.

Independent Filmmakers and Public TV's Mission

Public TV's role in funding and showcasing social-issue-based point-of-view documentary has had everything to do with documentary filmmakers taking coordinated, political action. Although public broadcasting was created with only the vaguest of mission language—to be noncommercial—documentarians have strategically argued its responsibility to represent diverse audiences and perspectives. This was present in the history, although not in the legislative language. The Carnegie Commission, the blue-ribbon group that laid the template for the service the law authorized, called for "excellence in the service of diversity."[13] Commissioners and many early leaders, such as Bill Moyers and James Day, perceived it as a mediating element in the public sphere.[14] The claim has continued to be invoked, sometimes strategically. CPB, which channels the federal dollars to stations and programs, announced in 2015—during the Obama Administration—on its website that "Digital, Diversity, and Dialogue are the framework for public media's service to America" and that it was founded "to champion the principles of diversity and excellence of programming, responsiveness to local communities, and service to all." The brutal realities of decentralization and limited taxpayer funding, however, have led to caution and compromise and a tight focus on the disproportionately upscale, older, white and female tenth of the viewership that donates to stations.[15]

But those ideals have been crucial for independent documentarians working within public TV. In its early days, independent filmmakers succeeded in getting on air films about controversial topics such as nuclear waste, women's and gay rights, and anticommunism as ideological bullying, as well as openly experimental documentary. By the later 1970s, though, after Nixon's battering and the defensive programming tactics of already conservative station managers, independent filmmakers—especially the social issue makers without other prospects—perceived avoidance of controversy and a bias toward the major coastal production centers. Especially after the election of Ronald Reagan, which focused conservative suspicion anew on public TV, the CPB began funding executive-produced documentary series and producing-station projects rather than individual filmmakers and their often unpredictable point of view. Independents protested loudly both within and beyond public broadcasting, and especially to Congress, throughout the later 1970s. Between 1976 and 1991, activists from federally recognized minority groups won line items in the CPB budget dedicated to supporting minority filmmakers, eventually forming five "minority consortia," each differently responding to constituents' issues. In 1978, filmmakers working primarily through the national membership organization Association of Independent Video and Filmmakers won a wrinkle in the congressional budget allocation for CPB saying that a "substantial" amount of program funding should go to independents.[16]

Over the next decade, the minority consortia began generating work from US minority perspectives, increasing the pool of documentary work fighting for airspace on a public TV where station managers often found no home for it. Independents argued—to public TV executives, to members of Congress, and to the general public—that their interests as filmmakers often overlapped with the responsibility of public television to present diverse perspectives from diverse parts of the United States.[17] By 1988, obstreperous independents had won a prime-time series on PBS, *POV*, partly with the help of existing documentary series executive producers (especially David Fanning, who as executive producer of a strongly branded series understood the value for him of other outlets for independents). Also in 1988, with the help of Representative Henry Waxman, who put together a bipartisan coalition in support, they won a dedicated allocation within CPB's budget. The line item was for a production wing focused on underserved audiences and underrepresented issues.[18]

This line item became ITVS, which still receives the majority of its funding directly from the federal-taxpayer-supported CPB. It is a coproducer of films it invests in rather than being a grantor. Many ITVS films also benefit from funding from the minority consortia, which have rebranded themselves as the National Multicultural Alliance. ITVS is required to give public television outlets the right of first refusal to its finished products, although it gets no guarantee of any outlet taking it. ITVS films now stock the two major public TV series for independent, point-of-view documentaries: *Independent Lens* (an ITVS series) and *POV*. Both series are carried in PBS's core schedule. ITVS and *POV* programs have won many journalistic and film awards.[19]

Diversity in Theory and Practice

Independent documentaries have often been in the political crosshairs, and precisely because ITVS is charged with funding independent and diverse productions, and also must commit to a claim of balance in representation in order to get productions on PBS and station schedules, ITVS is often implicated. The stage was already set when ITVS began. In 1991, Congressman Jesse Helms (R-NC) held up Marlon Riggs's *Tongues Untied* (1989), a confessional audiovisual poem shown on *POV*, about the experience of being Black and gay, as an argument for defunding public TV.

The brouhaha increased public broadcasters' preemptive alarm about independent documentary and claims of left-wing bias. PBS picked up conservative talk show host Tucker Carlson, in response, and for several years CPB encouraged conservative programming by sometime CPB staffer Michael Pack (who under the presidency of Donald Trump was controversially appointed to head America's public diplomacy services, the US Agency for Global Media). But ITVS survived. In 2002, Sally Jo Fifer became ITVS president, bringing political and management skills to address the specious charge that diversity was somehow bias. The ITVS board had established by 2003 that diversity was the organization's top priority, to be demonstrated through demographics of makers, subjects, and topics as well as through regional representation. This not only provided transparency in priorities but generated substantiating data. Fifer was able to show public broadcasters ratings data proving that ITVS programs brought in younger, more diverse audiences than other PBS shows. By 2016 ITVS-produced programs had won more Peabody awards (given for "the most powerful, enlightening, and invigorating stories in television, radio, and online media") than any other PBS series, including the veteran public affairs series *FRONTLINE*. [20]

The strategic conservative linkage of bias and diversity has continued, however. In 2012 the station leadership of WNET, which has featured billionaire David Koch among other wealthy patrons on its board, worked to drop *Independent Lens* and *POV* from the PBS prime-time lineup. This occurred soon after airing of Alex Gibney's documentary *Park Avenue* (2012), which focused on the one-percenters living in the same Manhattan building with David Koch. PBS appeared amenable to moving the series to a poorly watched time, off the core schedule. Only after renewed public filmmaker protests, both invoking and involving viewers, did PBS restore the series to the schedule.

In other cases, individual stations have pointedly preempted the two series when documentaries uncomfortable to a segment of their local audience appeared. For instance, all South Carolina public stations, which are connected in a network, as well as the Charlotte, North Carolina, public station, refused to run George Stoney, Judith Helfand, and Susanne Rostock's *Uprising of '34* (1995) apparently because its oral history of a textile strike there, brutally suppressed by textile owners, implicated still prominent families.[21] Southern stations generally refused to run Dawn Porter's *Spies of Mississippi* (2014), about FBI involvement in civil rights protests in the South, and other stations refused to carry it in its scheduled prime-time slot.[22]

In 2017, Congressman Andy Harris (R-MD) pointed (like Helms before him, without actually watching the programming) to three ITVS films as evidence of cultural liberalism. The three programs were Dean Hamer and Joe Wilson's *Kuma Hina* (2014), about a transgender Hawaiian teacher of traditional *hula*; Yoruba Richen's *The New Black* (2013), about organizing in the African American community of Maryland to reject a ban on same-sex marriage; and Heather Ross's *Baby Mama High* (2014), about a program to keep teen mothers in high school.[23]

So ITVS sits in a difficult position, between often obstreperous independent filmmakers frustrated with the limits of public television and a wary, risk-averse set of public TV stakeholders. Its process of selection demonstrates the gates and gatekeepers. Any filmmaker funded by ITVS must negotiate a set of gauntlets: peer recognition from fellow filmmakers in a peer-review panel for open-call projects (a result of insistence by filmmakers who lobbied for ITVS's creation); codesign with the on-staff ITVS coproducers, who are mandated to put filmmaker voice first but to maintain ITVS standards as well (they also must consider whether the format and framing will be acceptable to stations and PBS); legal review; and fact-checking. If the film is selected for *POV* or *Independent Lens*, PBS has final say on the lineup. As well, *POV*'s board of directors includes representatives from major stations and corporate leaders. ITVS also needs to work carefully and productively with the National Multicultural Alliance, whose members in more targeted ways also amplify and bolster independent documentarians. Any public attention to internal tensions to public broadcasting can jeopardize the trust ITVS has won with stakeholders.

Diverse Styles and Perspectives

Most executive-produced series on public TV, as noted, have evolved a framing and formula that prenegotiates most points of ideological controversy. ITVS, however, cannot use this approach, because its founding mission is to produce independent, one-off, point-of-view works to showcase underheard voices for underrepresented audiences. The range of styles are distinctive and diverse, while also being accessible to a lay audience, and have become, in some cases, pioneers of subgenres of documentary.

For instance, in the 1990s, while striving to leverage low-cost new video technologies and spread limited budgets, ITVS effectively became an incubator of the subgenre of personal memoir documentary, from Helfand's *A Healthy Baby Girl* (1997) and Billy Golfus and David E. Simpson's *When Billy Broke His Head . . . and Other Tales of Wonder* (1995) to the teen-to-teen personal storytelling of the eight-part series *The Ride* (1994). By 1993, a sixth of the submissions to ITVS were personal memoir. The form rapidly spread to commercial TV and theatrical documentary.[24]

ITVS documentaries have often participated in beyond-objectivity journalism, featuring an essay with an argument and often a personal perspective of the filmmaker. For instance, *Park Avenue* holds up the super-wealthy to scorn and, through the eyes of a doorman for the building where they live, contempt. (Among other things, the doorman reveals that the wealthy are terrible tippers, with David Koch the worst in the building.) Sonia Kennebeck's *National Bird* (2016) is a sobering and saddening look at the human cost of military drones, both on the bombed and the bombers, profiling three military whistleblowers whose own stories are three kinds of condemnation of the drone policies. Peter Galison and Robb Moss's *Containment* (2015) sounds the alarm about the unmet challenge of storing nuclear waste.

ITVS films have also featured historical documentaries that put underrepresented communities at the center. Examples include Jason Osder's *Let the Fire Burn* (2013), about the Philadelphia police and fire department's decision to let a poor African American neighborhood be destroyed in a standoff with a politico-religious sect; Benjamin Shors and Torsten Kjellstrand's *The Blackfeet Flood* (2016), about the worst natural disaster in Montana history and its effects on one Native family; Stanley Nelson Jr.'s *The Black Panthers* (2015), a recalling of a complex social and political movement; Johanna Hamilton's *1971* (2014), about antiwar resisters who broke into a draft office and released documents that revealed illegal FBI surveillance of US citizens; and Marco William's *Banished* (2007), about the all-too-common history of driving African Americans out of towns across the United States.

ITVS films have also featured hybridized versions of cinema vérité, close observational cinema that overlaps with personal voice journalism, personal essay, or biography. For instance, Anne De Mare and Kristen Kelly's *The Homestretch* (2014), a film about homeless teens' struggle to graduate high school in Chicago, mixes interview, archival material, and vérité footage to track the teens and their mentors. Joe Brewster and Michèle Stephenson's *American Promise* (2013), which followed the African American filmmakers' son and his best friend through twelve years of attendance at one of the most elite US schools, employs vérité, narration, and interviews with schoolchildren and others.

ITVS documentaries depend heavily on character-driven narratives, as do most general-interest documentaries, but they are framed within a context of their social implications. In Brad Barber and Scott Christopherson's *Peace Officer* (2015), an exploration of the dangers of militarizing the police and in particular SWAT teams, the lead character and de facto narrator is a former police chief who is also a relative of a mentally ill man killed by a SWAT team. But anecdotes and personal stories are used to tell a story of how SWAT teams have caused an outsized number of needless deaths, not only in Utah (where the story is based) but nationwide. Marta Cunningham's *Valentine Road* (2013) and Kelly Duane de la Vega and Katie Galloway's *Better This World* (2011) ask questions about juvenile criminal justice, in addition to exploring their particular narratives.

ITVS documentaries similarly put cultural celebrities and performances into a social context. The story of Greg Camalier's *Muscle Shoals* (2015) is the story of a sound arising from syncretic musical blending and borrowing from rich African American southern traditions. John Scheinfeld's *Chasing Trane* (2016) recovers a nearly forgotten understanding of the great jazz artist as a thinker and "spiritual warrior" about both society and art.

Documentaries Shaping a Public

ITVS has not only been a shaping force for social issue documentary that is reliably factual and transparent but also played a role in directly engaging Americans in shared problems and issues. It has thus taken on the challenge American philosopher John Dewey raised about public participation in democracy. He described the public as not merely an aggregation of individual opinion but a social body constantly in construction by conversation leading to action.[25]

ITVS has positioned its documentaries as interventions in public life, through engagement projects that have morphed with new platforms and possibilities. Discussion guides, community screenings and promotional partnerships are now both face-to-face and virtual. Communities connect virtually through ITVS's online viewing platform OVEE (which also allows real-time conversations and commentary.

Two recent studies at the Center for Media & Social Impact have measured engagement effects of ITVS documentaries. One measured the effects of using OVEE to engage targeted audiences demonstrated the utility of impact measurement of social issue films. The film *The Homestretch*, funded by ITVS and shown originally in PBS prime time, featured stories of several homeless teens in Chicago who succeed in graduating high school. Some 322 participants, teachers, and social work professionals joined the platform from forty states, coming from federal, state, and local government agencies and nonprofits dealing with homelessness, teens, and the challenge of raising graduation rates. Seventy percent valued the chance to share the experience with others around the country, and 21 percent valued the chance to talk honestly about a difficult problem. More than half said they would use the film in their own work.[26] In another study, researchers tracked community conversations convened by local public TV stations after viewings of *Always in Season*, an ITVS film by Jacqueline Olive about past and continuing lynchings in the US. They found that participants universally reported "breaking the silence" over race and racism in their own communities and expected to take action to address local issues after both viewing and discussing the film across racial and cultural lines.[27]

One study indicates that, at least in a time of crisis, viewers associate public broadcasting with public life. PBS and WNET's attempt to remove the independent documentary series from PBS prime time accidentally provided an opportunity to gauge how viewers perceive such programming when alerted it might become hard to find.[28] Filmmakers mobilized through their own networks and through networks of organizations they had worked with. They launched a petition that garnered more than three thousand responses. Internal negotiations among the stakeholders were influenced by the public action, and the result was a reprieve for the prime-time placement. Analysis of comments associated with the petition, from almost six hundred commenters who identified themselves as viewers, demonstrated strong associations between public TV, an informed citizenry, diverse perspectives, and civil discourse. These comments were unprompted; coders used discourse analysis to find themes. A sixth of them explicitly referenced the public mission of public TV, and others implied it. The themes of their comments fell into seven categories, of which the largest were the following three: "I find such programming meaningful" (299 comments), "This programming is core to public mission" (109 comments), and "Public TV's mission includes using public money to present material that commercial TV cannot afford to" (44 comments).

Sample comments included: "Such programs spark a desire in young film makers, to become socially, politically, and ethically conscious of the world around them and to provoke contemplation of these ideas in the viewer"; "Now more than ever our democracy needs a robust mixture of well-articulated points of view"; "stop this effort to eliminate these two venues that contribute to the life blood of democracy."[29]

In late 2014, when PBS and WNET proposed moving the series anew, a public mobilization again spotlighted the social function of public TV documentaries.[30] At a series of public hearings in a listening tour taken by public TV executives as a result of the pressure, makers were joined by nonprofit executives, representatives of organized labor, funders, journalists, and even film subjects. They all testified to the value of diverse voices on nationally distributed public TV.

In Washington, DC, the statement of representatives of CPB-funded minority consortia said, "The impact that public broadcasting has on diverse and minority communities through outreach is immeasurable, and must remain a resource for underrepresented groups in order to outline underrepresented issues." Representatives of groups ranging from disability rights to refugee services celebrated the connection between US residents and the public issues that connect them.[31]

Negotiating the Distance

Analysis of data generated by ITVS record-keeping documents the centrality of diversity. ITVS programming as seen in *Independent Lens* is more consistently diverse in makers and subjects across categories both than other documentary series within both public broadcasting and within commercial broadcasting. A study of 165 documentaries produced in 2014–2015 compared diversity of makers and subjects in ITVS programming with that in other public TV series (*Frontline*, *American Experience*, and *American Masters*) and in documentary series at two major commercial cable outlets for social issue documentary, CNN and HBO. ITVS programs tended more often to feature women and minority directors and subjects overall than other public TV programs and were more likely to have minority directors and subjects than commercial cable.[32]

But could diversity result in cultural minoritarianism, of primary interest to liberal coastal elites, as Representative Andy Harris's criticisms suggest? Another study suggested the opposite, that diversity drove toward geographical, demographic, and issue inclusion. It looked only at ITVS programs, focusing on geographic and demographic representation, compared with census data and with polling data about the top public issue concerns of the American public. ITVS programs' makers and programming are representative geographically throughout the United States, and programs take place slightly more often in rural areas than urban ones, as defined by the US census. Topics of the programs generally accord with concerns registered in national Pew polls of issues of concern, including public safety, education, and health.[33]

The Future of Documentary on Public TV

While independent documentarians have more options than ever before, it is possible that public television will continue to serve both as a showcase and as an incubator for independent documentary. Public TV has launched several digital-era experiments. PBS digital studios now has more than fifty original, openly available online series; they include *Hot Mess*, about climate change; *Two Cents*, about personal finance; and *Eons*, about natural history. ITVS has developed a game, *World without Oil*, to experiment with interactive platforms. It also launched a YouTube channel, Storycast, to showcase episodic series, such as Nicole Opper and Kristan Cassady's *The F-Word* (2017), following the adventures of a lesbian couple attempting adopt through the foster system, and Jenny Schweitzer's *Iron Maidens* (2015), about an all-girl robotics team at the Bronx High School of Science. Black Public Media, one of the minority consortia, created a wisely funny multiyear series, *Black Folk Don't . . .* (2013–), by Angela Tucker. This series, available openly on YouTube, features a variety of African Americans on a topic, ranging from yoga and skiing to getting places on time.

Conclusion

Public television has been crucial to the evolution of documentary filmmaking in the United States, in various ways throughout its sprawling, acronym-beset ecology. It is valuable because of its extraordinary national reach, and the high trust value associated with the PBS brand. It has legitimized and popularized subgenres of documentary, including the historical miniseries, the personal essay documentary, cinema vérité storytelling, the long-form investigative documentary, and nature programming. It has also cultivated generations of social issue, point-of-view filmmakers who see their work as participating in public life, and in the process created audiences who also become members of a public in engaging with their documentaries.

Notes

1. This analysis is informed by a long journalistic relationship with independent filmmaking in the United States and with public television, particularly ITVS. I began reporting on conflicts between independent filmmaker constituencies and public television as the cultural editor of the newspaper *In These Times* in 1978, at the beginning of the ten-year struggle by documentarians to create ITVS. I continued to follow that thread in reporting for my work as an editor of *American Film* and as a freelancer for the then leading trade publication for the field, *The Independent* (published by the Association of Independent Video and Filmmakers, the leading membership group that represented filmmakers). I have

served twice on the board of ITVS, from 2001 to 2007 and from 2014 to the present, with a term ending in 2023.

2. Peter Hamilton Consultants, "PBS Series Ranker for Eleven Strands," "Ratings Snapshot for US."
3. Peter Hamilton Consultants, "Realscreen 2015"; Cieply, "News Companies"; Cunningham and Silver, *Screen Distribution*.
4. Rainie, "About 6 in 10 Young Adults."
5. Chattoo, "State of the Documentary Field."
6. Barnouw, *Sponsor*.
7. Aufderheide, *Daily Planet*, 103–104.
8. Barnouw, *Sponsor*, 150.
9. Lembcke, "Burns and Novick"; Rosenberg, "Ken Burns' American War"; Bass, "America's Amnesia"; Edgerton, *Ken Burns's America*.
10. Benson and Anderson, *Reality Fictions*.
11. A major inspiration was the United Kingdom's Channel 4 blockbuster series *The World at War* (1973–1974), which was a major early success in a service established originally as a nonprofit public service to showcase work of independent filmmakers. Channel 4 resulted from independent filmmaker protests to the BBC about being shut out of opportunities at the BBC.
12. Else, *True South*.
13. Debrett, *Reinventing Public Service Television*, 142.
14. Day, *Vanishing Vision*.
15. Rowland, "Continuing Crisis"; Padovani and Tracey, "Report on the Conditions"; Balas, "From Underserved to Broadly Served"; Bullert, *Public Television*.
16. Aufderheide, *Daily Planet*.
17. Kidd, "Public Culture."
18. Aufderheide, *Daily Planet*, 99–120.
19. Aufderheide, "Documentary Filmmaking."
20. Lisa Tawil, Independent Television Service, personal correspondence, October 2, 2017.
21. Abrash and Whiteman, "Uprising of '34."
22. Akitobi, "PBS, 'Spies of Mississippi.'"
23. Schneider, "Diverse Documentaries."
24. Aufderheide, "Public Intimacy"; Lane, *Autobiographical Documentary*, 191–192.
25. Dewey, *Public and Its Problems*.
26. Chattoo and Howe, "Connecting Audiences."
27. Conrad, Chattoo, and Aufderheide, "Breaking the Silence."
28. Das, "PBS and WNET."
29. Aufderheide and Xie, "Public Television Viewers."
30. Lear, "Is PBS Neglecting Its Mission?"; Fisher, "Why PBS?"
31. Center for Media & Social Impact, "Public TV."
32. Chattoo et al., "Diversity."
33. Chattoo et al., "American Realities."

References

Abrash, Barbara, and David Whiteman. "The Uprising of '34: Filmmaking as Community Engagement." *Wide Angle* 21, no. 2 (March 1999): 87–99.
Akitobi, Emmanuel. "PBS, 'Spies of Mississippi,' and the Business of TV Programming Based on Racial Viewing Habits." *Indiewire*, February 11, 2014.

Aufderheide, Patricia. *The Daily Planet: A Critic on the Capitalist Culture Beat*. Minneapolis: University of Minnesota Press, 2000.

———. "Documentary Filmmaking and US Public TV's Independent Television Service, 1989–2017." *Journal of Film and Video* 71, no. 4 (2019): 3–14.

———. "Public Intimacy: The Development of First-Person Documentary." *Afterimage* 25, no. 1 (1997): 16.

———. "Public Television's Prime-Time Politics." *American Film (Archive: 1975–1992)* 6, no. 8 (April 1, 1983): 53–57, 62.

Aufderheide, Patricia, Jessica Clark, and Jake Shapiro. "Public Broadcasting & Public Affairs: Opportunities and Challenges for Public Broadcasting's Role in Provisioning the Public with News and Public Affairs." In *Media Re:Public*. Berkman Center for Internet and Society: Harvard University, 2008.

Aufderheide, Patricia, and Echo Xie. "Public Television Viewers and Public-Purpose Programming: Viewer Reactions to PBS Schedule Changes That Reduce Access to Independent Documentary." Washington, DC: Center for Media & Social Impact, 2012. http://cmsimpact.org/resource/public-television-viewers-and-public-purpose-programming-viewer-reactions-to-pbs-schedule-changes-that-reduce-access-to-independent-documentary/.

Balas, Glenda R. "From Underserved to Broadly Served: The Class Interests of Public Broadcasting." *Critical Studies in Media Communication* 24, no. 4 (October 1, 2007): 365–369.

Barnouw, Erik. *The Sponsor: Notes on Modern Potentates*. Classics in Communication and Mass Culture Series. New Brunswick: Transaction Publishers, 2004.

———. *Tube of Plenty: The Evolution of American Television*. Rev. ed. New York: Oxford University Press, 1982.

Bass, Thomas. "America's Amnesia." *Mekong Review*, no. 8 (2017). https://mekongreview.com/americas-amnesia/

Benson, Thomas W., and Carolyn Anderson. *Reality Fictions: The Films of Frederick Wiseman*. Carbondale: Southern Illinois University Press, 1989.

Bullert, B. J. *Public Television: Politics and the Battle over Documentary Film*. New Brunswick, NJ: Rutgers University Press, 1997.

Carroll, Rory. "How Big Tech Became the New Titan of Television." *Guardian* (US), September 15, 2017.

Center for Media & Social Impact. "Public TV and Independent, Point of View Documentary: Documents." School of Communication, American University. http://archive.cmsimpact.org/future-public-media/documents/field-reports/public-tv-and-independent-point-view-documentary.

Chattoo, Caty Borum. "The State of the Documentary Field: 2016 Survey of Documentary Industry Members." Washington, DC: Center for Media & Social Impact, School of Communication, American University, 2016. http://cmsimpact.org/resource/state-documentary-field-2016-survey-documentary-industry/.

Chattoo, Caty Borum, Patricia Aufderheide, Michelle Alexander, and Chandler Green. "American Realities on Public Television: Analysis of Independent Television Service's Independent Documentaries, 2007–2016." *International Journal of Communication* 12 (2018): 1541–1568.

Chattoo, Caty Borum, Patricia Aufderheide, Kenneth Merrill, and Modupeola Oyebolu. "Diversity on US Public and Commercial TV, in Authorial and Executive-Produced Social-Issue Documentaries." *Journal of Broadcasting and Electronic Media* 62, no. 3 (2018): 495–513.

Chattoo, Caty Borum, and Casey Freeman Howe. "Connecting Audiences with OVEE, an Online Screening Platform: An Assessment of the Homestretch PBS Documentary." Washington, DC: Center for Media & Social Impact, School of Communication, American University, 2016. http://cmsimpact.org/resource/connecting-audiences-ovee-online-screening-platform-assessment-homestretch-pbs-documentary/.

Cieply, Michael. "News Companies See Movies as Opportunity for Growth." *New York Times*, March 29, 2015. https://www.nytimes.com/2015/03/30/business/media/news-companies-see-movies-as-opportunity-for-growth.html.

Conrad, David, Caty Borum Chattoo, and Patricia Aufderheide. "Breaking the Silence: How Documentaries Can Shape the Conversation on Racial Violence in America and Create New Communities." Washington, DC: Center for Media & Social Impact, 2020.

Cunningham, Stuart, and Jon Silver. *Screen Distribution and the New King Kongs of the Online World*. Basingstoke, UK: Palgrave Macmillan, 2013.

Das, Angelica. "PBS and WNET Keep Independent Documentary in Primetime." Center for Media & Social Impact, School of Communication, American University, April 23, 2015. http://cmsimpact.org/blog/future-public-media/pbs-and-wnet-keep-independent-documentary-primetime.

Day, James. *The Vanishing Vision: The Inside Story of Public Television*. Berkeley: University of California Press, 1995.

Debrett, Mary. *Reinventing Public Service Television for the Digital Future*. Bristol, UK: Intellect, 2010.

Dewey, John. *The Public and Its Problems*. New York: Holt and Company, 1927.

Edgerton, Gary R. *Ken Burns's America*. 1st ed. New York: Palgrave, 2001.

Else, Jon. *True South: Henry Hampton and Eyes on the Prize, the Landmark Television Series That Reframed the Civil Rights Movement*. New York: Viking, 2017.

Engelman, Ralph. *Public Radio and Television in America: A Political History*. Thousand Oaks: Sage Publications, 1996.

Fisher, Daniel Clarkson. "Why PBS, and Viewers Like You, Must Continue Saving 'POV' and 'Independent Lens.'" *Medium*, September 8, 2015. https://medium.com/@danielclarksonfisher/why-pbs-and-viewers-like-you-must-continue-saving-pov-and-independent-lens-d48f3eca5cd5.

Garnham, Nicholas. *Emancipation, the Media, and Modernity: Arguments about the Media and Social Theory*. New York: Oxford University Press, 2000.

Keane, John. *The Media and Democracy*. Cambridge: Polity Press, 1991.

Kidd, Dustin. "Public Culture in America: A Review of Cultural Policy Debates." *Journal of Arts Management, Law, and Society* 42, no. 1 (January 1, 2012): 11–21.

Lane, Jim. *The Autobiographical Documentary in America*. Madison: University of Wisconsin Press, 2002.

Lembcke, Jerry. "Burns and Novick, Masters of False Balancing." *PublicBooks*, September 15, 2017.

Padovani, Cinzia, and Michael Tracey. "Report on the Conditions of Public Service Broadcasting." *Television and New Media* 4, no. 2 (May 1, 2003): 131–153.

Peter Hamilton Consultants. "The PBS Series Ranker for Eleven Strands: Average Audience and Trends, 2015–2018." DocumentaryBusiness.com, June 11, 2019. https://www.documentarytelevision.com/public-television/the-pbs-series-ranker-for-eleven-strands-average-audience-and-trends-2015-2018/.

———. "Ratings Snapshot for US Channels in 1Q'19: Average Primetime Audience & Distribution Footprints for 40 Factual Channels." DocumentaryBusiness.com, June 4, 2019. https://

www.documentarytelevision.com/ratings/ratings-snapshot-for-u-s-channels-in-1q19-average-primetime-audience-distribution-footprints-for-40-factual-channels/.

———. "Realscreen 2015. Ten Takeaways: More Delegates. Snow-Zilla. Uncertainty. Scale. Humble. Fear. Back to Content? Diversity." DocumentaryBusiness.com, February 6, 2015. https://www.documentarytelevision.com/commissioning-process/realscreen-2015-ten-takeaways-delegates-snow-zilla-uncertainty-scale-humble-fear-back-content-diversity/.

Rainie, Lee. "About 6 in 10 Young Adults in US Primarily Use Online Streaming to Watch TV." *FactTank*. September 13, 2017, http://www.pewresearch.org/fact-tank/2017/09/13/about-6-in-10-young-adults-in-u-s-primarily-use-online-streaming-to-watch-tv/.

Rosenberg, Alyssa. "Ken Burns' American War." *Washington Post*, September 14, 2017.

Rowland, Willard D., Jr. "Continuing Crisis in Public Broadcasting: A History of Disenfranchisement." *Journal of Broadcasting and Electronic Media* 30, no. 3 (Summer 1986): 251–274.

Schneider, Michael. "Diverse Documentaries under Attack as Congressman Questions Public Broadcasting 'Agenda.'" *Indiewire*, March 28, 2017.

Steel, Emily. "Netflix Bolsters Offerings in Documentary Genre." *New York Times*, July 28 2014. https://www.nytimes.com/2014/07/28/business/media/netflix-bolsters-offerings-in-documentary-genre.html.

Steigrad, Alexandra. "NBC Starts Documentary Unit to Attract Younger Audience." *WWD*, June 13 2017.

PATRICIA AUFDERHEIDE is University Professor of Communication Studies at American University. She is author of *Documentary Film: A Very Short Introduction* and (with Peter Jaszi) of *Reclaiming Fair Use: How to Put Balance Back into Copyright*.

PART II.
DOCUMENTARY ECOLOGIES

This section, devoted to documentary ecologies, brings together three different approaches to environmental documentary, considering the different aesthetic paradigms for visualizing the stakes and power of ecopolitics in the twenty-first century. The chapters included here address contemporary digital documentary via aerial, fly-over, and drone imagery (Zoë Druick); time-lapse cinematography (Devon Coutts); and infographics (Sabiha Ahmad Khan) as distinct formal techniques of spectatorial embodiment, visualization of slow violence and its effects, and data visualization, respectively. The section begins with Druick's historical investigation of popular long-form environmental documentaries. "On (Not) Falling from the Sky: Fly-Over Global Documentary as Capitalist Body Genre" considers a range of documentaries that have made extensive use of aerial views. From Godfrey Reggio's 1980s cult *Quatsi* trilogy and other panoramic global films, such as *Home* (2009) and *Samsara* (2011), and recent blue-chip environmental miniseries and documentaries (*Planet Earth* [2006], *Planet Earth II* [2016], *Life* [2007–2009]), Druick examines a subgenre of documentary invested in images of flight, mobility, and feelings of power and omniscience aligned with the aerial view. Druick reads these documentaries as a form of "body genre" of global capitalism, grounded in "proprioceptive aesthetics"—a form of cognitive mapping that stimulates a response that aligns our bodies with the cinematic apparatus itself. Although these technologized modes of looking might invite a "vernacular sublime" through the pleasure of virtual travel, Druick maintains that they fail to meet the demands of the social and environmental crises they evoke, in part because of their studious avoidance of any critique of the politics and consequences of capitalism itself.

Tracking environmental devastation through two more recent climate change documentaries *Chasing Ice* (2012) and *Chasing Coral* (2017), Coutts considers the problem of visibility, acceleration, deceleration, and slow violence, making the case for time-lapse cinematography as a powerful mechanism for visualizing the slow, seemingly invisible impacts of environmental destruction in powerful and accessible ways. Time lapse, he argues, has the potential to "represent slow violence to an audience increasingly in thrall to spectacle and acceleration" thereby making it recognizable as an urgent phenomenon in need of urgent attention. Expanding on the discourse about time-lapse photography and its ubiquity in ecodocumentary, Coutts reads its familiarity as an advantage: since it is no longer a novel aesthetic technique, perhaps it grants us access to think critically about a new dimension of experience, encouraging us to accelerate our response to effects that increasingly can no longer be said to be slow.

Finally, Khan focuses on Robert Kenner's popular ecodocumentary *Food, Inc.* (2008), which she describes as the "canonical cinematic expression of sustainable food politics" among a spate of recent documentaries about the environmental impact of industrial agriculture. Khan argues that the film generates a limited and complex "ecological consciousness," paradoxically undermined by its market-driven logic of food justice. At the heart of the film's eco-consciousness is the use of infographics, which she reads as a form of "visual activism" deployed across many food documentaries, particularly those produced around World War II, arguably the era that most accelerated the environmental impact of agriculture and the accelerated growth of agribusiness that we know today. The infographics in *Food, Inc.* operate on the visual logic of pastoral marketing in relation to Big Food. Although the film goes to great lengths to demonstrate the dubious mock pastoralism of Big Food's marketing strategies, Khan argues that it, nevertheless, paradoxically retains an investment in some ideal of human-nature relations. As a "spectacle of epistephilia," the infographic aesthetics of industrial food that the film displays exemplifies Timothy Morton's concept of "dark ecology," which Kahn describes as a "sinister approach to art that requires owning up to our complicity in the agro-environmental mess in which we find ourselves." Beyond more didactic critiques of the food industry that emerge in *Food, Inc.*, Kahn uses the frame of eco-kitsch to consider how animated sequences of food and supply might motivate a more ecologically sustainable public. Through their different emphases on specific techniques of the visible, Druick, Coutts, and Khan offer illuminating ways of thinking about tropes that extend across much of environmental documentary today, the political effect of such techniques marking a key point of contestation among them.

4

ON (NOT) FALLING FROM THE SKY
Fly-Over Global Documentary as Capitalist Body Genre

Zoë Druick

On June 7, 2015, the Smithsonian Channel aired the final installment in its *Aerial America* series of shows about each of the fifty states, which it had been televising for almost five years. By this point, one could say, the aerial fly-over, once a remarkable novelty, had become a fairly commonplace strategy, thanks in no small part to the Smithsonian museum itself, which has been screening the early IMAX film *To Fly* daily since its debut in 1976. Indeed, with the advent of Google Earth in 2001, satellite photography has become ubiquitous, and since 2015, camera-enabled consumer drone technology has made this view even more accessible.[1]

In some ways, these digital technologies of vision are extensions of the links between cinema and mobility that have been established since the inception of moving images—the traveling aspect of cinema appears prominently across a range of genres.[2] Early on, cinematic techniques were developed to provide spectators with the feeling of propulsion—the compression of physical distances and the transportation of the viewer by means of "sweeping, arcing, panning and canting" views—something that is further intensified by the promise of immersive technologies such as three projector Cinerama in the 1950s, IMAX since the late 1960s, Omnimax, and virtual reality today.[3] Such "vertiginous bodily orientations" and their resultant sensations are highly sought after by audiences.[4] IMAX, in which the "hyperbolic" technology itself is the star, literally takes camera movement to new heights.[5] The feeling of control over all we survey and of our powerful sense of becoming merged with the camera eye/I that allows viewers to flit across the globe while rooted in their seats are both a foundational part of the experience of cinema and of the "structure of feeling" of modernity.⁶ Perhaps the most quintessentially cinematic shot—the fly-over—often used as an establishing shot, has been refined with each new form of aircraft, from propeller plane to helicopter to satellite to drone.⁷ But until recently, it has been rare to find film and television productions that relied entirely on aerial photography.

While nonfiction cinema hasn't shied away from the aerial view (a common strategy in silent expedition films and city symphonies of the 1920s, for instance), it wasn't until Godfrey Reggio's *Koyaanisqatsi* in 1983 that nonfiction essay films adopted the mode. Since the mid-1990s, aerial documentaries have become more common (e.g., *Winged Migration* [2001]) until, most recently, aerial-dominant works such as *Planet Earth* (2006), *Home* (2009), and *Samsara* (2011) have arguably been seen by the largest audiences of any documentaries in history, across a variety of platforms. Partly this has to do with the globalization of platforms and, correspondingly, with a quest for subject matter that promises a global view. However, in what follows, I propose to consider the work of these popular documentaries not only in terms of the political economy of media or viewers' ability to comprehend global issues, such as environmentalism, but also in relation to the way they pleasurably engage the body of the viewer with feelings of power and omniscience by means of the technological "event" of the aerial view.⁸ Through their emphasis on the "proprioceptive aesthetic," they constitute, I suggest, a new kind of body genre.⁹

In a groundbreaking essay from the early 1990s, Linda Williams identified "body genres" as lowbrow cultural forms that aim to elicit bodily responses in the form of the release of fluids, such as tears, sweat, or sexual emissions, as well as involuntary chills and shudders.¹⁰ The aerial fly-over is arguably an increasingly ubiquitous perspective, if not a true genre, that provokes precisely such intense sensation and evokes a number of involuntary physiological responses. When watching a phantom ride or fly over, we often feel as though we are floating or falling through space even though we are safely in our seats. Depending on the duration, speed, angle, and altitude, our heartbeats may accelerate, we may begin to sweat, grip our seats (or our friends), hide our eyes, or display other physiological responses to the fear or thrill of heights. A fast-moving camera tends to put our bodies on high alert, as though at a precognitive level we feel we are about to be involved in an accident or disaster.¹¹

One significant difference from body genres as Williams conceptualizes them is that fly-overs and phantom rides do not require a body on screen with which to identify. Proprioceptive aesthetics, or "a sensation of my own body moving through on-screen space, at once weightless and frictionless, terrifying and illusory," stimulates our reactions through the identification of our bodies with the apparatus itself.[12] When we are wrapped up in our experience of thrilling sensation, critical engagement often retreats. As with flight simulation experienced when playing an air force video game, for example, the production of adrenaline and other physiological reactions are paramount, often taking precedence over reflection. Yet as anyone who has seen it will attest, the fly-over perspective provides the viewer with a strong sense of the power of the technological and even militarized gaze that at once makes up for and contains the viewer's fear. Our sense of power is further attested by the fact that we inevitably emerge from the fly-over unscathed.

While the analysis that follows partially relates to the particular conditions of capitalist media production in which the films and shows are made and circulated, it also takes into account the ways that technologized forms of expression work on the sensate body itself, helping to form embodied subjectivity in capitalism.[13] The contradictions between the stated humanitarian or ecological aims of any given production and the spectacular aerial aesthetics they offer may provide a useful site at which to undertake an exploration of capitalism, class, and media that goes beyond the question of representation or even relations of production to address the profoundly ideological phenomenology of technological power itself.[14]

Flying over the Planet

Since 2001, around the time of the globalization of the television market, there have been a series of high-intensity planetary wildlife documentaries on global television providers Discovery, BBC, National Geographic, Disney, and Netflix, including *Blue Planet* (2001), *Planet Earth* (2006), *Earth* (2007), *Life* (2007–2009), *Frozen Planet* (2011), *EarthFlight* (2011–2012), *Planet Earth II* (2016), and *Our Planet* (2019), all of which provide what Helen Wheatley calls "spectacular" high-resolution television, made for expensive home theaters.[15] Set to soaring soundtracks with narration by celebrities and renowned for their impressive ability to find and shoot camera-shy animals and obscure natural spectacles using new technological innovations, the shows provide "exotic" vistas and novel perspectives, including a preponderance of aerial photography taken from satellites, helicopters, balloons, and drones. These shows provide the pleasures of virtual travel and even boast tie-ins with tour companies.[16] They tend to keep humans off screen, along with "urgent problems such as climate change, habitat destruction, hunting and pollution."[17]

Fig. 4.1 The God's-eye view in *Planet Earth* (2006) emphasizes humanity's superiority to the natural world.

Planet Earth, for instance, is reported to be the most highly circulated documentary in history, selling millions of DVD box sets.[18] By emphasizing universal themes and focusing on the wonder of nature at a global scale, the series was specifically produced to "go global" and have a long shelf life.[19] Despite the lip service paid to the way the show exposes the wonders of nature, much of the press coverage of the series focuses on the technological innovation required to obtain the impressive shots. The shows were widely reported as relying on high-definition, light-weight, body-mounted camera-stabilizing rigs; Photron digital cameras capable of filming 2000 frames per second; heat sensitive thermal cameras for shooting in the dark; and emergent drone technologies. Seemingly, nothing is beyond the reach of the producers' recording equipment, which travels beneath the water and above the clouds, as easily exploring micro landscapes as macro. In every episode, life and death struggles caught on film deliver what Linda Williams calls with respect to pornography "maximum visibility."[20] With only the omniscient narrator to identify with and "the perspective of the camera that so often appears to be the narrator's eye, the viewer is constructed as omniscient and capable of penetrating the most inaccessible reaches of the natural world."[21]

As with other nature documentaries, although environmental problems are sometimes mentioned, they are rarely linked to histories of racism and colonialism. If the preservation of habitats and species is mentioned, it tends to be couched in terms of their usefulness to humans. By leaving humans out of the story, such shows either explicitly or implicitly suggest that humans are always disrupters of nature's "balance."[22] Thus, far from bringing the viewer to nature on its own terms, these shows are more like "extravagant animal operas" that emphasize humanity's technologically enhanced omniscience and superiority to the natural world.[23] This is borne out in the way in which technology is foregrounded in the series. There is a feeling of constant movement either within the frame or of the frame, including time lapse and slow motion. The series focuses on phenomena of massive scale, such as migrations, which are best observed from above. The planet is repeatedly shown in aerial view; satellites as well as the ubiquitous balloon and helicopter shots keep us floating atop the world. Through the organization of the material by ecosystem (e.g., mountains, oceans, caves, seas, islands, frozen lands), histories of material conditions in any one particular place are downplayed in favor of their timeless geological categorization.

Matching the God's-eye view, the soundtrack uses an omniscient and unseen narrator, the famous British naturalist David Attenborough, who provides the right balance of science and wonder, though never politics.[24] Attenborough upholds Sarah Kozloff's characterization of the heterodiegetic narrator as endowed with "power and pretensions to truth."[25] Never at a loss for words, Attenborough, who has been narrating British nature shows for five decades, "is like a knowledgeable and omnipresent museum guide."[26] When people do, rarely, appear on screen, it is always as anonymous actors who are either demonstrating long-standing Indigenous lifeways or as heavily technologized modern explorers (e.g., the "Caves" episode). Strains of world music contained within a symphonic musical frame are provided in the award-winning soundtrack by George Fenton.

While *Planet Earth* and its ilk do not touch on capitalism directly, they do express a particular anxiety of those living in the advanced capitalist world—to whom they are addressed—that the extractive and exploitative social and economic conditions in which we live somehow contradict the warm and protective feelings we may have about attractive animals and untouched nature more generally. As Richard Beck has noted: "The show does not simply depict uninhabited areas of the Earth; it depicts those areas in such a way as to block the formation of intellectual or conceptual links between them and the political or economic processes that continue to accelerate their degradation."[27]

By creating the most technologically advanced and sublimely impressive nature show yet produced, *Planet Earth*'s producers succeeded in attracting huge audiences domestically and internationally. Through its filming techniques, the show also situated itself in the tradition of the travelogue, expedition, and safari film. Flying over a pristine and untouched nature with enormous technological mastery conveys to the viewer—at a proprioceptive level—a sense of control over that which is actually out of control: unchecked capitalist expansion. Providing the viewer with satisfying experiences of powerful motility conveys the familiar feeling that to travel is to obtain knowledge, reinscribing the subject/object dichotomy of colonial humanism. The shows also inevitably evoke imperial nostalgia, longing for the things one has oneself helped to destroy, without compelling self-reflection in the viewer.[28]

Global Symphonies: *Home* and *Samsara*

Home and *Samsara*, two other very popular global documentaries of the early years of the twenty-first century, are indebted in different ways to the expedition film. Wildlife photographer, ecologist and goodwill ambassador for the United Nations environment program, Yann Arthus-Bertrand has made numerous films about Earth shot from helicopters with the goal of provoking environmental action. Perhaps his most iconic film, *Home* (2009), which was released simultaneously in theaters, on DVD, and on YouTube has been viewed by over 600 million people on YouTube alone, making it one of the most watched nonfiction films of all time.[29] Bertrand's work—including his 1999 book *Earth from Above*, which was an international best-seller; his films, such as *Human* (2015), *Terra* (2015); and his UN-sponsored database, *7 Billion Others*—fit comfortably into the category of "coffee table globalism" forged by *National Geographic*, the publication where he got his start. As he puts it, our relationship to nature is potentially unifying: "There is a universal quality about beauty; in front of a vast landscape, we all share the same feeling of wonder. When nature is beautiful, we are all moved by it."[30] You can see in his work a combination of the formal strategies of nature documentaries with the humanitarian framing more particular to French documentary traditions. According to Leon Sachs, Arthus-Bertrand inherits the nineteenth-century republican pedagogical tradition that attempts to attach civic values to object lessons. "*Home*'s global citizen," Sachs writes, "is in many respects a republican citizen on a planetary scale."[31] Sachs's argument is further bolstered by Arthus-Bertrand's production company's free distribution of a "pedagogical dossier" available online in six languages to help teachers use the film in their classes.

Fig. 4.2 Entirely photographed from the air, *Home* (2009) enacts a universal narrative about global humanism.

A cult of personality has grown up around Arthus-Bertrand.[32] He endows the aerial view with a "rhetoric of elevation in the moral sense of the term," presenting himself as a "spiritual aviator."[33] Shot in 120 locations in fifty-four countries, *Home* is a perfect emblem of the elite European male traveler's frictionless mobility and universal narrative about global humanism.[34] Every shot is taken from the air. However, unlike many aerial views, which are depersonalized, Arthus-Bertrand's perspectives continuously link the viewer back to him (and his stand-in narrators) as a strong teacher and concerned humanist. Yet in telling the story of environmental disaster as wrought by "Man" who has fallen from grace and lost his "harmonious relationship to his environment" in his quest for oil, the film replicates colonial humanism at a global scale replayed in the story of the Anthropocene.[35] All humans are equally to blame for environmental collapse. In this scenario there are only two states of being: harmonious and disastrous. However, absent a cognitive map of capitalism and global class relations, the film can provide only limited suggestions for reform of the system. Nevertheless, the filmmaker's flagrant use of technology to tell the story helps redeem its possibilities, without need for a reevaluation of capitalism itself.

A study of audience responses to *Home* undertaken in Italy with people of different nationalities emphasized that viewers appreciated the positivity of the film because they already felt like they were part of the environmental problem and wanted to be part of the solution as well.[36] This confirms a reading of the subject in capitalism as divided and conflicted. By seeing the Earth from space, they reported both feeling like astronauts and having a new sense of needing to care for the planet as "small, fragile thing."[37] This response evokes the relationship between a privileged, knowledgeable position and the feeling of a shift in scale that aerial imagery produces, raising the viewer to the level of a benevolent deity who can take care things that are, in reality, well beyond their individual control. At the least, these responses highlight the way in which the aerial viewpoint seductively includes the viewer in a technologized, ordered, and powerful, if not omniscient, perspective.

Arthus-Bertrand's work has been rightfully criticized for an optimistic techno-capitalist framework that contains its critical edge. The film's unresolved message about capitalism can be observed in the credit sequence where the word *HOME* itself is formed through an animation of the names of numerous large companies in the French fashion industry who helped crowd-fund it. Despite its stated humanist intentions, Arthus-Bertrand's work nevertheless sustains the colonial illusion that takes the aerial overview as a visual representation of superior knowledge and mastery. Technology in this sense does indeed function as ideology.[38] His work is thus a compelling illustration of the contradictions at play when looking in a way that embodies possession and mastery: one ends up telling a story about global ecological responsibility that doesn't identify global class relations.

Ron Fricke came to prominence for his work on the first two films in Godfrey Reggio's Qatsi Trilogy, *Koyaanisqatsi* (1983) and *Powaqqatsi* (1988). He extended that work with his films *Baraka* (1992; which was intended for IMAX) and *Samsara* (2011), in which the images, some of which were obtained from military satellites, are even more spectacular.[39] The films have been likened to travelogues and global symphonies and praised for not being typical issue documentaries. As one reviewer wrote, "With exotic imagery fit for the cover of *National Geographic*, the new film 'Samsara' ranges across the globe: there are fantastical tiered temples in verdant Myanmar and glorious Japanese mohawks, the natural wonders of Namibian sand dunes and orderly production lines of modern agribusiness in China and Europe. The locations are unnamed, and a rich, varied score is heard instead of political or social commentary. One striking image flows into the next, loosely organized according to the cyclical Hindu notion of birth and destruction that gives the film its Sanskrit title."[40]

In the press coverage, much is made of the large-format camera Fricke perfected to enable time-lapse panning shots and the scope of *Samsara*'s dozens of locations in twenty-five countries. The perpetual movement is reflected

Fig. 4.3 High-tech, aerial photography in *Samsara* (2011) valorizes difference and reinscribes it from a mobile and omniscient Western point of view.

in the title, which is taken from the Sanskrit word meaning "the ever-turning wheel of life," a term associated with South Asian subcontinent religions, including Tibetan Buddhism. The film is framed by the creation and destruction of a sand mandala by Tibetan monks, putting all we have seen into cosmic context as arbitrary and fleeting creation. While not afraid of harsh realities, the film "avoids taking up 'controversial' positions which might be detrimental to commercial success, adopting the viewpoint of an uninvolved witness." Likewise more concerned with "the aesthetic or emotional impact of its subjects than with the global political or economic conditions which account for them," *Samsara* found the sweet spot that enabled it to become a global phenomenon.[41]

In taking the "global panorama" to new heights, Ron Fricke's work is very much in the tradition of *National Geographic*.[42] *Samsara*'s seemingly random images of global squalor, sex trade workers, factory farming, and both industrial and nonindustrial workers as well as God's-eye views of environmental destruction, are mixed haphazardly in with proprioceptive sequences featuring fly-over shots of pristine forests, erupting volcanoes, heritage sites, and religious rituals. As Martin Roberts points out in relation to *Baraka*, Fricke's work is exemplary of the "capitalist First World's guilt at the social, economic, and cultural havoc it has wreaked on the world at large, coupled with nostalgia for a pristine, imaginary world prior to capitalist modernity."[43] Through the combination of non-Western themes and perspectives (e.g., the Sanskrit concept of *samsara*) and the deployment of the highest-grade military and industrial technologies of looking and flying, Fricke's work both valorizes difference and reinscribes it from a mobile and omniscient Western point of view, not unlike the nature films discussed earlier. Indeed, far from attempting to decenter the Western point of view, Roberts suggests that Fricke's work is an attempt to "reimpose a neo-colonial order on a world slipping increasingly beyond its control."[44] As in Reggio's work, the vision of global politics is largely reduced to a situation where the binary of tradition/nature versus modernity is mapped onto one of good versus evil. As the viewer is presumably already situated in "modernity," there is nothing to do but succumb to the inability to do anything but grit your teeth and experience the speed of life out of balance or to realize that all this, too, will, in the cosmic scheme of things, pass. The film's producer put it clearly when, in differentiating *Samsara* from global issue documentaries, he claimed, "We're not trying to say anything."[45]

Despite its claims to cover all of humanity, the film maintains a colonial expedition film logic of subject and object, as was clearly exposed by one enthusiastic reviewer, who noted: "Fricke knows that for all of his computerized camera movements and time-lapse photography, sometimes resting on a close-up of a Filipino inmate's eyes, a young African mother and child, or the single tear of a geisha slipping down her cheek is more emotionally powerful than anything technologically dazzling."[46] Fricke's reliance on expedition film conventions is apparent in the use of ethnographic portraiture at various points throughout the film: most of the portraits of mute subjects returning the camera's gaze are "natives"—women, children, and animals—all subjects typically found in the expedition film.[47]

What holds the film together, aside from its weak narrative thread of "continuous flow," is its musical score. The music of Michael Steams functions to unify the ultimately fragmentary visuals and is clearly based on the model provided by Philip Glass, which, from *Koyaanisqatsi* onward, set the sonic template for the global documentary or essay film. As with the aesthetic of Cold War humanism popularized by *The Family of Man* exhibit and publication, Glass's highly formalist music bonds the family of human music together through its rhythmic universalism. Although the modularity and circularity of his music is often ascribed to his interest in Indian music, it is also consonant with an expedition or view aesthetic, modular and nonnarrative Western forms.[48] In the ways in which Glass, Steam, Fenton, and other world music producers import sounds of authenticity into their Western musical frames, their work replicates perfectly an expedition aesthetic, as if having brought home a box of sonic souvenirs from world travels. Virtually all contemporary global expedition films use a combination of Western classical, postminimalist, and world music. The orchestration of difference through a camera presented as omniscient as well as the reliance on prominent soundtracks places these films squarely in the tradition of the city symphony—this time at a global scale.

While in many ways *Home* and *Samsara* are as different as the visions of their respective creators, in other ways they are actually quite comparable. Both made by well-heeled Euro-American auteur-adventurers who are closely associated with their bravery and technological prowess, these films convey strong ethical messages of a world "out of balance." Both directors utilize high-grade military surveillance and recording technologies, and both are committed to the aerial view. Unlike the use of aerial photography in *Planet Earth* to find and track elusive animal life and exotic vistas, both Arthus-Bertrand and Fricke use aerial photography to consider what "Man" or humanity has wrought on the earth—through large-scale agriculture, extractive development, urban living, and pollution. While Frick occasionally zeroes in with lingering still shots and slow pans of the authentic, Indigenous people he has contacted during his travels, Arthus-Bertrand prefers to maintain his eye in the sky (saving close-ups and interviews for other projects). As he flies over African villagers washing their clothes in a polluted river close to an oil refinery, they look up, small, ant-like, and, frankly, as dehumanized as the herds of animals shown from above in *Blue Planet*. Both films partake in a "melody of the world" structure where editing, music, and narration bring together a global story that is otherwise made up of extreme diversity.[49]

However, the global story evades issues of capitalism, imperialism, and global inequality in favor of a humanist story that suggests we're all in this mess together; that technology may have gotten us here but is also capable of getting us out; and that it will do so without the need for change at the level of relations of (re)production. *Samsara* presents no global issues explicitly, only implicitly through its universalist pretense to be able to be everywhere and see everything, and to find compelling natural beauty in the non-Western world. *Home* presents a heartfelt message of the necessity of global change that by illustrating the concept of the Anthropocene manages to avoid attributing fault to any state or corporate actors or naming any economic system.

Proprioceptive Aesthetics and Anticognitive Mapping

The global documentary's reliance on "proprioceptive aesthetics," the feeling of one's body moving quickly and powerfully through space, is telling, as is its emphasis on planetary scale.[50] In relation to narratives that don't actually thematize capitalism, the work thus risks replicating a terrifying feeling that the devastation of the Earth is being wrought by a force beyond our control, as though capitalism is just another sublime force of nature, without giving viewers a clear sense of how they may be implicated and, even more importantly, how they may intervene at a political level. I propose that this technical virtuosity produces something like a "vernacular sublime" where pleasurable experiences of mediated awe and even terror allow for the imagination of spectators' own power and control in limited ways which function at a precognitive or affective level.

To illustrate this point, we might fruitfully think about the limits of the concept of cognitive mapping—the influential aesthetico-political program provided by Fredric Jameson—in relation to this kind of representation. How, Jameson asks, do we conceptualize the "world space of multinational capitalism?" and what are the "totality of class relations on a global . . . scale"?[51] Although the ways in which power is distributed within the capitalist system is in some ways invisible—unlike, for instance, the symbols of monarchy—its effects on the world in the form of extraction, exploitation, war, and destruction must be ideologically reframed as ethical in popular culture to secure consent. One of the most insidious reframings has been provided by the colonial discourse of humanism itself, which has long been mobilized to justify economically motivated violence in the name of "moral, political, intellectual, educational, and social values."[52] This approach individualizes and relativizes the vastly discrepant situations of people around the world in relation to modernity (or, rarely, capitalism), but presents the struggle against inequality and injustice as one that necessitates the adoption of "universal" Western values. Insofar as this work obscures any understanding of the power relationships of global capital, it may be characterized as "anticognitive mapping."[53]

Part of the anticognitive mapping work of the global documentaries I have discussed stems precisely from the way they make us *feel*. IMAX films, which innovated propulsive movement into the scene as an event in itself, deploy the technology's tendency toward vertiginous movement into the frame rather than staying safely outside of the action as an onlooker.[54] Traveling shots like these bring the feeling of your heart or your stomach into your throat—the experience of the phantom-ride or fly-over aesthetic at its most basic. Enda Duffy characterizes this desire for speed as an essential part of capitalist modernity, "[Speed] as a desire clearly nurtured by capitalism—in every mass-cultural genre from car advertisements to car chase films—it may be *the* desire par excellence in Western culture that is fostered and tolerated in order to reconcile human subjects to their lot as actors in a 'dynamic' capitalist economic milieu."[55]

In their book *Cartographies of the Absolute*, Alberto Toscano and Jeff Kinkle observe that a comprehensive cognitive mapping of capitalism in film may be an impossible task. They argue that, despite its global reach, capitalism as such resists aesthetic representation because of its abstraction, its lack of an "easily grasped command-and-control centre."⁵⁶ It seems to spread as an intangible logic, vast and invisible. This often leads to a void filled with conspiratorial visions that tie global events up in a satisfying set of explanations rife with powerful and nefarious individuals. However, if cognitive mapping is a "precondition for identifying any 'levers', nerve-centres or weak links in the political anatomy of contemporary domination," as Toscano and Kinkle assert, then such visions are as useless for politics as blockbuster global environmental documentaries are.

Nevertheless, because of their global scope and ambitions and even, as in the case of *Home*, their pointed criticisms of wealth inequality, violent dispossession and environmental catastrophe, I would suggest that global documentary films seem to miss their mark more conspicuously than most. Moreover, because they purport to speak about the effects of global development or modernity, if not capitalism per se, they play a role in consolidating a problematic story of the Anthropocene.⁵⁷ In many ways, the films parallel the mainstreaming of the environmental movement; the stories they tell (or in the case of *Planet Earth*, only imply) about humans as sublime geological actors, changing the face of the earth, are capable of providing us with a site for the analysis of incomplete visions of a global totality.

Yet, as I have tried to suggest, any analysis of how capitalism is *represented* in film and television, such as that ably provided by Toscano and Kinkle, risks leaving out consideration of the ways in which cinema has emerged as an apparatus that helps to constitute capitalism's embodied spectator at the sensory level. The cognitive mapping approach, therefore, may be fruitfully complemented with the strand of scholarship considered here—the proprioceptive aesthetic—that considers the way that the cinematic apparatus operates at the level of the spectator's body. Considering the ways popular global documentaries mediate—at the level of affect—between our perception of our own bodies in space and perception of the world in which we live may help to concretize an assessment of precisely where this work forecloses political consciousness—most likely at a level beyond the realm of representation. As we've seen, no matter how much the texts profess to bring the viewer closer to nature or Indigenous others, on a proprioceptive level they actually manifest a vernacular capitalist sublime by articulating the rhythm of the viewer's bodily movement to the speed of technology, making it conspicuously independent from the slowness of most natural rhythms.⁵⁸

Drawing on humanist tropes of *The Family of Man* and associative forms of editing that link humans and animals in different parts of the word through commonalities, the genre of the global documentary has difficulty providing a cognitive map of the current capitalist system even as it obliquely addresses issues of environmental degradation, pollution and even exploitation. I have suggested that perhaps this inability stems from its roots in various aesthetic tendencies of Western imperialist ideology, such as a clear distinction between humans here at home and exotic nonhuman others whose lifeways are understood to be necessarily—if unfortunately—sacrificed on the altar of progress. They express something of an oblique realization, in Toscano and Kinkle's words, that the causes of "'our' social life are elsewhere, in the processes of extraction, dispossession and subjugation that constitute imperialism and colonialism" and that the "privileges of domination are accompanied by a poverty of experience and a deficit of knowledge."[59]

Nevertheless, as I've tried to suggest, even granted that these films and shows are incomplete documents of our global system, their gaps, inadequacies, and, indeed, contradictions may still convey something important about the culture that produced them. They are a revealing product of the globalization of the film and television markets, and the resultant production of images and sounds meant for viewers in many different cultural and linguistic contexts. They provide the thrills long associated with the phantom ride genre in general and IMAX in particular, coupling them with the framework of education and scientific understanding. They rely on the technologized modes of looking developed for conquest and war and teach us to be at home in a sublime mechanized gaze even as they thrill and shock us on a physiological level. But in relation to the social and environmental crises they evoke but never fully map and the politics they studiously avoid, they must also be seen as stories about the discomforts and denials of capitalism.

Notes

The author would like to acknowledge the research assistance of Gopa Biswas Caesar.

1. Dorrian, "On Google Earth," 295.
2. Ruoff, "Introduction," 2.
3. Richmond, *Cinema's Bodily Illusions*, 2; Roberts, "Baraka," 73.
4. Rabinovitz, "From Hale's Tours to Star Tours," 43.
5. Griffiths, "Time Traveling IMAX Style," 257.
6. Dorrian and Pousin, introduction, 1; Warner, "Intimate Communiqués," 11; Giblett, *Sublime Communication Technologies*, 2008.
7. Pinkerton, "Bombast."

8. Robic, "From the Sky to the Ground," 174.
9. Richmond, *Cinema's Bodily Illusions*, 6.
10. Williams, "Gender, Genre, and Excess." For a similar argument for the contemporary action film, see Christiansen, *Drone Age Cinema*, 12.
11. Rabinovitz briefly identifies *ride films* as a body genre in "From Hale's Tours to Star Tours," 43.
12. Richmond, *Cinema's Bodily Illusions*, 1.
13. See Crary, *Techniques of the Observer*; Duffy, *Speed Handbook*.
14. In this way, these productions are the exact opposite of what Scott MacDonald has termed *ecocinema*, which he defines as the idea of using cinema to provide experiences that "demonstrate an alternative to conventional media-spectatorship and help to nurture a more environmentally progressive mindset" ("Ecocinema Experience," 20).
15. Wheatley, "Limits of Television," 334.
16. Lippe-McGraw, "Tauck Tours."
17. Austin, *Watching the World*, 164.
18. *Planet Earth* was filmed in HD and cost £16 million to produce, making it the most expensive production in the BBC's history (Beck, "Costing Planet Earth," 63).
19. Mjos, *Media Globalization*, 131; Austin, *Watching the World* 122.
20. Williams, *Hardcore*, 48.
21. Armbruster, "Creating the World," 232.
22. Ibid., 226–228.
23. Siebert, "Artifice of the Natural," 43.
24. In response to critics, the BBC made a companion series about environmentalism, *Blue Planet: The Future* (2006), which was aired on a smaller network, BBC Four.
25. Kozloff, *Invisible Storyteller*, 96.
26. Siebert, "Artifice of the Natural," 49.
27. Beck, "Costing Planet Earth," 64.
28. Griffiths, "The Untrammeled Camera," 96; Staples, "Safari Adventure," 394; Rosaldo, "Imperialist Nostalgia," 108.
29. Crespo and Pereira, "Climate Change Films," 167.
30. Mun-Delsalle, "French Photographer."
31. Sachs, "Eco-Lessons," 134.
32. Lugon, "Aviator and the Photographer," 148.
33. Ibid., 150.
34. Sachs, "Eco-Lessons," 133.
35. Ibid., 137.
36. Crespo and Pereira, "Climate Change Films," 177.
37. Ibid., 177.
38. Duffy, *Speed Handbook*, 41.
39. Staples, "Mondo Mediations," 663.
40. Rapold, "Planetary Poetry," A12.
41. Roberts, "Baraka," 68. Fricke credits *Planet Earth* with location scouting for *Samsara* (Rapold, "Planetary Poetry," A12).
42. Roberts, "Baraka," 75. See also Lutz and Collins, *Reading National Geographic*.
43. Roberts, "Baraka," 69.
44. Ibid., 78.
45. Rapold, "Planetary Poetry," A12.
46. Walsh, "Samsara."

47. Staples, "Mondo Mediations," 667.
48. Lessard, "Cultural Recycling," 496.
49. Cowan, *Walter Ruttmann*, 82.
50. See Richmond, *Cinema's Bodily Illusions*.
51. Jameson, *Postmodernism*, 54, 416.
52. Bloom, *French Colonial Documentary*, 128.
53. Toscano and Kinkle, *Cartographies of the Absolute*, 176.
54. Griffiths, "Time Traveling IMAX Style," 239.
55. Duffy, *Speed Handbook*, 35.
56. Toscano and Kinkle, *Cartographies of the Absolute*, 24.
57. For a critique of the concept of Anthropocene, see Moore, "Rise of Cheap Nature," 78–115.
58. Richmond, *Cinema's Bodily Illusions*, 117.
59. Toscano and Kinkle, *Cartographies of the Absolute*, 16–17.

References

Armbruster, Karla. "Creating the World We Must Save: The Paradox of Television Nature Documentaries." In *Writing the Environment: Ecocriticism and Literature*, edited by R. Kerridge and N. Sammells, 218–238. London: Zed Books, 1998.
Arthus-Bertrand, Yann. *Home*. France: EuropaCorp, 2009.
Austin, Thomas. *Watching the World: Screen Documentary and Audiences*. Manchester: Manchester University Press, 2012.
Beck, Richard. "Costing Planet Earth." *Film Quarterly* 63, no. 3 (2010): 63–66.
Bloom, Peter J. *French Colonial Documentary: Mythologies of Humanitarianism*. Minneapolis: University of Minnesota Press, 2008.
Christiansen, Steen Ledet. *Drone Age Cinema: Action Film and Sensory Assault*. London: IB Tauris, 2017.
Cowan, Michael. *Walter Ruttmann and the Cinema of Multiplicity: Avant-Garde, Advertising, Modernity*. Amsterdam: Amsterdam University Press, 2014.
Crary, Jonathan. *Techniques of the Observer: On Vision and Modernity in the Nineteenth Century*. Cambridge, MA: MIT Press, 1990.
Crespo, Inês, and Ângela Pereira. "Climate Change Films: Fear and Agency Appeals." In *Transnational Ecocinema: Film Culture in an Era of Ecological Transformation*, edited by Tommy Gustafsson, 165–186. Bristol, UK: Intellect, 2013.
Dorrian, Mark. "On Google Earth." In *Seeing from Above: The Aerial View in Visual Culture*, edited by Mark Dorrian and Frédéric Pousin, 290–307. London: IB Tauris, 2013.
Dorrian, Mark, and Frédéric Pousin. Introduction to *Seeing from Above: The Aerial View in Visual Culture*, edited by Mark Dorrian and Frédéric Pousin, 1–10. London: IB Tauris, 2013.
Duffy, Enda. *The Speed Handbook*. Durham, NC: Duke University Press, 2009.
Fothergill, Alastair, dir. *Planet Earth*. UK: BBC, 2006.
Fricke, Ron, dir. *Samsara*. USA: Magidson Films, 2011.
Giblett, Rod. *Sublime Communication Technologies*. Basingstoke, UK: Palgrave Macmillan, 2008.
Griffiths, Alison. "Time Traveling IMAX Style: Tales from the Giant Screen." In *Virtual Voyages: Cinema and Travel*, edited by Jeffrey Ruoff, 238–258. Durham, NC: Duke University Press, 2006.

———. "The Untrammeled Camera: A Topos of the Expedition Film." *Film History* 25, no. 1–2 (2013): 95–109.

Jameson, Fredric. *Postmodernism; or, The Cultural Logic of Late Capitalism*. London: Verso, 1991.

Kozloff, Sarah. *Invisible Storyteller: Voice-Over Narration in American Fiction Film*. Berkeley: University of California Press, 1988.

Lessard, Bruno. "Cultural Recycling, Performance, and Immediacy in Philip Glass's Film Music for Godfrey Reggio's Qatsi Trilogy." In *Sound and Music in Film and Visual Media: An Overview*, edited by Graeme Harper, 493–504. New York: Continuum, 2009.

Lippe-McGraw, Jordi. "Tauck Tours Offering Vacations Inspired by BBC's 'Planet Earth II.'" *Condé-Nast Traveler*, March 21, 2017. https://www.cntraveler.com/story/tauck-tours-offering-vacations-inspired-by-bbcs-planet-earth-ii.

Lugon, Olivier. "The Aviator and the Photographer: The Case of Walter Mittelholzer." In *Seeing from Above: The Aerial View in Visual Culture*, edited by Mark Dorrian and Frédéric Pousin, 147–162. London: IB Tauris, 2013.

Lutz, Catherine, and Jane Collins. *Reading National Geographic*. Chicago: University of Chicago Press, 1993.

MacDonald, Scott. "The Ecocinema Experience." In *Ecocinema Theory and Practice*, edited by Stephen Rust, Salma Monani, and Sean Cubitt, 17–42. New York: Routledge, 2013.

Mjos, Ole. *Media Globalization and the Discovery Channel Networks*. New York: Routledge, 2010.

Moore, James W. "The Rise of Cheap Nature." In *Anthropocene or Capitalocene? Nature, History, and the Crisis of Capitalism*, edited by James W. Moore, 78–115. Oakland: PM Press, 2016.

Mun-Delsalle, Y-Jean. "French Photographer Yann Arthus-Bertrand Sends a Love Letter to Humanity in his Latest Film." *Forbes*, May 13, 2016. https://www.forbes.com/sites/yjean mundelsalle/2016/05/13/french-photographer-yann-arthus-bertrand-sends-a-love-letter-to-humanity-in-his-latest-film-human.

Pinkerton, Nick. "Bombast: Everywhere with Helicopter." *Film Comment*, February 20, 2015. https://www.filmcomment.com/blog/bombast-everywhere-with-helicopter.

Rabinovitz, Lauren. "From Hale's Tours to Star Tours: Virtual Voyages, Travel Ride Films, and the Delirium of the Hyper-real." In *Virtual Voyages: Cinema and Travel*, edited by Jeffrey Ruoff, 42–60. Durham, NC: Duke University Press, 2006.

Rapold, Nicolas. "Planetary Poetry, Woven into a Movie." *New York Times*, August 17, 2012, Arts 12.

Richmond, Scott C. *Cinema's Bodily Illusions: Flying, Floating and Hallucinating*. Minneapolis: University of Minnesota Press, 2016.

Roberts, Martin. "'Baraka': World Cinema and the Global Cultural Industry." *Cinema Journal* 37, no. 3 (1998): 62–82.

Robic, Marie-Claire. "From the Sky to the Ground: The Aerial View and the Ideal of the Vue Raisonée in Geography during the 1920s." In *Seeing from Above: The Aerial View in Visual Culture*, edited by Mark Dorrian and Frédéric Pousin, 163–187. London: IB Tauris, 2013.

Rosaldo, Renato. "Imperialist Nostalgia." *Representations*, no. 26, special issue (Spring 1989): 107–122.

Ruoff, Jeffrey. "Introduction: The Filmic Fourth Dimension: Cinema as Audiovisual Vehicle." In *Virtual Voyages: Cinema and Travel*, edited by Jeffrey Ruoff, 1–24. Durham, NC: Duke University Press, 2006.

Sachs, Leon. "Eco-Lessons: Yan Arthus-Bertrand's HOME and the Republican Pedagogical Contract." In *The Environment in French and Francophone Literature and Film*, edited by Jeff Persels, 133–142. Amsterdam: Rodopi, 2012.

Siebert, Charles. "The Artifice of the Natural: How TV's Nature Shows Make All the Earth a Stage." *Harper's Magazine* (February 1993): 43–51.
Staples, Amy. "Mondo Mediations." *American Anthropologist* 96 (1994): 662–668.
———. "Safari Adventure: Forgotten Cinematic Journeys in Africa." *Film History* 18, no. 4 (2006): 392–411.
Toscano, Alberto, and Jeff Kinkle. *Cartographies of the Absolute*. Winchester, UK: Zero Books, 2015.
Walsh, Katie. "'Samsara' Tells the Story of Our World with Stunning Visuals and Spiritual Heft." *IndieWire*, February 8, 2012. http://www.indiewire.com/2012/02/sbiff-review-samsara-tells-the-story-of-our-world-with-stunning-visuals-spiritual-heft-113187.
Warner, Marina. "Intimate Communiqués: Melchior Lorck's Flying Tortoise." In *Seeing from Above: The Aerial View in Visual Culture*, edited by Mark Dorrian and Frédéric Pousin, 11–25. London: IB Tauris, 2013.
Wheatley, Helen. "The Limits of Television? Natural History Programming and the Transformation of Public Service Broadcasting." *European Journal of Cultural Studies* 7, no. 3 (2004): 325–339.
Williams, Linda. "Gender, Genre, and Excess." *Film Quarterly* 44, no. 4 (Summer 1991): 2–13.
———. *Hardcore: Power, Pleasure, and the "Frenzy of the Visible."* Berkeley: University of California Press, 1989.

ZOË DRUICK is Professor in the School of Communication at Simon Fraser University. She is author of a number of books, including *Projecting Canada: Government Policy and Documentary Film at the National Film Board*; *Allan King's "A Married Couple"*; and the coedited volume *Cinephemera: Archives, Ephemeral Cinema, and New Screen Histories in Canada*.

5

ACCELERATING DECELERATION
Slow Violence and Time-Lapse Cinematography

Devon Coutts

The story of the tortoise and the hare conjures a familiar image in the contemporary West. As the story goes, a tortoise, fed up with being teased for its slowness, challenges a hare to a race. The hare falls asleep, arrogantly assured of its triumph, while the tortoise plods inexorably on to victory. The fable's message is simple: slow and steady wins the race. But put another way, the fable cautions against underestimating the power of slowness in the face of intemperate acceleration. In our contemporary political and environmental climate, this is a lesson that we would do well to remember. If cultural theorists such as Rob Nixon and Paul Virilio are correct, the Western technocultural and military-industrial complex has been asleep for far too long, while the environmental devastation left in its wake is slowly but surely catching up.

In *Slow Violence and the Environmentalism of the Poor*, Rob Nixon makes the crucial claim that the aftereffects of violent incursions on people and environments are themselves a kind of violence. The problem Nixon highlights is primarily representational, as he struggles to discover a way to elevate the long-term effects of climate change, toxicity, or war into public consciousness. Nixon identifies the source of the problem in the acceleration of technology and culture that causes our attention spans to atrophy—a view that he shares with philosopher of speed, Paul Virilio. Virilio's analysis complements Nixon's critique by framing speed as a kind of violence. Virilio's account of modern accelerationism helps to elucidate why a culture of speed struggles to acknowledge slow violence as a problem. Both Nixon and Virilio point to a need to decelerate, but neither offers a satisfactory answer to what deceleration would accomplish or how we might actually begin to enact it—beyond ridding ourselves of technology altogether. The inadequacy of this answer prompts the question: How can we represent slow violence to an audience increasingly in thrall to spectacle and acceleration in a way that will incite lasting change?

This chapter takes up Nixon's concept of slow violence in order to grapple with its representational challenges and to present a potential answer to his difficult problem. By seeking first to understand the precise problem of representing slow violence, it becomes possible to think through potential strategies for granting it greater visibility. According to Virilio, the basis of the problem arises in the parallel development of motion picture technology with technologies of war. Due to their mutual influence, Virilio claims that representational technology can be nothing but a violent tool feeding further acceleration. However, we cannot simply accept uncritically that motion picture technology is inherently violent. I argue that the best way to turn toward a process of deceleration is to begin from within acceleration itself. Examining time-lapse cinematography as a technique for visualizing climate change indicates one way we might harness acceleration to serve the need to redress the effects of slow violence convincingly to a broad audience.

On a less conceptual level, the problem of representing slow violence is very similar to the problem faced by environmentally engaged films to communicate complex scientific data in an accessible way. In the final sections of the chapter, I shift to two case studies to examine how some recent documentary films have used time-lapse cinematography to respond to the challenge of data visualization. As I will discuss, time-lapse sequences can be used as a highly effective means of communicating an issue in an interesting, direct, and affectively powerful way. Jeff Orlowski's 2012 film, *Chasing Ice*, and its thematic successor, *Chasing Coral* (2017), demonstrate how time-lapse cinematography can act as an emotionally impactful tool to inspire audiences to think critically about our impact on the environment and potentially mobilize change.

Slow Violence and Representation

In his introductory chapter to *Slow Violence and the Environmentalism of the Poor*, Rob Nixon explicitly outlines his chief concern: to enable us to "rethink—politically, imaginatively, and theoretically" the notion of slow violence. However, his definition of slow violence as "a violence that occurs gradually and out of sight, a violence of delayed destruction that is dispersed across time and space, an attritional violence that is typically not viewed as violence at all," implies that rethinking slow violence is not the most imperative goal.[1] It seems, rather, that the issue is not of *re*thinking slow violence but of actually acknowledging it directly as a kind of violence. That is to say, the issue at the heart of Nixon's critique is to find a way for us to conceptualize slow violence in the first place. Nixon's project, and his problem, then, is to find a way to make slow violence not only thinkable but recognizable as an urgent phenomenon requiring our immediate attention. Today, instances of slow violence include climate change in general, toxic waste dumping, nuclear radiation, and other long-standing effects of wars waged since the early twentieth century.

Nixon identifies the Western tendency to place economic and technological interests over environmental or social concerns as a main cause of the current culture of acceleration. He argues further that the representational techniques employed by Western media play an active role in obscuring the problem. According to Nixon, the media is the field on which a "battle over spectacle" is conducted, which is decisive "for the foresight with which public policy can motivate and execute precautionary measures."[2] How, then, Nixon asks, "when public policy is shaped primarily around perceived immediate need . . . can we convert into image and narrative the disasters . . . of indifferent interest to the sensation-driven technologies of our image-world?"[3] The media itself "lacks the attention span to follow war-inflicted catastrophes that take years or generations to exact their toll," which prevents those catastrophes from entering public consciousness beyond the short duration of their initial appeal.[4] The increasing speed of our news reports exemplify the accelerated pace of culture in the West, and the rapid imagery seems to be replacing our capacity to remember these issues for longer than they appear on our screens. Thus, speed (of coverage, delivery, impact, etc.) and spectacle become the hallmarks of imagistic power, as our representational technologies strategically obscure the seriousness of their own ecological impact both historically and materially.

Even so, the representational problems of slow violence cannot be reduced simply to a failure of gaining Western recognition. Nixon notes that many of the effects of slow violence are concentrated in areas that Western audiences find it easy to ignore, but this is not exclusively the case. Landmines from the First World War still lie with the dead in Flanders Fields, and disturbing reminders of climate change arise yearly in the property damage caused by forest fires and hurricanes. The difficulties of representing slow violence as an imminent threat are, to an important degree, inherent to the concept. Slow violence is older than anyone now living and can be traced back centuries—for instance, to when humans first began to alter the climate during the Industrial Revolution by releasing excessive amounts of carbon into the atmosphere. The violence of environmental devastation is not immediately evident, unlike the instantly destructive forces of war, but the aftereffects on people and environments are all the more damaging for their insidious onset. As Nixon demonstrates, even negative commentaries on the effects of technology and acceleration on culture remain in thrall to acceleration's obscuring and obliterative potential. Using the example of the Gulf War, Nixon critiques technophiles and technophobes alike in their failure to acknowledge "the environmental and epidemiological ethics of its duration." Nixon specifically criticizes Paul Virilio for distancing the Gulf War from its physical effects and treating the "war on the ground as inconsequential, local, and quick."[5] Yet apart from the fact that Virilio consistently overlooks the long-term environmental implications of the rapidly increasing complexity of military technology, his insights into speed and technology bear certain similarities to Nixon's critique of the media and accelerationism. This similarity warrants further attention, since reading both together produces a more comprehensive account of the challenges in representing slowness to an accelerated culture.

Virilio, Cinematic Acceleration, and the Violence of Vision

In large part, Virilio overlooks the long-term environmental effects of military technology, but it is precisely this lack of emphasis that allows him to illustrate the problems inherent in representing slow violence. As Anne Friedberg notes, Virilio's 1984 text, *War and Cinema*, "predicted, in an advance guard of seven years, the military logistics of the yet-to-be-waged first Gulf War," referring to his account of the correlation between the development of war technology and the refinement of cinematic "sight machines."[6] For Virilio, cinematic techniques and military techniques are inextricably linked, to the extent that cinema is inherently a kind of military technology.

Virilio links the conduct of warfare to a kind of visual production, as in modern warfare, one can take a picture in the same movement that one fires a gun. Film and photography radically expand the perceptual field, allowing one to record and reproduce vast landscapes, but by virtue of the fact that they are mediated through a screen, the actual environment appears more virtual than real. Accordingly, when war machines combine with image-capture technology, the result is a whole new kind of spectacle—as when war makers became filmmakers and battlefield imagery became news and propaganda. The sight machines resulting from their combination, such as the satellite, act like disembodied eyes, surveying the terrain from above without ever touching down and taking stock of the situation on the ground. Image-capture technology co-opts our perceptual modes, taking over for vision but, in so doing, renders the violence at an insurmountable distance for both spectator and soldier. Thus, according to Virilio, technology that expands our visual field turns vision into a weapon. Through the scope of the gun, the abstraction of the radar, the distance of the satellite, or any other modern cinematic instruments for conducting war, "*the function of the weapon is the function of the eye*."[7] Since the power to see becomes the power to strike anywhere, at any time, with little to no warning, vision itself becomes violent.

But as an all-seeing gaze, real-time image capture can only see what is visible. As Nixon's critique reveals, the problem with the distant technological gaze is that despite its ubiquitous eyes, it cannot see the threat posed by slow violence. The onset of slow violence is precisely *slow* and is, therefore, invisible to the media culture that is accustomed to spectacle and speed. Indeed, speed must be linked to spectacle, just as, by Virilio's account, it must be linked to politics and warfare. In a kind of inversion of Nixon's point, Virilio writes, in *Speed and Politics*, that speed is a kind of violence that when coupled with imagistic war technology, destroys space as well as time. The domination of space by visual technology is evident in the ability of the modern military to almost instantaneously launch an attack on any part of the world. As a result, spatial distance effectively collapses, moving the "field" of conflict into the virtual "nonplace" of speed.[8] The modern arms race is, then, a race to conquer speed, since modern technology has enabled the total collapse of spatial distance as a strategic point of defense.

Yet as Nixon indicates, modern warfare's remote conduct does not make its *effects* merely virtual. The problem is that the sight machines move too fast to see any effect that does not manifest immediately. Taken to extremes, both speed and slowness escape our perceptual registers, such that the kind of violence that moves too slowly to be seen is incommensurable with the speed that blurs our vision. The problem with representing slow violence to an accelerated culture results from the fact that both the very slow and the very fast are invisible to us and to each other. Virilio notes that "*in the current context, to disarm would . . . mean first and foremost to decelerate*, to defuse the race toward the end."[9] Nixon similarly argues that we first need to slow down if we are to begin to address slow violence. "Today," Virilio writes, "the reduction of warning time that results from the supersonic speeds of assault leaves so little time for detection, identification and response" that time to react, time to intervene, is the most valuable currency in modern politics.[10]

The time to react and to intervene is imperative when it comes to redressing slow violence. Resolving the conflict between the acceleration that makes slow violence invisible to us will thus depend on our ability to find a way to shrink the distance between the two, ending the race before we run out of time to redress the harm.

The problem with which I began was that of representing slow violence, of finding a way to make its effects not only visible but also understandable as the effects of violence. Virilio problematizes vision in his account of technology, claiming that cinematic sight machines can only ever be violent. However, Virilio's critique merely highlights the first part of the problem with regard to visibility, in that his sight machines do not help us understand what they show us. It is not enough to see a ravaged landscape or a former battlefield—*we must also understand that what we see is a problem*. The rate at which slow violence is tangibly affecting the environment makes it all the more urgent that people take notice. If we are to be able to redress its effects in any lasting way, it seems our attempts to represent slow violence would benefit from a little bit more acceleration. In my view, altering technology's impact on the world has a greater chance of success if we turn toward a process of disarmament from within technology itself—in harnessing the representational power of the moving image to redress the harms of slow violence. The camera, after all, is a more efficient eye—and therein lies both the danger and the potential of moving image technology. I want to claim, contra Virilio, that just because cinematic techniques intersect with military techniques does not mean that war is the only thing for which cinema can be used. In the next sections, I shift my analysis to the realm of cinema more explicitly. I explore the possibility that through the use of time-lapse cinematography, we can begin to think about how to shrink, rather than exacerbate, the distance between our actions and their effects on the environment.

Time Lapse as a Representational Technique

When framed in the context of cinema, the representational problem of slow violence begins to look a lot like the problem of data visualization. Data visualization is a problem for any film that needs to explain complex information and frame it in a compelling and understandable way. More specifically, as Sean Cubitt discusses, visualizing data is a problem for environmentally engaged films, which seek to represent scientific data in an easily accessible, accurate, and interesting way.[11] It is not enough to show an audience a data set and let the numbers speak for themselves. Merely seeing lines on a graph or an increasing or decreasing number sequence will neither teach audiences about an issue nor convince them that it is important. Data visualization in films must do two things at once: it must present *and* explain the information. In other words, effective data visualization allows audiences to both see and understand the problem under discussion. In environmental films, the data being represented is scientific information about some aspect of the global ecological crisis. In Nixon's view, every aspect of the ecological crisis is an example of slow violence. Thus, every film that struggles to effectively visualize the scientific data that represents climate change confronts the representational challenges inherent in slow violence.

However, the representational challenges of slow violence add another dimension to the problem of data visualization. It is not only a matter of seeing and understanding that slow violence is a problem but also one of convincing people that slow violence is a problem *that must be addressed*. That is to say, the problem of representing slow violence includes communicating the imperative to act. When it comes to representing the violence of ecological devastation, then, data visualization must do three things: it must present information, explain the information, and inspire the audience to act. This last requirement is particularly challenging, since pure data usually lacks the emotional force to inspire audience mobilization. As will become evident when I turn to the case studies at the end of the chapter, time-lapse cinematography has the power to successfully synthesize all three of these requirements in an emotionally impactful way.

Cubitt invokes the time-lapse technique as an example of an effective mode of data visualization, though he mentions it only briefly, as just one example of how numerical data can be presented. His survey of potential modes of data visualization is useful in highlighting the variety of ways one can present complex information, but in my view, the representational capacities of the time-lapse technique go beyond merely displaying numerical data. Time-lapse cinematography (or photography) allows one to project imagery at a much more rapid pace than it was recorded, "resulting in a revelation of motion [or change] ordinarily imperceptible to unenhanced human sight."[12] Typically, a time-lapse sequence "consists of sequential photographs taken at a set interval (i.e. one photo every second, one photo every 24 hours)."[13] Films are usually projected at twenty-four frames per second, but in a time-lapse sequence, the frame density is much lower: rather than twenty-four frames per second, it could show twenty-four frames over twenty-four seconds, each depicting a separate image of the same place over a corresponding twenty-four hours. The resulting sequence would depict a whole day's worth of change in less than thirty seconds, enabling a viewer to actually see what would normally be an invisible, gradual series of changes. The time-lapse technique thus appears as a clear front-runner in the methods available to us to shrink the distance between the slow processes of environmental degradation and our limited human vision.

As I discuss in greater detail with reference to the case studies, time-lapse technology effects a radical shift in perspective in that it grants us access to a timescale that is normally beyond our capacity to comprehend. A process taking place over many years is slow from a human perspective, but on the vast time scale of the Earth, even a whole human lifetime is hardly equivalent to a second. With time-lapse technology, we have the ability to represent Earth time in a way that is recognizable and understandable in human terms. Within a sequence, we can both visualize and understand the violence of long-term environmental degradation as the precise kind of violence that it is—slow violence. These qualities, when used in the service of representing phenomena such as climate change, can help us encourage people to reflect on the violence of insidious processes in an effective way. Seeing a time-lapse sequence brings the subject matter to life in a unique and dazzling manner, as it presents clear evidence of the minutiae of a process, be it of growth or deterioration. The coupling of the striking visuals with the intuitive narrative of growth or decline makes time lapse interesting, immediate, and convincing and lends it the ability to not only deliver information but also give viewers the emotional impetus to act.

Time-Lapse Cinematography in Action

In what follows, I examine the efficacy of using time-lapse cinematography to renegotiate the way we think about our impact on the environment in Jeff Orlowski's two recent films, *Chasing Ice* and *Chasing Coral*. These films demonstrate that it is now possible to produce stunning time-lapse sequences of processes that would otherwise escape mass notice. In both of these films, the problem of data visualization is front and center. In *Chasing Ice*, Orlowski follows photographer James Balog, and his Extreme Ice Survey team, as they take time-lapse technology to unprecedented levels in order to achieve their goal of visualizing climate change. *Chasing Coral* builds on the successes of the technique in *Chasing Ice* and works to bring into view the effects of climate change on the ocean by emphasizing the phenomenon of coral bleaching. Considering both together shows how harnessing the communicative, representational, and affective capabilities of data visualization techniques can help us reengage with the physical environment.

Chasing Ice: *Preserving the Memory of the Land*

One of the core structural elements of *Chasing Ice* is a confrontation with the problem of data visualization. The difficulty of representing scale haunts the film's attempts to communicate compelling evidence about the speed at which the glaciers are disappearing. The struggle to emphasize magnitude is tangible in the series of attempts the film's creators make to frame it, first in narration, then with edited still photographs, next with graphs and charts, and finally with time-lapse sequences. Their attempts begin where Balog's project begins—at the Solheim glacier. Balog returns to the Solheim glacier six months after he had photographed it initially and finds it severely diminished. The film cuts between action shots of Balog exploring the glacier, setting up his equipment, and photographing the ice. All of this is constantly accompanied by Balog's voice-over narration telling us how he came to understand that the ice contained the story of climate change, interspersed with facts about normal glacier behavior. He tells us that a small amount of diminishment in the summer is normal and is balanced out by growth in the winter—but the rate of retreat in just six months rendered the glacier unrecognizable. Balog recounts to the audience how seeing the reduction of the Solheim glacier convinced him to forego graphs and computer models in favor of photographic evidence of the phenomenon of climate change itself. *Chasing Ice* thus documents Balog's attempt to provide the public with, in his words, "believable, understandable visual evidence" for climate change—something that "grabs you in the gut."

The film first tries to visualize Balog's astonishment using still photographs altered to give us a sense of scale. We see a photograph of a person in a yellow coat standing on the glacier, dwarfed by the mountain of ice that fills the frame. The image then zooms out to show the full picture, in which the person is only visible as a square of yellow in the midst of the grays and browns of ice and rock. A white line appears next to the person with the words "six feet" to present a stark comparison with the glacier that is now outlined with an orange line. The next shot is a picture from six months later, taken even farther away to encompass more of the landscape. The line and the words measuring the human are now hardly visible, and the human is not visible at all. The orange line measuring the original size of the glacier remain, but a large section at the top now shows only sky. To further emphasize the point that the glacier has severely diminished, we then see a series of different before and after photos showing their respective subjects presented side by side in a single frame. It can be clearly seen that the glacier in the "six months later" photos is significantly smaller and contains little to no ice.

As a mode of data visualization, before and after photographs that contain interpretive aids such as outlines and measurements are quite effective. They communicate precisely what the filmmakers wish to explain in a clear and direct manner in a single image. They convey instantly a collection of numerical data regarding, in this case, the percentage left of the glacier after six months. But even when showing something as shocking as a glacier reduced by half in a short period of time, before and after photographs edited with lines and measurements are visually bland. The same problem appears later on in the film when the filmmakers employ computer models to explain how ice core scientists extract and analyze ancient ice to measure the correlation between the rise in parts per million of carbon dioxide and the rise in global temperature. A voice-over from glaciologist Dr. Tad Pfeffer explains this process to us, accompanied by an animated chart with blue and red lines representing carbon parts per million and global temperature moving at a steady rate until they rise together far above the gridline of the chart. Displaying the objective fact of the glacier's recession incites an intellectual response that might convince some viewers that there is a problem, but it does not promote an affective reaction strong enough to achieve Balog's goals to make the audience feel the depth of the problem. Despite its objective effectiveness, Balog and Orlowski decided not to rely on before and after photographs or computer models as their central means to grab the audience "in the gut." Rather than using still photographs or numerical data animated in computer models to document the changed landscape, Balog wanted to produce video clips showing the landscape actually changing. His idea quickly grew into a larger project, the Extreme Ice Survey (EIS), which photographed the transformation of nine glaciers from Iceland to Alaska over the course of four years, from 2007 to 2011.

Orlowski saves the time-lapse sequences for the climax of the film and only shows them during the final fifteen minutes. This final segment features Balog on his 2011 media tour, during which he presented the results of the EIS project to various North American audiences. We viewers join the filmed audiences as the time lapses are unveiled. The results of the project are visually stunning time-lapse sequences showing the glaciers retreating at an alarming pace. The film cuts between shots of Balog on the news and on stage, shots of the actual time-lapse sequences, and reaction shots from groups and individual audience members. When the time lapses are shown, it is immediately evident that they are the most effective of the various methods employed in the film to visualize the problem. The visceral astonishment that the time lapses are meant to invoke is exemplified in one reaction shot in particular. At around the sixty-one-minute mark, we see a young boy standing before a screen, staring upward with his mouth agape in silent horror as the glaciers disappear right before his eyes.

The time lapses transform the glacier recession into an active process rather than a completed set of scientific facts. The longest time lapse depicts the recession of the Columbia glacier by almost two and a half miles over the course of three years. As Balog explains to us in voice-over, they had to pivot the camera twice in order to capture the extent of the recession. The sequences display each pivot of the camera, and we witness three times in total what looks like solid ice transform into water, until water is all that remains in the frame. After projecting the Columbia glacier sequence, the film shows us a before and after photograph like the one discussed earlier, including lines and measurements to depict the extent of the change. But the context for seeing this data has been utterly transformed by the preceding time lapses. The time lapses add an affective element that prepares audiences to understand and appreciate what the scientific data means in a visceral way.

By employing time lapses, *Chasing Ice* achieves more than just a showcase of an effective method of data visualization—it shows the powerful affective dimension of time-lapse cinematography in itself. Through the sequences, the film succeeds in bringing the glaciers to life for the audience just in time to watch them die. This has the effect of conveying the immensity of the loss that has already happened, and in emphasizing that the loss of the glaciers is still ongoing. Here, time lapse succeeds in becoming a tool to communicate the effects of the slow violence contributing to the melting glaciers, and the urgency of the problem. Watching the glaciers disappear in a time lapse shifts the interpretative focus from something finished that we can study, to something that is happening and will continue to happen unless we can figure out a way to slow it down. Communication in this expansive visual way opens the possibility for action, on the basis that raising awareness of the dangers of climate change has the potential to mobilize action against it.

Chasing Coral: *Any Problem Can Be Solved with a Little Creative Thinking*

Chasing Coral, like *Chasing Ice*, has data visualization as one of its central foci. *Chasing Coral* follows the same general structure as *Chasing Ice*: it begins with a project to raise awareness about an environmental problem, interviews scientists and experts to gain insight into the problem, showcases the process of obtaining time-lapse footage, and finally, reveals the time-lapse sequences to the audience. However, there are notable differences between the two with regard to their approaches to communicating and visualizing the central problem. Melting glaciers are a common metonym for climate change in general, but the discussion often ends with the glaciers causing the sea levels to rise. In *Chasing Coral*, Orlowski seeks to investigate deeper into the consequences entailed by our warming oceans and, in a sense, build on the project he began with *Chasing Ice*. In this film, he takes the time-lapse cameras beneath the waves of the rising sea to highlight the effects of climate change on coral reefs. In many ways, this is a more difficult task than emphasizing the danger of the melting glaciers was.

The project the film begins with is the XL Catlin Seaview Survey: a free, online, publicly accessible database containing extensive panoramic views of underwater landscapes. According to its founder, former advertising agent turned underwater photographer Richard Vevers, the public were engaging with the imagery without realizing that there was a problem affecting the oceans. It is immediately obvious that there is a problem when we are confronted with visual evidence of a glacier shrunken to a fraction of its original size. It is not immediately obvious that there is a problem when confronted with images of colorful versus bleached coral. For all the average viewer knows, the two images could just be pictures of two different kinds of coral. Orlowski's second film thus seeks to bring our attention to the phenomenon of coral bleaching, which has been the cause of death to over 50 percent of the world's reefs since the first recorded event in 1979. The first task of *Chasing Coral*, then, is to engage and educate the audience about why it matters that corals are dying, which involves casting light on the rising temperature of the oceans as one of the most dangerous effects of climate change. Like the melting glaciers, coral acts as a gauge of climate change in general, since corals only bleach when the water temperatures rise too rapidly for them to adapt. But while it takes years for the melting glaciers to manifest as a problem, coral bleaching events take place within mere weeks. As such, rather than using time-lapse sequences to make climate change visible, the project in *Chasing Coral* tries to make visible the fact that climate change itself is accelerating.

To accomplish its primary pedagogical task, *Chasing Coral* takes advantage of a larger variety of more sophisticated data visualization techniques than were available during the production of *Chasing Ice*. Additionally, rather than saving the time lapses to be revealed at the end of the film, Orlowski uses the sequences throughout *Chasing Coral* for a larger variety of purposes. It is interesting to note that the greater sophistication of the data visualization techniques was itself a product of the acceleration in technological development between 2012 and 2017. Thanks to increasing sophistication in digital production, *Chasing Coral* is able to communicate its data in a much more visually appealing manner. As well as time lapse, the film employs infographics, computer-generated 3D models, heat maps, and animated graphs, to name the most frequently used methods. On the whole, *Chasing Coral* presents its data in an interactive manner, for example, by inserting an internet search bar to mark an expository transition. Including approximations of interactivity allows the film to invite the viewer to enter into the research that the film is presenting on a personal, individual level, just as one might through a casual search on Google. The interactive style is sustained through the conjunction of animated infographics, 3D models, and time-lapse sequences. The film employs this constellation of techniques to great effect in support of coral reef biologist Dr. Ruth Gates's explanation of the anatomy of coral.

As the film moves from imagery of coral polyps under a microscope into a 3D model of the structure of corals, we see their skeletons and their polyps laid out graphically while we listen to Dr. Gates explaining how a coral is not a plant but an animal that lives in symbiosis with the plants within its tissues. These plants are microalgae, and as they photosynthesize, they produce food for the coral. Left to their own devices, corals have no set life span—they continue to live for as long as their environment supports them. In the next sequence, the time lapses show us the corals growing and changing according to their own self-sustaining life cycles, still accompanied by voice-over from Dr. Gates. When subjected to the speed of the time lapse, the corals' seemingly stable, plant-like appendages come alive in ways we would normally never see—and the accompanying visuals prove their stunning vitality. The corals seem to dance in the time lapses, growing and changing at high speeds and in high definition right before our eyes. Corals, we also learn, are huge sophisticated structures that form the center of a vast ecosystem of other underwater creatures. It is their structural importance in the oceans that make their loss so detrimental to the health of the planet.

Heat maps and animated graphs help Orlowski visualize for the audience where the affected regions are and why rising temperatures are a problem. Via an animated graph tracking ocean temperatures from the late 1800s to the present, we see that the lines on the graph only enter red zones within the past thirty years, and we note the increasing frequency in the past decade. But it is only after establishing that the corals are in fact living creatures that play a massive role in maintaining the structural integrity of the ocean that *Chasing Coral* shifts to show Orlowski and Vevers's race to capture visual evidence of the speed at which coral dies during bleaching events. Just as he does in *Chasing Ice*, Orlowski must bring the phenomenon to life before the scientific aspects can be understood on an affective level. *Chasing Coral* ultimately champions the cause of redressing the effects of climate change before it is too late to save the world's underwater ecosystems. And it does so by advocating for personal, physical action in combination with technological innovation. The climactic scenes of *Chasing Coral* feature time-lapse sequences that were captured not by automated machines but, rather, as the result of human resourcefulness and dedication to a cause. Due to unforeseen challenges that force them to leave behind their sophisticated automated equipment, Orlowski and camera technician Zack Rago must manually photograph the reefs using regular underwater cameras over the course of approximately one month.

In Orlowski's hands, camera equipment becomes a way to personally engage with the environment and to rehabilitate it as a physical entity in need of care. The time lapses underscore the immediacy and the tragedy of the accelerated rate of loss that the world's corals continue to undergo. However, the *Chasing Coral* team were limited to only a few affected regions. So, as the film's final interactive element, Orlowski released an online callout message prior to the release of the film to enlist help from all over the world in documenting local bleaching events. He includes the submitted footage in a montage sequence near the end of the film not only to give further evidence of the enormity of the threat to the world's corals but also as a message of global cooperation. Orlowski's public outreach initiative expands the scope of the problem to a global scale, while encouraging localized involvement through social media. By asking people living in or near affected areas to document the bleaching events in their own backyards, whether through regular photography, video recording, or homemade time lapse, Orlowski effectively extends the platform to allow local initiatives to have global reach. Initiatives such as the Catlin Seaview Survey and Orlowski's social media outreach show that virtual terrains need not distance us from the physical landscape. Popular outreach initiatives as seen in *Chasing Coral* can instead expand our field of both action and vision and encourage us to accelerate our responses to effects that can no longer be said to be slow.

Bringing Us Up to Speed: The Acceleration of Deceleration?

Based on the successes of *Chasing Ice* and *Chasing Coral*, it is clear that as a technique, time-lapse cinematography has the potential to not only expand our understanding of the problems in our accelerating world but also begin to redress them. Viewing slow phenomena, such as melting glaciers, in a time-lapse sequence not only reveals minute changes in an otherwise apparently static landscape but can also assist us in learning to think differently about our impact on the environment. Similarly, viewing living coral in time lapse alongside sequences depicting the speed of their death emphasizes the imperative that we act more quickly to redress the deterioration of our world's ecosystems. In Orlowski's films, a truly global picture emerges to reveal the extent of the problem of climate change, both above and beneath the surface of the oceans. His successes in using time lapse to visualize, communicate, and personalize complex issues also highlights the ability for representational technology to shrink the distance between audiences and the physical environment and potentially open the way for new kinds of collaboration to take place.

The question guiding this analysis regards the use of time-lapse cinematography as an effective representational strategy for redressing slow violence. The problem of representing slow violence stems, according to Rob Nixon, from the acceleration of Western technoculture and, thus, implies the need to decelerate if we are to be able to redress its harms. However, the effects of slow violence are themselves accelerating, as is represented so well in Orlowski's films. The use of time-lapse cinematography in *Chasing Ice* and *Chasing Coral* provides us with examples of how the technique is able to represent invisible processes and incite visceral, affective responses. Time lapse inserts an emotional dimension into traditional methods of data visualization that is essential in inspiring audiences to take the problems seriously. It seems that now more than ever, we would benefit from a bit more acceleration—that is, if such acceleration is channeled into different arenas than it has been in the past. In the current climate crisis, it becomes evident that accelerating the rate at which we try to decelerate the effects of climate change is necessary if we are to have a chance of finding more sustainable outcomes.

Notes

1. Nixon, *Slow Violence*, 2.
2. Ibid., 66.
3. Ibid., 3.
4. Ibid., 200.
5. Ibid., 202.
6. Friedberg, "Virilio's Screen," 188–189.
7. Virilio, *War and Cinema*, 20; italics in the original.
8. Virilio, *Speed and Politics*, 149.
9. Ibid., 153; italics in the original.

10. Ibid.
11. Cubitt, "Everybody Knows This Is Nowhere," 280.
12. Lavery, "No More Unexplored Countries," 2.
13. Persohn, "Exploring Time-Lapse Photography," 501.

References

Cubitt, Sean. "Everybody Knows This Is Nowhere: Data Visualization and Ecocriticism." In *Ecocinema Theory and Practice*, edited by Stephen Rust, Salma Monani, and Sean Cubitt, 279–296. New York: Routledge, 2013.

Friedberg, Anne. "Virilio's Screen: The Work of Metaphor in the Age of Technological Convergence." *Journal of Visual Culture* 3, no. 2 (2004): 183–193.

Lavery, David. "'No More Unexplored Countries': The Early Promise and Disappointing Career of Time-Lapse Photography." *Film Studies* 9, no. 1 (Winter 2006): 1–8.

Nixon, Rob. *Slow Violence and the Environmentalism of the Poor*. Cambridge: Harvard University Press, 2011.

Orlowski, Jeff. *Chasing Coral*. USA: Cos. Exposure Labs, Argent Pictures, Code Blue Foundation, EarthSense Foundation, Kendeda Fund, Sustainable Films, 2017.

———. *Chasing Ice*. USA: Cos. Exposure Labs, Diamond Docs, 2012.

Persohn, Lindsay. "Exploring Time-Lapse Photography as a Means for Qualitative Data Collection." *International Journal of Qualitative Studies in Education* 28, no. 5 (2015): 501–513.

Virilio, Paul. *Speed and Politics*. Translated by Mark Polizzotti. Los Angeles: Semiotext(e), 2006.

———. *War and Cinema*. Translated by Patrick Camiller. London: Verso, 1989.

DEVON COUTTS is a PhD student in Philosophy at SUNY Stony Brook.

6

FROM ELEGY TO KITSCH

Spectacles of Epistephilia in *Food, Inc.* and Early Food Documentaries

Sabiha Ahmad Khan

Food, Inc. (2008) memorably ends with a call to action urging viewers to "vote to change this [food] system. Three times a day," emphasizing that they "can change the world with every bite."[1] This call to action invites viewers to invest the mundane act of eating with revolutionary meaning. In fact, the film's production company, Participant Media, commissioned a report to document the impact of *Food, Inc.*, which, since the film's release, had played a major curricular role in its now-defunct community engagement effort, Takepart.[2] Survey participants, most of whom came from the narrow demographic of white middle-class women without children, felt the film's call to action was accessible.[3] They reported feeling better about their ability to intervene in the existing food system and have an impact on the environment. The idea that simply buying and consuming the so-called right foods would change the food system in the United States provided the participants with what an investigator on the study called a "near-future hope" and "proximal alternate reality."[4] However, this seamless movement between eating and voting, and the hope that movement generates, belies a number of fissures in the utopic, seemingly progressive vision of politics underlying the film's main critiques of the industrial food system.[5] I argue that these fissures are useful for understanding the limits of the popular appeal of *Food, Inc.*, ironically through its invocation of the populist agenda of good food for all.

The increasing scrutiny and awareness of the environmental effects of agribusiness inserts *Food, Inc.* into a broader debate about how local, sustainable agriculture could potentially help to stave off the effects of climate change, not to mention feed the human population. Viewed within this ecocritical frame, *Food, Inc.* and its ilk provide a rich archive of visual meditations on the way in which food documentaries, by covering "all aspects of the food cycle, from production to disposal," showcase how "food mirrors individuals' and societies' relationship with nature."[6] Reading *Food, Inc.* for its underlying theory of the relationship between humans and nature is instructive for developing a model of popular engagement—political, alimentary, and environmental—in the Anthropocene.

But given the scope and scale of anthropogenic climate change, the ability to imagine worlds, actual or cinematic, beyond the Anthropocene—what will likely amount to human extinction—is fraught with contradictions.[7] As the canonical cinematic expression of sustainable food politics, *Food, Inc.* warrants an ecocritical reading that embodies what Nicole Seymour has described as the "new task for ecocinema: not just external representation, but . . . self-reflection *as a form of ecological consciousness.*"[8] This paper argues that *Food, Inc.* generates a limited "ecological consciousness" that is underwritten ironically by a market-based logic of food justice. I argue that the heart of *Food, Inc.*'s ecological consciousness is not narratives of people's victimization at the hands of Big Food but the infographics used to critique that industry.[9] The infographics act as a nascent form of what Nicholas Mirzoeff has called "visual activism," which describes how people "actively use visual culture to create . . . new ways to see the world," much as internet memes are deployed.[10] As the uncanny reprisal of early and World War II–era food documentaries—arguably the era that most accelerated the environmental impact of agriculture—*Food, Inc.*'s particular vision of the food system as articulated through its infographics is key to understanding the film's potential for popular engagement in the Anthropocene.

* * *

Food, Inc.'s infographics operate overwhelmingly on the visual logic of unveiling the pastoral marketing rhetoric of Big Food.[11] It includes the spectator on its journey deep into the duplicitous world of food manufacture from the very start. The opening credit sequence famously consists of smooth point-of-view tracking shots from the perspective of a shopper pushing a grocery cart. Food labels depict vividly cartoonish pastoral scenes replete with red barns and rolling hills. Plenitude is the overall visual logic of the sequence, with shelves and freezers lined from top to bottom with various food items. The spectator, standing in as the shopper in question, occasionally pauses to contemplate the latest special on offer. Meanwhile, the voice-over intones that meat is no longer sold with bones, and tomatoes are not real but "notional." The sequence ends by cross-fading from a photographic mural of a lush green field to a dismal feedlot. Nothing is as it seems in the grocery store. Stuck in a seemingly infinite course from aisle to aisle, the shopper-spectator is on a Sisyphean errand: doomed to push the cart eternally only to be denied repeatedly the purity and goodness of his or her purchases.[12]

The film sees its investigative purpose as exposing the "deliberate veil" that the food industry places over its own production processes.[13] Unveiling is problematic because it presumes an uncomplicated relationship between appearance and reality and does not acknowledge the functioning of ideology or fantasy in the film text.[14] If *Food, Inc.* sees itself as a documentary film, then it is certainly such in the way that, in the words of André Bazin, "film is always a social documentary": "the recognition of our collective dreams, illusions, and, I dare say, worst thoughts."[15] The "dreams," "illusions," and "worst thoughts" that the food industry creates—the pastoral margarine, the "notional" tomato, the pneumatic chickens, the cornucopia of corn-based processed consumables—paradoxically co-constitute the very fantasy of sustainability that the food film is trying to promote.

Food films such as *Food, Inc.* that advocate for sustainable solutions on the level of individual consumer choice, according to Julie Guthman, exemplify the "agrarian paradox" of the California-based organic food movement. The paradox lies in the fact that this movement has disavowed its industrial nature despite being constrained by industrial processes because of limits on land valuation.[16] Guthman writes that such writings and films have an underlying sense of "naturalism" that blends "seamlessly" with politics.[17] Like the ecological jeremiads of Rachel Carson's *Silent Spring* and Davis Guggenheim's *An Inconvenient Truth*, films about sustainable food put forth contradictory views of the environment: that it's a thing of innate beauty worthy of our regard and that it's a place in need of human control and intervention.[18] As Robin L. Murray and Joseph K. Heumann have argued, contemporary food films, such as *Food, Inc.* and *King Corn*, and even their historical antecedents, such as *The Plow That Broke the Plains* (1936), indulge in a sense of "environmental nostalgia" that doesn't account for the industrial realities of the current food landscape.[19] The result, as Timothy Morton has argued, is a temporally disjointed form of elegiac mourning for the death of a beautiful object that has not yet passed.[20] By denying the industrial agricultural landscape through a mournful sense of loss, elegy casts aside the industrial as an abject, undesirable entity. Yet because of its abject status, the industrial ironically holds together the illusion of sustainable organic agriculture through the "agrarian paradox."

Food, Inc. fully embraces the contradictory elegiac and Edenic vision of wholeness characteristic of Guthman's "agrarian paradox" and views the conditions of production in Big Food as a violation of that. *Food, Inc.*'s critique of the monocultural agriculture on which Big Food depends would seem to be environmentally sound. But it relies on what Guthman has characterized as a trend in much food writing: that "food politics has become a progenitor of a neoliberal anti-politics that devolves regulatory responsibility to consumers' via their dietary choices."[21] *Food, Inc.* consistently focuses on the individual point of contact between buyer and seller, which helps explains why the film lauds Walmart's stocking of organic foods, despite its global reach.[22] In *Food, Inc.*, sustaining market diversity—ironically, through economies of scale—is key to sustaining agricultural and, by extension, biological diversity.

Implicit in all this is the view that the environment, like neoliberal markets, is self-regulating and self-equilibrating, which falls squarely in the popular pastoral idea of nature as unchanging and whole.[23] This elegiac structure is thematized and visualized throughout the film in the rhetoric of unveiling Big Food's mock pastoralism. While the film acknowledges that food marketing exploits the warm feelings associated with pastoralism, it does not dismiss pastoralism as its ideal of human-nature relations. The film's championing of sustainable farmer Joel Salatin's methods speaks to the embrace of the pastoral.[24] In a way, *Food, Inc.*'s resistance to shaking off the cloak of pastoralism is evidence of what Timothy Morton has called the "Oedipal logic" of ecological awareness.[25] Rather than generate a sense of ecological awareness, the prospect of escape recapitulates the delusion of the Hegelian "beautiful soul," that the bad stuff (political, environmental, industrial) is "out there" somewhere while the good stuff is here and local.[26] In other words, a direct critique of agriculture only causes further entrapment itself within that logic.

There is something predictable and even potentially boring about *Food, Inc.*'s binary vision of food activism. Jennifer Barker views *Food, Inc.*'s visual strategy as "positively tame" compared to *Super Size Me*, which centers the aesthetic of the grotesque to illustrate vividly the negative effects of fast food on Morgan Spurlock's body.[27] *Food, Inc.*, Barker argues, focuses not on portraying but on performing disgust by taking the high road and refusing to dwell on the abjection of industrial food production.[28] A *New York Times* review of the film notes that the end titles, for instance, a kind of "final checklist . . . registers as far too depressingly little."[29] The individual act of buying and eating organic seems to be at a depressingly distant scalar disconnect to the all-encompassing systemic nature of the problems with industrial food. And yet the respondents to the Takepart survey reported having a sense of a "near-future hope" by the end of the film, which one could interpret as a nascent form of ecological "self-reflection."[30] The "proximal alternate reality" of a "near-future hope" feels good because it invests the place and moment of consumption with seemingly infinite political possibility despite its banality.[31]

The results of the Takepart survey suggest that consumerism may in fact be the way into "self-reflection" precisely because of its banality. Timothy Morton has argued that "the very consumerism that haunts environmentalism—the consumerism that environmentalism explicitly opposes and indeed finds disgusting—provides the model for how ecological awareness should proceed."[32] *Food, Inc.*'s boring qualities stem in part from what Morton has described as a kind of ecological "ennui" that is in fact "the quintessence of ecological awareness": "the abject feeling that I am surrounded and penetrated by other entities."[33] This impression is not lost on an NPR (National Public Radio) review of the film, which warns spectators that "every frame makes you choke on your popcorn."[34] The "citizen food consumer" whom *Food, Inc.* addresses, according to Belinda Smaill, is therefore a consumer in both senses of the word: both as a knowledgeable economic agent and as an embodied eater.[35] For Smaill, the implications of *Food, Inc.*'s paradoxically domesticated hailing of the viewer is that the documentary form itself can not only appeal to reason but also "foreground sensorial meaning as a way of accessing the world."[36]

A *New York Times* review observes that the hyperawareness that *Food, Inc.* generates in the spectator induces responses reserved for the most grotesque of genre films: "Forget buckets of blood. Nothing says horror like one of those tubs of artificially buttered, nonorganic popcorn at the concession stand."[37] By drawing attention to the horrific conditions of the multiplex alimentary experience, the reviews highlight the way in which *Food, Inc.* literally makes spectators reflect in real time about the ecological and environmental implications of the popcorn they are stuffing in their mouths. So as much as *Food, Inc.* and films like it attempt to label industrial food as the "bad stuff" and local food as the "good stuff," there is an engaging quality to the very artifice behind the industrial food that *Food, Inc.* shuns.

What precipitates from *Food, Inc.*'s separation between bad and good food is what Morton refers to the "uncanny valley" of the in-between, the stuff where zombies and monsters of the industrial food system reside.[38] In *Food, Inc.*, the monstrosities of the industrial food system, and the rhetorical fodder for the film's argument against industrial agriculture, are pastoral marketing, the "notional tomato," the conditions of poultry houses, feedlots, chickens with enormous breasts to meet consumers' hunger for white meat, E. coli in ground beef, the proliferation of corn- and soy-based processed foods, the dollar menu, and GMO trademarked seeds. Belinda Smaill regards the focus in *Food, Inc.* on such "abject" food products as a way of laying bare the "breakdown of meaning ... needed for [animals] to be perceived as food."[39] I argue that the "breakdown of meaning" can serve as a useful category of engagement—an embrace of the abject products of the food industry that speak to our worst fears—GMOs, food scares, and that we ourselves will become what we eat.

The aesthetics of industrial food that *Food, Inc.* cultivates through its infographics therefore begins to exemplify literary scholar Timothy Morton's notion of "dark ecology," a sinister approach to art that requires owning up to our complicity in the agro-environmental mess in which we find ourselves.[40] As Rachel Laudan has argued, acknowledging our collective reliance to the industrialized food system ultimately makes that system accountable for figuring out a way to churn out healthy, sanitary, sustainably produced food.[41] I argue that *Food, Inc.*'s visualization of industrial processes and their products, by relying on scale and plenitude or *copia* as its overriding visual rhetoric, begins to approach Morton's dark ecology but shuts it down in favor of a stark melodramatic narrative of good and bad actors, good and bad food.

* * *

While *Food, Inc.*'s impulse toward consumerism begins to confront the industrialization of the food supply, it simply doesn't go far enough and falls back on melodramatic means of explaining the social problem of agricultural and environmental degradation. As Linda Williams argues, melodrama is the dominant mode of US culture that draws sharp contrast between good and bad actors in "the search for moral legibility."[42] In *Food, Inc.* the contrast is between good (organic, local) and bad (industrial, processed) food and good (white male journalists, advocates, business owners, and organic farmers) and bad (Big Food) actors on this dramatic stage.[43] One symptom of *Food, Inc.*'s melodramatic approach is that it unwittingly mutes the voices of the animal, vegetable, and undocumented "others" on whom middle-class nourishment seems to depend in the United States.[44] The one family of color in *Food, Inc.* is shown in "caricature," to be trapped between having to choose between medicine and the dollar menu since vegetables at the supermarket are too expensive.[45] While this cash-strapped situation is a common one, the film makes it appear as a zero-sum game to be solved within the confines of the nuclear family. The film does not allow room to think about the way in which the family's cultural or broader community context could serve as a viable resource.[46] To focus on actors and citizens as individual consumers above all else does not account for difficulties in accessing food in food deserts or clever workarounds and problem solving around day-to-day provisioning.[47] With the market as the savior of this melodramatic narrative of the food industrialists versus their hapless consumer-victims, there is a trust that the market is self-regulating and has possibly even an innate moral sense that good will triumph over evil in the name of equilibrium.

The consumer-focused vision of *Food, Inc.* feeds into what Jodi Dean calls a neoliberal "free trade fantasy" that buying more organic, locally grown food from retailer giants such as Walmart benefits all involved parties.[48] The neoliberal vision of *Food, Inc.*, in turn, jibes well with melodrama's focus on the possibility of hope as something that depends on an individual display of an "archaic sort of virtue" as opposed to systemic changes.[49] And this yearning for the display of virtue is something that Williams argues "can musically be felt in terms of patterns of anticipation and return."[50] The movement forward in the narrative, which is dominated by the "rescue, chase, or fight," is mirrored by the delay of resolution and a wallowing in the feeling of "too late."[51] Even though the film's narrative is dominated by stories of fights against Big Food, the title cards at the end of *Food, Inc.* save us as shoppers in the nick of time, and everyone wins, neoliberal style, in the process.[52]

That temporal dimension to melodrama in part helps explain why the participants in the Takepart survey of *Food, Inc.* may have expressed a sense of "near-future hope" that their individual actions could help change the food system as a whole.[53] That same sense of hope motivates the environmental elegy that Morton critiques for its paradoxical relationship to time. Like elegy, melodrama, in Williams' terms, seeks to "return to the time of origins and the space of innocence."[54] Elegy similarly involves a double temporality: weeping for the present (as the past) from the vantage point of the future.[55] In trying to visualize the villainy of Big Food in duping the public with pastoral marketing, *Food, Inc.* unwittingly falls into the pastoral trap through its temporal melodramatic and elegiac narrative rhythms.

Food, Inc. tries to debunk these pastoral fantasies by arguing by accretion that the scale of production in Big Food is responsible for all sorts of environmental and health horrors. Throughout the film, a number of infographics demonstrate the ways in which economies of scale in the food industry have completely changed the products themselves. To illustrate the dramatic consolidation of the meat industry, an infographic shows many cows on conveyor belts headed toward their industrialized deaths and zooms in on one

Fig. 6.1 A sampling of infographics in *Food, Inc.* (2009) illustrating the scalar quandaries posed by industrial agriculture.

representing the meat industry in the 1970s and another representing the meat industry today, both shown to be a patchwork of meat companies. One graphic compares the growth of a chicken in 1950 to one grown at the time of the film's production. The growth of the contemporary chicken's breasts especially vastly outpaces that of the 1950s chicken due to the now contemporary consumer preference for white meat. Yet another graphic shows the variety of products that can be made with corn, from ketchup to crackers to charcoal briquettes. These food items and household objects pop onto the screen, pirouette, and then recede into the background. In all these examples, the sheer number of products belies the standardized and industrialized processes that create them, seemingly out of sheer will.

These highly mediated infographics are starkly different from other moments in the film that explicitly elicit the emotion of the spectator: the chicken farmer driven to bankruptcy; the chickens condemned to a short, suffocating life in a crowded hoop house; the shaky, vignetted, secret footage of the chicken wranglers; the heart-wrenching story of the young boy who died of *E. coli* poisoning and his tirelessly advocating mother; Oprah being sued under draconian veggie libel laws; or the immigrant family who is forced to choose between medicine and food from fast-food value menus. Williams argues that in melodrama, the action of the plot is punctuated by "ephemeral spectacles" that express a pathos "in which audiences admire the show."[56] These spectacles alternate with the frenetic action of the plot. The net effect between the actions and spectacle is what Williams calls a "visceral form of ethics" that "is felt as good" by viewers.⁵⁷

But rather than depart from the realist mode of the rest of the film, these "spectacles of epistephilia," to build on Bill Nichols's coinage, plunge deeper, in Mortonian fashion, into a higher-fidelity recording of the state of the human-nature connection in the Anthropocene.⁵⁸ That human-nature connection, according to Timothy Morton, is a nauseatingly oppressive one where humans cannot shake the influence and presence of things and waste because they are connected to one another through the mechanism of consumption. Morton writes: "Consumerism is the specter of ecology. When thought fully, ecological awareness includes the essence of consumerism, rather than shunning it. Ecological awareness must embrace its specter."⁵⁹ In the course of informing viewers of the excesses of industrial food, the infographics in *Food, Inc.* actually stimulate an appetite for the familiar junk food sitting at home in their pantries. As the film reviews I discussed earlier mention, *Food, Inc.*, through its phenomenology of guilt, prompts viewers to "choke on their popcorn" and reflect on the snacks on offer at the multiplex.⁶⁰ Even food systems scholar Julie Guthman admits that reading and learning about so-called pure food from Michael Pollan and other popularizers of the sustainable food movement "in a funny way makes [her] crave some corn-based Cheetoes."⁶¹ *Food, Inc.* dramatizes this tension between rejecting and desiring the abject refuse produced by Big Food in its twirling, popping industrial food products.

In a documentary film that sees itself as productively enabling social change, there is something fundamentally ineffectual and possibly even silly about food that spins, pops and twinkles as pure spectacle without going anywhere or doing anything. Jack Halberstam has identified such moments of silly animation in Pixar films that thematize political revolt—"Pixarvolt"—as possessing a paradoxical political power that he calls the "queer art of failure."⁶² What is queer about the politically charged, yet silly animation in these Pixar films is their rejection of heteronormative, binary systems that are defined by success and productivity.⁶³ Similarly, the infographics of *Food, Inc.*, by rejecting narrative resolution, societal problem-solving, and productivity, reject the neoliberal values underlying *Food, Inc.*'s social engineering project. In their ineffectualness to the advancement of the film's plot, the "spectacles of epistephilia" in *Food, Inc.*, provide a counter-narrative to agrilogistics, whose focus on maximizing the productivity of crops arguably ushered in the era of the Anthropocene.

In this way, the animated infographics in *Food, Inc.* unwittingly enact what Annabelle Honess Roe has described as the "critical political possibilities of animation within a live-action context."⁶⁴ At first, the infographics in *Food, Inc.* appear to serve the "mimetic" function of animated sequences within live-action films or TV news, which work seamlessly to supplement archival material or sociohistorical context otherwise unrepresentable through live-action footage.⁶⁵ But paying attention to the particular aesthetic style of the animated infographics in *Food, Inc.* allows the viewer to reconsider those sequences, in Cristina Formenti's terms, as "tools for conveying emotions and therefore for dramatizing the events recounted."⁶⁶ The style of the animated infographics in *Food, Inc.* explicitly depends on the kitschy aesthetics of advertising for its visual appeal. The abject industrial foods featured in these infographics, because undesirable, in aesthetic terms take on the attributes of kitsch. These moments of kitsch, therefore, act as instances of Mirzoeff's notion of "counter-visuality" by providing critical responses to the pastoral elegy that organizes the majority of the film. While elegy involves a temporal nostalgia, kitsch involves an embrace of the uncanny—the more one focuses on the good stuff, the more one craves the bad stuff. The chorus-like repetition of the infographics throughout the film in turn rhythmically underscores their uncanniness. As an aesthetic acknowledgment of the repressed rather than an appeal to purity, the uncanny nature of kitsch is, according to Morton, key to cultivating an ecological awareness.⁶⁷

The kitsch of *Food, Inc.*'s infographics is a style that—as the film's reviewers make clear—underscores the ways in which going to the movies, in Vivian Sobchack's terms, is always an "embodied experience . . . in which our sense of the literal and the figural . . . may sometimes be perceived in uncanny discontinuity, but most usually configures to make undifferentiated sense and meaning together."⁶⁸ In this way, the animated infographics, like more critical animated documentaries, "convey subjective experiences that are irreducible to language or image."⁶⁹ By returning to these moments of familiar, yet embarrassingly tacky infographic kitsch, *Food, Inc.*, unwittingly performs a political act by, in Morton's words, "reintroduc[ing] the uncanny into the poetics of the home."⁷⁰ Unlike the calls to action at the end of the film, which explicitly call on viewers to eat the right thing, the infographics stimulate ecological awareness by reminding viewers of the cozy and somewhat oppressive proximity of the bad food that surrounds them and the extent to which they are imbricated within the industrial food system.

* * *

The film's kitschy visual mirroring of the false cornucopian plentitude that Big Food markets to the masses marks an uncanny return to the point of

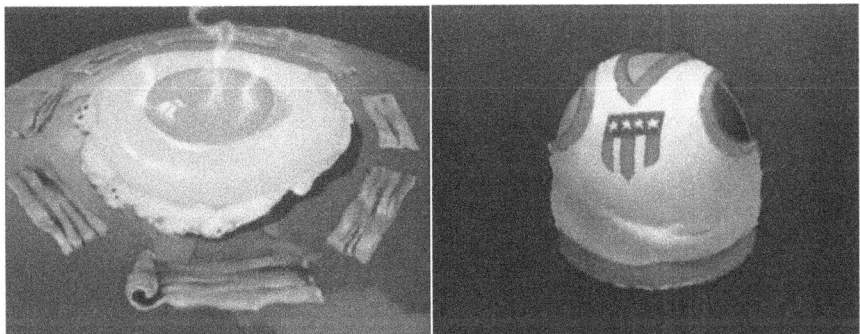

Fig. 6.2 Stills from *Food Will Win the War* (1942) relying on a hyperbolic form of infographic to illustrate the outsized US contribution to the war effort in terms of food production.

origin for the current industrialized food system, World War II. The infographics in *Food, Inc.* are part of a longer history of food films before and during World War II that relied on animated food for rhetorical power. Food production during World War II marks a deepening of the link between food production and anthropogenic climate change that set the stage for the Green Revolution during postwar Reconstruction and the postcolonial period.[71] The logic undergirding wartime food propaganda, therefore, prioritized agrilogistical maximization: that is, altering the entire food system to get the most nutrients for the buck.[72] To this end, the Disney Studios film *Food Will Win the War* (1942), for example, boasts about the US contribution of food to the Allied forces in Europe. The visual rhetoric of that film relies on a repetitious, statistically accurate form of hyperbole designed to bolster support for US involvement in the war, arguing, for instance, that if the 50 billion eggs produced annually at that time "were made into one huge fried egg, it would cover all the United States and Canada" (fig. 6.2).[73] Many of the estimates of US food production reach outlandishly planetary proportions, with the wheat produced being sufficient to make enough pasta to knit a sweater to keep the Earth warm (fig. 6.2). It is worth noting the prescience of this image—that human food production could actually alter weather on a planetary scale.

The logic of unveiling that guides *Food, Inc.*'s investigative impulse has wartime antecedents as well. Jean Negulesco's *Food and Magic* (1943) draws attention to the issue of wartime food waste using the conceit of a magic show that relies on stop-motion animation to stress to the on- and off-screen audience the urgency of its public service announcement. "Magic" acts as the recurring motif for illustrating to the audience the ease with which food, "ammunition as vital as bullets," can be saved, wasted, and consumed.[74] The

Fig. 6.3 A female character in *Food and Magic* (1943) is "magically" confronted with the immense scale of food waste in the United States.

stop-motion animation, edited together with the magician's snap of his fingers, transforms one loaf of bread into a mountain. The magician taunts a woman in the audience with the mountain, implying that the volume points to either her hearty appetite or her food waste: "There, madam, is the amount you cause to disappear every week." The woman protests that she possibly could not have consumed or wasted so much bread. The woman's figure is dwarfed by the amount of bread, a visual trick that argues for the urgency of addressing food waste. This type of alimentary prestidigitation, like in *Food, Inc.*, relies on a logic of unveiling not only the degree and scale of food-related issues but also the way in which food itself has a magical effect on its eaters. That said, the overall tone of the film remains comic despite the urgency of the issue at hand.

The spectatorial excesses of topics that stimulated the appetite were very much on the mind of British documentary filmmaker Paul Rotha, whose *World of Plenty* (1943) and *The World Is Rich* (1947) argued for postwar peace by ensuring the equitable distribution of food around the globe according to needs and wants rather than the whims of the free market.[75] Rotha's films resonate with now contemporary food films in the sense that they have been

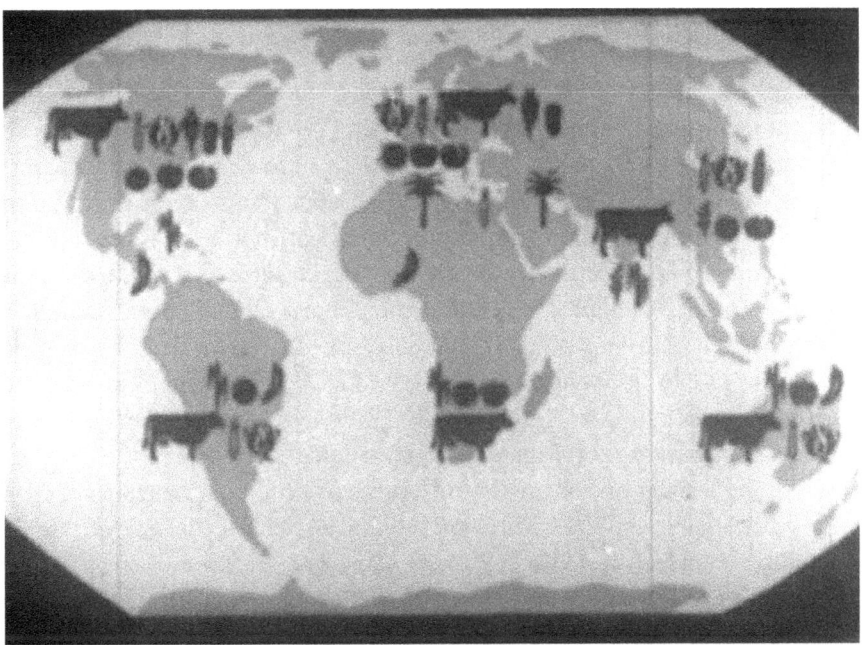

Fig. 6.4 A world map in in Paul Rotha's *World of Plenty* (1943) uses ISOTYPE animation to argue for the effortless path to peace that the international commodity trade could provide in the postwar period.

read as precursors to global movements, such as Slow Food, that help establish "global ethical engagement" on the level of everyday concerns like eating.[76] The film uses animated diagrams called ISOTYPES (International System of Typographic Picture Education), originally developed by Austrian sociologist Otto Neurath but adapted for film in collaboration with Paul Rotha. Neurath's wife and collaborator, Marie L. Neurath, writes about how the ISOTYPE animations are designed to inspire "a laughter of surprise . . . [that] illustrates something that is otherwise published (or hidden away) in statistical tables."[77] The same rhetoric of unveiling that courses through *Food, Inc.* is present here. Food commodities similarly pop on the screen in cartoonish fashion. The difference is that Neurath associates revelation with "the laughter of surprise" rather than the disgust that *Food, Inc.* inspires.

Rather than aim for verisimilitude, Rotha focuses on stimulating interest in the topic of food and health through rather avant-garde means that infused many early British documentaries.[78] As if to anticipate audience objection to the animations, *World of Plenty* includes a multivocal voice-over in which an authoritative male British voice dialogues with an American everyman over the validity of the animated diagrams. The British narrator explains: "They tie production to consumption by distribution." The skeptical American respondent challenges his phrasing as being too elitist: "Why do you have to talk that way? All they mean is, they send the food where it's wanted." Later, the American, confused by the animation, quips, "You can prove anything with diagrams. Give me half an hour with Walt Disney, and I could pay my income tax and never feel it!" The dialogic voice-over has the effect of calling into question the representational apparatus of the entire film. By breaking the fourth wall, *World of Plenty* draws attention to its status as a cinematic construction. Unlike *Food, Inc.*, which uses the rhetoric of unveiling to delineate sharply between illusion and truth and delays the search for truth by tugging at the viewer's emotional heartstrings, *World of Plenty* aims to represent the truth while questioning its ability to do so. The playful tone of *World of Plenty* offers an alternative to *Food, Inc.*'s self-importance.

Looking back at one of the first instances of a food documentary, Edgar Anstey's *Enough to Eat? The Nutrition Film* (1936), which is an early example of the illustrated lecture genre of documentary, one gets a view of a genre-in-the-making and the values and anxieties about food underpinning the form itself.[79] *Enough to Eat?* arguably was the *Food, Inc.* of its day in terms of impact and controversy. Sponsored by the Gas, Light, and Coke Company of Great Britain, *Enough to Eat?* was based on the impactful *Food, Health and Income* (1936) report by John Boyd Orr, whose work linking malnutrition to poverty earned him the Nobel Peace Prize after the war. In *Enough to Eat?*, as in *Food, Inc.*, consumption of the wrong combination of foods, based on the nutritional sciences of the time, threatens to unravel the social fabric. And though the images in *Enough to Eat?* follow the 1930s documentary "pattern . . . between image and concept," they do so with an eye to calling attention to the cinematic apparatus of the film instead of claiming to debunk illusion with truth as *Food, Inc.* does.[80] In doing so, the film privileges infographics as a way of countering the medium-specific effects of cinema that Rotha, too, was intent on limiting and draws focus away from the melodramatic frame that social problems seem to invite. Instead, the film focuses on the non-human or contextual elements of malnutrition, including aspects like food expenditure and the nutrients that make up the foods. This contextual approach critiques the spectral excesses of cinema, instead highlighting the materiality of the problem at hand through artistic techniques that paradoxically lack an indexical relationship to the social world.

The tone of *Enough to Eat?* does not devolve into hysteria-producing melodramatics, but stays even-keeled despite the alarming findings of the

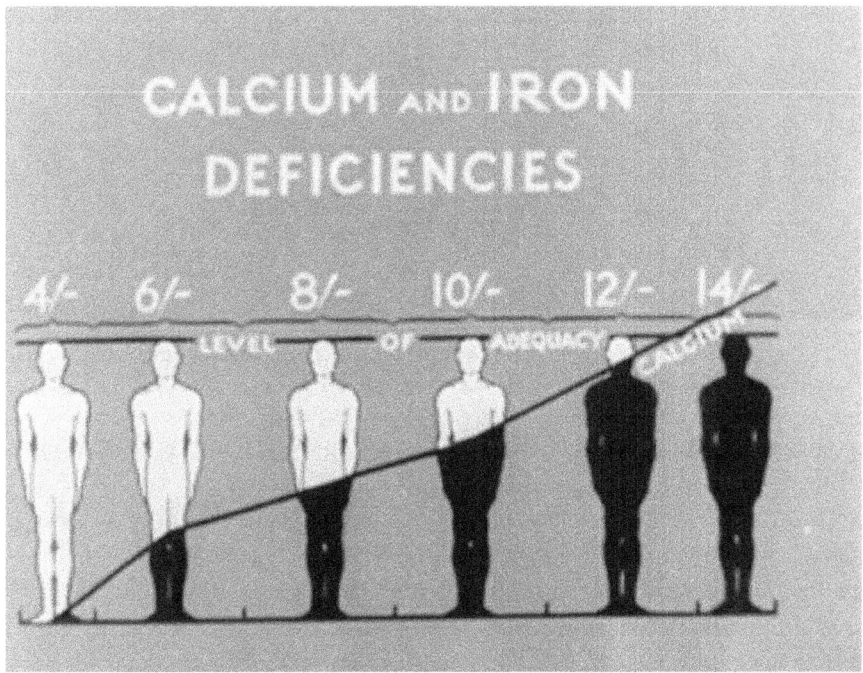

Fig. 6.5 An infographic in *Enough to Eat?* (1936) demonstrates a correlation between income and nutrition.

report on which the film is based. The on-screen narrator, Julian Huxley, public scientist extraordinaire and secretary of the London Zoological Society, argues against showing "harrowing pictures" of starving children presumably because he prefers that the film appeal to reason rather than to emotion but also because he sees that horrific images do not adequately represent the problem of malnutrition, which he explains was "less obvious and spectacular in its effects but much more widespread." Instead, Anstey asserts that the "gray drama" of the facts is all that is needed to communicate the reality of malnutrition in Great Britain. For example, the film features an antecedent to Rotha and Neurath's ISOTYPE animation that shows calcium and iron deficiencies in people according to their weekly food expenditure. The animation subscribes to Huxley's cautioning against melodramatic live-action photography that has the counterintuitive effect of distancing spectators from the problem at hand. The figures are faceless statuettes representing populations spending increasingly more amounts of money per week on food. The image is radical for its depiction of both the poor and the wealthy in the exact same abstracted style. An animated line intersects each figure to represent

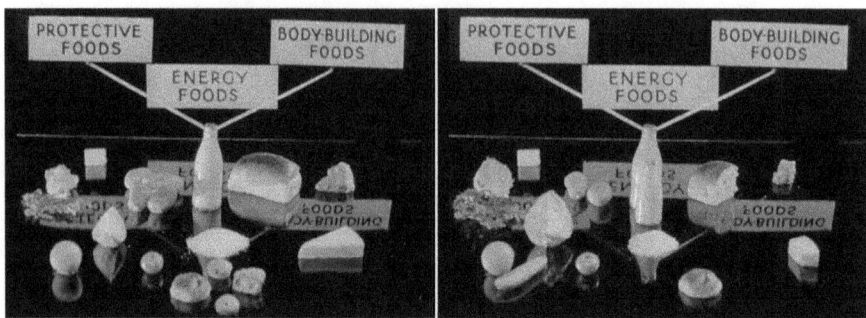

Fig. 6.6 Adjacent shots in *Enough to Eat?* (1936) use stop-motion photography to visualize actual versus ideal diets for children in the United Kingdom during the interwar period.

the degree of nutritional deficiencies per group with the effect of the most vulnerable being visible and the least vulnerable obscured in shadow. Rather than exploit images of the poor to advance the cause of national health, *Enough to Eat?* renders the abstracted figures into digestible tidbits of information. Data literally becomes food in a sequence in which various types of food groups pop off-screen to illustrate the ideal diet for a child. A loaf of bread magically halves itself while a head of lettuce doubles in size. The use of stop-motion animation here playfully gestures toward an off-screen human mouth chomping on the foodstuffs in question while calling attention to the cinematic apparatus that allows for such camera tricks. As in *Food and Magic*, the instantaneity with which the food disappears and appears on screen carries the rhetorical import of the film without the weight of drama: that the health gap between rich and poor is a function of income alone and can be remedied with strategic government subsidies.

These graphics serve as antecedents to the type of infographic kitsch that pulses throughout *Food, Inc.* As Rotha's, Anstey's, and Huxley's comments demonstrate, these "spectacles of epistephilia" are symptomatic of an anxiety about the melodramatic effects of cinematic images on spectators within the context of the "social problem film," which was intended to balance between popular appeal and the formation of an informed citizenry. In contrast, *Food, Inc.* sees itself as unambiguously unveiling the secrets of the food industry and directing consumers to act in a way to change the food industry through its melodramatic narrative, which appeals to what Williams describes as the dominant language of American democracy. Yet the kitschy animated infographics in *Food, Inc.*, which have come to be a conventional aspect of the genre of the "social problem film," act as an unwitting critique of the melodramatic rhythm that marks the rest of the film. The rhetoric of unveiling in

Food, Inc. presumes that food marketing is a visualization of food that can't be trusted and needs to be rejected. Yet, according to Timothy Morton, food marketing and consumerism paradoxically contain the specter of ecological awareness because they acknowledge the material relation of humans to the natural world. While Eric Schlosser's voice-over calls attention to the "pastoral fantasy" of food marketing, the film overall underestimates the power of the pastoral fantasy in its own narrative rhythms. In warning the spectator to beware of how food is represented on an industrial scale, the film invites spectators to view the film's own representation of food through a critical lens. In this way, the infographics in *Food, Inc.* provide a space of "counter-visuality" for viewers to redefine their relationship to food and, by extension, the more-than-human world that makes up food. By featuring the most abject and industrial objects of *Food, Inc.*'s own critical gaze, the infographics help stimulate ecological awareness in the popular consciousness.

Notes

1. Kenner, *Food. Inc.*
2. Takepart, "Welcome, *Food, Inc.* Fans!" On the importance of audience surveys for ascertaining the "political impacts of visual modes" associated with environmentalism, see Ivakhiv, "Green Film Criticism and Its Futures," 13.
3. Blakley et al., *Changing Appetites and Changing Minds*, 7.
4. Nahm, "Hope."
5. For readings of *Food, Inc.* that do not take its progressive vision at face value, see Barker, "Chew on This," 70–73; Flowers and Swan, "Eating at Us," 244–247; Lindenfeld, "Can Documentary Food Films," 382–383; Murray and Heumann, "Contemporary Eco-Food Films," 46–49; Smaill, "New Food Documentary," 88–89.
6. Carson, Baron, and Bernard, *Appetites and Anxieties*, 9.
7. See Mirzoeff, "Visualizing," 213–232; Cohen, "*Arche-Cinema* and the Politics of Extinction," 239–265.
8. Seymour, "Irony and Contemporary Ecocinema," 73.
9. On the formal dimensions of *Food, Inc.*'s critique of Big Food, see Barker, "Chew on This," 86–87; Lindenfeld, "Can Documentary Food Films," 378–379; Murray and Heumann, "Contemporary Eco-Food Films," 47; Smaill, "New Food Documentary," 91–92.
10. Mirzoeff, "Visualizing," 292–293.
11. Murray and Heumann, "Contemporary Eco-Food Films," 47.
12. For various characterizations of the grocery story scene in *Food, Inc.*, see Barker, "Chew on This," 86; Lindenfeld, "Can Documentary Food Films," 381; Murray and Heumann, "Contemporary Eco-Food Films," 48.
13. Murray and Heumann, "Contemporary Eco-Food Films," 48.
14. Grosoli, "Andre Bazin," 6.
15. Ibid., 7.
16. Guthman, *Agrarian Dreams*, 274.

17. Guthman, "Commentary," 263.
18. Opie and Elliot, "Tracking the Elusive Jeremiad," 10.
19. Murray and Heumann, "Contemporary Eco-Food Films," 44.
20. Morton, "Dark Ecology of Elegy," 254.
21. Guthman, "Commentary," 264.
22. Guthman, "Neoliberalism," 1172; Guthman, "Commentary," 263.
23. Garrard, *Ecocriticism*, 56–58.
24. Barker, "Chew on This," 79–80; Murray and Heumann, "Contemporary Eco-Food Films," 49.
25. Morton, "Oedipal Logic of Ecological Awareness," 17.
26. Morton, *Ecology without Nature*, 116–119.
27. Barker, "Chew on This," 70.
28. Ibid., 70–71.
29. Dargis, "Meet Your New Farmer."
30. Nahm, "Hope."
31. Ibid.
32. Morton, *Dark Ecology*, 125.
33. Ibid.
34. Edelstein, "For Health or Profit."
35. Smaill, "New Food Documentary," 82.
36. Ibid., 83.
37. Dargis, "Meet Your New Farmer."
38. Morton, *Dark Ecology*, 136.
39. Smaill, "New Food Documentary," 89.
40. Morton, *Dark Ecology* 5.
41. Laudan, "Plea for Culinary Modernism," 43.
42. Williams, "Melodrama," 55.
43. Flowers and Swan, "'Eating at Us,'" 244–245.
44. Barker, "Chew on This," 77–78; Flowers and Swan, "'Eating at Us,'" 246.
45. Flowers and Swan, "'Eating at Us,'" 246.
46. See Peña, *Mexican Americans*; Khan, "Cultivating Borderland Memories," 89–115.
47. Flowers and Swan, "'Eating at Us,'" 246.
48. Dean, "Enjoying Neoliberalism," 59.
49. Williams, "Melodrama," 74.
50. Ibid.
51. Ibid.
52. Ibid.
53. Nahm, "Hope."
54. Williams, "Melodrama," 74.
55. Morton, "Dark Ecology of Elegy," 254.
56. Williams, "Melodrama," 57.
57. Ibid., 74.
58. Nichols, *Representing Reality*, 174; Morton, *Ecology without Nature*, 142.
59. Morton, *Dark Ecology*, 125.
60. Dargis, "Meet Your New Farmer."
61. Guthman, "Can't Stomach It," 79.
62. Halberstam, *Queer Art*, 29.
63. Ibid., 96.

64. Honess Roe, "Interjections and Connections," 284.
65. Honess Roe, *Animated Documentary*, 26; Hight, "Primetime Digital Documentary Animation," 14.
66. Formenti, "Sincerest Form of Docudrama," 109.
67. Morton, *Ecology without Nature*, 169.
68. Sobchack, *Carnal Thoughts*, 76.
69. Honess Roe, *Animated Documentary*, 137.
70. Morton, *Ecology without Nature*, 177.
71. See Perkins, *Geopolitics and the Green Revolution*.
72. See Collingham, *Taste of War*.
73. Luske, *Food Will Win the War*.
74. Negulesco, *Food and Magic*.
75. Rotha, *World of Plenty*; Chapman, *New History of British Documentary*, 120–121; Aitken, "'World without End," 669–670.
76. Aitken, "World without End," 658.
77. Neurath, "Isotype in Films."
78. Miller, "Documentary/Modernism," 226–241.
79. Anstey, *Enough to Eat? The Nutrition Film*. For the broader context of *Enough to Eat?* and other scientific films, see Boon, "Documentaries and the Social Relations of Science," 73–109.
80. Purdon, *Modernist Informatics*, 150.

References

Aitken, Rob. "A 'World without End': Post-War Reconstruction and Everyday Internationalism in Documentary Film." *International History Review* 35, no. 4 (2013): 657–680.
Anstey, Edgar, dir. *Enough to Eat? The Nutrition Film*. UK: Gas, Light, and Coke Company, 1936. Available online at Wellcome Library. "*Enough to Eat? The Nutrition Film*." YouTube video, May 24, 2013, 21:03. https://www.youtube.com/watch?v=0rqQBQ2jDE4.
Barker, Jennifer Marilynn. "Chew on This: Disgust, Delay, and the Documentary Image in *Food, Inc.*" *Film-Philosophy* 15, no. 2 (2011): 70–89.
Blakley, Johanna, Grace Huang, Sheena Nahm, and Heesung Shin. *Changing Appetites and Changing Minds: Measuring the Impact of "Food, Inc."* Media Impact Project, USC Annenberg Normal Lear Center, February 2012. https://learcenter.org/wp-content/uploads/2016/06/Food-Inc-Summary-Report.pdf.
Boon, Timothy. "Documentaries and the Social Relations of Science." In *Films of Fact: A History of Science Documentaries in Film and Television*, 73–109. New York: Wallflower Press, an imprint of Columbia University Press, 2008.
Carson, Diane, Cynthia Baron, and Mark Bernard. *Appetites and Anxieties: Food, Film, and the Politics of Representation*. Detroit: Wayne State University Press, 2014.
Chapman, James. *A New History of British Documentary*. New York: Palgrave Macmillan, 2015.
Cohen, Tom. "*Arche-Cinema* and the Politics of Extinction." *boundary 2* 44, no. 1 (2017): 239–265.
Collingham, Lizzie. *The Taste of War: World War II and the Battle for Food*. New York: Penguin, 2013.
Dargis, Manohla. "Meet Your New Farmer: Hungry Corporate Giant." Review of *Food, Inc.* Directed by Robert Kenner. *New York Times*, June 11, 2009.

Dean, Jodi. "Enjoying Neoliberalism." *Cultural Politics* 4, no. 1 (2008): 47–72.
Edelstein, David. "For Health or Profit, but Not Necessarily for Both." Review of *Food, Inc.* Directed by Robert Kenner. *Fresh Air*, June 18, 2009.
Flowers, Rick, and Elaine Swan. "'Eating at Us': Representations of Knowledge in the Activist Documentary Film *Food, Inc.*" *Studies in the Education of Adults* 43, no. 2 (Autumn 2011): 235–250.
Formenti, Cristina. "The Sincerest Form of Docudrama: Reframing the Animated Documentary." *Studies in Documentary Film* 8, no. 2 (2014): 103–115.
Garrard, Greg. *Ecocriticism*. New York: Routledge, 2011.
Grosoli, Marco. "Andre Bazin: Film as Social Documentary." *New Readings* 11 (2011): 1–16.
Guthman, Julie. *Agrarian Dreams: The Paradox of Organic Farming in California*. Berkeley: University of California Press, 2014.
———. "Can't Stomach It: How Michael Pollan et al. Made Me Want to Eat Cheetoes." *Gastronomica* 7, no. 3 (Summer 2007): 75–79.
———. "Commentary on Teaching Food: Why I Am Fed Up with Michael Pollan et al." *Agricultural and Human Values* 24 (2007): 261–264.
———. "Neoliberalism and the Making of Food Politics in California." *Geoforum* 39, no. 3 (May 2008): 1171–1183.
Halberstam, Jack. *The Queer Art of Failure*. Durham, NC: Duke University Press, 2011.
Hight, Craig. "Primetime Digital Documentary Animation: The Photographic and Graphic within Play." *Studies in Documentary Film* 2, no. 1 (2009): 9–31.
Honess Roe, Annabelle. *Animated Documentary*. New York: Palgrave Macmillan, 2013.
———. "Interjections and Connections: The Critical Potential of Animated Segments in Live Action Documentary." *animation: an interdisciplinary journal* 12, no. 3 (2017): 272–286.
Ivakhiv, Adrian. "Green Film Criticism and Its Futures." *ISLE: Interdisciplinary Studies in Literature and Environment* 15, no. 2 (July 2008): 1–28.
Kenner, Robert, dir. *Food, Inc.* New York: Magnolia Pictures, 2009. https://www.hulu.com/movie/food-inc-1beef04f-564c-444f-bcc2-a483eb610975.
Khan, Sabiha Ahmad. "Cultivating Borderland Memories, from Field to Screen." *Food and Foodways* 24, no. 1–2 (2016): 89–115.
Laudan, Rachel. "A Plea for Culinary Modernism: Why We Should Love New, Fast, Processed Food." *Gastronomica* 1, no. 1 (2000): 36–44.
Lindenfeld, Laura. "Can Documentary Food Films Like *Food Inc.* Achieve Their Promise?" *Environmental Communication: A Journal of Nature and Culture* 4, no. 3 (2010): 378–386.
Luske, Hamilton, dir. *Food Will Win the War*. Burbank, CA: Walt Disney Studios; Washington, DC: United States Department of Agriculture, 1942.
Miller, Tyrus. "Documentary/Modernism: Convergence and Complementarity in the 1930s." *Modernism/Modernity* 9, no. 2 (2002): 226–241.
Mirzoeff, Nicholas. "Visualizing the Anthropocene." *Public Culture* 26, no. 2 (2014): 213–232.
Morton, Timothy. *Dark Ecology*. New York: Columbia University Press, 2016.
———. "The Dark Ecology of Elegy." In *The Oxford Handbook of Elegy*, edited by Karen Weisman, 251–271. New York: Oxford University Press, 2010.
———. *Ecology without Nature*. Cambridge, MA: Harvard University Press, 2007.
———. "The Oedipal Logic of Ecological Awareness." *Environmental Humanities* 1 (2012): 7–21.
Murray, Robin L., and Joseph K. Heumann. "Contemporary Eco-Food Films: The Documentary Tradition." *Studies in Documentary Film* 6, no. 1 (2012): 43–59.
Nahm, Sheena. "Hope and the Big Picture: A Near Future Approach to Social Change." *Digest: A Journal of Foodways and Culture* 2 (Summer 2013). http://digest.champlain.edu/vol2/rn2_2.html.

Negulesco, Jean, dir. *Food and Magic*. Los Angeles, CA: Warner Brothers, 1943. Available online at Oscars, "Academy War Film Collection: Food and Magic." YouTube video, November 11, 2015, 9:21. https://youtu.be/YnzYNwuzxrY.

Neurath, Marie L. "Isotype in Films." Isotype Revisited, October 2009. https://isotyperevisited.org/1946/06/isotype-in-films.html. Originally published 1946.

Nichols, Bill. *Representing Reality*. Bloomington: Indiana University Press, 1991.

Opie, John, and Elliot, Norbert. "Tracking the Elusive Jeremiad: The Rhetorical Character of American Environmental Discourse." In *The Symbolic Earth: Discourse and Our Creation of the Environment*, edited by James Gerard Cantrill and Christine L. Oravec, 9–37. Lexington: University of Kentucky Press, 1996.

Peña, Devon G. *Mexican Americans and the Environment*. Tucson: University of Arizona Press, 2005.

Perkins, John H. *Geopolitics and the Green Revolution: Wheat, Genes, and the Cold War*. New York: Oxford University Press, 1997.

Purdon, James. *Modernist Informatics*. New York: Oxford University Press, 2016.

Rotha, Paul, dir. *World of Plenty*. London: British Ministry of Information, 1943. Available online at Indiana University Libraries Moving Image Archive, "World of Plenty," 44:43. https://collections.libraries.indiana.edu/IULMIA/items/show/55.

Seymour, Nicole. "Irony and Contemporary Ecocinema: Theorizing a New Affective Paradigm." *Moving Environments: Affect, Emotion, Ecology, and Film*, edited by Alexa Weik Von Mossner, 61–78. Waterloo, CAN: Wilfrid Laurier University Press, 2014.

Smaill, Belinda. "New Food Documentary: Animals, Identification, and the Citizen Consumer." *Film Criticism* 39, no. 2 (Winter 2014/2015): 79–102.

Sobchack, Vivian. *Carnal Thoughts: Embodiment and Moving Image Culture*. Berkeley: University of California Press, 2004.

Takepart. "Welcome, *Food, Inc.* Fans!" Accessed November 7, 2020. http://www.takepart.com/foodinc/.

Williams, Linda. "Melodrama Revised." In *Refiguring American Film Genres: History and Theory*, edited by Nick Browne, 42–88. Berkeley: University of California Press, 1998.

SABIHA AHMAD KHAN is Assistant Professor in the Department of Communication at the University of Texas at El Paso.

PART III.
SHORT FORMS AND WEB PRACTICES

This section moves online to examine short forms and web practices. Under other circumstances, these works might be considered instances of digital documentary, but in light of the current hegemony of digital formats for capture, completion, and distribution of media, the use of *digital* as a definitional term seems anachronistic at best. Instead, we are interested in how the affordances of online publishing and viewing have shaped the evolution of popular documentary expression. While speed, economy, and scale continue to lure a wide range of creators to the web, we do not take it for granted that *online* is synonymous with *popular*. Rather, this section explores a range of practices that contribute a specific lexicon to the field of popular documentary.

Anthony Kinik's chapter, "Errol Morris, the *New York Times*, Docmedia, and Op-Docs as Pop Docs," offers an exploration of the integration of documentary shorts and newspaper journalism. Focusing on the Op-Docs and Retro Report series created for NYTimes.com—and singling out the widely disseminated but less celebrated Op-Doc contributions by Errol Morris—Kinik investigates the tensions between Morris's auteurist preoccupations and the more common, institutionally driven reportage formats of the *Times*. Kinik uses the case study of Morris to examine the evolution of electronic journalism as it becomes cross-fertilized with the diverse stylistic conventions of TV, documentary, video blogging, and YouTube, culminating in an eroding distinction between journalism and documentary. His chapter goes beyond aesthetics to argue that the convergence of newspaper journalism and documentary filmmaking has located the two as partners in an ideological struggle that may well determine the evolving status of truth in an embattled fourth estate.

In "Popular Music and Short-Form Nonfiction: Is the Web a Forum for Documentary Innovation?," Michael Brendan Baker considers how the rapid proliferation of online music video production, facilitated by new video compression technologies, has subtly reshaped the popular music documentary today. With online music video production being one of the strongest drivers of online video activity, Baker traces a brief history of its evolution over the past twenty years, highlighting the influence of corporate interests (e.g., American Express, Vevo, Red Bull Music Academy) and journalism sites like Pitchfork Music as well as the role of independent productions, including *The Take Away Show* and *Southern Souls* via digital platforms such as YouTube and Vimeo. Although new technologies and delivery systems might suggest the expansion of aesthetic innovation, Baker reads much of the proliferating short-form music documentary on the web as crystalizing around existing representational practices. Appropriating the concept of *remediation* as a framework, Baker explores the influence of earlier media, particularly established forms of the feature-length documentary, in relation to the vernacular style of contemporary short-form web productions.

In her chapter "From the Essay Film to the Video Essay: Between the Critical and the Popular," Allison de Fren looks at the emerging genre of video essays, a scholarly form that has found audiences beyond academia, bridging the cinephilic and popular, artistic and entertaining. Presenting case studies of the genre's most celebrated and prolific creators, de Fren positions video essays as sharing a historical legacy with essay films. Within the field of documentary studies, essayistic film and video have been recuperated and celebrated by scholars such as Michael Renov for putting forward an expanded range of filmmaking subjectivities. So too, in her mapping of the emergent phenomenon of videographic criticism, de Fren embraces the diversity of voices that have gravitated to the form, defining and expanding its role as an intermediary between fan culture and media scholarship. Charting a two-way movement between academia and popular culture, de Fren analyzes work by figures such as Kevin B. Lee, whose popular success and extraordinarily prolific output led him to an academic appointment, contrasted with the celebrated stylist Kogonada, who abandoned his academic pursuits in favor of virtuosic supercuts and works commissioned by the Criterion collection that eventually landed him at the helm of a feature film that premiered at Sundance in 2017. Also in the mix is filmmaker and scholar

Thom Andersen, whose long-form personal-critical video essay *Los Angeles Plays Itself* (2003) has been credited with elevating the form to the status of art while also inspiring responses such as Tony Zhou and Taylor Ramos's *Vancouver Never Plays Itself* (2015). De Fren analyzes the artistry and artifice of the video essay as a form of popular documentary and part of a distinct legacy of the essay film, revealing both the pleasures and contradictions of this hybrid form.

7

ERROL MORRIS, THE *NEW YORK TIMES*, DOCMEDIA, AND OP-DOCS AS POP DOCS

Anthony Kinik

Showdown

In the sixth and final episode of *Wormwood* (2017), Errol Morris's genre-bending Netflix Original docudrama, a feature interview with Seymour Hersh, the groundbreaking investigative journalist, turns into something of a showdown—and a standoff. Morris is investigating the strange case of Frank Olson, a military scientist and Central Intelligence Agency (CIA) associate who died under mysterious circumstances in 1953, plummeting from an upper-story window of a hotel in New York City while on a business trip. Decades later, in 1975, the case of Olson's apparent suicide was complicated further when the news broke that he had been the victim of the CIA's secretive MK-Ultra program and its experiments with LSD. It was Hersh who had first revealed the CIA's "massive, illegal" domestic espionage program in 1974—including the exploits of MK-Ultra—and one year later, he was also the one who helped bring the new details of the Olson case to light.[1]

However, instead of resolving the case, Hersh's work, together with the government's release of formerly classified materials and an official apology from President Gerald Ford, set Olson's son Eric on a forty-year quest to discover the truth of his father's death. It is this obsessive and convoluted quest, with all its *Hamlet*-like intrigue, that is the real subject of *Wormwood*. In this regard, even though Morris developed a radically new form for his latest project—one that features well-known actors, extensive use of scripted dialogue, and elaborate dramatizations and reenactments, highly sophisticated

Fig. 7.1 Seymour Hersh in conversation with Errol Morris, *Wormwood* (2017), episode 6.

editing and collage effects, and an eclectic and powerful soundtrack—*Wormwood*'s concerns should be familiar to those who've followed Morris's career. The series shares the same set of interests as all of Morris's major works since *The Thin Blue Line* (1988): the road to establishing the truth of any contentious matter is long and winding and littered with obstacles and challenges of all kinds; those who travel this road often get lost along the way or are preyed on by footpads, cutthroats, and other unsavory characters.[2]

Morris's project was prompted by some shattering discoveries that were unearthed by Eric Olson himself in 2014: his father's death wasn't an accident or a suicide, and it wasn't simply the unfortunate result of experiments with LSD. Olson's death wasn't even a simple murder, although there most certainly was foul play involved. Instead, it was the product of what Eric Olson calls "a fully authorized institutional decision," and the LSD tale had been concocted and circulated by the CIA itself, through unwitting agents like Hersh, as a cover story to obscure a much more damning tale. Eric Olson contacts Hersh in the wake of his bombshell findings, and, perhaps not surprisingly, the veteran journalist is reluctant to be involved at first—after all, his reputation is on the line.

It is within this charged context that Morris's interview with Hersh takes place. Morris is ostensibly recording Hersh's testimony, but he's also acting as an advocate for Eric Olson, and simultaneously transforming the esteemed journalist into much more than a talking head. Hersh admits that he was duped by the CIA in the mid-1970s—it was still relatively early in his career, and he was still a little naive—and he verifies that a source confirmed Olson's conclusion, but he remains unable to go to press with the matter. This prompts him to lecture Morris on "Journalism 101": he may agree with Eric that "something heinous happened to [Frank] Olson," but he doesn't "know that in a way that I can publish," making his personal beliefs in this matter—and anyone else's, as far as Hersh is concerned—beside the point. Minutes later, Morris presses his subject further. Doing so leads Hersh to give his interviewer a further lesson on the topic of investigative journalism:

> MORRIS: For me, part of the story is the fact that you can't tell the story.
>
> HERSH: That's not a new phenomenon. That's a very serious issue. I do operate at different levels than other people because I can get information. People trust me.[3] They trust my judgment. I'm old. I told you, I'm seventy-nine. I've been doing this goddamn thing for, you know, 350 years. Something like that. Don't make this a big deal about journalism. . . . The source is more important than the story—always. Always.

The fact that Morris was nearly seventy at the time seems to have eluded Hersh. But in addition to the stature of the two individuals involved, what I find fascinating about this exchange is that it pits journalism and documentary filmmaking—two of the most prominent examples of what Bill Nichols and others have labeled "discourses of sobriety"[4]—against one another, and it does so at an interesting moment in time. Hersh's appearance in *Wormwood* is filled with frustration and disdain, with eye-rolling and condescension. He allows himself to be interviewed, but he seems to regard documentary filmmaking as a lesser form of inquiry. Hersh's performance is also filled with a certain lack of self-knowledge—a theme that is central to Morris's work. Among other things, Hersh doesn't seem to realize that Morris is accomplishing much of what Eric Olson is seeking on his behalf: he's getting Seymour Hersh, the acclaimed journalist who helped reveal—then unwittingly impede—the Frank Olson case, to state on the record that he agrees with Eric Olson's discoveries and that he, too, believes that Frank Olson was executed. In a sense, Morris is "publishing" Hersh on this matter. He also gets him to utter the closest thing to a Rumsfeldian "unknown knowns" moment as *Wormwood* has to offer.[5]

> HERSH: The mechanism of this process. . . . If I'm right that [Frank Olson] was done in, there was a mechanism—it wasn't ad hoc.
>
> MORRIS: What do you mean by a mechanism?
>
> HERSH: See, I knew you were going to ask that question. What do you mean by, "What do you mean"? A mechanism. There was a procedure.
>
> MORRIS: A mechanism to eliminate an undesirable.
>
> HERSH: Mm-hmm. Why not?

Fig. 7.2 History, collage aesthetics, and reenactments in *Wormwood* (2017).

In the end, Hersh testifies that Eric Olson's account was confirmed by one of his most trusted CIA sources, *on camera*. Hersh might not be in a position to provide details, but this exchange is *Wormwood*'s equivalent to the famous tape recorder finale in *The Thin Blue Line*, in which David Harris—without providing any details—appears to confess *on tape* to Morris that he framed Randall Adams for the murder of police officer Robert Wood and that he might actually have been Wood's murderer.

At a glance, *Wormwood* seems like a historical project, one that is focused primarily on a relatively obscure case that occurred well over sixty years ago, during the early years of the Cold War and the CIA—its elaborate historical reconstructions all have to do with this period—and, therefore, one that has little to do with the present situation. But like so many of Morris's other historical projects—*The Fog of War* (2003), for instance—the series is actually "vitally important" and incredibly timely.[6] After all, as a tale of whistleblowers, of the power struggle between the press and the federal government (especially the White House, the intelligence community, and the Pentagon), of covert operations as organized crime and the government execution of extralegal and illegal "justice," and of nuclear anxiety, *Wormwood* has plenty that resonates with US politics in the early twenty-first century. Later, when it is revealed that Frank Olson was involved quite specifically in the development of a covert campaign of biological warfare against North Korea, the immediate relevance of *Wormwood* becomes hauntingly clear.

In any case, there's no indication in Hersh's uneasy demeanor that he recognizes Morris as either an equal or a fellow traveler. Hersh's reactions were likely driven by his own feelings of guilt and shame—over having been duped, over having taken so long to admit that he'd been used, over having insulted the Olson family,[7] over having started Eric Olson on this self-destructive forty-year quest. But whatever the case, he never acknowledges that he and Morris have rather similar interests and are part of the same general project. After all, if Hersh was one of the protagonists of the investigations into the Abu Ghraib scandal,[8] Morris was the one who created what is arguably the most powerful film on the matter, *Standard Operating Procedure* (2008)—one that shared Hersh's conviction that the focus on "a few bad apples" was a whitewash—and simultaneously transformed it into a philosophical inquiry into the nature of photography in the digital age.

There's also no acknowledgment that Morris has worked in print media as a journalist, that he was a regular contributor to a leading US newspaper for years, or that the newspaper in question was one with which Hersh himself had a long and eventful association: the *New York Times*.[9] Morris has produced a number of short films for the *Times*'s online Op-Docs section, but his most significant contributions came as a blogger for the paper's online Op-Ed section, where he published a series of long-form essays on the elusive (and controversial) nature of photography. These posts include a couple on the Abu Ghraib affair, and the series as a whole would go on to form the basis of Morris's thought-provoking and deeply affecting book on photography and documentary representation: *Believing Is Seeing: Observations on the Mysteries of Photography* (2011).

Finally, there's no admission that the distinction between journalism and documentary filmmaking has largely collapsed in the second decade of the twenty-first century, that documentaries are now a common part of the online version of print media like newspapers and magazines, or that newspapers and magazines are now in the business of supporting and exhibiting documentaries. Here, Hersh is hardly alone. The fact that documentaries of all kinds—prosaic, poetic, philosophical, pointedly political, and so on—and in all different styles have become a mainstay of the online editions of leading newspapers and magazines, like the *New York Times*, the *Washington Post*, the *Guardian*, the *New Yorker*, and the *Atlantic*, has not gone entirely unnoticed, but it has been underreported and underanalyzed.

In what follows, I'd like to suggest that the convergence of the newspaper and the documentary has had significant repercussions for both print media and nonfiction filmmaking, for journalism and for documentary studies, and that the online version of the *New York Times* has been a particularly fascinating laboratory for such experimentation. Analyzing the introduction of documentary studies and, later, actual documentary films into the space of the *Times* 2.0 provides a revealing glimpse into how these partnerships and allegiances have formed and what, specifically, they've generated. In particular,

I place a great deal of emphasis on the online version of the *Times* Opinion page and the advent of the Op-Docs series, with, in both cases, the contributions of Errol Morris as my central focus. Here, once again, we find something of a blind spot, even among those who have studied Morris's career closely. With some notable exceptions, there has been a tendency to overlook or to underappreciate these online projects, and it is my contention that the significance of these editorials, blog posts, and Op-Docs deserves much closer scrutiny.

Docmedia

Back in the late 1990s and early 2000s, opinions were starkly divided when it came to the fate of the documentary in the digital era, as they were in other realms affected by rapid technological evolution. In one camp, there was a considerable amount of consternation over how the documentary would fare if the internet, and especially the arrival of Web 2.0, brought about the demise of television, the medium that had done the most to support the production of documentaries globally for decades. In the other, there was a considerable amount of optimism that this brave new digital world would help bring about novel ways of producing, distributing, and exhibiting documentaries as well as entirely new forms of reception and interaction. David Hogarth, in his 2006 book *Realer Than Reel: Global Directions in Documentary*, seemed to address the doomsayers when he wrote, "We often hear that we are living in a post-documentary age." Like Linda Williams and others before him, he argued that "audiovisual truths and the way we perceive them [were being] fundamentally transformed by new types of cultural mediation and reflexivity."[10] Hogarth could see bright new vistas ahead, however, and he cautioned that film and media studies would have to adjust and adapt, and reject "fixed, exclusivist" definitions of documentary form, or risk missing the boat.[11] Web 2.0 was still in its infancy, but already Hogarth was arguing that a new era had dawned for the documentary, one that was no longer attached to a particular medium the way things had been "in the cinema or broadcast eras."[12]

More recently, scholars have begun to study what impact a more highly developed, more expansive Web 2.0 has actually had on the field of documentary, and in some cases this has resulted in freewheeling utopian pronouncements. Take the late Peter Wintonick's "New Platforms for Docmedia: 'Variant of a Manifesto,'" his digital-era ode to Dziga Vertov's manifestos of the 1920s. Channeling Vertov at his most provocative, Wintonick argues that not only has the documentary field been altered but, in fact, the concept of documentary—and even the term *documentary*—is now null and void. In their place, Wintonick proposed that we had entered the "Now

Media" era and that the documentary had been supplanted by "Docmedia," a multimedia, multiplatform set of texts and practices that was particularly representative of "the future and the now." Indeed, as Wintonick put it, "Docmedia is Now Media."[13] In spite of his extreme language, Wintonick's vision of this new landscape was considerably more inclusive than Vertov's—it had more to do with getting rid of monolithic definitions of documentary and embracing the seemingly infinite variations and permutations that have cropped up in recent years. Writing in the same collection, Jon Dovey and Mandy Rose also celebrated the fragmentation of the documentary field as well as the great variety of "distinctive documentary forms" that had been made possible. Instead of focusing on the "voice of documentary," as had been common in earlier times, they focused their attention on issues of interactivity, on how digital media have made it possible for documentaries to "stage a conversation."[14]

In both of these essays, an emphasis is placed on new permutations, on cutting-edge versions, and there is less of an emphasis on the variety of spaces and places documentaries are now turning up. Dovey and Rose refer to this development as a more "straightforward" notion of online, and they seem to suggest that while this version does "[offer] documentary more distribution possibilities," they find it "click-driven" and conventional, and it is clear that interactive documentaries are more compelling to them.[15] However, what's missing in such discussions is that even the most traditional approaches to documentary might undergo a significant transformation depending on how and where one encounters them, and that these new contexts might make for collisions and combinations capable of producing startling effects. Such developments might not be as eye-catching and buzzworthy as VR or interactivity, but that doesn't mean there isn't something revolutionary about them.

In 2002, when Steven Spielberg included animated "e-paper" editions of *USA Today* in *Minority Report* as part of his retro-futurist vision of 2054, it felt to many viewers at the time that such technology might actually be decades away.[16] However, today many of our digital edition newspapers actually are fully animated, covered as they are with advertisements, interactive graphs, maps, slide shows, illustrations, and, indeed, videos, and while the digital newsprint that Spielberg imagined has yet to come into existence and still seems unlikely, digital newspapers can now be found across a variety of different platforms, and, thus, in an infinite variety of contexts. For our purposes, if videos are now a mainstay of the most sophisticated online newspapers and magazines, it must be pointed out that virtually all of these videos fall under the category of documentary representation. In other words, some version of "2054" is already very much with us, and indeed, this mediascape is one that is rich in Docmedia.

Writing in 1999, in an afterword to *Collecting Visible Evidence*, the groundbreaking collection he edited with Jane M. Gaines, Michael Renov commented on the "blurred boundaries" that were defining the field of documentary due to recent technological developments. Renov argued that such blurring, such collapsing of high and low, fiction and nonfiction, was nothing new, and he invoked Walter Benjamin's cultural criticism, and the essay "The Author as Producer," in particular, as evidence:

> Optimistic even in the face of fascist advances, Benjamin singled out the newspaper as that literary vehicle capable of replacing depth with breadth and of dissolving the conventional distinction between author and public. As always, Benjamin captures both sides of the equation at once, both blessing and curse: yes, breadth might displace depth—a significant loss for intellectual life—but that circumstance was balanced by heightened public access to the means of production. In the newspaper, letters to the editor and opinion pieces could mingle freely with professional news coverage; literary qualification could begin to become public property. The newspaper was the "theatre of the unbridled debasement of the word" but also its salvation.[17]

Renov noted that in the late twentieth century, it was the video camera and the internet that were making possible what Benjamin had called "the literalization of the conditions of living." What was unimaginable to Renov and others at the time was the way the internet might actually bring about not only the widespread collapse of the newspaper industry but also, in its wake, the convergence of the documentary and the newspaper, the folding of the documentary *into* the newspaper. Indeed, Renov's discussion of the politics of digital media, the newspaper, and the documentary would prove prescient.

Op-Docs

Andrew Rossi's documentary *Page One: Inside the New York Times* (2011) provides a highly illuminating portrait of a group of reporters and editors who are simultaneously racing to cover the digital shakeup of the news media (WikiLeaks, news aggregators, the war on Old Media, etc.) while trying to ensure that the Gray Lady does not fall victim to the technological revolution.[18] There's a moment in the film when David Carr, the paper's late, great Media Desk writer, quips about the release of a new, tablet-friendly version of the *Times*. Despite his media savvy, Carr was something of a digital skeptic, and in this scene he confronts Brian Stelter, who was then a media correspondent for the *Times* and the film's primary digital enthusiast—and, thus, a frequent punching bag for Carr—as he navigates the online edition on his iPad.

> CARR: That is a great reading experience. You know what it reminds me of?
> STELTER: What?
> CARR: A newspaper.

Carr was being facetious, of course, because already at the time *Page One* was shot, the look and feel of the online edition of the *Times* was changing rapidly and dramatic experiments were either being initiated or were being discussed and tested. One of these features that was being expanded was the inclusion of *nonfiction* video content.

The same year as the release of *Page One*, 2011, the Opinion section of the *New York Times* launched a new project: Op-Docs. This series of short documentaries on diverse topics stood out for its wide array of techniques and approaches as well as for bringing together the talents of both established, well-known filmmakers—such as Laura Poitras, Alan Berliner, Stanley Nelson, and Heidi Ewing—and little-known, up-and-coming ones. As *Page One* had made clear, the years 2009 and 2010 were pivotal ones. The nation was still very much in the throes of the Great Recession, the newspaper industry was in a tailspin, online-only news sources and news aggregators were clobbering what remained of the establishment press, and the *New York Times* was desperately trying to restructure and reorganize: laying off employees and forcing others into early retirement, downsizing and consolidating, developing a new business model, and generally rethinking their mandate. But they were also busy trying to reinvent themselves and attempting to remain relevant by developing new formats (including the tablet-friendly version that David Carr mocked so witheringly), new features, and new dimensions and by embracing multimedia with increased enthusiasm.[19] Tellingly, the Op-Docs series presented itself in the form of "seasons"—just like the television shows and podcasts that were fueling the trend toward binge consumption of the media—and while Season 1 began somewhat tentatively, in terms of form and scope, the series soon became much more ambitious and began to draw increased attention and, eventually, acclaim.[20]

Conceived as an "online video forum for emerging and established filmmakers and artists to share their views," according to Kathleen Lingo, the executive producer of Op-Docs from 2015 to 2018, the series was intended to add bold new dimensions to the Opinion section and bring it, and the *Times*, into the twenty-first century.[21] The experiment seemed to work.[22] An already legendary Opinion section was augmented by the sudden introduction of short documentaries, and the quality of the films and the "fresh perspectives" they provided began to generate a following, "[capturing the] public imagination and [sparking] dialogue online and offline in dramatic new ways," according to Lingo.[23] One of the most interesting aspects of Op-Docs is that it wasn't just about patching in some videos in a cynical attempt to increase traffic for the online edition of the *Times* (although, there's no question that such issues are of vital importance to newspapers in the digital age)—it really did have a lot to do with expanding the definition and the purview of "print" journalism. Thus, these films are not merely released by the *New York Times*, they are "published" by the newspaper on a very specific date, and filmmakers who submit their work to the Op-Docs division have to comply with the same journalistic standards that the rest of the contributors to the *Times* do, including meticulous fact-checking.[24] In other words, no compromises were being made. Video content—*documentary* video content—wasn't about replacing the newspaper; it was about expanding the newspaper. It was about "[extending] the mission of *The New York Times* in new ways."[25]

Morris 2.0

When A. O. Scott's review of *Wormwood* appeared in the *New York Times* in late 2017 under the title "'Wormwood' Confirms That Errol Morris Is Our Great Cinematic Sleuth," the use of the word *our* was likely meant to suggest America or the American public, but it could just as easily have been a reference to the *Times* itself. For over a decade, in addition to continuing to be one of the world's leading documentary filmmakers (and an increasingly prolific one), Morris was a feature contributor to the newspaper's Opinion section. Morris's involvement with the *Times* became a regular engagement when he began to publish a series of carefully researched, well-illustrated, and meticulously documented blog posts—some of which were epic in scale—for the paper's online Opinionator column ("a gathering of opinion from around the web"). Morris had contributed to the *Times* earlier, and the first of these Op-Ed pieces, "Not Every Picture Tells a Story," from November 2004, introduced a line of argument, and a fixation with photography, that has been a mainstay of his work ever since: "Photography, because of its causal relationship to the world, seems to give us the truth or something close to the truth. I am skeptical about this for many reasons. But even if photography doesn't give us truth on a silver platter, it does make it harder for us to deny reality. It puts a leash on fantasy, confabulation and self-deception. It provides constraints and borders. It circumscribes our ability to lie—to ourselves and to others."[26] His contributions to the *Times* remained sporadic, however, until 2007, by which time the Opinionator section had

Errol Morris, the New York Times, *Docmedia*, and Op-Docs as Pop Docs | 127

Fig. 7.3 Errol Morris's essay "Liar, Liar, Pants on Fire" (2007) as it appears in the online edition of the *New York Times*.

been launched. The *Times* was in the process of revamping its online edition, of building its content and giving it more of an independent identity, and it began to take better advantage of Web 2.0's vast multimedia opportunities. Suddenly, it was possible for someone like Morris to not only publish op-eds in the *Times* but also create longer, more densely layered texts that combined his own observations with interviews and quotations and made great use of photographs, clippings, documents, illustrations, maps, charts, artifacts, and other pieces of evidence.

Morris responded with his first Opinionator column, "Liar, Liar, Pants on Fire," and there, he followed up on the line of inquiry he had commenced with "Not Every Picture Tells a Story" nearly three years earlier: "Pictures are supposed to be worth a thousand words. But a picture unaccompanied by words may not mean anything at all. Do pictures provide evidence? And if so, evidence of what? And, of course, the underlying question: do they tell the truth?"[27] As this passage indicates, this was a column having to do with photographs and context, with the captioning of photographs, and with whether photographs have an intrinsic truth value to them. But this time, it featured a looser, more personal, and more playful tone ("This may seem hopelessly obvious, but I have this saying—and I believe there's something to it—that there is nothing so obvious that it's obvious."), and this time it was augmented with photographs, newspaper clippings, and an illustration (a recruitment poster from 1915). Not long afterward, Morris stepped things up further, publishing longer, more detailed, and more probing stories. These posts included historical studies, such as the three-part series "Which Came First, the Chicken or the Egg?" from September 2007, which used Roger Fenton's 1855 Crimean War photographs, and the debates that have surrounded them, to initiate a discussion about the tricky nature of photographs as evidence, as well as the seven-part series "The Case of the Inappropriate Alarm Clock" from October 2009, which dealt with the Depression-era photographs of the Farm Security Administration and how photographs got caught up in the raging political battles of the day. But they also included contemporary inquiries, such as Morris's "Will the *Real* Hooded Man Please Stand Up" from August 2007, his first study of the Abu Ghraib scandal and its aftermath, and "The Most Curious Thing" from May 2008, his second, an article that dealt in detail with the notorious "thumbs-up" photograph of Sabrina Harman and how it was used to "fuzz up" the scandal. Thus began a relationship with the *New York Times* that has resulted in a remarkable, and remarkably diverse, body of work—a body of work that has addressed war and photographic evidence, fraudulence and fakery, photography and the presidency, early computing, typefaces, reenactments in film, and the two Donalds (Rumsfeld and Trump), among other topics. And not long after, Morris would begin to discuss issues of documentary representation in the *Times* with moving images and sound, in addition to still images and text.

To date, Errol Morris has contributed eight films to the *Times*'s award-winning Op-Docs series—running the gamut from personal profiles to public service announcements. However, his most significant contributions to Op-Docs have been two films dealing with the assassination of President Kennedy—*The Umbrella Man* (season 1, November 21, 2011) and *November 22, 1963* (season 2, November 20, 2013), which commemorated the forty-eighth and fiftieth anniversaries of this epochal event, respectively—and another film having to do with military laboratories and the smallpox virus: *Demon in the Freezer* (Season 5, May 17, 2016). These films build on themes that have been a constant in Morris's work since his first contributions to the *Times* Opinion section as well as in many of the feature-length films he's produced over the same period. Thus, Morris's two JFK assassination films both feature Josiah "Tink" Thompson, the author of *Six Seconds in Dallas: A Micro-Study of the Kennedy Assassination* (1967), a writer and historian with whom Morris shares a philosophical bent and a history as a private investigator. Both films are shot in the style of Morris's episodes for *First Person* (2000–2001), his short-lived television series that made one long interview with a single individual the basis of each episode, while also making great use of his Interrotron machine. Thus, each of these films consists of a single interview with Thompson[28]—no other interviews are featured—and, otherwise, each film is made up of photographs, documents, clippings, archival footage, the minimal use of reenactments, and the elegiac sounds of solo piano works by Arvo Pärt (*The Umbrella Man*) and Philip Glass (*November 22, 1963*). *The Umbrella Man*, as its title suggests, focuses on a mysterious figure who could be seen in the Zapruder film and in other photographic and cinematographic records of Dealey Plaza, standing under an open black umbrella on a bright, sunny day, directly in front of the spot where Kennedy was first hit with a bullet. Who was this "umbrella man," what was he doing there in that particular spot, and was he part of some kind of conspiracy? The story of the "umbrella man" is just one of countless bizarre elements connected to the assassination of President Kennedy, and as Thompson explains, in 1967 it prompted John Updike to write a column for the *New Yorker*'s "Talk of the Town," where he speculated that there may be a quantum dimension to historical inquiry, just as there's a quantum dimension to physical reality.[29] Over footage of a microscope and of some of the strange organisms one can see with one, Thompson states the theory this way: "If you put any event under a microscope, you will find a whole dimension of completely weird, incredible things going on. It's as if there's the macro level of historical research where things sort of obey natural laws and usual things happen and unusual things don't happen. And then there's this other level where everything is really weird." As *The Umbrella Man* makes clear, not only is the presence of this mysterious individual strange, but the answer to the mystery is equally bizarre—almost beyond human comprehension.

In the film *November 22, 1963*, Thompson builds on his comments in *The Umbrella Man*, arguing that that fateful day in American history marked a "tectonic shift." He admits that he's gone back to giving that day in Dallas a lot of thought in recent years and that he's been wondering why the details of that case aren't any clearer now, in the early twenty-first century, than they were forty to forty-five years ago. He's also thought a lot about how November 22, 1963, differs from other momentous dates, like December 7, 1941, and September 11, 2001. Thompson comments: "What was different about November 22nd . . . was, right from the beginning, we couldn't put a 'why?' answer on it.

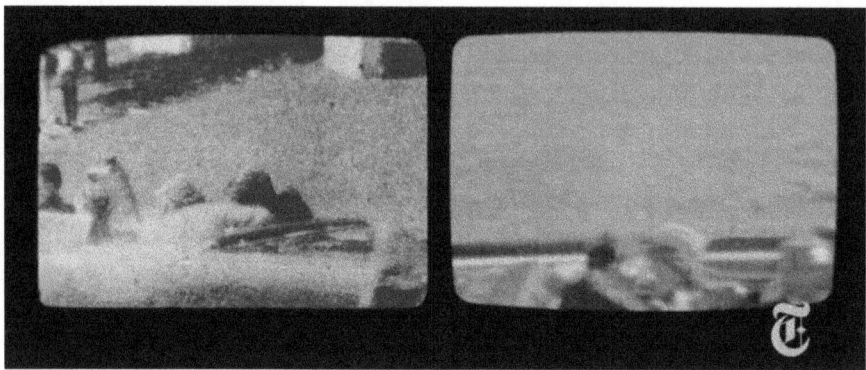

Fig. 7.4 Split-screen aesthetics and the JFK assassination in Errol Morris's *November 22, 1963* (2013).

It seemed to be beyond that." However, even if the why of the events in Dallas remains elusive, Thompson believes that researchers should at least be able to get closer to a more fine-grained account of *what* actually happened. As he explains, what occurred in Dealey Plaza had to have happened one way and not another, and researchers have a considerable amount of documentary material to work with.

In addition to the Zapruder film, there were at least twenty-five to thirty individuals who produced still photographs and motion picture footage as the motorcade passed through the plaza. Conspiracy theorists are constantly debating which of these records hold the truth and which are fakes, but according to Thompson, the records support one another—they provide a "self-authenticating evidentiary basis" for a close analysis of those six seconds in Dallas, one grounded in photographic and cinematographic documents. As with so many other Morris projects, the moral is that the truth may be fragmentary, it may be contingent, but it is not unknowable; it is possible to reconstruct it—maybe even when it comes to November 22, 1963.

Morris's most recent film for Op-Docs, *Demon in the Freezer*, holds the distinction of having been the two hundredth film release in the series. Morris celebrated the occasion with his boldest and most ambitious Op-Doc yet. *Demon in the Freezer* deals with the ongoing debates over what is to be done with laboratory stocks of smallpox that have been preserved since the virus was officially "eradicated" in 1979 to great fanfare. What Morris discovers is that, as in the case of nuclear warfare, the United States and the Soviet Union both had extensive biological warfare divisions, and that here, too, the Cold War never really came to an end. When Morris asks D. A. Henderson of the Johns Hopkins Bloomberg School of Public Health what the rationale is for

Fig. 7.5 Mise-en-scène and screen culture in Errol Morris's *Demon in the Freezer* (2016).

holding on to this most dangerous of viruses, he notes that it's the same argument that's made about nuclear weapons. This prompts Morris to blurt out, "Mutually assured destruction with germs!" as his film takes on absurd and disturbing *Dr. Strangelove*–like dimensions. In terms of production values and approach, *Demon in the Freezer* sits somewhere between *Standard Operating Procedure* and *Wormwood*, with maybe a dash of *Tabloid* (2010). Like both *Standard Operating Procedure* and *Wormwood*, it features the extensive use of digital animation—in this case, used primarily to provide 3D, moving-image models of viruses. Like *The Fog of War* and *Wormwood*, audio and audiovisuals from archival documentaries and television news coverage figure prominently. As one would expect, photographs, clippings, diagrams, illustrations, and other artifacts are also a crucial aspect of Morris's presentation, but, here, much of this material is handled through a "simulation microfiche reader" technique that Morris had used on earlier projects like *The Fog of War* and *Tabloid* and that he would go on to use to great effect in *Wormwood*. And lastly, Morris also makes a point of displaying archival television coverage on period television sets, which are shown in full view, and set against period decor, in exactly the same way that he does in projects like *Tabloid* and *Wormwood*, thereby creating some sense of what it felt like to catch this news the first time around (say, in 1979), when you watched it on a twenty-one-inch Sony Trinitron.

Instead of privileging a single interview subject, Morris provides four interviews in *Demon in the Freezer*, two of which—the case in favor of destroying America's smallpox stocks (Henderson) and the case against it (Peter Jahrling, of the United States Army Medical Research Institute of Infectious Diseases)—are given roughly equal weight. As counterpoint, Morris presents a Russian scientist, Serguei Popov, who found himself coerced into joining the biological warfare division of the ultrasecret KGB-monitored Vector Institute back in the 1980s, as well as an American scientist, Lisa Hensley, who has worked with Jahrling for years despite some misgivings. Ultimately, while *Demon in the Freezer* is ostensibly about the smallpox virus, and therefore about infectious diseases and the quest to eradicate them through the use of vaccines and other means, it also addresses a number of other issues: regimes of secrecy, the perils of scientific and military hubris, the threat of biological warfare, and the even greater threat posed by insecure individuals in positions of great power. In fact, at one point Morris asks Henderson quite pointedly about where the real threat lies.

> MORRIS: The demon in the freezer—is it us? Is it man?
> HENDERSON: Well [chuckling nervously], that's a good point.

According to Henderson's account, the history of modern warfare—which Morris illustrates with archival footage of nuclear blasts and air raids over Southeast Asia—has been one of stages: first nuclear weapons, then chemical weapons, and finally biological weapons. And his concluding pronouncement is ominous: "I think we can anticipate we're going to have some very complicated and very difficult problems." Morris is clearly sympathetic to Henderson's views on the US military establishment, and on human nature more generally, and in retrospect, *The Devil in the Freezer* is an obvious precursor to *Wormwood*. After delving into the Olson case, however, Morris's understanding of the history of modern warfare appears to have changed, for as *Wormwood* makes clear, America's secret biological warfare program was there all along—it was contemporaneous with the nuclear program and a crucial, if little-known, aspect of the Cold War.

Conclusion

As has been widely reported, commented on, and agonized over, we live in an era of "fake news" and "alternative facts," an era where the White House has declared the news media to be the "enemy of the people" and the "official opposition party."[30] Right-wing attacks on the news media, the mainstream media, and the "lamestream" media have been around for decades—arguably, since the heyday of the Pentagon Papers, Watergate, and Seymour Hersh's reports on My Lai and domestic spying at the CIA—but over the last few years, it's safe to say that an all-out war on the press has been declared and is underway. And in spite of the fact that some Republicans have expressed some discomfort with this state of affairs and have sought to distance themselves from this culture war's most extreme proponents—including the president—the GOP itself has backed these attacks and lent credence to them. Meanwhile, a parallel universe of alternative facts; shoddy, decontextualized, and recontextualized statistics; doctored and misrepresented images; and actual fake news has taken hold—one that already includes a major US broadcaster and appears to be growing exponentially and one, it must be noted, that also features an extensive documentary arm. Through his long-standing association with the Opinion section of the *New York Times*, Errol Morris not only forged a connection with the realm of print journalism, but he introduced serious discussions of documentary representation—including the politics that surround them and their stakes—into this realm. Whether they realize it or not, the documentary filmmakers who have contributed to the Op-Docs series at the *Times* have been placed into a similar partnership and allegiance with a print journalism corps under fire. This means that they've also been placed into a wide-ranging ideological struggle with those trying to undermine any faith in the "liberal" press, in any notion of a fourth estate, and even in any notion of the truth. Obviously, this is a struggle of the greatest magnitude, and it's one where Morris's work on documentary representation and the pursuit of the truth has taken on increased importance. It's exactly where responsible documentary filmmakers, and those who study them, should be placed.

Postscript

With all this in mind, it is maybe not surprising that Morris's film, *American Dharma* (2018), which went into limited release in November 2019 after having premiered at the Venice Film Festival in September 2018 and then struggled to get a distribution deal, is a full-length feature film about Steve Bannon, his thought, and its repercussions. Together with Roger Stone, Bannon, the alt-right gadfly and former Breitbart chairman, Trump 2016 campaign chief, and White House *chef militaire*, is the man who is most often credited with having orchestrated the dramatic turnaround that led to Donald Trump's shocking election victory in 2016. He was also an architect of Trump's war on the press and on "the elite media," with the *New York Times* being a favorite target. But Bannon was also a filmmaker and (purportedly) a Hollywood executive and dealmaker, and in addition to being a serious film buff, he also happens to be an avowed fan of Morris's documentary technique.[31] *American Dharma* builds on Morris's widely discussed fascination with "pariah" figures like Fred Leuchter (*Mr. Death* [1999]), Robert McNamara (*The Fog of War*), Lynndie England (*Standard Operating Procedure*), Donald Rumsfeld

(*The Unknown Known* [2013]), and Joyce McKinney (*Tabloid*).³² Here, however, there's a new urgency to the tone, in large part because it's much less of a historical study than so many of his other best-known films are, as the crisis in question is still unfolding.

It is perhaps for this very reason that Morris's voice is the most present (and invasive) it has ever been—his uncharacteristically testy and adversarial demeanor indicates a new level of panic and anxiety with regards to the War on Truth. Morris has been accused by some critics of providing Bannon with yet another platform for his ideas and of having aided and abetted his legendary powers of self-mythologization by devoting a documentary to him, "[reinforcing] the idea that he is a political mastermind, as opposed to a fringe figure who may have gotten lucky in one election."³³ Such accusations may go some way toward explaining Morris's distribution woes. Less charitable critics have suggested that Morris may have actually been outwitted by Bannon or, at least, tricked into contributing to Bannon's postfactual "sludge" instead of developing a cinematic agent that might counteract it, and in many ways, I'd have to agree with them.³⁴ Morris makes a valiant effort to update his fixation with artifacts and evidence for the digital age. Gone is the "simulation microfiche reader" approach he'd used on previous films. Here, instead, the film focuses on digital files, on windows, and on the clicking-and-dragging that we use to navigate our computer interfaces. And while I'm sure Morris 2.0 is adept, even knowledgeable, when it comes to modern computing and the peculiarities of internet culture circa 2018, Bannon appears to have a particularly savvy (and cynical) grasp of this domain.

Given his career trajectory and his concerns, Morris's attraction to Bannon is easy to understand. It's not for nothing that John Milton's *Paradise Lost* and its depiction of the machinations of Satan and the rebel angels is an important point of reference for the film. What originally struck me as curious from the standpoint of this chapter was Bannon's willingness to take part in Morris's project. Didn't he realize that the distinction between journalism ("the enemy of the people") and documentary had collapsed? Didn't he realize that he's dealing with a *Times* man? Now, having seen *American Dharma*, I'm left with the impression that maybe Bannon was all too aware of who he was dealing with. In any case, Morris never challenges Bannon on how he reconciles his radical spin on freedom of speech with his radical attacks on freedom of the press, and he never brings up the *Times*, nor any of his work for the "newspaper of record," textual, audiovisual, or otherwise.

Notes

1. Hersh, "Huge CIA Operation Reported," 1.
2. Plantinga, "Philosophy of Errol Morris," 44–46; 47–48.
3. Hersh has always been highly controversial, and as David Carr and others have pointed out, Hersh's journalistic method is partly to blame for this. See Carr, "Dogged Reporter's Impact."
4. Nichols, *Representing Reality*, 3.
5. The reference here is to Errol Morris's 2013 profile of Donald Rumsfeld (and his propensity for curious wordplay), *The Unknown Known*.
6. Scott, "'Wormwood' Confirms."
7. Back in 1975, Hersh apparently referred to the Olsons as "the most goddamned uncurious family in the United States," according to Eric Olson.
8. Hersh, "Torture."
9. According to David Remnick of the *New Yorker*, Bob Woodward and Carl Bernstein described Hersh as being "unlike any reporter they had ever met." On the one hand, he had no qualms about publicly denouncing Henry Kissinger as being guilty of war crimes. On the other, Hersh was both "openly attracted and repelled by the power of the *New York Times*"—the very newspaper through which he had been reporting on the Watergate scandal.
10. Hogarth, *Realer Than Reel*, ix. See also Williams, "Mirrors without Memories," 9–21.
11. Hogarth, *Realer Than Reel*, ix–x.
12. Ibid., 125–126.
13. Wintonick, "New Platforms for Docmedia," 376.
14. See, e.g., Bill Nichols's "The Voice of Documentary." Dovey and Rose, "This Great Mapping of Ourselves," 374.
15. Ibid., 368.
16. Ebert, "Spielberg & Cruise & The Movies."
17. Renov, "Documentary Horizons," 317.
18. See TakePart, "Page One"; Kinsley, "Hyperactive Fly."
19. For a related behind-the-scenes look at the *Times*, see Folkenflik, *Page One*.
20. Among other accolades, the series has won numerous awards, including two Emmys (in the News and Documentary category), a Peabody, an International Documentary Association prize, and a World Press Photo Multimedia Award. Flood, "How *New York Times*"; *New York Times* Company, "Kathleen Lingo Named."
21. Hooper, "Introducing."
22. After a successful stint with Op-Docs, including acting as its executive producer, Lingo was named the *New York Times*'s "first editorial director for film and TV" in November 2018, according to a press release from the *New York Times* Company. In this new role, she was charged with "shaping" and expanding "what The New York Times looks like on screen"; see *New York Times* Company, "Kathleen Lingo Named."
23. Ibid.
24. Flood, "How *New York Times*."
25. Ibid.
26. Morris, "Not Every Picture."
27. Morris, "Liar, Liar."
28. Actually, both films are made up of the same interview, apparently, as Thompson is dressed in exactly the same clothes, and the lighting and studio set-up are identical.
29. Updike, "Talk of the Town," 51.

30. Grynbaum, "Trump Strategist"; Grynbaum and Sullivan, "Trump Attacks"; Green, "CNN's Jim Acosta."
31. Bruck, "How Hollywood Remembers."
32. Croce, "Errol Morris."
33. Kenigsberg, "What Makes Steve Bannon Tick?"
34. Brody, "Errol Morris."

References

Brody, Richard. "Errol Morris Lets Steve Bannon Off the Hook." *New Yorker*, October 1, 2018. https://www.newyorker.com/culture/the-front-row/american-dharma-reviewed-errol-morris-lets-steve-bannon-off-the-hook.

Bruck, Connie. "How Hollywood Remembers Steve Bannon." *New Yorker*, April 24, 2017. https://www.newyorker.com/magazine/2017/05/01/how-hollywood-remembers-steve-bannon.

Carr, David. "Dogged Reporter's Impact, From My Lai to Abu Ghraib." *New York Times*, May 20, 2004. https://www.nytimes.com/2004/05/20/arts/dogged-reporter-s-impact-from-my-lai-to-abu-ghraib.html.

Croce, Fernando F. "Errol Morris on *Standard Operating Procedure*." *Slant*, May 3, 2008. https://www.slantmagazine.com/film/nonstandard-operating-procedure-an-interview-with-errol-morris/.

Dovey, John, and Mandy Rose. "'This Great Mapping of Ourselves': New Documentary Forms Online." In *The Documentary Film Book*, edited by Brian Winston, 367–375. Basingstoke, UK: BFI/Palgrave MacMillan, 2013.

Ebert, Roger. "Spielberg & Cruise & The Movies." RogerEbert.com, June 16, 2002. https://www.rogerebert.com/interviews/spielberg-and-cruise-and-the-movies.

Flood, Brian. "How New York Times Op-Docs Change the Way Film and News Media Intersect." *The Wrap*, January 18, 2017. https://www.thewrap.com/how-new-york-times-op-docs-change-the-way-film-and-news-media-intersect/.

Folkenflik, David, ed. *Page One: Inside the "New York Times" and the Future of Journalism*. New York: Public Affairs, 2011.

Gaines, Jane M., and Michael Renov, eds. *Collecting Visible Evidence*. Minneapolis: University of Minnesota Press, 1999.

Green, Lloyd. "CNN's Jim Acosta Takes Trump's Bait Again." *Guardian*, June 11, 2019. https://www.theguardian.com/us-news/2019/jun/11/the-enemy-of-the-people-review-cnn-jim-acosta-trump.

Grynbaum, Michael M. "Trump Strategist Stephen Bannon Says Media Should 'Keep Its Mouth Shut.'" *New York Times*, January 26, 2017. https://www.nytimes.com/2017/01/26/business/media/stephen-bannon-trump-news-media.html.

Grynbaum, Michael M., and Eileen Sullivan. "Trump Attacks *The Times*, in a Week of Unease for the American Press." *New York Times*, February 20, 2019. https://www.nytimes.com/2019/02/20/us/politics/new-york-times-trump.html.

Hersh, Seymour M. *Chain of Command: The Road from 9/11 to Abu Ghraib*. New York: HarperCollins, 2004.

———. "Huge CIA Operation Reported in US Against Antiwar Forces, Other Dissidents in Nixon Years." *New York Times*, December 22, 1974, 1, 26. https://timesmachine.nytimes.com/timesmachine/1974/12/22/432151792.html.

---. "Torture at Abu Ghraib." *New Yorker*, May 10, 2004. https://www.newyorker.com/magazine/2004/05/10/torture-at-abu-ghraib.
Hogarth, David. *Realer Than Reel: Global Directions in Documentary*. Austin: University of Texas Press, 2006.
Hooper, Riley. "Introducing: Kathleen Lingo, Producer of NY Times Op-Docs." *Vimeo Blog*, December 17, 2015. https://vimeo.com/blog/post/introducing-kathleen-lingo-producer-of-ny-times-op.
Kenigsberg, Ben. "What Makes Steve Bannon Tick?" *New York Times*, October 31, 2019. https://www.nytimes.com/2019/10/31/movies/american-dharma-review.html.
Kinsley, Michael. "A Hyperactive Fly on a Newsroom Wall." *New York Times*, June 18, 2011. https://www.nytimes.com/2011/06/17/movies/page-one-inside-the-new-york-times-review.html.
Morris, Errol. *Believing Is Seeing: Observations on the Mysteries of Photography*. New York: Penguin Press, 2011.
---. "Liar, Liar, Pants on Fire." *New York Times*, July 10, 2007. https://opinionator.blogs.nytimes.com/2007/07/10/pictures-are-supposed-to-be-worth-a-thousand-words.
---. "The Most Curious Thing." *New York Times*, May 19, 2008. https://opinionator.blogs.nytimes.com/2008/05/19/the-most-curious-thing.
---. "Not Every Picture Tells a Story." *New York Times*, November 20, 2004. https://www.nytimes.com/2004/11/20/opinion/not-every-picture-tells-a-story.html.
Morris, Errol, dir. *American Dharma*. Cambridge, MA: Fourth Floor Productions, 2018.
---. "Errol Morris: Demon in the Freezer." *New York Times* video, May 17, 2016, 17:56. https://www.nytimes.com/video/opinion/100000004412128/errol-morris-demon-in-the-freezer.html.
---. "November 22, 1963." *New York Times* video, November 20, 2013, 13:51. https://www.nytimes.com/video/opinion/100000002563395/november-22-1963.html.
---. *The Thin Blue Line*. 1988. New York: Criterion Collection, 2015.
---. "The Umbrella Man." *New York Times* video, November 21, 2011, 06:36. https://www.nytimes.com/video/opinion/100000001183275/the-umbrella-man.html.
---. *Wormwood*. Los Gatos, CA: Netflix, Inc., 2017. https://www.netflix.com/watch/80059446.
New York Times Company. "Kathleen Lingo Named Editorial Director for Film and TV." November 15, 2018. https://www.nytco.com/press/kathleen-lingo-named-editorial-director-for-film-and-tv/.
Nichols, Bill. *Blurred Boundaries: Questions of Meaning in Contemporary Culture*. Bloomington: Indiana University Press, 1994.
---, ed. *Movies and Methods, Volume II: An Anthology*. Berkeley: University of California Press, 1985.
---. *Representing Reality: Issues and Concepts in Documentary*. Bloomington: Indiana University Press, 1991.
---. "The Voice of Documentary." In *Movies and Methods, Volume II: An Anthology*, edited by Bill Nichols, 258–273. Berkeley: University of California Press, 1985.
Plantinga, Carl. "The Philosophy of Errol Morris: Ten Lessons." In *Three Documentary Filmmakers: Errol Morris, Ross McElwee, Jean Rouch*, edited by William Rothman, 43–59. Albany: SUNY Press, 2009.
Remnick, David. Introduction to *Chain of Command: The Road from 9/11 to Abu Ghraib*, by Seymour M. Hersh, ix–xix. New York: HarperCollins, 2004.
Renov, Michael. "Documentary Horizons: An Afterword." In *Collecting Visible Evidence*, edited by Jane M. Gaines and Michael Renov, 313–325. Minneapolis: University of Minnesota Press, 1999.

Rossi, Andrew, dir. *Page One: Inside the New York Times*. New York: Magnolia Pictures, 2011. DVD.

Rothman, William, ed. *Three Documentary Filmmakers: Errol Morris, Ross McElwee, Jean Rouch*. Albany: SUNY Press, 2009.

Scott, A. O. "'Wormwood' Confirms That Errol Morris Is Our Great Cinematic Sleuth." *New York Times*, December 14, 2017. https://www.nytimes.com/2017/12/14/movies/wormwood-review-errol-morris-peter-sarsgaard.html.

TakePart. "Page One: Inside the *New York Times*." Accessed November 23, 2020. http://www.takepart.com/pageone/.

Updike, John. "The Talk of the Town." *New Yorker*, December 9, 1967, 51–55. http://archives.newyorker.com/?i=1967-12-09#folio=050.

Williams, Linda. "Mirrors without Memories: Truth, History, and the New Documentary." *Film Quarterly* 46, no. 3 (Spring 1993): 9–21.

Winston, Brian, ed. *The Documentary Film Book*. Basingstoke, UK: BFI/Palgrave MacMillan, 2013.

———. Introduction to *The Documentary Film Book*, edited by Brian Winston, 1–29. Basingstoke, UK: BFI/Palgrave MacMillan, 2013.

Wintonick, Peter. "New Platforms for Docmedia: 'Variant of a Manifesto.'" In *The Documentary Film Book*, edited by Brian Winston, 376–382. Basingstoke, UK: BFI/Palgrave MacMillan, 2013.

ANTHONY KINIK is Associate Professor of Film Studies in the Department of Communication, Popular Culture and Film at Brock University. He is editor (with Steven Jacobs and Eva Hielscher) of *The City Symphony Phenomenon: Cinema, Art, and Urban Modernity between the Wars*.

8

POPULAR MUSIC AND SHORT-FORM NONFICTION

Is the Web a Forum for Documentary Innovation?

Michael Brendan Baker

In the latest white paper prepared by Cisco Systems, one of the largest technology conglomerates in the world, it was revealed 82 percent of all internet traffic in 2017 was video and predicted the figure will grow four-fold within the next five years. By that time, a million minutes of video content will stream across global networks every second of every day.[1] With this in mind, while it is impossible to enumerate the number of videos presently available on the internet across myriad platforms and services, it should suffice to say that for most people around the world, the moving image resides on the web. But a funny thing happened with the gradual transformation of the internet into a forum for video. Where once new technologies and means of delivery would prompt the exploration of new horizons of aesthetic possibility ad infinitum, video on the web has, for the most part, crystallized existing representational practices. The internet delivers video, yes, but has it necessarily reshaped the moving image?

One specific space in which the internet has fostered incredible growth is in the production of documentary. Professionals and amateurs alike are using the web to post and share nonfictional projects in numbers rivaling that of conventional producers. Generally, when we speak of innovation in the context of the moving image, we discuss the development of new technologies and the impact of these technologies on representational strategies. But what if, in addition to these concerns, we considered this space in terms of the opportunities it provides filmmakers for the examination of subjects and subject matter underserved (or entirely ignored) by filmmakers and videographers working within the explicitly commercial environment of feature-length productions?

In the absence of the clear commercial imperatives of feature-length film production and distribution, the creators of short-form documentaries—a format that has historically encountered myriad obstacles in reaching larger audiences—are well-positioned to explore and innovate new aesthetics within a highly accessible, popular forum.

Documentary on the web—not to be confused with web-docs or the interactive documentary, which adapts the conventions of nonfiction to the dynamic spaces of new media and the internet—propagates already established and widely popular nonfiction forms including reality-style programming, historical examination, sports biographies, and the popular music documentary. Music-related video is one of the strongest drivers of online digital video over the last decade.[2] The growth of the category is nothing short of staggering as commercial outlets and independent producers alike have pursued nonfictional storytelling on the web. However, the question remains whether the corpus exhibits any of the aesthetic innovation we might expect to see in such a space or whether creators are taking the opportunity to examine subject matter—for example, non-Western locales, nonwhite identities, and nonnormative expressions of gender and sexuality—largely unattended by documentarians working in feature-length commercial film and television. The popular music documentary, despite its timeless popularity, is one category of work that has been particularly lacking both in terms of the creativity of its expression and the breadth of subject matter it examines, in part because of the commercial imperative that drives the production of so many music documentaries. Perhaps the conventions of the popular music documentary, when adapted to the imperatives of noncommercial web distribution and exhibition, beget stylistic innovation and encourage a diversity of representational strategies brought to bear on an array of popular musical subjects.

Commercially robust, steeped in history, and at times critically acclaimed, the popular music documentary is ubiquitous in popular culture and invariably accessible in its address to audiences. It is an aesthetically rich corpus notable for its innovation in the area of sound and moving image technology and the ways in which it reflects a complex system of sociocultural and industrial interactions.[3] Through the 2000s, the nonfictional treatment of musical subjects became a popular and ever-growing segment of online videos as the genre experienced something of a renaissance due, in part, to its profile and success at film festivals and in nontheatrical spaces, such as home video and streaming. The web is particularly well-suited as a distribution and exhibition space for popular music documentaries as it allows for the focused targeting of preconstituted fan audiences and communities that are central to the genre's past successes and ongoing viability. By the end of the decade, refined approaches to form and subject matter fostered in part by digital technology—and the rapid evolution of video compression, which permanently established the web as a distribution and exhibition space—had subtly reshaped the popular music doc, its conventions coalescing to a vernacular style immediately recognizable to audiences across any number of boundaries. I favor the term *vernacular*, as it captures the conventionalization of particular production workflows and representational strategies across professional, semiprofessional, and amateur lines. The term also accents the ways in which the formulae of the rockumentary genre—the dominant popular music documentary category—and its strategies for the visual representation of musical performance, in particular, have taken on an ordinariness that is accessible to creators and audiences alike across the globe.

It is neither practical nor productive to address short-form music documentaries produced for the web in their totality—they number in the thousands, if not tens of thousands. Instead, the methodology adopted here identifies and analyzes works that are representative of the larger spheres of production and reception. These shorts, ranging in length from several minutes to slightly less than an hour, straightforwardly adapt the storytelling structures and representational strategies of the feature-length music documentary to the distribution outlets, viewing behaviors, and larger media flows of the internet.[4] This chapter presents a brief history of the short-form popular music documentary as it has evolved online over the past twenty years, highlighting the role played by independent productions, including *The Take Away Show* and *Southern Souls*, and journalism outfits like Pitchfork Media and the influence of corporate interests, including Vevo, American Express, and the Red Bull Music Academy. It is not my intention to quantify the dynamic and ever-expansive catalog of professionally produced and offered-by-amateur popular music shorts inhabiting the web. Instead, by highlighting several key series produced in diverse contexts at a critical juncture in the development of the format, it is possible to sketch the broader contours of the corpus and explore its relationship to both established forms of the feature-length music documentary and of popular documentary more generally.

To deal with nonfictional web shorts as "cinematic" seems self-evident despite the networked nature of their distribution and exhibition. David Rodowick describes the persistence of cinema, in part, as those representational strategies and structural features of the moving image shaped by the physical properties of the first era of motion pictures that nonetheless remain foundational in the age of digital video. "Our audiovisual culture is currently a digital culture," writes Rodowick, "but with a cinematic look. And cinema, too, is increasingly just another element of digital culture."[5] If the internet is the medium of this digital culture, Jay David Bolter and Richard Grusin's theory of remediation provides us with a way of understanding the relationship between digital media and "older" regimes of audiovisual representation and allows us to conceptualize new media in terms of how it *contains* established forms such as the popular music documentary. Bolter and Grusin posit "what is in fact new [about new media] is the particular way in which each innovation rearranges and reconstitutes the meaning of earlier elements."[6] Citing Bloom's theory of influence, Bolter and Grusin contend it is the remediation of a medium (and within a medium) that offers insight to the practice of representation in earlier media.[7] The act or process of remediation reveals the influence of the earlier media—its technology, techniques, and practices—on new media. The remediation of nonfictional visual representations of popular music within the context of web productions reveals much about the influence of existing representational strategies on emerging spaces within the visual culture of popular music and confirms the inescapable weight of that history on its representation within new mediums.

Art historian E. H. Gombrich describes the relational link between artworks in terms of *schema* and *revision*.[8] The innovation of a schema, an identifiable pattern found in an artwork, can be both copied straightforwardly or adapted and elaborated on through revision, thus allowing the original idea to solicit new responses and provoke further revision.[9] Central to this dynamic is the role problems play in the founding of *schema* and their subsequent revision. With this in mind, I would suggest strategies for the visual representation of popular music in nonfiction film and video are produced through a process described by David Bordwell (and recently historicized by Colin Burnett) as the "problem-solution" model of film style. Bordwell, who invokes Gombrich's work within his formalist history of film style, asks the historian of film style to move beyond the simple identification of formal patterns and pose questions about what motivates particular strategies and their evolution over time: "One shot versus several; single versus multiple camera positions; fairly flat versus relatively deep compositions; distant views versus close ones; spatial and temporal continuity versus continuity. Can we pick out plausible patterns of change running from our earliest [example] to our most recent one? Are there overall principles governing these differences?"[10]

The degree to which some of these compositional and editorial techniques are relevant within the context of nonfiction filmmaking may be limited, but the way such structural and stylistic elements cohere as generic convention is particularly germane to the present discussion because many of the visual cues adapted by and elaborated on by creators of popular music docs on the web are explicitly generic ones. Folding Gombrich's model of schema and revision into the study of remediated texts, by way of Bordwell's "problem-solution" model of film style, allows one to balance considerations of visual style, genre convention, and contemporary audiovisual practices when addressing the question of influence and the weight of moving image history on new media.

Documentary films about popular music and related idioms usually feature some combination of performance footage, interviews, and undirected material. The ever-growing number of media objects invested in the documentary representation of popular music in theaters, at home, and online suggest we are in the midst of the category's resurgence and expansion. These films originally emerge in the 1960s as part of a larger shift in the character and content of Western youth culture and popular music, signaled by Burt Stern's seminal work of film reportage, *Jazz on a Summer's Day* (1960). The category's ascent to the status of the theatrical documentary par excellence through the latter part of the 1960s and the 1970s occurs directly in proportion to the growth of pop and rock music as cultural and economic forces.[11] A series of high-profile films, soundtrack releases, and box-office successes in the 1970s permanently establish the rockumentary, specifically, as a mainstream nonfiction film genre with an identifiable stable of classics (*Dont Look Back*, dir. D. A. Pennebaker, 1967; *Monterey Pop*, dir. D. A. Pennebaker, 1968; *Gimme Shelter*, dir. Albert Maysles, David Maysles, and Charlotte Zwerin, 1970; *Woodstock*, dir. Michael Wadleigh, 1970; *The Concert for Bangladesh*, dir. Saul Swimmer, 1972; *The Last Waltz*, dir. Martin Scorsese, 1978) before diminishing opportunities for theatrical distribution in the era of the Hollywood blockbuster were mitigated by new exhibition outlets in the form of home video and cable television.

As I've written elsewhere, five broad currents and trends typify the popular music documentary.[12] Biographies are an explicitly hybrid form encompassing interviews, live performance sequences, and observational footage. These films derive their allure from the featured artist's status within popular music culture and popular culture at-large. Concert and other performance-based films span the gamut from rigorously choreographed and composed audiovisual spectacles to low-budget, sparsely edited, fan-made films and videos. By any conservative measure, the concert documentary is the largest category of work within the corpus. A companion to both the biography and concert currents is the "tour film" or "making-of" film. Unlike biographies, which span an artist's entire career, or the concert film that generally represents a single event, these films are focused on the events surrounding a whole tour or the act of making a single album or planning a special event. A fourth trend within the category are ethnographic studies of popular music, its subgenres, and subcultures. While other types of music documentary serve as documents of a particular musical culture and its participants, exercises in ethnography make explicit claims about the value of the research object and the filmmaker's purpose for documenting the music, musicians, and audiences in question. The compilation format, or archival project, is the most common made-for-television music documentary, but it is less often produced for theatrical release. More than any other type of popular music documentary, the compilation format relies on the structure and expository mode of address of classical documentaries with the subordination of the images to a singular rhetorical position and a reliance on didactic commentary.[13] While a single film might adopt various approaches resulting in hybrid forms and subgenres, popular music documentaries are often best described by the approach that governs its structure and mode of address to the audience.

Notwithstanding the experimentation and innovation that naturally resides in such a large and diverse corpus of work, the popular music documentary is a decidedly conservative form in terms of its narrative structures and visual style. The basic sonic and photographic strategies of the genre—conventionalized in the late 1960s and early 1970s—were subject to very little revision or reinvention in the decades that followed their emergence. Behind-the-scenes moments are largely observational in nature, interviews are garden-variety talking heads, and the soundtrack honors the professional practices of the recording studio in combination with live audio production. Meanwhile, the visual representation of musical performance within the corpus is largely limited to two basic approaches. As I've written elsewhere, the journalistic strategy for the visual representation of musical performance is "typified by its clear compositional qualities (e.g. stable camera position; sharp focus; balanced lighting) and commitment to a coherent representation of both the performer and performance space. . . . It strives to provide an unambiguous photographic record of the performance and is amenable to conventions of analytical editing."[14] The impressionistic strategy, on the other hand, "offers a highly stylized, often abstract representation of the performance. There is less an interest in documenting the space of the performance than in communicating an emotional or psychological dimension of the music through formal techniques often evinced in experimental practice (e.g. instability of the frame; unusual compositions; unconventional focus and lighting; plastic cutting)."[15]

The audiovisual aesthetics of this latter approach might now be described as postclassical in terms of its linkage of traditional cinematic practices and music video stylistics developed over several decades. Carol Vernallis's model detailing "intensified audiovisual aesthetics" expands on Bordwell's discussion of intensified continuity—"traditional continuity amped up, raised to a higher pitch of emphasis"—in postclassical cinema, shifting the discussion from narrative filmmaking to nonnarrative works, such as music videos.[16] Vernallis argues the intensified audiovisual aesthetics of these works move beyond conventional film style through a "heightened" use of traditional and still-emerging sound and image techniques that "create rifts in form that permeate all the way to deep structure."[17] However, I believe new approaches to form and subject matter fostered in part by digital technology (and the rapid evolution of video compression, which permanently established the web as a distribution and exhibition space) have only subtly reshaped the popular music documentary, its conventions best understood as a vernacular style immediately recognizable to audiences across generational boundaries.

The preponderance of nonfiction musical shorts and features now produced and distributed primarily with digital and networked technologies demonstrate two especially curious results of the ubiquity of visual representations of popular music performance as it relates to documentary aesthetics. The first is an emptying out of conventional formal stylistics that results in material fitting neither the journalistic nor the impressionistic strategies for the visual representation of musical performance previously outlined. A new generation of cinematographers and videographers such as France's Mathieu Saura—aka Vincent Moon—foreground the presence of increasingly mobile cameras within the space of the performance in ways that were truly unattainable (if not completely unimaginable) to previous generations of documentarians, effectively collapsing the observational style of classic rockumentaries on varying degrees of interactivity in a manner that calls attention to itself. These new works reimagine the *liveness* of popular music performance by situating the artist in commonplace environments (e.g., private homes, elevators, cafés, public transit, tourist attractions) and capturing the performance in a single continuous take. It is not the illusion of copresence between the performer and home audience but rather the copresence of the performer and the filmmaker as creative force who serves as a surrogate for the viewer as she carves out the performance from quotidian spaces.[18] In online series such as *The Take Away Show* and *Southern Souls*, on-location performances appear to occur spontaneously: there is no clear introduction of the performers apart from on-screen text and no establishing of the technical means by which the performance will be executed (e.g., sound recording devices, additional cameras), just blind faith (or an existing investment in the brand or filmmaker) that sound and image will be effectively captured and communicated in a way that preserves the emotion or energy of the performance. The second consequence of this profusion of music documentary production is a disavowal of the notion (which gradually emerges within music videos and overtakes the long-form music video format) that the musical performance need not be represented at all. The highly stylized, fictional scenarios featuring popular music soundtracks that defined music videos through the 1980s and 1990s are giving way to a reinvestment in nonfictional representations of musical performance and the observational and interactive modes of representation that defined the visual style of popular music documentaries in the late 1960s and 1970s.

It is fair to suggest the earliest instance of a short-form popular music documentary on the web receiving widespread viewership and critical cache is *The Take Away Show*, a self-described video podcast produced by La Blogothèque, a music blog based in France. The series now stands as one of the web's preeminent sources of nonfictional representations of musical performance; in 2017, it boasted over 113 million YouTube viewers with a subscriber list of over 360,000.[19] Launched in 2006 in partnership with Blogothèque editor Christopher Abric, founding director Vincent Moon took to the streets of Paris to document touring musicians using an approach to production not unlike the more well-established techniques of field recording. During his time with *The Take Away Show*, Moon produced over two hundred videos featuring a range of artists including Arcade Fire, Grizzly Bear, Sigur Ros, and REM. While the series occasionally placed international artists in the spotlight, the majority of Moon's *Take Away Shows* featured rock and pop artists from North America and the United Kingdom. *The Take Away Show* evolved into something of an internet-phenomenon and received recognition in mainstream press (e.g. *New York Times Magazine*; the *Guardian*), which only amplified its profile in popular culture.

The *New York Times* declared, "Moon proved it's possible to reinvent an old, tired format (the music video) using the very thing (the Internet) that supposedly killed it."[20] However, while it is true that the internet as a distribution platform is central to the story of *The Take Away Show*, I believe it is necessary to consider these filmed performances nonfiction shorts as opposed to music videos, primarily because the representational strategies adopted by

Fig. 8.1 A performance appears to occur spontaneously in Arcade Fire's *The Take Away Show* (March 2007).

Moon are profoundly indebted to the documentary tradition. These are not music videos. The schema adopted and revised by the filmmakers is not that of the music video of the last thirty years but rather the observational documentary dating back to its postwar invention. Moon developed an intimate visual style showcasing an unrehearsed single-take handheld camera technique, a distinct audial approach, and a viral distribution strategy via YouTube and Vimeo that made entries in the series nearly ubiquitous in the years following its original launch. Moon does not interact with the performers, but neither does he conceal his presence or the artfulness of his cinematography. It is a stylistic approach cum representational strategy that immediately brings to mind the musical sequences of an iconic contemporary fiction film, *Once* (dir. John Carney, 2007), as much as it does any music documentaries of the period, and echoes some of the greatest musical moments of canonical observational documentaries of the 1960s. With an archive presently boasting over four hundred musical shorts, *The Take Away Show* serves as a stylistic and philosophical foundation on which subsequent waves of popular music documentarians can innovate.

The format and aesthetic pioneered by *The Take Away Show* proliferates across the web. There are a number of copycat series, but perhaps the most interesting (and industrious) of these is *Southern Souls*, a high-profile Canadian-based progeny of *The Take Away Show*. Creator and director Mitch Fillion effectively transferred Moon's approach to the southern Ontario music scene with the primary purpose of documenting both emerging Canadian artists and iconic performers (e.g., *Sloan: Live at Massey Hall*).[21] At the time of writing, *Southern Souls* has subtly transformed itself from a documentary series into a platform, boasting an archive of over 1,300 videos available via Vimeo featuring a national slate of artists primarily from the fields of folk, country, and indie rock along with commissioned work from Fillion and his collaborators. Moon, meanwhile, used *The Take Away Show* as a springboard toward a career in feature-length documentary filmmaking and is now widely credited with remediating the "music video" in the age of DIY digital video production and the web. He uses his platform and prestige to explore traditional music cultures and music-based rituals around the globe.

Pitchfork Media began as a music review blog in the mid-nineties and is now among the most influential, most read English-language music publications on the web. Originally a DIY independent venture, the site was purchased by Conde Nast in 2015, becoming part of a larger corporate entity. In 2008, the site launched Pitchfork.tv to organize the streaming of music videos from featured artists on the site and began producing a substantial volume of original content in 2012. While most of this content is focused on live performance, there was an early and ongoing commitment to documentary-style projects. The original video content produced by Pitchfork represents what is likely the largest and most viewed collection of nonfictional popular music shorts available on the web; chief among the site's original documentary video series are *Pitchfork Classic*, *Liner Notes*, and *A Brief History Of*.[22]

Pitchfork Classic consists of only three films, nearly feature-length, and represent Pitchfork's most ambitious individual projects with production values mirroring those of theatrical features and television broadcast. Rigorously researched, these films comprise a rich tapestry of audiovisual materials gleaned from personal archives and label resources in their examination of the conception, production, release and legacy of an alternative album now deemed a classic in the eyes of fans and critics alike. These three films—the earliest, *Pitchfork Classic: The Flaming Lips' "The Soft Bulletin"* (dir. R. J. Bentler, 2013)—have an average audience of a half million views and represented the most watched original material produced by the site until the launch of Pitchfork's more conventionally organized short-form series of the last several years. The *Classic* series demands the viewer's attention, are difficult to excerpt and share on social media, and are certainly expensive to produce, so it is perhaps understandable that Pitchfork's investment in original productions remained overwhelmingly focused on short-form documentary projects in the years that followed.

Liner Notes, consisting of twenty-two episodes at the time of writing, offers viewers a concise capsule history of canonical albums in under five minutes. The series is, in many ways, Pitchfork's version of audiovisual click-bait and a response to the labor-intensive, comprehensive approach of the *Classic* series. Through narration, archival photographs, and recordings, viewers are provided a superficial summary of the album's production, marketing and release, and a brief argument about the album's impact on music history. Stylistically, there is little to distinguish one episode from the next, and the substance of each episode is tailored to those not particularly well versed in the history and mythology of the music and musicians under review. It must also be said the focus of this series is the popular music canon of North America and western Europe to the exclusion of the rest of the world. Pitchfork's *A Brief History Of*, created by R. J. Bentler (vice president of video programming and executive producer of all Pitchfork video content), does not correct this narrow view of popular music history, but it is noteworthy as an example of animated documentary, an exceptional form within the world of nonfiction. Each episode of the series addresses its subject matter with a clear comedic impulse and is often structured in the form of a young student's multimedia presentation to his classmates. Generally, each 2D computer-animated short is concerned with a genre, subgenre, or subculture of popular music (e.g., goth, dad rock, emo music) and adopts the representational strategies of the compilation format to address the audience with both humor and insight. One episode, "A Brief History of Goth" (Joren Cull, 2016), was the winner of People's Voice Award in Animation at the Twenty-First Annual Webby Awards in 2017, a testament to the artistry and sophistication of the project as well as to the profile and power Pitchfork Media holds within the marketplace. Director and multihyphenate Cull voices an affected teen made up like Edward Scissorhands who takes his class through a PowerPoint presentation chronicling the history of the alternative rock idiom most closely associated with Siouxsie and the Banshees and the Cure. As the young student speaks, a carousel of cartoonishly stylized line-drawn album art and band photos appears in a frame within the frame. The narrator's vocal fry and monotone delivery addressing such a niche topic become a humorous send-up of the voice-of-God narrator so central to this expository mode of address. With its fictionalized premise and informational content, *A Brief History Of* is a hybrid form that challenges any easy definition of what constitutes documentary and subtly reshapes the audience's perception of how popular music history is visualized within a nonfictional space. Viewership of these shorts is substantially larger than that of earlier Pitchfork.tv productions in large part

Fig. 8.2 A young student gives classmates a crash course in pop music history in *A Brief History of Goth*, Pitchfork TV (October 2016).

because of the ubiquity of social media and the ever-increasing opportunities to share these shorter works across a number of platforms and devices.

Arguably the highest-profile entrant in the field of online popular music documentary is American Express with *Unstaged*, a series of live performances "filmed" by noted film directors for live internet streaming via Vevo, the branded YouTube channel—ranked number one in viewership globally—formed in December 2009 as a joint partnership between Sony Music Entertainment, Universal Music Group, and Abu Dhabi Media.[23] The series debuted with two high-profile events in 2010—Arcade Fire directed by Terry Gilliam and John Legend and the Roots directed by Spike Lee—and continued with two to three streaming events per year through 2014, featuring high-profile artists, including Duran Duran (with David Lynch), The Killers (with Werner Herzog), Tim McGraw (with Bennett Miller), My Morning Jacket (with Todd Haynes), and Pharrell (with Spike Lee). As this partial list demonstrates, the selected artists represent the upper echelon of mainstream North American popular music and the "name" directors consist entirely of men who occupy a privileged position within contemporary American cinema. Aesthetically, these live streams are conservatively styled with conventional camera positions, standard set and lighting designs, and prevailing concert sound practices. The individual filmmakers and the series as a whole do little more than re-create the concert film within the dynamic space of an online streaming event. Viewers would be forgiven for confusing these internet events for videocassette recordings of live concerts from the 1980s. The true appeal of these events is equally the name recognition of the musical acts and celebrity directors and the simultaneity with which the viewer at home witnesses the concert performance as a consequence of the networked technologies delivering the experience. Returning to Bolter and Grusin's conception, the live musical event is remediated as a moving image yet celebrated as the original as a consequence of our willingness to accept the mediated event's implicit claim that it is, in fact, "live" and therefore authentic in a way that is distinct from a prerecorded audiovisual spectacle.[24]

Strictly speaking, the *Unstaged* series are live streaming events, not concert films, and they are feature-length productions. At their most successful, these live streams attract over 1.6 million live YouTube viewers and work to foster audience engagement using novelties such as browser-based interaction and mobile apps.[25] They draw overwhelmingly on the representational strategies and visual style of the most conventional of concert films, exhibiting nothing resembling Bordwell's postclassical style or Vernallis's intensified audiovisual aesthetics. What is most striking about the series is not how the original live stream is presented but rather how the shows are archived. Located at American Express Music, the live streams are no longer offered in their entirety and are instead served to visitors in playlists variously comprising individual song performances, backstage material, and promotional materials originally circulated in advance of the original live stream.[26] The business logic informing this decision is likely rooted in a particular (and increasingly outmoded) way of monetizing web traffic: the increased page views of multitudinous abridged content is thought to be more valuable than the longer engagement encouraged by extended formats. As a result, these paratextual short-form audiovisual artifacts effectively replace the feature-length streaming event and obscure it for all except those who originally viewed the concert online or in person. In this way, the nonfictional shorts efface any historical value of the feature-length original within the popular imagination; any technological innovation demonstrated by the *Unstaged* series is undermined by these negative impacts.

The closest cousin of Pitchfork.tv's documentary series—and the nearest equal to the combined corporate might of American Express and Vevo—was perhaps the audiovisual production arm of the Red Bull Music Academy (RBMA, 1998–2019). Once a global, itinerant annual music festival and conference focused on DJ culture and electronic music, the now-defunct RBMA—a sponsored entity founded by the Austrian energy drink company in 1998—produced dozens of short documentary films, web series, and at least one feature-length documentary (*What Difference Does It Make? A Film about Making Music*, dir. Ralf Schmerberg, 2014). The online video portion of the initiative, and the production of music documentaries in particular, was an outgrowth of RBMA's original mandate to archive video recordings of keynote lectures and make them available online; these materials are now archived online following the discontinuation of the initiative. As a result of both its particular musical focus and the global nature of the initiative, the RBMA addressed subject matter and non-Western artists in a way that Pitchfork.tv has failed to do to this point in its history. *Diggin' in the Carts*, for example, a short-form documentary series launched late in 2014, examines Japanese video game music. Comprising six episodes, the series adopts a conventional mix of talking heads and illustrative footage (both archival and contemporary) but does so with a cast of interviewees representing a true diversity of personalities and perspectives while the subject matter itself is utterly unique. The playful, bouncing, ping-ponging aesthetic of so much Japanese video game music is neatly echoed in the presentation of the interview material and supporting footage. RBMA's most ambitious series, *Atlas Unfolded*, follows DJ and producer João Barbosa (a.k.a. Branko, of Portuguese electronic dance group Buraka Som System) in a vérité-style as he travels the world documenting the musicians and music communities that inform his creativity. Individual short films include *Ata Kak: Time Bomb* (dir. Nathan Corbin and Tony Lowe, 2017), the story of a Ghanaian musician discovered in the West by way of a mysterious cassette recording, and *Afro-Peruvian Beats* (dir. Tito Cabellos, 2017), an ethnographic portrait of young DJs and producers in Peru reclaiming their musical heritage. This commitment to bringing non–North American vernacular musics to the attention of English-language documentary audiences placed the Red Bull Music Academy at the vanguard of the popular music documentary on the web and differentiated this work from that of Pitchfork.tv, the *Unstaged* series, and others before it.

Early in its history, popular music documentaries served as fertile grounds for experimentation in the visual representation of music and musical performance and played a critical role in both visualizing and historicizing popular music. These films were among the most beloved and widely seen nonfiction films, representing some of the most visible instances of documentary in popular culture. At critical moments in its evolution, the popular music doc saw new technologies serve briefly as the catalyst for new representational strategies but these sparks of creativity only rarely prompted the exploration of previously un- and underrepresented musical styles and communities. In the 1970s, small-gauge motion picture photography provided the means by which amateur cinematographers and semiprofessional filmmakers could explore subcultural music communities and noncommercial musics; several canonical works of the original punk movement were captured in such a way (*The Punk Rock Movie*, 1978; *The Decline of Western Civilization*, 1981). In the 1980s, this pattern repeated itself with the introduction of commercially available videocassette recorders; in this extended moment, fan-documentation became the most lively area of the popular music doc with projects such as *Heavy Metal Parking Lot* (1986) becoming revered cult classics. This migration of the production practices from large-format to small-gauge analog film, and subsequently from film to video, is mirrored by the migration of the moving image to digital video formats in the late 1990s and the web several years later. However, the question remains whether or not this shift brought with it a similar expansion of subject matter and representational strategies.

The web has become a vibrant space for the production and distribution of documentary and the popular music documentary is enjoying a renaissance as it contributes to the ascendance of digital video online. However, several key popular music documentary series encompassing the first decade of digital video's migration to the web suggest stylistic innovation is the exception to rule, and those innovative approaches we do discover are quickly conventionalized and subsumed within the new vernacular of the short-form popular music documentary. Moreover, they suggest the proliferation of the short-form pop music doc across the web has not brought with it a concomitant diversification of subject matter addressed by documentarians. The aesthetic triumph of *The Take Away Show* was, in many ways, a return to representational strategies dating back to the early development of observational filmmaking, while the global outlook of the Red Bull Music Academy documentary series has not been adopted by other major players in the marketplace. Technological innovation in the areas of livestreaming and interactivity as credited to *Unstaged*, meanwhile, was undermined by the simplistic nature of the paratextual nonfictional shorts made available after the original event. Virtual reality (VR) is the latest technological frontier addressed by makers of popular music documentaries, but it remains to be seen what impact VR will have on the space and whether or not audiences will support it. In September 2017, the *New York Times* released *The National: Something Out of Nothing*, a twelve-minute VR film focusing on the band live in concert and at work in their private studio; ignoring the hook of VR technology, the short film is a straightforward observational music documentary. Pitchfork announced earlier the same year the launch of a branded VR channel in partnership with Inception, a leading provider of 360-degree and virtual reality entertainment media, but has committed only to the production of music videos. And so, as we face the next wave of popular music documentary on the web—and short-form docs, in particular—we are left to consider the same questions posed at the outset. Are the opportunities and technologies afforded documentary filmmakers by digital video and the web reshaping the form in a meaningful way? Does the vernacular nature of the popular music doc stifle creativity as new stylistic approaches are quickly subsumed by the representational strategies that defined the category over the last half century? Have popular music documentarians on the web thus far failed to engage with subject matter largely unattended by those working in feature-length commercial film and television? Is the web, as so many assume, truly a forum for innovation in the field of documentary?

Notes

1. Cisco, "Cisco Visual Networking Index."
2. See Rhys, "MTV Reunites with Vevo."
3. See Baker "Rockumentary."
4. The academy defines a feature-length film as any motion picture over forty minutes in length (Academy of Motion Picture Arts and Sciences, "90th Academy Awards").
5. Rodowick, *Virtual Life of Film*, 133.
6. Bolter and Grusin, *Remediation*, 270.
7. Ibid., 49.
8. Gombrich's discussion takes place within the context of a larger consideration of representation in the visual arts and architecture and the causes of historical change within those fields.
9. Gombrich, *Art and Illusion*, 74.
10. Bordwell, *On the History of Film Style*, 2.
11. Baker, "Rockumentary," 183.
12. See ibid.
13. Nichols, *Representing Reality*, 34.
14. Baker, "Rockumentary," 97.
15. Ibid., 116.
16. Bordwell, *On the History of Film Style*, 16.
17. Vernallis, *Unruly Media*, 39.
18. Originally defined by Philip Auslander in the context of mediatized spaces or audiovisual events in which the performers and audience are both physically and temporally copresent to one another—a distinction that became necessary with the advent of recorded sound—the concept of *liveness* is adaptable to the digital age with reference to "an interaction produced through our engagement with [an] object and our willingness to accept its claim [that it is, in fact, 'live']" (Auslander, *Liveness*, 9).
19. See La Blogothèque, "About."
20. Goodman, "Video Explorer."
21. Kenny, "Mitch Fillion."

22. See Pitchfork TV, "About."
23. Rhys, "MTV Reunites with Vevo."
24. See Auslander, "Sound and Vision."
25. See Mitchell, "American Express."
26. A small number of *Unstaged* events remain available as feature-length concert videos, but these represent a small percentage of the American Express Music library; see American Express Music website.

References

Academy of Motion Picture Arts and Sciences. "90th Academy Awards of Merit for Achievements During 2017." Accessed January 21, 2020. https://www.oscars.org/sites/oscars/files/90aa_rules.pdf.

American Express Music. Accessed October 2, 2017. http://amexmusic.com. Page no longer available.

Auslander, Philip. *Liveness: Performance in a Mediated Culture*. New York: Routledge, 1999.

———. "Sound and Vision: The Audio/Visual Economy of Musical Performance." In *The Oxford Handbook of New Audiovisual Aesthetics*, edited by John Richardson, Claudia Gorman, and Carol Vernallis, 605–621. New York: Oxford University Press, 2012.

Baker, Michael Brendan. "Rockumentary: Style, Performance, and Sound in a Documentary Genre." PhD diss., McGill University, 2011.

Bolter, Jay David, and Richard Grusin. *Remediation: Understanding New Media*. Cambridge: MIT Press, 1999.

Bordwell, David. "Intensified Continuity Visual Style in Contemporary American Film." *Film Quarterly* 55, no. 3 (Spring 2002): 16–28.

———. *On the History of Film Style*. Cambridge: Harvard University Press, 1996.

Burnett, Colin. "A New Look at the Concept of Style in Film: The Origins and Development of the Problem-Solution Model." *New Review of Film and Television Studies* 6, no. 2 (August 2008): 127–149.

Cisco Systems. "Cisco Visual Networking Index: Forecast and Methodology, 2017–2021." Accessed January 21, 2020. https://www.cisco.com/c/en/us/solutions/collateral/service-provider/visual-networking-index-vni/white-paper-c11-741490.html.

Fox, Killian. "Rock'n'Roll to Go." *Guardian*, October 27, 2007. https://www.theguardian.com/music/2007/oct/27/popandrock.netmusic.

Gombrich, E. H. *Art and Illusion: A Study in the Psychology of Pictorial Representation*. Princeton, NJ: Princeton University Press, 2000.

Goodman, Lizzie. "The Video Explorer." *New York Times Magazine*, June 19, 2011. http://www.nytimes.com/2011/06/19/magazine/vincent-moons-take-away-videos.html.

Kenny, Amy. "Mitch Fillion and the Birth of Southern Souls." *Hamilton Spectator*, November 19, 2012. https://www.thespec.com/whatson-story/2191127-mitch-fillion-and-the-birth-of-southern-souls/.

Khanna, Vish. "Red Bull Music Academy," *Exclaim!*, October 30, 2007. http://exclaim.ca/music/article/red_bull_music_academy.

La Blogothèque. "About." Accessed October 2, 2017. https://www.youtube.com/user/LaBlogotheque/about.

Mitchell, Julian. "American Express Scores Big with Unstaged Series, Getting Fans Involved around the World." *Forbes*, September 30, 2015. http://forbes.com/sites/julianmitchell

/2015/09/30/disclosure-sam-smith-and-lion-babe-deliver-electrifying-show-for-amex-unstaged/.
Nichols, Bill. *Representing Reality: Issues and Concepts in Documentary*. Bloomington: Indiana University Press. 1991.
Pitchfork TV. "About." Accessed October 2, 2017. https://www.youtube.com/user/pitchforktv/about.
Rhys, Dan. "MTV Reunites with Vevo, Now Has Licensing Deals from All Four Majors." *Hollywood Reporter*, March 6, 2012. http://www.hollywoodreporter.com/news/mtv-vevo-music-videos-facebook-youtube-297178.
Rodowick, D. N. *The Virtual Life of Film*. Cambridge, MA: Harvard University Press, 2007.
Somaiya, Ravi. "Pitchfork Media Becomes Part of Condé Nast Stable." *New York Times*, October 14, 2015. https://www.nytimes.com/2015/10/14/business/media/conde-nast-buys-pitchfork-media.html.
Vernallis, Carol. *Unruly Media: YouTube, Music Video, and the New Digital Cinema*. New York: Oxford University Press. 2013.

MICHAEL BRENDAN BAKER is Professor of Film Studies at Sheridan College. He is editor (with Thomas Waugh and Ezra Winton) of *Challenge for Change: Activist Documentary at the National Film Board of Canada*.

9

FROM THE ESSAY FILM TO THE VIDEO ESSAY

Between the Critical and the Popular

Allison de Fren

The audiovisual essay, a descendant of the "essay film," is gaining popularity as a way to think and write about film and media among a broad range of practitioners who once occupied distinct spheres, including filmmakers, scholars, students, critics, cinephiles, and fans. While its antecedent was "positioned at the crossroads of 'documentary, avant-garde, and art film impulses'"[1] and often confined to noncommercial channels of distribution, the audiovisual essay circulates within an expanding online network in which the lines between noncommercial and commercial, as well as between amateur and professional, are increasingly blurred.

Drawing on a series of case studies, this essay examines some of the strategies that the digital audiovisual essay borrows from its cinematic forebears as well as how it has evolved formally, structurally, and narratively to appeal to online and increasingly mobile viewers. In the process, it explores how practitioners stake ground and negotiate terms within an expanding field of popular interest as well as how they work with and around copyright laws. I am particularly interested in the relationship between present and past—that is, how audiovisual essays create conversations with earlier essay films and how those conversations are made relevant and responsive to contemporary viewers, whose interests and viewing habits may be at odds with the spectatorial and critical aspirations of the original texts.

What unites the examples presented is that each attempts to navigate the uneasy terrain between the critical and the popular, with work falling along a continuum between academically oriented *videographic criticism*—a term used by the peer-reviewed journal *[In]Transition*—and the fan-based supercuts and formal dissections currently proliferating on YouTube.[2] Although the tension between criticality and popularity also marked the first essay films, there has been a radical democratization of the form with the advent of digital and networking technologies, opening up the practice to all who wish to participate and increasing the number of viewers, sometimes into the millions.[3] Still, many of the most successful audiovisual essayists, as the examples provided will attest, are those for whom the practice began as an extension of some form of media professionalism—whether filmmaking, editing, criticism, or scholarship—and evolved to become a mainstay of their professional activities. How they financially sustain their evolving practice, how they reconcile their creative and critical agenda with the free-for-all race for online and mobile viewership—with its attendant pressures to "go viral"—and how they protect their work within an ephemeral media environment with shifting copyright regulations, are questions of mounting interest. As we will see, within the increasingly competitive, complex, and cross-platform sphere of social and mobile media, essay films are often invoked as a reminder of the craft's origins or as a benchmark from which to trace its evolutionary trajectory and assess its current status, even when the demands of online distribution make it difficult to follow suit.

While all the practitioners on whom I focus use the audiovisual essay to reflect on film and other media, not all of the essay films with which they dialogue are similarly focused. Whether or not an essay film is specifically about film, however, there is an inherent reflexivity in the act of drawing attention to one's thoughts about a topic, which often extends to the medium and the ways in which it enables or limits the ability to communicate. As Timothy Corrigan has noted, the power of the essay, whatever the medium, lies in its dialogic relationship with "representational assumptions," involving "practices that undo and redo film form, visual perspectives, public geographies, temporal organizations, and notions of truth and judgment."[4] It was the reflexive, dialogic, and experimental use of the cinematic apparatus to probe for truths beyond the indexical real that, for some scholars, first distinguished the "essay film" from what might otherwise have been categorized as documentary, although the relationship between the two—and the extent to which they can be viewed as separate genres—remains a subject of ongoing discourse. As compared with the empirical grounding of documentary, the essay film tends to inspire metaphors of fractured vision and perceptual distortion—evoking such terms as *refractive*, *prismatic*, and *kaleidoscopic*—suggesting a more playful, less committed relationship to realism and the facts as well as a way of seeing and thinking facilitated by formal experimentation. Along these lines, Nora M. Alter suggests that what defines the essay film is the "cognitive anamorphosis" it produces through multiple and shifting vantage points and the complex and sometimes contradictory layering of images and sounds. Like visual anamorphosis, a technique used in painting to subvert realism through the distortion of perspective and creation of multiple points of view, the various methods—formal, structural, and narrative—by which the essay film produces cognitive estrangement set it apart from the "the relatively clear line of argumentation," evidence building, and storytelling "in documentary productions."[5] The essay film's perceptual anomalies are, however, not for their own sake, according to Alter, but for the purpose of ideological critique and the desire "to intervene intellectually in the standing order of things."[6] It thus has a distinct and often real-world agenda even if its methods are oblique.

Alter goes on to suggest that the essay film's critical aims "have in numerous cases been forgotten or cast aside as the genre has become more popular."[7] Because the same technological developments that have fueled that popularity have also given rise to the increasing essayistic consideration of film and other media, I will draw particular attention to their affordances and constraints and the tendencies they encourage. The relatively recent ability to access, replay, and remix a global media archive has resulted, in particular, in an online explosion of supercuts and send-ups that highlight the textual or formal patterns and themes of popular film texts and directors. Even for those who aspire toward criticality, the capacity of digital and networking technologies for discovering, isolating, and sharing new insights about films and media texts makes it difficult to avoid becoming recursively engaged in an interplay of images and sounds that reinforce and reproduce themselves, increasingly in shorter, more eye-catching forms. Such tendencies work against the "cognitive anamorphosis" by which essay films direct their spectators to concerns that are beyond the frame (and thus beyond "the cultural enterprise promoting the prominence, success, and prestige of marketable products"), and they therefore become a notable source of tension in audiovisual essays that are in conversation with essay films, since the latter serve as models toward which the former aspire.[8]

One gets a glimpse of the different ways of seeing encouraged by the essay film and audiovisual essay in *Terrence Malick's City Symphony* (2016; hereafter, *TMCS*) by Conor Bateman, which announces in its title its debt to the city symphonies of the early twentieth century. Bateman—whose video essays are an extension of a varied career in and around independent film and the Australian film festival circuit—has argued explicitly for producing work outside "the YouTube/academia divide." He suggests that the necessity of achieving either virality or scholarly recognition prevents audiovisual essays from fulfilling what he considers their greatest promise: to engage viewers in a "process of discovery."[9] Bateman has used essay films in his own work as touchstones for the kind of audiovisual explorations he endorses in his writing. *TMCS* emulates, in particular, *Manhatta* (1921), a short cine-poem often described as "the first avant-garde film produced in the United States."[10] A collaboration between the painter Charles Sheeler and photographer Paul Strand, *Manhatta* conjures a typical day in lower Manhattan from a nonnarrative progression of shots—the first of which show the arrival of workers to the city on the Staten Island ferry. Similarly, Bateman's audiovisual essay culls and reassembles shots of Los Angeles (LA) from Malick's *Knight of Cups* (2015), an experimental drama in which some scenes were shot on a handheld camera in unstaged public places throughout the city. In the spirit of the city symphonies, in which "the city plays itself," Bateman frees the film's mise-en-scène from the narrative pull of individual protagonists to focus on the camera's movement through the sun-drenched micro-environments that comprise LA's sprawl, from the iron, glass, and concrete of downtown to the sand and water of the beachfront. And like the city symphonies, which celebrated the "everyday reality" of the metropolis and the ability of the *kinoglaz* or "cinema eye," as Dziga Vertov called it, to reveal the truths of modern life, *TMCS* prompts viewers to scan for the truths beneath the establishing shots and location settings of Malick's film. Film truth is, in both cases, not supplied by a voice-over or linked to facts but is discovered in seeing anew through the power of camera work, visual montage, and juxtaposition. But whereas the city symphonies invite new perspectives on and ways of seeing the city and, through it, industrial modernity, Bateman's audiovisual essay invites a new perspective on Malick's film. Its title, *Terrence Malick's City Symphony*, provides the only interpretive frame, one that suggests our takeaway should be as much, if not more, about the auteur behind the roving shots we are viewing as about the city they are capturing, thus generating a heightened awareness of his choices and the resulting impression of Los Angeles—and by extension the Hollywood film industry—being conveyed.

In assigning Malick as the author of the latent city symphony within *Knight of Cups*, Bateman circumscribes within an auteurist endeavor the shots of LA that he frees from the film's narrative. This focus on the auteur as a mode of film production and consumption, while integral to the histories of both the essay film and audiovisual essay, was an outgrowth of mid-twentieth-century technological and theoretical developments and was, thus, largely unexplored at the time of the city symphonies from which Bateman draws inspiration. Even in Vertov's *Man with a Movie Camera* (1929), whose introductory credits describe the subsequent work as "excerpts from the diary of a cameraman," the titular cameraman—who is shown at work throughout the film—is unnamed and iconic, his role subsumed by the overarching celebration of the liberatory potential of the kino-eye, which Vertov viewed as superior to the human eye. The rise of the auteur is often traced technologically to portable cameras, such as the Arriflex and Eclair 35mm Cameflex, and theoretically to Alexandre Astruc's 1948 manifesto, "The Birth of a New Avant-Garde." In it, he heralds the cinema as a "caméra-stylo" or "camera-pen" for rendering the inner world of the filmmaker, "a form in which and by which an artist can express his thoughts, however abstract they may be, or translate his obsessions, exactly as he does in the contemporary novel or essay."[11] As Christian Keathley has noted, "This declaration stimulated a new generation of filmmakers—notably, those of the French New Wave—to an unprecedented level of creative work, expanding not only on cinema's already established analogy with the novel, but also exploring Astruc's other possibility—the essay."[12] While auteurism and the essay film would, thereafter, develop in tandem, the audiovisual exploration of the filmmaker *as* auteur was tied to even later developments: first, the archival preservation of classic films and their supporting production and promotional materials; and second, the increasing distribution of both in proximity to one another via digital technologies.

To the extent that a nexus point exists in the intersecting histories of the essay film and the online audiovisual essay about film, it is in the output of the company that pioneered the codistribution of films and paratextual supplements, the Criterion Collection. Founded in 1984, Criterion's mission was, from the beginning, to bring to a wider audience "the defining moments in cinema," including foreign, classic, and critically rediscovered films—as well as such foundational essay films as Orson Welles's *F for Fake* (1975), Chantal Akerman's *News from Home* (1976), and Chris Marker's *Sans Soleil* (1983)—which it made available outside of arthouse settings, first on laserdisc and then on DVD. As part of this mission, it included high-quality master elements—such as shooting scripts, storyboards, production stills, and design sketches—which expanded both appreciation for and understanding of the cinematic texts they accompanied. The mainstay of these materials was the production of screen-specific commentary, both by filmmakers and film scholars and critics. While the commentary track would become a standard value-added "extra" of the commercial DVD beginning in the late 1990s, it was inaugurated over a decade earlier by Criterion on the laserdisc for *King Kong* (1933), which featured critical commentary by film historian, Ronald Haver. Criterion eventually began releasing its titles on DVD, but it took pains to distinguish its supplementary materials from those on commercial DVDs, eschewing the "making of" featurette that promised to take viewers "behind the scenes" and instead drawing out the film's larger archival, critical, and contextual frame in order to reinforce its authorial presence and cultural significance. As Mark Parker has noted, the DVD packaging of Criterion films were "infused with something of an ethos, an attitude toward film that mingled the enthusiasm of a fan, the nostalgia of a cinema lover, the responsibility of a teacher, the precision of a bibliographer, and the insight of a scholar,"[13] establishing each as a cultural artifact worth collecting and studying.

Criterion's multimodal approach to film appreciation and analysis—what some have called "film school in a box"—now marks the current landscape of audiovisual essays, whose practitioners, including film fans, critics, scholars, and teachers, both shape and are shaped by their newly acquired access to film archives and editing equipment, privileges once reserved for professionals. Film scholar Laura Mulvey, who provided the commentary on Criterion's 1994 laserdisc release of Michael Powell's *Peeping Tom* (1959), noted early on how digital technologies—with their ability to slow down, freeze, and repeat film scenes at will—could unearth hidden meanings of equal value to the film lover and the film scholar and critic, while drawing out the latent tendencies of one within the other. In this context, "textual analysis [might] cease to be a restricted academic practice and return . . . to its origins as a work of *cinephilia*, of love of cinema."[14] Although she was writing before the proliferation of online audiovisual essays, her insights were prescient in that most of what one currently finds online—from fan-based supercuts to videographic scholarly criticism—is in the service of a dedicated cinephilia as well as a revived auteurism. This tendency is, in fact, exemplified by Kogonada, an academic turned audiovisual essayist turned filmmaker, who was commissioned by Criterion as part of its online strategy.[15] Unlike the other essayists discussed here, Kogonada neither writes about audiovisual essays nor references essay films in his work. He is, however, an important practitioner who helped popularize the form, generating renewed interest in Criterion's niche catalog among a born-digital audience.

In his role as digital pied piper—disseminating video essays online intended to lead viewers back to Criterion's website—Kogonada has eschewed the audio commentary that Criterion pioneered. Although there is some variation in his work, the majority of his audiovisual essays are artful supercuts

Fig. 9.1 Criterion innovated the critical commentary track on its 1984 laserdisc release of *King Kong* (1933). The remastered 2010 release on Blu-ray added more features, including audio commentary by special effects master Ray Harryhausen.

that, with fetishistic precision, draw out the formal proclivities and thematic fixations of famous auteurs, evident in titles like *Hands of Bresson* (2014), *Eyes of Hitchcock* (2014), and *Godard in Fragments* (2016). Like Bateman's essay film–inspired work, his video essays tend to be more observational than expository, making their points through variations on a theme rather than voice-over or explanatory text. Indeed, with a few notable exceptions, they fall squarely within the "poetic register," an interplay of images and sounds that forms an expressive continuum with the "explanatory mode," in which language (whether written or spoken) is privileged.[16] Although such poetic explorations make the most of "multi-media technologies and the rich audiovisual possibilities they offer," they also, as Keathley notes, risk "an opacity that means potentially going unrecognized as criticism."[17] Despite having a background in film studies, criticism has been neither Kogonada's mandate nor his goal. At the 2016 Berlinale, where he made a rare appearance for the panel, "In Reference to Visual Essays," he was asked why he chose primarily to highlight the tendencies of directors without commenting on them. He replied that when making video essays, he leaves his academic hat behind, stating, "I don't really have a desire when I'm making any of this, to teach . . . I just want to be a starting point for conversation." In describing his own work, Kogonada has drawn an analogy between its presentational style and the preparation of sushi: "With sushi, every cut matters. And so do the

Fig. 9.2 Like many of Kogonada's video essays, *Hands of Bresson* (2014) is a poetic supercut that underscores a repetitive motif within the auteur's signature style.

ingredients. Those two ongoing choices are the difference. What you select, and how you cut it."[18] In this sense, his video essays both invoke and emulate the auteurs on whom they focus through the cultivation of a signature style. And while there is no doubt that his work has generated interest in Criterion films, the palatable morsels he has delivered also stand on their own, sometimes replacing the larger fare they are intended to showcase, and he has been treated as an auteur in his own right.

The production of Kogonada as auteur represents a Web 2.0 twist on Catherine Grant's observation that digital and DVD culture often serve as "Auteur Machines."[19] As she notes, the immediacy of the intertextual frame they provide for experiencing cinematic texts has the potential for "engendering different, more comprehensive forms of auteurism than were previously possible," including "the actual 'production' of auteurs, that is, the bringing into discursive existence commercially- and critically-defined 'significant directors.'"[20] While she focuses on the film director whose commentary track has been the key aspect of contemporary DVD culture, her insights might be extended to the online audiovisual essayist, who produces an entirely new work rather than, as in director commentary, an accompaniment and aural rewriting of a film. Indeed, the autonomy of Kogonada's vision is underscored by the fact that his work for Criterion garnered enough support for him to make his first narrative feature film, *Columbus* (2017), which premiered at Sundance.[21]

Although many other audiovisual essayists have attracted fans and a following, Kogonada was in the unusual position of having both a platform and artistic freedom—Criterion owns the electronic rights to the films he has explored audiovisually, while giving him a great deal of creative license—enabling him to develop a signature style in relation to the work of the auteurs through whom he has found inspiration. By contrast, the approach taken by other essayists is often partly dictated by the way their audiovisual essays are funded and distributed, and these constraints are thrown into relief when they are in conversation with essay films. A particularly good example of the tensions that get played out between an audiovisual essay and its cinematic role model is *Vancouver Never Plays Itself* (2015, hereafter *VNPI*) by Tony Zhou and Taylor Ramos, a playful variation on a theme established by Thom Andersen in *Los Angeles Plays Itself* (2003, hereafter *LAPI*), considered by many as an exemplar of the film essay whose topic is film. Zhou and Ramos's approach to the audiovisual essay also provides a comparison with the lyrical compositions of Kogonada, since they helped popularize a rapid-fire voice-over style dubbed "hyper-narration."[22]

Both *LAPI* and *VNPI* examine how the home cities of their makers are portrayed in film and television, and both take a first-person expositional approach to making their points. Although conceptually related, however, the two works encourage very different modes of spectatorship. The film *LAPI* builds its case reservedly and methodically over the course of nearly three hours, backed by supporting evidence drawn from over 200 Los Angeles–set feature films, some well-known and others obscure. The video essay *VNPI* employs a fast-cut editing style to match its hypernarration, breezing through footage from eighty-five different media texts in just over nine minutes. While the former circulated primarily within arthouse and academic circuits, the latter was disseminated on YouTube, attracting over a million online viewers in less than a year. This difference in approach is not only attributable to the means of distribution (or lack thereof) available at the time of their release, but also the background of the creators and the impetus for their work. Unlike *LAPI*, which is considered filmmaker-critic Andersen's magnum opus, *VNPI* is one of nearly thirty videos made by Zhou and Ramos over the course of two and a half years (April 2014 to September 2017) for their now retired YouTube channel *Every Frame a Painting*. The impetus for the series was, according to the pair, the difficulties they were having in their respective careers—Zhou is a film editor and Ramos an animator—of "communicating visual ideas to non-visual people." As Zhou explained in a post-mortem article about the series: "Many people can't understand something until you show it AND explain it to them. Eventually I would just go to a computer, pull up a YouTube clip, sit next to them and point out specific things (this is how the Spielberg Oner video started). One day I thought: 'I wish someone would make video essays this way—like someone sitting next to you, demonstrating visual literacy.' And that was how the idea of *Every Frame a Painting* was born."[23] The resulting series provided a master class on film form, with each video essay produced in conformance with an overarching tone and style. The presence of Zhou served as a connective through-line; he provided his own voice-over, opening each video with the signature line, "Hi, my name is Tony and this is *Every Frame a Painting*." His chummy, upbeat performance stands in contrast to the deadpan delivery of Encke King in *Los Angeles Plays Itself*, whose fractious and nonperformative quality has led many to the mistaken conclusion that the voice-over was provided by Andersen himself. The VO for the latter, moreover, maintains a declarative mode of address throughout, a likely extension of the fact that the film grew out of lectures that Andersen had given at California Institute of the Arts, where he has taught for over thirty years. What began, according to Andersen, as an academic critique of the 1997 filmic adaptation of the James Ellroy novel *L.A. Confidential* would, in the resulting essay film, become an erudite, subjective account of the representational offenses that the film industry has committed at the expense of the city of Los Angeles and its residents. By comparison, *VNPI* drifts in and out of second person, simultaneously appealing to film lovers and filmmakers. The main point of the essay, that Vancouver is often a location in film and television but rarely a setting, is delivered in ways that could be construed as either critical or instructional, for example, when Zhou asks "How do you fake one city as another without the audience noticing?" and then provides exemplary instances of the technical camouflage used to disguise Vancouver as a variety of American cities, including Seattle, San Francisco, and New York. This how-to approach is also reflected in the titles of some of the other video essays in the series, such as *Jackie Chan—How to Do Action Comedy* and *Edgar Wright—How to Do Visual Comedy*, each engaging in critique less as an end in itself than a means of delivering working advice on film form.

While the accessible approach and fast-paced sequencing of the video essays on *Every Frame a Painting* seem specifically geared toward capturing new subscribers (and indeed, viewer subscription on the YouTube channel passed the one million mark before it was retired), Zhou has stated that most of the stylistic choices made by him and Ramos, including rhythm, pacing, interplay of VO and image, and number and length of clips, were reverse engineered in accordance with YouTube's copyright policies: "I spent about a week doing brute force trial-and-error. I would privately upload several different essay clips, then see which got flagged and which didn't. This gave me a rough idea what the system could detect, and I edited the videos to avoid those potholes. So something that was designed to restrict us ended up becoming our style."[24] The irony of their signature style is that, while it made their series widely popular, it was also a contributing factor in its demise. In their postmortem, Zhao and Ramos describe the double-edged sword of their internet success—both the excitement of attracting a large following and the ways in which it created a vice grip, limiting their sense of creative freedom and contributing to their decision to end the series in December 2017. The demands of addressing both their fan base and YouTube's copyright policies made it difficult, for example, to cover the work of more obscure filmmakers they admired, such as Andrei Tarkovsky, whose films require viewer patience and cannot be made legible without playing longer shots than YouTube's bots would allow.

In *LAPI*, on the other hand, Andersen gives himself as much time as he needs to make his points, sacrificing accessibility on the altar of critical depth. His film is edited without concern for copyright, providing an intermission a little over halfway through its 169-minute run time. For this reason, its distribution remained limited. The film first premiered at the Toronto Film Festival and, after enjoying an enthusiastic festival run, maintained a largely underground existence and cult following in which it was circulated among cinephiles and architecture buffs on bootleg DVDs and YouTube links. It wasn't until the film's tenth anniversary that Andersen remastered it, reedited what he "found annoying" in the original, and released it on DVD and Apple iTunes.[25]

Still, according to Zhou and Ramos, whatever compromises they might have made to maintain their large viewership, their core commitment was to produce independent work. As they note, they eschewed commercial sponsorship and largely self-funded their series with supplementation from the crowdfunding site Patreon. Moreover, the work itself, while tailored for online distribution and reception, was informed by the tradition of the essay film, as exemplified not only by *VNPI*, but also *F for Fake: How to Structure a Video Essay* (2015). Marking the midpoint of the series, the latter offered a primer on the evolving craft of the audiovisual essay via a confession by Zhou that many of their best moves were stolen from Orson Welles's *F for Fake* (1973), which is itself an essay film organized around confessions by professional forgers. From *F for Fake*, Zhou extracts two rules for structuring video essays that, he argues, are so universally effective, they would work equally well for a narrative feature film or an animated television show. This point is then illustrated, and the two rules elaborated, through video and audio clips of Trey Parker, cocreator of the animated series *South Park*, and film director John Sturges, each discussing narrative storytelling. The first rule, explained by Parker in a video clip of a class given at New York University, concerns the importance of cause-and-effect logic. When outlining a story, rather than adding one event after the next in a disconnected, ad hoc fashion—that is, this happens "and then" that happens—every event that occurs in the narrative should either cause or get modified by every subsequent event. As Parker puts it, "what should happen between every [storytelling] beat that you've written down is either the word 'therefore' or 'but.'" The second rule is illustrated through audio commentary by Sturges—excerpted, significantly, from Criterion's laserdisc release of *Bad Day at Black Rock* (1991)—in which he discusses the importance of having two story lines advancing in parallel. Suspense is built by playing them off one another: "you reach the peak of one, you go to the other . . . when it loses interest, drop it; 'meanwhile back at the ranch.'" As Zhou notes, *F for Fake* is an exemplar of these storytelling rules, "except [Welles] doesn't connect scenes, he connects thoughts. Even though this movie is an essay, each moment has the connective logic of a *South Park* episode." As in many other *Every Frame a Painting* installments, this one ends with a second person how-to takeaway: "remember, video essays aren't essays, they're films, so you want to structure and pace them like a filmmaker would: *therefore* and *but, meanwhile back at the ranch.*"

While this audiovisual essay provides, in an entertaining format, indispensable guidance for other essayists and a useful pedagogical tool for teachers, it also exemplifies the critical limitations of Zhou and Ramos's form-versus-content approach to the series. By focusing on the universal applicability of the film's structure, they lose opportunities to draw out its subversive real-world agenda. Another audiovisual essay on *F for Fake* serves as a good point of comparison. *F for Fake and the Death of the Author* (2015) by Kyle Kallgren, the producer of the YouTube video essay channel *Brows Held High*, addresses directly the objectives of the film, which were—as Jonathan Rosenbaum states in his liner notes for its 2005 Criterion DVD release—to undermine "many cherished beliefs about authorship and the means by which 'experts,' 'God's own gift to the fakers' validate such notions."[26] Kallgren appears in the video essay, as does Welles in the film, establishing his authorial presence, only to undermine his own authority after stopping his analysis midstream: "Before I go on, I want to throw off any airs of expertise that I might be putting on. My undergrad work was in theater, not in film. My grad work was in film but more in film production than film theory. . . . I've never been published by anyone other than myself. . . . Basically, everything I'm saying right now is the opinion of a film fan who just kind of taught himself film theory." After suggesting that there are more useful critics on the internet "that I would rather you watch than watch me," and offering viewers the opportunity to turn off the video, he pauses momentarily, sheepishly asks, "Still here?" and then resumes his analysis of *F for Fake*, using it as a springboard for an extended inquiry into authenticity and authorship, all the while playfully imitating the film's digressive tendencies.

Kallgren thus casts light on the concerns of the original film while also drawing attention to its legacy, an online environment of audiovisual essays where the work of autodidacts and fans mingles with that of credentialed scholars, relativizing what is considered expertise. In doing so, he achieves the same kind of prismatic study of truth and illusion that makes Welles's "film about trickery" one of the most admired and cited essay films, while also demonstrating why any essayistic attempt to pay homage to it must ultimately grapple with the film's own mistrust of the ways that aesthetic value is conferred. Kallgren's approach is not only reflexive; it is also in line with what Corrigan calls "refractive cinema," a category he reserves for essay films that interrogate art or film, "overlapping their representations of other artistic and aesthetic experiences with their own cinematic processes and frequently reflecting those processes as a reflection on film itself."[27] This work is, Corrigan argues, even when formally pleasing, functionally anti-aesthetic: "These films ask us not to think so much about the aesthetics of film—the genius behind it, artistic strategies, or its emotional and imaginative communications. Rather, refractive cinema tends, in a variety of ways, to draw attention to where film fails or, more precisely, where and how the cinematic can force us beyond its borders and our borders, can force us to think about a world and ourselves that necessarily and crucially exist outside the limits of the cinema."[28] As the essay film does more than merely reflect and comment on the world, refractive cinema does more than reflect and comment on the cinematic world. Rather, it shatters it like a mirror or sets it against itself, like a hall of mirrors, dispersing "the image through a social space" outside the frame. This "abjection" of the cinematic runs counter to the majority of audiovisual essays, whose concerns rarely extend beyond the world of the films they explore, however intertextual, and the auteurs who made them. The essay film's "refractive" potential has been championed most strongly by practitioner and critic Kevin B. Lee, who has argued that it is only when the online audiovisual essay confronts its own propensities for visual distraction that it is able to perform "a drop-kick through the looking glass of the screen into the world around it."[29]

Lee is the most prolific audiovisual essayist of all time, having made over 350, a level of output that, in part, prompted the *New York Times* to dub him the "King of the Video Essays." "Ambassador" is an equally fitting title since he has served as curator of and spokesman for audiovisual essay programs in numerous international forums, including film festivals, museums, and academic institutions, while also mentoring the work of dozens of other practitioners. He began his varied career as a filmmaker-turned-critic, starting a blog in 2006 titled *Shooting Down Pictures* in which he set out to watch and discuss every one of the 1,000 "greatest films" cited on the website They Shoot Pictures Don't They? For each, he wrote a critical essay supplemented with photos and clips, eventually progressing to video essays, which he began posting to YouTube in 2007, only two years after the site's launch. He not only worked solo but also collaborated with dozens of other critics, inspiring some to begin making video essays themselves. In January 2009, YouTube shut down his site for copyright infringement, a move that ended up helping generate interest in his work, since many of the critics with whom he had collaborated spoke out on his behalf, pressuring YouTube into reinstating his account and subsequently helping to legitimize the audiovisual essay as a form of criticism.

In 2010, Lee was hired by then-arthouse streaming site Fandor as chief video essayist, where he became the founding editor of its online digital magazine, *Keyframe*. While there, he created hundreds of video essays and commissioned numerous works by others, but his relationship with Fandor remained tenuous due, in large part, to the tensions between its bottom line and his own. Lee has spoken candidly about not only his difficulty supporting himself on the weekly videos he made for Fandor but also the weekly hit counts they placed on his work. He has also recounted, with some irony, the story of his first viral video essay for the site, *The Spielberg Face* (2011). As he tells it, Lee found himself in the nearly impossible position of generating hits for what, at the time, was a catalog of independent films, and in a desperate bid to keep his job, he chose to focus on the popular director. He posted his audiovisual essay at the start of a workday, was invited to an afternoon lunch by an executive from Fandor who proceeded to fire him, and thereafter returned to the office to pack his things, only to discover that his video essay had generated more traffic than the site had ever received before. His success prompted Fandor to hire him back as a part-time editor and contributor, but his commitment to criticality continued to put him at odds with the site's increasing demands for viewership.

The Spielberg Face is, in fact, a study in this tension. Reminiscent of a work by Kogonada, it isolates a pattern in the director's oeuvre, a proclivity for close-ups in which a single character gazes off-screen with a beatific expression, "eyes open, staring in wordless wonder," as the camera slowly dollies forward. Lee draws attention to "the Spielberg face" not only as a cinematic tendency but also as one of many heavy-handed tactics used by the director for emotional signaling, the latter underscored through both voice-over narration and strategically placed text. At the 2016 Berlinale panel "In Reference to Visual Essays," Lee acknowledged that as successful as *The Spielberg Face* was, it would likely have generated twice as much interest if he had dispensed with narration and made it a supercut.[30] He then underscored the importance that he places on creating a more critical position for the viewer, in this case, "about the way Spielberg uses a particular kind of rapturous expression to manipulate audience response."

Fandor, however, did not heed the message of Lee's first viral hit for it and continued to seek out strategies for capturing eyeballs, the majority of which, its marketing research suggested, were trained on mobile devices. As a result, Lee's video essays became shorter—from ten to five to two minutes long—and, shortly before he left the site, he dispensed entirely with voice-over narration and was experimenting with animated block text as a way of appealing to mobile phone users. What prompted him finally to leave his position was the removal by the site of approximately 280 video essays in January 2017, some made by him and others by the video essayists whose work he had commissioned, a purportedly preemptive move related to music licensing that conveniently eliminated work that didn't fit the increasingly mainstream image they were cultivating. Lee quit in protest and subsequently worked with Audiovisualcy, Catherine Grant's "Videographic Film Studies" Vimeo channel, to identify, collect, and link to the Fandor-commissioned video essays, many of which were reposted by their makers. Later in the year, Fandor shuttered *Keyframe* entirely in a final bid to broaden its appeal "beyond cineastes to Movie Fanatics" (a bid that failed; in 2018, the company laid off most of its staff and sold its assets).[31]

After leaving Fandor, Lee pursued an advanced degree, became the first artist-in-residence at the Harun Farocki Institut in Berlin, and thereafter took an academic appointment. Now free of the bottom-line pressures of commercial work, his audiovisual essays have become increasingly oriented toward social activism and political engagement. Musing about his transformation from cinephile to activist, he notes that the turning point was the 2009 shutdown of his YouTube account: "From that moment the act of making a video

Fig. 9.3 In *The Spielberg Face* (2011), Kevin B. Lee takes a more critical approach to the supercut by using text and voice-over to comment on the rapturous expression repeated in countless Spielberg films.

essay became something I took less for granted, with my attention redirected toward underlying economic and industrial factors that govern their fate. This shift of one's field of vision, resulting in the ability to see anew, has always been the quality of the video essay I cherish most."[32] However much he has had to compromise on criticality, the use of image and sound to find a new way to see and hear has long been at the heart of Lee's practice. Unlike others either working in or theorizing the field, he has been relatively agnostic about form, sidestepping disagreements around VO narration, didacticism, and formal experimentation, while advocating for a working definition that "errs on the side of inclusiveness"—namely, that "an essay film explicitly reflects on the materials it presents, to actualise the thinking process itself."[33] At the same time, his work has increasingly gestured beyond what many consider "the two primary markers of the form—reflexivity and subjectivity"—toward refraction.[34] As Corrigan notes, refractive cinema expands the "typical essayistic formulation of something like 'thoughts occasioned by' or 'thoughts on' a particular public experience" by opening up "a kind of abstracted zone for thinking through and about film as a critical experience in itself, thinking through the very terms of cinematic thinking."[35]

Lee both echoes and enacts Corrigan's ideas about refraction in the video essay *The Essay Film—Some Thoughts of Discontent* (2014). It wends between two parallel tracks, one questioning what an essay film is, and the other questioning the place of audiovisual criticality in a contemporary

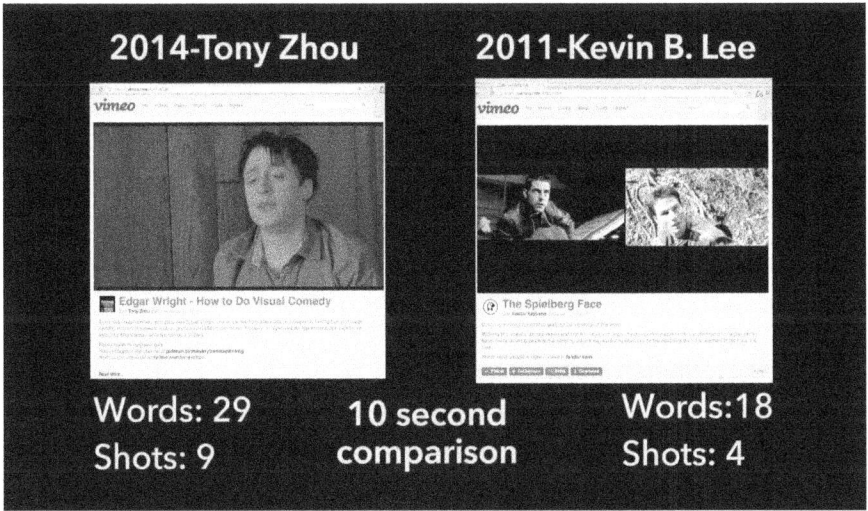

Fig. 9.4 In this side-by-side comparison of word/shot count in video essays by Zhou/Ramos and himself, Kevin B. Lee underscores the relative speed of their hypernarration and editing, suggesting that it produces a "cognitive treadmill effect" that forces viewers to keep up. From *What Makes a Video Essay Great* (2014).

online environment of audiovisual spectacle and proliferating media. "If we are submerged in sounds and images," it asks, "can we use them to stay afloat" and, if so, how? Lee draws from over twenty essay films, assembling excerpts in a play of image, sound, voice-over, and text—all the tools in the film essayist's arsenal—as if thinking through what the essay film might teach the contemporary audiovisual essay that has inherited its legacy. To the extent that it presents an answer, it is in the words of Kodwo Eshun of the Otolith Group, which scroll upward like ending credits: "the essayistic is not about a particular generic fascination for voice-over or montage, the essayistic is dissatisfaction, it's discontent with the duties of an image and the obligations of a sound." Eshun's words are followed by a montage of clips from iconic essay films, ending in a black screen over which Lee speaks, suggesting that what defines the essay film is its refusal to "take sounds and images for granted, so that behind the screen one feels a mind at work, letting us see and hear how it thinks." This thought about cinematic thinking is then refracted by a series of film clips interspersed with three intertitles—"with the screen," "through the screen," "beyond the screen"—the last three words extending beyond the frame so that the letters are cut off. The next and last clip of the video essay is a scene from *F for Fake* in which Orson Welles makes a coin disappear in a magic trick, as if to illustrate the "abstracted zone" beyond image and sound toward which both the essay film and his audiovisual essay aspire.

Lee's emphasis on audiovisual discontent is, by his own admission, at odds with most other practitioners of the form, although, as the previously discussed case studies demonstrate, digital technology and online distribution have fed a host of conflicting impulses. On the one hand, DVD culture and digital editing encourage a cinephilic contemplation that often results in works of aesthetic and auteurist appreciation, sometimes even achieving artistic status in their own right. On the other, increasing competition for viewership, commercialism, and the prohibitions of networked distribution, demand brevity and the sacrifice of content for sensory impact, contributing to an ever-expanding internet torrent of eye candy. Although markedly different in intent and approach, both impulses arguably undermine the refractive attributes of the essay film, whose critical possibilities are what initially drew Lee and many others to the audiovisual essay in the first place.

Notes

1. Paul Arthur in Rascolli, "Essay Film," 39.
2. See the *[In]Transition* website.
3. As Alter has noted, a number of early examples—including Walter Ruttman's *Berlin: Symphony of a Metropolis* (1927) and Hans Richter's *Inflation* (1928)—were funded as "quota films." These films were made to satisfy the required number of national films that had to be shot before foreign films could be imported and distributed, and were often screened before, and thus tied to the popularity of, feature films.
4. Corrigan, *Essay Film*, 4.
5. Alter, *Essay Film after Fact and Fiction*, 7.
6. Ibid., 12.
7. Ibid., 12.
8. Adorno, "Essay as Form," 62–63.
9. Bateman, "Publish or Perish."
10. Horak, "Avant-Garde Cinema," 203.
11. Astruc, "Birth of a New Avant-Garde," 13.
12. Keathley, "La Caméra-stylo," 179.
13. Parker and Parker, *DVD and the Study of Film*, xiii.
14. Mulvey, *Death 24x a Second*, 144.
15. The pseudonym *Kogonada* is a heteronymic tribute to Kōgo Noda, the screenwriting partner of filmmaker Yasujirō Ozu, whose work was the focus of the video essayist's abandoned doctoral dissertation.
16. Keathley, "La Caméra-stylo," 181.
17. Ibid., 183.
18. Kogonada in Erlich, "Supercut Guru Kogonada."

19. She borrows the term from Barbara Klinger, who was writing before the advent of digital technology.
20. Grant, "Auteur Machines?," 103.
21. A video essay that Kogonada made on the Japanese auteur Hirokazu Kore-eda caught the attention of director Chris Weitz, who subsequently became one of the first coproducers of *Columbus*.
22. As discussed in Lee, *What Makes a Video Essay Great?*
23. See Zhou, "Postmortem."
24. Ibid.
25. Foundas, "Los Angeles Plays Itself."
26. Rosenbaum, *Discovering Orson Welles*, 294.
27. Corrigan, *Essay Film*, 181.
28. Ibid., 191.
29. Lee, "Video Essay."
30. Lee acknowledged the greater appeal of Kogonada's approach, noting that while Kogonada's video essays have garnered multiple Vimeo staff picks, his have never gotten any.
31. Fandor CEO Larry Adem in Kaufman, "Fandor Is Moving Toward the Mainstream."
32. Lee, "Critique, Protest, Activism."
33. Lee, "Video Essay."
34. Rascolli, "Essay Film," 34.
35. Corrigan, *Essay Film*, 195.

References

Adorno, Theodor W. "The Essay as Form." In *Essays on the Essay Film*, edited by Nora M. Alter and Timothy Corrigan, 62–63. New York: Columbia University Press, 2017.

Alter, Nora M. *The Essay Film after Fact and Fiction*. New York: Columbia University Press, 2018.

Alter, Nora M., and Timothy Corrigan, eds. *Essays on the Essay Film*. New York: Columbia University Press, 2017.

Anderson, Steve F. "Fair Use and Media Studies in the Digital Age." *Frames Cinema Journal* 1, no. 1 (2012). http://framescinemajournal.com/article/fair-use-and- media-studies-in-the-digital-age/.

Astruc, Alexandre. "The Birth of a New Avant-Garde: La Caméra-Stylo." In *The New Wave*, edited by Peter Graham, 12–23. New York: Doubleday, 1968.

Bateman, Conor. "Publish and Perish: Video Essays in the Age of Social Media." *4:3*, February 20, 2017. https://fourthreefilm.com/2017/02/publish-and-perish-video-essays-in-the-age-of-social-media/.

Corrigan, Timothy. *The Essay Film: From Montaigne, After Marker*. Oxford: Oxford University Press, 2011.

Erlich, David. "Supercut Guru Kogonada: How He Leapt from Small Screens to Sundance NEXT with the Mysterious 'Columbus.'" *IndieWire*, January 18, 2017. https://www.indiewire.com/2017/01/kogonada-columbus-john-cho-haley-lu-richardson-interview-sundance-2017-1201769859/.

Foundas, Scott. "'Los Angeles Plays Itself' A Decade Later." *Variety*, September 23, 2013. http://variety.com/2013/film/news/los-angeles-plays-itself-a-decade-later-1200661848/.

Grant, Catherine. "Auteur Machines? Auteurism and the DVD." In *Film and Television after DVD*, edited by James Bennett and Tom Brown, 101–115. London: Routledge, 2008.

Grant, Catherine, and Christian Keathley. "The Use of an Illusion: Childhood Cinephilia, Object Relations, and Videographic Film Studies." *Photogénie*, June 2014. http://www.photogenie.be/photogenie_blog/article/use-illusion.

Horak, Jan-Christopher. "Early American Avant-Garde Cinema." In *American Film History: Selected Readings, Origins to 1960*, edited by Cynthia Lucia, Roy Grundmann, and Art Simon, 200–214. New York: Wiley, 2015.

[In]Transition. A Media Commons Project with JCMS. Accessed November 24, 2020. http://mediacommons.futureofthebook.org/intransition/.

Kaufman, Anthony. "Fandor Is Moving Toward the Mainstream, and Bracing for the Backlash." *IndieWire*, May 11, 2017. http://www.indiewire.com/2017/05/fandor-mainstream-keyframe-closed-backlash-exclusive-1201815695/.

Keathley, Christian. "*La Caméra-stylo*: Notes on Video Criticism and Cinephilia." In *The Language and Style of Film Criticism*, edited by Alex Clayton and Andrew Klevan, 176–191. London: Routledge, 2012.

Kendrick, James. "What Is the Criterion? The Criterion Collection as an Archive of Film as Culture." *Journal of Film and Video* 53, nos. 2–3 (Summer–Fall 2001): 124–139.

Lee, Kevin B. "Critique, Protest, Activism, and the Video Essay." *NECSUS*, May 28, 2017. https://necsus-ejms.org/critique-protest-activism-and-the-video-essay/.

———. "In Dialogue: Eric Faden and Kevin B. Lee." In *The Videographic Essay: Criticism in Sound and Image*, edited by Christian Keatheley and Jason Mittell. Kino-Agora 9. Montreal: Caboose, 2016.

———. "Video Essay: The Essay Film—Some Thoughts of Discontent." *Sight and Sound*, August 8, 2014. http://www.bfi.org.uk/news-opinion/sight-sound-magazine/features/deep-focus/video-essay-essay-film-some- thoughts.

———. "What Makes a Video Essay Great?" Video Essay Catalog No. 269. Vimeo video, January 15, 2017, 07:06. https://vimeo.com/199577445. Originally published December 28, 2014.

Losilla, Carlos. "The Absent Image, The Invisible Narrative." Frankfurt Papers. The Audiovisual Essay: Practice and Theory of Videographic Film and Moving Image Studies. September 2014. http://reframe.sussex.ac.uk/audiovisualessay/frankfurt-papers/carlos-losilla/.

McWhirter, Andrew. "Film Criticism, Film Scholarship and the Video Essay." *Screen* 56, no. 3 (Autumn 2015): 369–377.

Mulvey, Laura. *Death 24x a Second: Stillness and the Moving Image*. London: Reaktion Books, 2006.

Nichols, Bill. *Representing Reality: Issues and Concepts in Documentary*. Bloomington: Indiana University Press, 1992.

Parker, Mark, and Deborah Parker. *The DVD and the Study of Film: The Attainable Text*. London: Palgrave Macmillan, 2011.

Ramos, Taylor, and Zhou, Tony. "Postmortem: Every Frame a Painting." *Medium*, December 2, 2017. https://medium.com/@tonyszhou/postmortem-1b338537fabc.

Rascolli, Laura. "The Essay Film: Problems, Definitions, Textual Commitments." *Framework* 49, no. 2 (Fall 2008): 24–47.

Rosenbaum, Jonathan. *Discovering Orson Welles*. Berkeley: University of California Press, 2007.

Tracy, Andrew, Ginette Vincendeau, Katy McGahan, Chris Darke, Geoff Andrew, Olaf Möller, Sergio Wolf, Nina Power, and Nick Bradshaw. "Deep Focus: The Essay Film." *Sight and Sound*, August 2013. http://www.bfi.org.uk/news-opinion/sight-sound-magazine/features/deep- focus/essay-film.

Trope, Alison. "Footstool Film School: Home Entertainment as Home Education." In *Inventing Film Studies*, edited by Lee Grieveson and Haidee Wasson, 353–373. Durham, NC: Duke University Press, 2008.

Van Den Berg, Thomas, and Mikloss Kiss. *Film Studies in Motion: From Audiovisual Essay to Academic Research Video*, July 2016. http://scalar.usc.edu/works/film-studies-in-motion/index.
Vertov, Dziga. *Kino-Eye: The Writings of Dziga Vertov*. Berkeley: University of California Press, 1985.
Zhou, Tony. "Postmortem: Every Frame a Painting." *Medium*, December 3, 2017. https://medium.com/@tonyszhou/postmortem-1b338537fabc.
Zoller Seitz, Matt. "Copy Rites: YouTube vs. Kevin B. Lee." *Slant Magazine*, January 13, 2009. https://www.slantmagazine.com/house/article/copy-rites-youtube-vs-kevin-b-lee/.

ALLISON DE FREN is Associate Professor in the Department of Media Arts & Culture at Occidental College. Her audiovisual essays have been published in a variety of online journals and screened internationally.

PART IV.
AUTEURS, POLITICS, AND POPULARITY

This section brings together three essays on auterism, politics, and popularity: two on celebrated auteurs of documentary studies Errol Morris and Laura Poitras and one on the understudied oeuvre of Lauren Greenfield. Jonathan Kahana directs his attention to Morris's post-9/11 War Trilogy, including the hugely successful, Oscar-winning *The Fog of War: Eleven Lessons from the Life of Robert S. McNamara* (2003) and the considerably less popular *Standard Operating Procedure* (2008) and *The Known Unknown* (2013). Kahana tracks the evolution of Morris's signature combination of interview and reenactment to argue that underlying the troubled audience responses to figures from the American military establishment, such as Robert McNamara and Donald Rumsfeld, lies a revealing and powerful erosion of irony as a rhetorical tool of documentary expression. In the dialectical pairing of interview and reenactment that characterizes these films, Kahana develops a model of counterperformativity, provocatively borrowing from Paul de Man a nuanced linguistic calculus for distinguishing among confession, testimony, and "the excuse" across the trilogy.

Next, we turn to Shilyh Warren's "Vérité: Lauren Greenfield and the Challenge of Feminist Documentary," an examination of the work of photographer and documentarist Lauren Greenfield, whose extensive catalog includes decades of monographs, short films, multimedia exhibitions, advertisements, and the feature-length documentaries *Thin* (2006), *Queen of Versailles* (2012), *Generation Wealth* (2018), and *The Kingmaker* (2019). Warren considers the academic neglect of Greenfield's work, asking why—despite her recurrent and persistent exploration of feminist themes and subjects—Greenfield's films appear to be out of step with contemporary theoretical trends at the intersections of feminism, documentary and aesthetics in academic scholarship. Situating Greenfield's popular aesthetic as a form of feminist vérité with slick, mainstream visual elements that resemble reality TV, Warren argues for the value of framing the artist's interest in capitalist consumption, coercion, and excess with respect to the lives of women and girls in American culture. This essay offers an illuminating meditation on "the disconnect between objects and methods" that persists in academic scholarship, particularly in the chasm between women's filmmaking (mainstream and otherwise) and feminist film theory today. Warren deftly reads the critical neglect of Greenfield's work as consistent with the marginalization of popular forms of documentary and feminism compared with privileged documentary practices, canonized feminist auteurs, and what she calls the canonized archive of "correct" feminist counter cinema.

In the final essay of the section, S. Topiary Landberg considers the changing landscape of popular, post-9/11 award-winning documentaries of the last decade, including *Persepolis* (2007), *Waltz with Bashir* (2008), *Standard Operating Procedure* (2008), *Exit through the Gift Shop* (2010), and *Faces Places* (2017), reading a paradigmatic shift across many social-realist, progressive political documentaries toward what she calls an "antirepresentational turn." Concentrating on Laura Poitras's Academy Award–winning documentary, *Citizenfour* (2014), Landberg interprets this antirepresentational ethos as a form of ironic pedagogy that problematizes and reverses prevailing ideas about the politics of representation. As an allegory for the way that the National Security Agency and the American government treats US citizens and the right to access information, *Citizenfour*'s antirepresentational tactics demonstrate the degree to which aesthetics and style can be powerfully connected to theme. Beyond their auteurist frames, what brings these three chapters together is the provocative way their analyses interrogate pathways and roadblocks to the popular, both inside and outside the academy.

10

ERROL MORRIS AND THE ENDS OF IRONY

Jonathan Kahana

Standard Operating Procedure (dir. Errol Morris, 2008) opens with an ironic remark by one of its principal interviewees, Tim Dugan, who looks directly into Morris's camera and says, "I wouldn't recommend a vacation to Iraq any time soon." Irony piles on irony over the course of the film, where, as Morris comments, reenactment was everywhere: in the very detainment of "enemy combatants" at Abu Ghraib, itself an element in the reconstruction of the Iraqi prison system in order to house American detainees during the American occupation; in the "bad apples" restaging of sexual humiliations perpetrated on detainees; and in the subsequent reenactment by US military and diplomatic officials of national humiliations in apologetic public statements in a war already "based on humiliation." In his director commentary on the DVD version of *Standard Operating Procedure*, Errol Morris, who frequently refers to the actions captured in the infamous photographs at Abu Ghraib as "reenactments," calls one of the images an "ironic . . . picture of American foreign policy." Morris's word choice is striking. What do we make of the use of the term *irony* in the work of documentary? Are they merely indices of false meaning or something else? How does ironic speech perform in the genre that is supposed to be filmmaking at its most genuine, at its most serious, and at its most plainspoken? Is there a name for this apparently new form of documentary?

The term *performative documentary* has been in vogue for some time, perhaps starting with the critical reception of Jennie Livingston's documentary about queer ball culture in New York City in the 1980s, *Paris Is Burning*, reference to which seems to mean a documentary that contains human figures who pose, gesture, dance, act, or in some other way make a mildly or overtly theatrical display of themselves so that the viewer becomes at least slightly confused about whether there is any difference between the "character" in whose body a person appears, documented in their filmed image or their recorded sound, and the ontologically embodied, historical person *represented* by that "character"; as in, for example, the description of an interview that has "a highly constructed, performative feel"[1] or the idea that "documentaries are a negotiation between filmmaker and reality and, at heart, a performance."[2] This use of the term comes initially from the language philosophy of J. L. Austin, where *performative* is the name for a special kind of utterance, one with the capacity to both *state* an action and *perform* that action. "We should say," explains Austin in "Performative Utterances," "that in saying what I do, I actually perform that action";[3] although confusing matters somewhat, he writes elsewhere of a distinction between the "performance of an act *in* saying something as opposed to performance of an act *of* saying something."[4] A promise is a statement that, in being stated, makes something happen: a performative utterance could, for instance, be a bet, a pronouncement of marriage, the passing of sentence by a judge, or the conferral of a degree by a university official.[5]

To be absolutely clear about this, I do not think that documentary film and video can make performative utterances in the sense in which Austin intends or in the sense intended by theorists of theater and performance and the film and video theory that depend on these theories of performing in the theatrical sense. I do, however, believe that documentary is capable of something I will call the *counterperformative* and that these sorts of cinematic or videographic utterances have frequently appeared in the film and television work of director Errol Morris. These formulations give voice to an utterance that is not exactly, or not at all, what the subject of speech means by the utterance yet still *recall* a performative utterance. The syntax in Morris's filmmaking has often had the quality of a *counterperformative*—a cinematic utterance that operates like a "doing" as much as, or more than, a "saying," even though its configuration as a statement should militate against it making the kind of sense or having the determinative force to make things happen in reality that we expect from a performative speech act.[6] I mean the "counter" in "counterperformative" to function something like the way that the "counter" in "counterpublic" functions: to invert or negate the positive sense of the term, while still suggesting that if action *can* be a property of a language or medium of speech, the undoing of action can too. This is what, in his writing on irony and excuses, Paul de Man calls a "radical negation" of a statement's agency.[7] Morris has long been intrigued with these odd, self-canceling formulations, and they have figured frequently in his work, as with his observation in the recent telefilm *Wormwood* (2017), where he refers to the state's admission that its use of LSD in the death of an army scientist was "a way for the government to take responsibility and not take responsibility." Counterperformatives are related, in fact, to counterpublics, as we shall see.

I will suggest as well that two of these negative speech acts, the excuse and irony, can also serve as counterperformatives in the rhetoric of documentary film, in ways that inform the meanings of Morris's filmmaking and audience reception of it. Furthermore, and counterintuitively, this undoing effect—where syntax militates against sense—can perhaps be seen at its strongest in one of Morris's least popular and most poorly reviewed films, the "war" film *Standard Operating Procedure* (2008). Here, one might reasonably expect a veteran director like Morris to be considerably more attuned to his public and to have a more sensitive finger on the pulse of an American citizenry several years into an increasingly unpopular and seemingly endless conflict. In his well-funded, highly polished, and widely circulated series of feature releases for commercial theaters—not to mention his successful and prolific sideline in television commercials—we might expect to find that Morris had achieved the apotheosis, not the nadir, of the "popular" documentary film. Among the reasons for this surprising shift in documentary fortunes for Morris, we might count a generalized turn by Morris away from performativity and irony. The second of these was often cited in popular criticism of popular cinema, including documentary, as an effect of the tragedies of September 11, 2001, if not of a broader cultural suspension of the postmodern condition of irony as such, declared dead by *Time* magazine on Monday, September 24, 2001, followed shortly by the purported death of postmodernism itself.[8] In both the linguistic-philosophical (speech acts) and commonsense (theatrical, dramatic, overtly gestural) senses, "performativity" more or less disappeared from Morris's commercial-theatrical documentary releases with his feature-length interview with Donald Rumsfeld, *The Unknown Known*.[9]

This chapter—which develops and expands on an earlier formulation dealing only with *Standard Operating Procedure*—places these developments in the language philosophy of documentary in the larger context of the popular films of Errol Morris and, in particular, a set of commercial nonfiction feature films made by Morris in the decade following the opening of the US multifronted war on terror in the wake of the 2001 terrorist attacks on New York and Washington: *The Fog of War: Eleven Lessons from the Life of Robert S. McNamara* (2003), *Standard Operating Procedure* (2008), and *The Unknown Known* (2013). Morris has, seemingly jokingly, referred to different sets of three of the films he made in this period as one or another kind of "trilogy," and there is some justification for this label: in the timing of these films and their subjects, deeply and increasingly unpopular wars in Southeast Asia, South Asia, and the Persian Gulf, one might see faint outlines of auteurist concepts like the series, or the obsession. And it is true that although they do not all centrally address the same military conflict, each film makes use of forms of historical explanation that have become the director's stock in trade: the interview and dramatic reenactment.

Morris remains, through the aural and visual signatures of his films and television ads, one of the most recognizable and best-known auteurs of contemporary documentary, winning an Academy Award for *The Fog of War*, an honor that some, including Morris himself, considered industrial-commercial validation long overdue. One could argue that a better way to create ties between the films in this decade-long period of work, which includes the poorest-reviewed and, in terms of theatrical box office revenues, least popular of all of the director's feature films, is simply as failures: failures to build and connect with both critical and popular cinema audiences over an ostensible object of mutual revulsion,[10] the authorized and unauthorized military entanglements of the period. This critical and popular failure can be perhaps more precisely ascribed to the serious attention that Morris gives to state speech and, in all three, the director's putatively sympathetic treatment of figures sometimes excoriated as war criminals and widely viewed as self-exculpating apologists for imperial aggression and terror, a sympathy nursed by the decline of irony in the director's work and in its stead the emergence of the counterperformative mode.

Irony

Morris has often employed an ironic voice and syntax in his films, particularly through the "creative treatment" of archival and stock footage and through increasingly redundant stagings of historical incidents in reenacted scenography. Irony does not construct so much as *re*construct meanings,[11] making assertions out of words and phrases that at first appear to mean something different than what they say on their surface. Morris's form of documentary has long seemed one of the most prominent and successful—popular—examples of a perverse, not to say cynical, style of contemporary documentary, one that functions as the "radical negation"[12] of the possibility of factual assertions and truth claims in documentary. *The Thin Blue Line* (1988) is the best example of an ironic approach to documentary in Morris's work, in particular for the reenactments, which, although they allow many sources and witnesses to "say what they mean" in their version of the killing of the police officer for which Randall Dale Adams is wrongfully arrested, tried, and put on death row, never actually re-create an accurate account of the murder. In this way, the reenactments ironize the very truth claim inherent in documentary that usually serves as a "contract" between filmmaker and viewer, incidentally guaranteeing a bond between what is heard in documentary and what is seen.

One can find lessons of this sort on the operation of irony in documentary presented throughout Morris's documentary oeuvre, as with the historically specific examples of Cold War irony that Morris uses as little flourishes on his eleven "lessons" in strategic rhetoric, as modeled by Robert McNamara. A racially inflected instance occurs in *The Fog of War*, at a moment where sound editing, archival footage, and historical anecdote come together in a brief articulation of the Orientalist fear of Asian masses. In an interview, McNamara explains how his and the US Army's zeal for efficiency led to the development of the B-29 bomber, a plane that could fly for long distances at high altitudes, and thus produce high numbers of enemy deaths without much loss of American pilot life. "The airfields [for mid-journey refueling of the B-29] were built with Chinese labor," explains McNamara; "it was an insane operation." Footage, presumably of this "insane operation," shows rows of Chinese workers toiling at the work of breaking individual rocks to surface the runways and isolated sound effects offer a patina of verisimilitude. Over images of the laborers waving to the camera while wearing heavy yokes of stones, McNamara recalls that "I can still remember them hauling these huge rollers to crush the stone to make them flat: a long rope, somebody would slip, the roller would roll over them, everybody'd laugh and go on." If the telling of this cruel story, about which nothing is funny, weren't irony enough, McNamara reveals yet another irony at the end of the anecdote: that the operation was a complete waste of time and was abandoned in favor of another method of shortening the planes' flights. But a more subtle irony of politics here seems to be McNamara's and the film's idea that there is something funny or trivial about life and its loss to "the Asian," a sense of humor evoked in the childish sound effect of the hammer and the grinning, waving archival subjects who were then rolled to death by their countrymen, the larger implication being that in a mass political system *less* democratic than ours, ironies are just foisted on you.

A similar moment of political irony occurs a little later in the film, when it comes around to the question of McNamara's guidance of the Vietnam War. When the film takes up events that led to the Gulf of Tonkin Resolution, which gave the president the unilateral authority to declare war in August

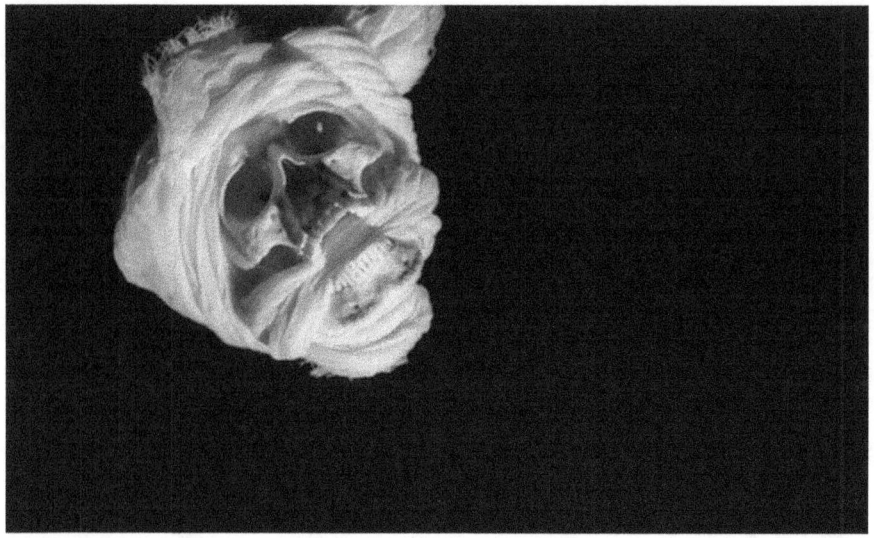

Fig. 10.1 In a reenacted gesture symbolic of the use of irony in Morris's *Fog of War* (2003), Robert McNamara drops a human skull down a stairwell to observe how it breaks.

1964, it again makes use of interview sound, and archival sound and footage to fashion a historical account of the events that took place on August 2, 1964, when the commander and sailors of the USS *Maddox* mistakenly believed that it had been attacked by North Vietnamese torpedoes. Morris titles this chapter of the film "Believing and Seeing Are Both Often Wrong," and he and McNamara agree that "we see what we want to believe." To both men, the turn of phrase—as inimical to the empirical principle of documentary as any statement could be—seems also to contain a buried irony: that in statecraft, foreign or domestic, actions can be authored (as Hannah Arendt said of Nazism) by no one; an erroneous exchange of information, about an exchange of hostilities that didn't take place, can precipitate a political event. Wayne Booth calls this sort of irony—where the irony grows larger than can be contained by its user's initial, merely double intention—*unstable irony*.[13]

In two of Morris's earliest films, *Gates of Heaven* (1978) and *Vernon, Florida* (1981), a flat, contourless voice (affectless in both Bill Nichols's sense, the "voice" of the film, and in the plain sense of voices as sounds on the soundtrack) ironizes the documentary enterprise as such, by intimating, with an audiovisual voice of deadpan frontality, that the odd characters who populate its scenes beggar belief and implicitly asks the viewer to engage in the contract of trust despite evidence on the screen that these people are too strange to be true. In her recent book *Green Documentary: Environmental Documentary in the 21st Century*, Helen Hughes cites an explanation of verbal irony that maintains that an utterance can be understood by a listener to skew ironic when uttered in a "flat or deadpan intonation, slower tempo, lower pitch level, and greater intensity than the corresponding literal utterances and is generally seen as a cue to the speaker's mocking, sneering, or contemptuous attitude."[14] If "intonation" and "utterances" can be broadened to include both visual and sonic (verbal and musical) aspects of a documentary film's overall pattern of what Bill Nichols called its "voice," it is hard not to read these early films as ironizing "straight" documentary,[15] and *The Thin Blue Line* as finding ironies in an already vexed situation of testimony, where the interview is used to peel away the layers of speech in subjective statements in documentary. Rather than finding that "the personal" aspect of a character's speaking self betrays something "realer" than what their words might initially allow, the interview in Morris's later interview-based films becomes a kind of onion: beneath the surface, just more superficial layers, about which "truth" is often the least effective question to ask. In this, Morris can be seen as the continuation of a manner of interview-based filmmaking practiced to perfection by another skeptic of the personal, Emile de Antonio. As Nichols reminded us in his 1983 essay "The Voice of Documentary," de Antonio "does not invariably accept the word of witnesses, nor does he accept the rhetorical strategies . . . that limit historical understanding to the personal." In a de Antonio film, "characters do not emerge as the autonomous shapers of a persona destiny."[16] Citing examples from films by de Antonio and others, Nichols argues that the "voice" of a film of this kind is able to "make witnesses contend with one another to yield a point of view more distinctive to the film than to any of its witnesses (since it includes this very strategy of contention)."[17] Thus, Nichols's "voice" of documentary is implicitly, to some extent, an ironic mode of expression.

Similarly, describing one of the earliest and best examples of an ironic voice in documentary, the narration of Luis Buñuel's 1932 film *Land without Bread*, Bill Nichols characterizes the film as a "documentary" (the quotation marks are Nichols's) that "winks" at its audience: "Ostensibly a condescending, judgmental description of a remote, primitive region of Spain, Las Hurdes, the film piles winks upon winks to signal that Buñuel's target is not this allegedly backward region but the blatantly ethnocentric attitudes adopted toward such regions by their colonizers."[18] Nichols's succinct gloss on *Land without Bread*'s mixed message about the Hurdanos and, by extension, about documentary itself is that the film remains "in possession of a truth the images often confirm, sometimes deny, and that the viewer hesitates to believe," placing the viewer in a "double bind" in which she finally doesn't know whether or not to believe and trust the film: to treat it, in other words, as a documentary.[19] Morris isn't a surrealist, but his anti-realist bent follows in Buñuel's footsteps. Indeed, a most powerfully absurdist version of the documentary interview in Morris's handling of it is the confessional guise of the interview that appears toward the very end of *The Thin Blue Line*, David Harris recounts a highly condensed, pseudo-symptomatic version of his autobiography in which a traumatic childhood is to blame for his violent adulthood. Here, the personal is used as an excuse by Harris in a story meant to explain his violent nature: at the age of three, Harris's older brother fell in a pool and drowned, leading Harris, he supposes, in an explanation for which he himself seems to have no enthusiasm, to have fallen out of favor with his father. ("I guess my dad, I don't know, maybe he couldn't get rid of the responsibility or the guilt or something, I don't know what it was . . . I was there, and maybe I reminded him of that all the time, you know, growing up, and it was hard for me to get any acceptance from him.") Morris uses a similar tactic in another film, *Tabloid* (2010), about another sensational crime that may or may not have occurred, and it could perhaps be said that the closing lines proffered by Harris to Morris about Adams—"Didn't believe him, huh? Criminals always lie"—is not only the final word in the seemingly unsolvable mystery but also the motto of all documentary of a certain postmodern stripe after 1988.

If the soft-sell television spot is the epitome of postmodern irony, Morris is something of a lynchpin between advertising and contemporary documentary. Consider that in addition to his legitimate documentary work, Morris is also a much sought-after director of advertisements for television and web broadcast. He has shot over a thousand commercials for a wide variety of clients.[20] Morris told an interviewer for *Advertising Age* that he "enjoy[ed] thinking about how to put across an idea about branding and marketing."[21] His embrace by and of advertisers is hardly surprising, given the power of branding in his documentary work, from the iconic Burger King milkshake reenactment in *The Thin Blue Line* forward. Morris has described a direct line from his use of reenactments in *The Thin Blue Line* to the appeal, for advertisers, of his style of "visual storytelling,"[22] and their attraction to his distinctive way of conducting interviews "with so-called real people."[23] Some of these advertisements borrow the truth-seeking device of the "Interrotron," Morris's method of directing the gaze of interviewees directly into his camera lens. In these cases, irony takes the form of a degree of emotion inappropriate to a television advertisement—either blasé or exuberant—from the "so-called real" subject of the spot, who resembles one of the ordinary people who appear in some of Morris's films.

Excuses

Another counterperformative trope is favored by Morris in addition to irony. In his documentary and commercial work prior to *The Unknown Known* and *Standard Operating Procedure*, he relies heavily on the excuse. According to de Man, irony is performative because it "consoles and promises" *as* it excuses.[24] Theorists of Morris's work have commented on its force in the (post) modernist documentary. But unlike the tongue-in-cheek reenactments in films where they are used to illustrate scenes or ideas for which no images exist (the "event horizon" of a black hole in *A Brief History of Time* [1992], electricity running through an execution device or the "hanging" of a bag of sand in *Mr. Death: The Rise and Fall of Fred A. Leuchter, Jr.* [1999]), the duplicative reenactments in *Standard Operating Procedure* reiterate events for which ample photographic evidence exists. The ironic tone of both the reenactments and Morris's own questions is significantly diminished by comparison with his earlier films: here, they appear repetitive and redundant rather than reflexive or ironic.

Like most of the major American pans of *Standard Operating Procedure*, J. Hoberman's review in *The Village Voice*—under the headline "Errol Morris Lets Torturers Off Easy"—preoccupied itself with Morris's "obtrusive mannerism."[25] The aesthetic premise of these critiques—that in making a documentary with the industrial and stylistic resources of commercial entertainment cinema, Morris violated a law of genre separating documentary from other forms of screen culture—was accompanied by a kind of moral formalism, the suggestion that what Richard Schickel referred to as the film's "production values" were the moral equivalent of the ethical and legal transgressions of its subjects.[26] In her *New York Times* review, Manohla Dargis was especially scornful of Morris's apparent embrace of Hollywood style and production methods, referring to the film as a "blockbuster" and a "costly-looking production" requiring the services of a "costume designer, a wardrobe stylist, six hair and makeup people, an action consultant, an armorer, 5 set dressers, 7 animal handlers, 10 prop makers, 33 cast members and Danny Elfman, the longtime composer for Tim Burton." Dargis concluded her review with particular attention to Morris's use, since *The Thin Blue Line*, of reenactments shot in the manner of dramatic fiction:

> But nothing he has done previously approaches the level of fetishistic detail he achieves here, whether he's showing us beautifully backlighted dust motes dancing in the prison air or an exquisitely photographed pearl of blood dangling from a brutalized prisoner's, or rather actor's, nose. The close-ups of the snarling, barking guard dogs summon memories of Stephen King's "Cujo," which makes

Fig. 10.2 "It was Charlie Foxtrot without a doubt." Civilian interrogator Tim Dugan sets the stage for Abu Ghraib and American military morale in *Standard Operating Procedure* (2008).

sense, given that Mr. Morris's epistemological quest has led him to reimagine Abu Ghraib in the vernacular of a cheap Hollywood horror flick. If nothing else, the dogs and their trainers serve as a reminder that Mr. Morris is, in his own singular fashion, very much in the entertainment business.[27]

In highlighting Morris's use of *photogenie*, however, these reviews did the film a certain poetic justice, even as they helped discourage audiences from seeing it in theaters. Compared with *The Thin Blue Line* and *The Fog of War*, two of Morris's more successful theatrical releases, *Standard Operating Procedure*, its "blockbuster" methods notwithstanding, did poorly at the box office, taking in $324,217 from its worldwide release. *The Unknown Known* did even worse, with a worldwide theatrical gross barely above $300,000.[28] Taking seriously its juridical poetics, we ought to first consider what it means that *Standard Operating Procedure* not only allows convicted criminals and agents of the brutal American occupation of Iraq to speak in their own voices but also to do so without contradiction by their victims; academic or journalistic experts on the war, the military, or the region; or the editorial voice of a narrator. This directorial choice provides a sympathetic context for their testimony, giving the subjects' complaints, fears, and reasons for acting in seemingly inhuman ways emotional and intellectual credence—even, one could say, honoring and dignifying the speakers and their words by turning them into the stuff of low or high cinematic art. On this aspect of style, Dargis is correct: the lavish reenactments recall, depending on one's frame of reference, torture porn or the beatific museum installations of Bill Viola. Against itself, I argue, *Standard Operating Procedure* employs the counterperformative excuse.

The trope is announced from the very beginning of the film, which opens with remarks by one of the ostensibly critical observers among the film's small cast of characters, Tim Dugan, a civilian interrogator employed at Abu Ghraib by the CACI corporation. Dugan's psychologistic opening remarks invite the viewer to hear the testimony that will follow as evidence of a traumatic situation; as an overture or epigraph, his remarks establish that not only the historical and autobiographical statements that follow but also the textual "voice" of the documentary itself will function as an excuse for the actions depicted and described.[29] Dugan begins in medias res, and the part of his interview that we hear first is—uncharacteristic, for a Morris film— truncated so that it sounds quite clearly like the response to a question rather than a self-contained statement.

Although we can guess what Dugan means by *it*, in the phrases "it was Charlie Foxtrot, without a doubt . . . I'd never seen anything like it"—and I think that the point is precisely that we know quite well already to what *it* refers—the initial obscurity of the referent literally begs the question while highlighting the absent cause, or provocation, of Dugan's memory. The reflections that follow—"I never thought I'd ever see American soldiers so depressed and morale so low" and "You gotta consider yourself dead, and . . . if you're there and you consider yourself already dead, you can do all the shit you have to do"—prefigure the Abu Ghraib veterans in the rest of the film as survivors of a traumatic experience, and prepare the viewer to hear their voices as evidence of their experience of a state in which agency and action are separated from will and consciousness. Both of Dugan's rueful expressions of belatedness frame the film to come as a paradox: either too late to solve the mystery represented by the photographs or able to explain it only if the photographs and soldiers' voices are treated as evidence of what in the United States is called a "preexisting condition," one that well predates the production of the Abu Ghraib torture scenes or the enlistment of the Reservists of the 372nd Military Police Company, back to the national-popular use made of trauma theory in the wake of the September 11 attacks and before that to the psychic history of American military operations in Vietnam and other conflicts. In each of these crises, documentary cinema has played a role in establishing an excuse for violence.

Once thought of only as an individual affliction, one that was an exclusive concern of medicine and psychiatry, trauma is now used by many disciplines, as well as in the popular imagination, to name a collective condition, so pervasive as to function at times like a historical periodization. Medical anthropologists Didier Fassin and Richard Rechtman declare trauma "the universal language of a new politics of the intolerable,"[30] and although the "new" discursive event to which they refer is the acceptance of post-traumatic stress disorder in 1980 by the American Psychiatric Association, this historical paradigm could also describe the past decade in our discipline, which seems to agree that trauma is a fundamental concept for understanding screen culture since September 11, 2001.[31]

Take for example the framing gesture of Julia Lesage's sixty-page *Jump Cut* essay on "Torture Documentaries," where Lesage declares that the "traumatic event" of the "U.S. involvement in torture" is "*the* issue of our time, especially in the United States." Before an official or authoritative history of the torture era is written, Lesage claims, documentary films will establish the outlines of a public sphere of debate about this state-authored "catastrophe."[32] In a climate of official silence, sophistry, and legal subterfuge from their government about its embrace of torture, good Americans, Lesage suggests, will learn not only the truth from PBS's *Frontline*, or from films like *Ghosts of Abu Ghraib* (dir. Rory Kennedy, 2007), *Taxi to the Dark Side* (dir. Alex Gibney, 2008), and *Standard Operating Procedure* but also from such films how to "face" this truth. Such descriptions of a decade-long crisis, with its own audiovisual symptomatology, configure a national-popular condition of trauma, a state in which the condition of being a good American flows directly from the production or consumption of documentary images of international violence. *Standard Operating Procedure* certainly *entertains* this idea of a traumatic *episteme* of documentary. But I think the film also offers, or at least evokes, a quite different historicization of trauma, of torture, and of the relation of both to truth, as we use the term in documentary studies, somewhat obsessively and somewhat unthinkingly. The prevalence of the rhetoric of the excuse, as counterperformative, throughout the film, is in keeping with this premise.

The harshest reviews of *Standard Operating Procedure* took issue with the use of film style in the reenactments, and tended to separate out the reenactments from the rest of the film; even when critics remarked (in negative ways) on the interviews, their objection was to the postproduction treatment of them. But the (redundant) relation of the reenactments to the (quite frequently reiterative) content of the interviews is key to the film's aims, and to distinguishing these aims from those of the other films in which many of the same characters appear. By contrast with Morris's work since *The Thin Blue Line*, these reenactments frequently recall what we have already heard on another track of the film, serving only to amplify, exaggerate, or aestheticize facts or ideas delivered as testimony. In this way, various forms of narration in the film create a self-enclosed economy of discourse about torture at Abu Ghraib, a system within which the statements of the accused have the effect not of confessions but of excuses. To restate my thesis as a question: what is it about Morris's subjects and the encounter with bureaucratic state speech that prompts this tropological shift in his dramatic signature, from irony to the excuse?

The excuse is a particular kind of speech act, one that—unlike the confession—makes no reference to external conditions or measures of truth, or, more precisely, carries with it its environment of authenticity. "To confess," writes de Man, "is to overcome guilt and shame in the name of truth."[33] The confession appeals to its listener to hear the confession as a pathbreaking statement of the way things are or the way they happened, one that sets the record straight, or overcomes a self-deception. The most important aspect of the excuse, on the other hand, is not its (absolute) truth claim, but its (relative) ethical claim, since every excuse says "I had good reason to do the thing which to you seems wrong." The excuse is thus the more radical speech act: although the confession attests to a change (of heart) in its speaker, it does so in reference to social standards—reality, the good, the past—which are shared by speaker and listener. The excuse, on the other hand, invites the listener to reconsider both historical and ethical givens and standards; to entertain *another* explanation of what happened and what it means now.

And since, as de Man observes, the excuse "states a suspicion . . . that might lead to an impossibility to know,"[34] interviews that perform excuses in the guise of confessions have been important to the development of a kind of radical history in documentary. Testimony and confession have, of course, a long history of use as settings for documentary speech, one that extends back well beyond Morris's use of these performance situations. In the United States, these two tendencies were amply displayed in political documentary of the late 1960s and 1970s, when, borrowing tactics of consciousness-raising and "coming out" from the feminist and gay and lesbian movements and their counterparts in documentary, films like *Interviews with My Lai Veterans* (dir. Joseph Strick, 1970) and *Winter Soldier* (dir. Winterfilm Collective, 1972), gathered together American veterans of the war in Vietnam, and gave them the opportunity to admit to the torture, rape, and murder of prisoners and civilians, a series of horrifying performances whose aim was twofold: to provide vivid, firsthand support for the moral case against the war, and to corroborate arguments made by veterans' groups that veterans were suffering from the effects of what they had seen and done even after returning home.

More distant in time, but perhaps closer in method to *Standard Operating Procedure* is an older film about soldiers as victims, John Huston's 1946 Army Signal Corps film about the treatment of war neuroses, *Let There Be Light*. Like *Standard Operating Procedure*, *Let There Be Light* makes use of both interviews and reenactments and establishes an equally hermetic world; as with Morris's film, *Let There Be Light* uses the combination of staged interviews and dramatic sequences to suggest that if the actions and affects of traumatized soldiers were abnormal, they could be made sensible to the ordinary moviegoer in the terms of mainstream fiction cinema, giving the semiotics of trauma the currency of a national-popular cultural form. And there is nothing ironic in these previous films' use of the subject of trauma.

This barbaric history of scientific theater is summoned throughout *Standard Operating Procedure*, but perhaps most unnervingly when the film examines the infamous "Man on the Box" image, a sequence in which Sabrina Harman and Megan Ambuhl explain how the alleged torture of a detainee nicknamed "Gilligan" by the guards was, in Harman's words, "just words." Here again, underscored by the cruel pun on "justice," *Standard Operating Procedure* displays its awareness that the speech act is undone by counterperformativity. Harman and Ambuhl insist that the charade of electrification was "necessary" but also harmless, since no current ran through the electrical wires, and that there were so few hard feelings between torturers and victim that "Gilligan" became a kind of "buddy" of the soldiers, given pleasant work that he enjoyed doing, an explanation which is an exemplary case of the confession that functions as an excuse. Although the women ostensibly reveal unknown, even self-indicting, truths about the ugly images—more than one photograph was taken of the abuse; the victim was in no danger; he was found innocent of any crime; later, everyone became friends, which allowed the soldiers to exploit "Gilligan" further—these admissions are also meant to absolve the women telling the story of blame for what the viewer *thinks* she sees, a strategy of exculpation operated both verbally and performatively, down to Harman's appropriately inappropriate laughter about the incident, as if narrating it into the camera brings up mixed and unfamiliar (which is to say spontaneous, or sincere) emotions. The reenactment that illustrates the story has two functions. Its obvious function is to point out the fictional aspect of the witnesses' confessions and excuses by suggesting a parallel between these autobiographical fictions and the cinematic re-presentation of certain details of the historical incident, itself a cruel theatrical fiction enacted upon a naive and reluctant member of its cast, a man who plays a character with a variety of names: the "Hooded Man," the "Man on the Box," "Gilligan," "Ali Shalal

Qaissi," "Abdou Hussain Saad Faleh." Only a couple of these names are spoken in the film, but Morris knows and uses all of them elsewhere.[35] Since the "Gilligan" incident, and the mystery of the true identity of the man under the hood were, as Morris has said, the impetus for the film, it would seem reasonable to assume that the highly stylized, even cliché, use of cinematic technique in the reenactment—slow motion, for instance, or the score's references to Barber's "Adagio for Strings," or the Mickey Mouse–like foley effects—is intended to provoke the questions: what is the true source of this image which "everyone" has already seen "everywhere"? And how do we "unmask" it?: versions, we might say, of Buñuel's enduring question (from *Land without Bread*), "why is this absurd picture here? Apparently, as the film has shown us, it isn't enough to ask directly those who created it, since, as we hear, they will answer with a confession that is also an excuse.[36] The operative paradox of this dialectical pairing of interview and reenactment is that cinema is not the best medium to teach us how to see behind mass-produced images, even though it constantly promises to teach us how to see what is all-too-familiar in new ways.

Like many films in the cycle of American documentaries about the Iraq war and the war on terror, the dark tone of *Standard Operating Procedure* is a crude measure of its politics, which are, generally speaking, a politics of radical distrust: distrust in officially stated national prerogatives and distrust in official explanations of the means by which such plans can be judged necessary or effective. And like many documentaries made in a climate of suspicion, *Standard Operating Procedure* begins from a kind of confessional impulse toward the problem of darkness, seeking to establish what de Man calls "the clarified atmosphere of a truth that does not hesitate to reveal the crime in all its horror."[37] But de Man also says of the excuse that it "ruins the seriousness of any confessional discourse by making it self-destructive,"[38] and *Standard Operating Procedure*, likewise, constantly refuses (or fails) to put documentary evidence—whether speech, footage, or photography—on display in a way that could be judged "more true" or more serious than those sounds and images in the film which seem to make it unserious entertainment. When Robert Sklar writes, in his *Cineaste* review of *Standard Operating Procedure*, that Morris's interview with Brigadier General Janis Karpinski "brings human energy to a film that otherwise seems to concoct its excitement artificially," he gets to the heart of the distress that the film causes many viewers, although I think the point works even better when stated in reverse: *because Standard Operating Procedure* embraces artifice and the cinematic tools of excitation, it is capable of explaining how cinema generates "human energy."[39] In this way, *Standard Operating Procedure* illustrates how easily entertainment and punishment are integrated in the documentary; which is, after all, one of the worst things one can say about the Abu Ghraib photographs themselves.

Perhaps unsurprisingly, then—for it seems the film in the "war trilogy" least informed by a sense of irony—*The Unknown Known* more or less dispenses with reenactment. Apart from the historical irony with which a number of former presidential advisors, including Rumsfeld, return to the White House under Bush's son, Morris treats very little of what Rumsfeld says during his interview as ironic, despite his contention, in the film and elsewhere, that Rumsfeld is just as much of an unreliable narrator as the main characters in Morris's previous films. Indeed, most of the reconstructions of history in *The Unknown Known* are achieved without reenactment, and instead with the use of Rumsfeld's "memory" in the interview and with footage from other media appearances by Rumsfeld, where his memory of previous situations or statements is demonstrated to be lacking.

At just the moment that American film culture decided that the disappearance of irony from public discourse amplified the public appetite for documentary (and what Nichols has called its "sobriety"), Morris has seemed headed in the opposite direction. To what can we attribute this "linguistic turn" in the three feature documentary films Morris produces in the long wake of September 11, *The Fog of War*, *Standard Operating Procedure*, and the "endlessly frustrating" thirty-three-hour interview with Rumsfeld, *The Unknown Known* (2013)?[40] For one thing, all seem burdened by the second Bush administration's abuse of truth in state speech, which, judging by the evidence of the recent *Wormwood*, Morris views as the return of a recurring problem in modern presidential administrations. Shortly after the release of *The Unknown Known*, Morris told a reporter, "I could give up the interviewing thing. I'm tired of it, I really am tired of it."[41] It's not a coincidence that this feeling of exhaustion comes for Morris at the end of a decade of conflict: between the United States and its adversaries in the seemingly endless War on Terror and between the speaking subject of the state and an American media public seemingly unfazed by years of attacks at the highest level of government on truth and "discernible reality."[42] Whether such attacks and the numbing Twitter feed of certainties about national insecurity that issue daily from the White House spell the end of documentary irony for Morris remains to be seen. They have at least changed the ends to which irony has seemed for so long to be profitable and useful to him and made him one of the most distinctive voices in American documentary.

Notes

1. Anderson, "Past in *Ruins*," 83.
2. Ellis, *Documentary*, 45–46.
3. Austin, "Performative Utterances," 235.
4. Austin, *How to Do Things*, 99.
5. Austin, "Performative Utterances," 235. See also Ward, "Drama-Documentary."
6. What Butler calls "cinematic performativity" in her analysis of *Paris Is Burning* can bring one of the film's characters "back, as it were, into visibility, although not to life." See *Bodies That Matter*, 133.
7. On *radical negation*, see note 11 of this chapter. On *counterpublic*, see Warner, *Publics and Counterpublics*, 118–119.
8. See for example Didion, *Fixed Ideas*, 11.
9. The use of actors and "stagy" reenactments makes a return in his 2017 docudramatic miniseries for the Netflix streaming service, *Wormwood*. The brief reappearance of Donald Rumsfeld in that series, as one of the Ford-administration officials who pushed to cover up the CIA's involvement in the suicide of a military scientist twenty years before, is less a historical irony than a sad commentary on the continuities of dynastic power in American government.
10. On the effect of revulsion, see Nichols, "Letter to Errol Morris," 181–190.
11. See Booth, *Rhetoric of Irony*, 6.
12. "A more radical negation than one would have in an ordinary trope such as synecdoche or metaphor or metonymy" is one of the ways that Paul de Man defines *irony*. See "Concept of Irony," 165. In the chapter titled "Irony, Paradox, and the Documentary: Double Meanings and Double Binds" in his book *Speaking Truths with Film*, Nichols writes, similarly, that "irony and paradox typically arise from the statement of one thing and the negation of that same statement figuratively." See Nichols, *Speaking Truths*, 166.
13. Booth, *Rhetoric of Irony*.
14. Hughes, *Green Documentary*, 100–101.
15. Nichols, "Voice of Documentary," 639–641.
16. Ibid., 647.
17. Ibid., 646.
18. Nichols, "Irony, Paradox," 168.
19. Nichols suggests that the lurid recent film about mass murders committed by the Indonesian state and paramilitaries acting as its agents, *The Act of Killing* (2012), has supplanted *Land without Bread* as the cardinal example of irony in documentary (Nichols, *Speaking Truths*, 175).
20. See Nudd, "Errol Morris Reflects." A number of spots directed by Morris are viewable at his personal website, errolmorris.com.
21. Nudd, "Errol Morris Reflects."
22. Ibid.
23. Ibid.
24. Man, "Concept of Irony," 165.
25. Hoberman, "Errol Morris."
26. Schickel, "*Standard Operating Procedure*."
27. Dargis, "We, the People behind the Abuse."
28. The box office figures are taken from BoxOfficeMojo.com.
29. Nichols, "Voice of Documentary," 639–641.
30. Fassin and Rechtman, *Empire of Trauma*, 93.

31. See, for instance, Prince, *Firestorm*; Wegner, *US Culture in the Long Nineties*; Kaplan and Wang, *Trauma and Cinema*; and the introduction to Walker.
32. Lesage, "Torture Documentaries."
33. Man, "Excuses (*Confessions*)."
34. Ibid., 280.
35. See Morris, "Will the Real Hooded Man."
36. In this respect, I am in agreement with Nichols, when he writes that what we hear from the guards is "not confession, contrition, and the assumption of full responsibility . . . but tales of rationalization, victimization, and denial": in other words, excuses. See Nichols, "Letter to Errol Morris," 183.
37. Man, "Excuses (*Confessions*)," 279.
38. Ibid., 280.
39. Sklar, Review of *Taxi*, 52.
40. Nicholson, "Point for Rumsfeld."
41. Ibid.
42. The felicitous phrase *discernible reality* is taken from remarks by an aide of President George W. Bush to journalist Ron Susskind for an infamous article about the Bush administration written for *New York Times Magazine*. See Susskind, "Faith, Certainty, and Presidency."

References

Anderson, Steve F. "The Past in *Ruins*: Postmodern Politics and the Fake History Film." In *F Is for Phony: Fake Documentary and Truth's Undoing*, edited by Alexandra Juhasz and Jesse Lerner, 76–87. Minneapolis: University of Minnesota Press, 2006.
Austin, J. L. *How to Do Things with Words*. Cambridge: Harvard University Press, 1962.
———. "Performative Utterances." In *Philosophical Papers*, edited by J. O. Urmson and G. J. Warnock, 233–252. Oxford: Oxford University Press, 1961.
Booth, Wayne. *A Rhetoric of Irony*. Chicago: University of Chicago Press, 1974.
Bruzzi, Stella. *New Documentary*. 2nd ed. London: Routledge, 2006.
Butler, Judith. *Bodies That Matter: On the Discursive Limits of "Sex."* New York: Routledge, 1993.
Dargis, Manohla. "We, the People behind the Abuse." *New York Times*, May 2, 2008.
Didion, Joan. *Fixed Ideas: America Since 9.11*. New York: New York Review of Books, 2003.
Ellis, John. *Documentary: Witness and Self-Revelation*. Milton Park, UK: Routledge, 2012.
Fassin, Didier, and Richard Rechtman. *The Empire of Trauma: An Inquiry into the Condition of Victimhood*. Translated by Rachel Gomme. Princeton, NJ: Princeton University Press, 2009.
Hoberman, J. "Errol Morris Lets Torturers Off Easy." *Village Voice*, April 22, 2008.
Hughes, Helen. *Green Documentary: Environmental Documentary in the 21st Century*. Bristol, UK: Intellect, 2014.
Kaplan, Ann E., and Ban Wang, eds. *Trauma and Cinema: Cross-Cultural Explorations*. Hong Kong: Hong Kong University Press, 2004.
Lesage, Julia. "Torture Documentaries." *Jump Cut: A Review of Contemporary Media* 51. http://ejumpcut.org/currentissue/index.html.
Man, Paul de. "The Concept of Irony." In *Aesthetic Ideology*, edited by Andrez Warminski, 163–184. Minneapolis: University of Minnesota Press, 1996.

———. "Excuses (*Confessions*)." In *Allegories of Reading: Figural Language in Nietzsche, Rilke, and Proust*, 278–301. New Haven, CT: Yale University Press, 1979.
Morris, Errol, dir. *Standard Operating Procedure*. Culver City, CA: Sony Pictures Home Entertainment, 2008. DVD.
———, dir. *Wormwood*. Los Gatos, CA: Netflix, Inc., 2017. Streaming.
Morris, Errol. "Will the Real Hooded Man Please Stand Up." Opinionator, *New York Times*, August 15, 2007. http://opinionator.blogs.nytimes.com/2007/08/15/will-the-real-hooded-man-please-stand-up/.
Nichols, Bill. *Blurred Boundaries: Questions of Meaning in Contemporary Culture*. Bloomington: Indiana University Press, 1994.
———. *Introduction to Documentary*. 3rd ed. Bloomington: Indiana University Press, 2017.
———. "Irony, Paradox, and the Documentary: Double Meanings and Double Binds." In *Speaking Truths with Film: Evidence, Ethics, Politics in Documentary*, 164–180. Berkeley: University of California Press, 2016.
———. "Letter to Errol Morris: Feelings of Revulsion and the Limits of Academic Discourse." In *Speaking Truths with Film: Evidence, Ethics, Politics in Documentary*, 181–190. Berkeley: University of California Press, 2016.
———. *Speaking Truths with Film: Evidence, Ethics, Politics in Documentary*. Berkeley: University of California Press, 2016.
———. "The Voice of Documentary." In *The Documentary Film Reader*, edited by Jonathan Kahana, 639–641. New York: Oxford University Press, 2016.
Nicholson, Amy. "Point for Rumsfeld: Errol Morris Tells Us He's Tired of Interviewing People." *Village Voice*, April 2, 2014. https://www.villagevoice.com/2014/04/02/point-for-rumsfeld-errol-morris-tells-us-hes-tired-of-interviewing-people/.
Nudd, Jim. "Errol Morris Reflects on Apple, Miller High Life and Other Great Commercials He's Made." *Adweek*, August 3, 2017. https://www.adweek.com/creativity/errol-morris-reflects-on-the-great-ads-hes-made-and-wants-to-make-more/5/.
Prince, Stephen. *Firestorm: American Film in the Age of Terrorism*. New York: Columbia University Press, 2009.
Schickel, Richard. "*Standard Operating Procedure*: Too Much Style?" *Time*, April 24, 2008.
Sklar, Robert. Review of *Taxi to the Dark Side/Standard Operating Procedure*. *Cineaste* 33, no. 3 (Summer 2008): 50–52.
Susskind, Ron. "Faith, Certainty, and Presidency of George W. Bush." *New York Times Magazine*, October 17, 2004.
Walker, Janet. *Trauma Cinema: Documenting Incest and the Holocaust*. Berkeley: University of California Press, 2005.
Ward, Paul. "Drama-Documentary, Ethics and Notions of Performance: The 'Flight 93' Films." In *Rethinking Documentary: New Perspectives, New Practices*, edited by Thomas Austin and Wilma de Jong, 191–203. New York: McGraw-Hill, 2008.
Warner, Michael. *Publics and Counterpublics*. New York: Zone Books, 2002.
Wegner, Philip. *Life between Two Deaths, 1989–2001: US Culture in the Long Nineties*. Durham, NC: Duke University Press, 2009.

JONATHAN KAHANA was Associate Professor of Film and Digital Media at the University of California, Santa Cruz. He is author of *Intelligence Work: The Politics of American Documentary* and editor of *The Documentary Film Reader*.

11

VÉRITÉ

Lauren Greenfield and the Challenge of Feminist Documentary

Shilyh Warren

For the past two and a half decades, photographer and filmmaker Lauren Greenfield has become one of the most astute reporters on the vulgarity and ecstasy of the American dream, particularly as it affects the psychic and material lives of women. Greenfield and her still and moving cameras have peered into the intimate spaces of youth culture, gender performance, wealth, and consumerism. There she finds women and girls mercilessly shaped by the pressures of a materialist culture obsessed with living in the extreme. Her extensive catalog of work includes several monographs, multimedia exhibitions, short films, and four feature-length documentaries, *Thin* (2006), *Queen of Versailles* (2012), *Generation Wealth* (2018), and *The Kingmaker* (2019). *Queen of Versailles* and *Generation Wealth* enjoyed theatrical releases, a rare feat for documentary films, for films by women filmmakers, and doubly so for documentaries by women filmmakers.

Despite her commercial and critical success, Greenfield—like other popular women documentarians—has been almost completely ignored by both documentary and feminist scholars. Given her sustained focus on gender, transnationalism, consumerism, capitalism, and race, this lacuna seems surprising. Very few women directors have achieved the career success that Greenfield has attained, fewer still whose work centers on issues of gender, class, and race. Yet scholarly attention to her work is practically nonexistent. Why? The claim I make here is that Greenfield's successful career has developed in tension with the anticapitalist and antirealist commitments of both feminist theory and documentary scholarship, which have been slow to develop analytical practices commensurate with what I'm calling the "feminist vérité" evident in Greenfield's films. Hailed by critics as her signature style, vérité paradoxically begins to explain both her success in the marketplace and her neglect by feminist scholars.

Neither documentary studies nor feminist film studies have paid very much attention to the contemporary success of popular women documentarians such as Greenfield, Amy Berg, Lucy Walker, Heidi Ewing, Rachel Grady, Gabriela Cowperthwaite, and others. Historically, women have made greater inroads and represent a larger percentage of directors in the world of documentary than in popular features. However, the distance between women filmmakers and academic scholarship in documentary and feminist studies has narrowed little over the past few decades. In the case of popular feminist documentary especially, the accessibility and marketability of vérité make it suspect to feminist film studies. In contrast, I argue that in Greenfield's films, we see a crucial example of feminist politics and popular form. Although she downplays the feminist politics of her work, Greenfield's obsession with whiteness girls and women, mothers and daughters, and the material imperatives of the American dream has produced a critical and fascinating archive of popular documentary feminism that pressures the enduring questions of women's documentary filmmaking: questions about how and why gender matters and interrelates with other axes of oppression, how to negotiate the ethics of representation, how to read the relationship between form and content, and how to evaluate the desire to catalyze revolutionary thinking, feeling, and action.

Intimate Reality in *Thin*

Thin (HBO, 2006) opens with severe white letters on a black screen: "Eating disorders affect an estimated five million people in the United States. As many as one in seven women with anorexia will die from the illness." Didactic marshaling of empirical evidence, however, is not the primary aim of this harrowing documentary. Rather, *Thin* also enacts a feminist mode of inquiry and analysis, gathering a chorus of women's voices and bodies to share deeply personal struggles with body image and mental illness at a residential treatment center in South Florida. The opening sequence transitions from an exterior shot of a dark building to an interior world of harsh fluorescent lights: as viewers, we are also invited in from outside, into the core of trauma, invasive care, and struggle with survival that women experience inside. Over the course of the documentary, we follow four women through treatment and recovery journeys that are in turn tragic and inspirational,

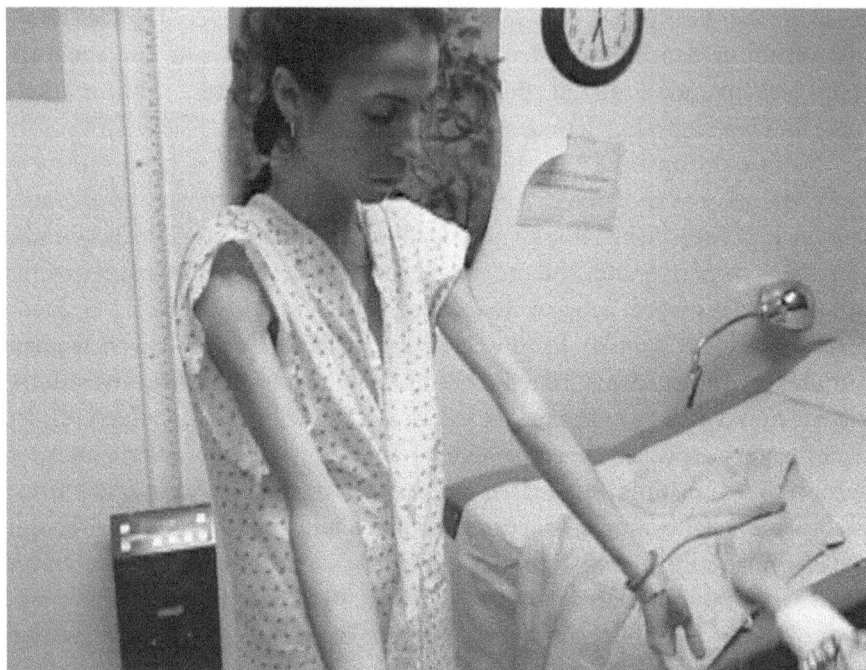

Fig. 11.1 Daily inspections survey the bodies of women for vitals and evidence of self-harm in *Thin* (2006).

hopeful and wearying. *Thin* confronts viewers with a familiar and also extreme example of the way women both conform to and resist narratives about the currency and value of female embodiment. The captivating documentary is a distressing portrait of a flawed, profit-driven institution, a cultural disease, and four women caught in the sticky trap of a culture obsessed with women's bodies.

As Greenfield tells it, her work has consistently been driven by a desire to document the way that capitalism shapes identity, both for those clamoring at the margins of the global economy as well as those who loll around in plush luxury at its center. She rightly notes that capitalism seeks to make loyal and vulnerable customers of us all, often by preying on the cultivated insecurities of girls and women. And as much as capitalism drives the obsessions and desires of young women, in *Thin*, Greenfield suggests that the brutal economies of health insurance and pharmaceuticals also interrupt the progress of their treatment. In other words, *Thin* is as much about the suffering of young mentally ill women as it is about the voracious cycles of capitalism that produce and maintain gender inequity and gendered vulnerabilities more broadly.

That *Thin*—a feminist critique of media, healthcare, and capital—should find itself comfortably in the mainstream on HBO, a premier cable channel, also tells us that Greenfield's debut documentary adheres to expectations of the mainstream audience and mainstream curators, particularly in terms of its style. Greenfield's combination of observational filmmaking, interviews, and fast-paced, glossy camerawork places her in the unique position of being both feminist and popular, mainstream and radical.

At the Renfrew Habilitation Center, women with life-threatening eating disorders are treated by nutritionists, therapists, and pharmacists. The narrative arc of the documentary begins at the crack of dawn when nurses wake women in order to weigh them, check their vitals, and ask questions about their physical and emotional health. Throughout these sessions, the women's bodies are hauntingly similar, each thin woman bracing herself against the morning cold. The film crew remains at a remove, recording the scene in an unobtrusive and observational manner. However, the intimacy of the process, and the knowledge we gain about the appearance, risk, and vulnerability of these women, establishes a compassionate closeness with each subject. Squeezed into the small space of the examination room with the film crew and the filmed subjects, we sense spatially that we are being let in on the inside of a secret—the public secret of starving women's bodies. This opening sequence closes with a visual analog to onomatopoeia that registers thinness in the faintest font for the film's title: THIN.

In the scenes that follow, we are introduced to four main characters—Shelly, Polly, Brittany, and Alisa. Ranging in age, life experiences, class, and education, these four white women will become painfully familiar to us as the film crew records them in group, individual, and family therapy. Observational footage captures the women eating, playing, gossiping, smoking, breaking rules, and coming to terms with the severity of their obsessions. Interspersed with this footage are interviews with each woman, and occasionally *Thin* includes textual details about the histories and potential futures of the women. These techniques, and especially the combination of vérité and interviews, converge within the popular framework of televisual documentaries pioneered by HBO.

Greenfield originally explored this subject in *Girl Culture*, the photographic project that inspired her to make *Thin*. Pitched as part gallery exhibit and part educational installation, the photographs that comprised *Girl Culture* brought Greenfield into a national conversation about gender, body image, and documentary, eventually landing the young filmmaker at HBO, where veteran producers R. J. Cutler and Sheila Nevins nurtured Greenfield's ambition. A hotbed of televised documentary in the late 1990s and early 2000s, HBO's twin interests in educational and sensational nonfiction projects found their match in Greenfield's politically conscious and stylistically mainstream work. HBO produced *Thin* in the early 2000s, when the cable network was building its documentary credibility. Drawing from the success of reality TV, the network hoped to reach its more educated audience with "sensational" material that nonetheless carried the weight and currency of socially conscious documentary. HBO began establishing its cable credibility as a producer of documentary content in the late 1990s, under Nevins's leadership. Nevins used the financial leverage of the successful company to attract acclaimed independent filmmakers, such as Barbara Kopple, Alan and Susan Raymond, Albert Maysles, Jon Alpert, and Lee Grant, generating a profile of HBO as a "quality" cable network.[1] *Thin* fits this profile well. At times, the film lingers uncomfortably on the more sensational aspects of eating disorders: the skeletal bodies of the women, the shocking numbers on their scales, their attempts to control and purge food. Individual and group therapy sessions overflow with tears and accusations. Family meetings reveal trauma and shame. Even the film's interspersed interviews sometimes drum up gossip and innuendo "behind the scenes," drawing from the formula of reality TV. Sly editing decisions (the juxtaposition of patients and nurses all talking about diets) and cutaways (to pharmaceutical ads, for example) implicate the institution and the medical-industrial complex in our disordered gender culture.

But *Thin* also has a serious feminist mission at its heart: the desire to spark a conversation about the way this disordered food and body culture destroys women physically and emotionally by yoking them to internal preoccupations about the shape of their thighs and upper arms, thereby removing them from the trajectory of successful adulthood. "I'm 28 and I have no periods and the body of a young girl," laments one patient, visibly shaken by her reality. *Thin*, like much of Greenfield's landmark work, is acclaimed for being "both sensational and educational," but the work is less often noted for its fierce feminist politics. Body image, which Greenfield examines at the extreme in *Thin* but also as a pervasive and insidious force in *Girl Culture*, *kids + money*, and *Queen of Versailles*, is clearly a staple feminist issue, since eating disorders disproportionately affect women and girls and have roots in the misogynistic objectification of women's bodies. Moreover, *Thin* clearly indicts the medical-industrial complex that claims to cater to these young women but through a maze of insurance requirements and restrictions that often forecloses successful care, especially for women of limited financial resources.

Paradoxically, Greenfield's slick televisual style, which makes her accessible to wide audiences and attractive to major funders, has also played a role in impeding her reception as a serious artist among film scholars. Susan Murray's work on televised documentary suggests that the nexus of reality TV and documentary has often clouded the discursive treatment of films like *Thin*, since "documentary is seen as a valid and productive social as well as an artistic endeavor, while reality TV is often vilified or dismissed."[2] To date, academic scholarship on *Thin* has come primarily from social scientists who read the film as a vital (but uncomplicated) representation of eating disorders, reminding us how comfortably vérité fits with the famed "discourses of sobriety," described by Bill Nichols, and furthermore how some subjects (the gendered experiences of women) might get read as "sociologically" relevant while others achieve the status and treatment of "art."[3]

The Underbelly in *Queen of Versailles*

In 2012, *Queen of Versailles* (Evergreen Pictures, 2012) opened the Sundance Film Festival and went on to earn Greenfield the Best Director Award in the US Documentary Competition. A provocative portrait of a Florida family on track to build the largest house in America when the financial crisis of 2008 derailed their ostentatious ascent, *Queen of Versailles* was snapped up almost immediately by Magnolia Pictures, screened theatrically worldwide throughout 2012, and has earned over $2 million.[4] Certainly higher-grossing documentaries abound, but terribly few of these are directed by women or focus on issues central to women's lives. *Queen of Versailles*, as its title suggests, is very much about the woman at its core. This significant accomplishment by a woman documentary filmmaker was nonetheless met with lukewarm coverage by the press. Industry reviewers, for example, tended to praise the film's schadenfreude but denigrate its conventional vérité look and style. *The Hollywood Reporter* predictably compared the film's style to the tiresome antics of reality TV and suggested that *Queen of Versailles* would find its most receptive audiences on the small screen.[5] The *New Yorker* also focused on the vérité techniques of the film but commended *Queen* as an allegorical reassessment of the myth of the American dream, which encourages rich and poor alike to reach beyond our means, sometimes to the point of breaking.[6]

Queen of Versailles opens with a striking montage of extreme wealth in action (personal jets, speed boats, fur coats, enormous mansions). Eventually, the opening credits of *Queen* settle on a portrait of a younger Jackie Siegel, the society wife and mother at the heart of the film's story, looking appropriately regal in a black-and-white photograph in an ornate gilded frame. Evident here and in the title, *Queen of Versailles*, is the film's central interest in the woman of the house—and not just any house, but the largest house in America, which Jackie Siegel and her timeshare mogul husband are building in Central Florida. By focusing intensely on Jackie's quotidian affairs—the house, the dogs, the children, meals, exercise, holidays—and more importantly on Jackie's "everyday-ness," *Queen of Versailles* operates as both a portrait of a family and a mirror held up in the face of American culture. Greenfield interlaces observational footage of Jackie as she moves through her privileged life (with girl-next-door tastes), with interviews with the family members, employees, and friends, raising surprisingly pointed questions about gender, class, and race and, in particular, the way white wealth and the superlative vision of white femininity depends on the exploited labor of women of color.

The narrative arc of the film begins with the wealthy couple at the top of their game. They throw a lavish party for the entire cast of the Miss America pageant, for example. The camera details the luxurious soirée with shots of expensive food, famous people, and the Siegels' enormous cardboard check for $25,000 to the Miss America Foundation. Scenes of David Siegel shamelessly flirting with and harassing the young women guests start to reveal the patriarch of the family as a distasteful misogynist mogul, obsessed with appearances and easy money, disparaging of women and especially his wife. Later, scenes in the underbelly of the Siegel's Westgate signature timeshare high rise in Las Vegas show scores of employees passionately offering working-class people cheap mortgages that they cannot afford. When Greenfield, behind the camera, asks David Siegel why he's building the largest house in America, he replies pompously, "Because I can." Of course, by the end of the film when the titular American Versailles is in foreclosure, a morose David jokes that the documentary ended up being a "riches to rags" story instead of the expected inverse tale of a mogul and his mansion. Yet it is the riches-to-rags version of the story that makes it such an illuminating study of white femininity, White patriarchal capitalism, and its staggering dependence on the labor of less privileged women of color.

Fitting for a movie about a house, scenes of the family at home dominate *Queen of Versailles*. It is here that the film's study of white femininity is sharpest. Although Jackie does not work outside the home, she is a woman constantly on the move. The gendered labor Jackie performs takes place within a rigid framework in which she is expected to maintain her looks and the entirety of the domestic realm while her crotchety husband retains complete control over their volatile finances. The relationship is completely traditional and misogynist to the core. When he is not grumpily hiding away in his man cave, David consistently makes sexist jokes, threatens to trade Jackie in for younger women, propositions Miss America, and shuts his wife completely out of his business. In many scenes, she ventures into his office trying to coax him, kiss him, support him, or love him and is constantly met with a sneer and a cold shoulder, which she miraculously shakes off. She tans, Botoxes, and has her hair and nails done. She works out and shows off her body. She helps throw parties. She manages the household help. She revels in the attention of the camera and the filmmaker.

After the crisis, the Siegels have to reduce their household staff dramatically, and the house descends into filth and chaos: dog feces litter the carpets, lizards and fish die in their tanks, clothes pile up on bathroom and bedroom floors. At one point Jackie pulls out a cooking pot and wisecracks, "I guess I'm the chef now." Throughout these scenes, Jackie maintains a calm, smiling presence, joking with her eight children and trying valiantly to please and appease her cantankerous husband. Observational footage shows her constantly on the move, bustling around the house as well as out and about in the limo, shopping and making beauty visits, stopping at McDonald's for obscene amounts of chicken nuggets and French fries. The film skillfully builds a sympathetic portrait of Jackie, who retains a warm, affable personality despite her hyperbolic wealth. And yet, Greenfield also makes it clear that Jackie's notable gendered labor, which is primarily affective and aesthetic, would be impossible without the work of other, less privileged women.

Several of the Siegels' female employees are interviewed and highlighted in the film, especially Marissa Gaspay and Virginia Nebab, the Filipino nannies who have cared for the children since birth. Both of the nannies admit to feeling deeply attached to the Siegel children. "I'm not the biological mom," says Marissa as she attends to Drew, one of the Siegel boys who loves to sleep with her, "but I feel like I'm a mom." In another telling sequence, Jackie admits that having eight children only seemed like a good idea because she had so many nannies to care for them. Later, Virginia tells her side of the story. She moved to the United States from the Philippines to support her family back home. Family snapshots show Virginia with the white Siegel babies in her arms as she explains in voice-over how attached the children are to her and how they tell her, "Nanny, I love you." Virginia's interview takes place in the children's playroom, toys piled high all around her as she smiles, saying, "I really love them like my own." As she continues her story, however, tears start to roll down her cheeks, and she is soon crying over the cruel paradox of feeling closer to her employer's children than she does to her own. A snapshot

Fig. 11.2 Virginia Nebab, pictured with one of the Siegel children in *Queen of Versailles* (2012), laments that her work for one of the wealthiest families in the United States has prevented her from raising her own children in the Philippines.

of her smiling young son the last time she saw him at seven years old cuts to an image of him now, nineteen years later, a full-grown man. "I miss them," she sighs.

These sharp sequences cut deeply through the soft flesh of the documentary. Throughout her work, Greenfield balances the soft with the sharp as she investigates cultural practices at the nexus of whiteness and gender. In this way, she captures the self-damaging cultural practices of women like Jackie who are "hinged between racial privilege and gender oppression," in Kimberly Lamm's terms.[7] Other times, Greenfield turns over the visible side of privilege to reveal the cruel patterns of oppression that sustain the slick facade of wealth. "I have come to almost all of my subject matter," she explains, "from a cultural perspective and I always . . . was attracted to the idea of social documentary."[8] These tendencies in Greenfield's work, which place her at the nexus of feminist critique and popular documentary form, carry the torch of feminist documentary, especially as it emerged in the political climate of the 1970s, into the present.

About-Face in *Generation Wealth*

Greenfield's latest work, *Generation Wealth* (Evergreen Pictures, 2018), also has iterations as a multimedia exhibition and massive photo book. The film offers a retrospective of her career, including photographs, interviews, and videos that highlight what she calls the "influence of affluence" as it shapes lives around the globe, from her hometown of Los Angeles to the far corners of Shanghai.⁹ The monograph *Generation Wealth* wears its subject matter boldly on its shimmering gold cover and includes over 650 lush and saturated photographs. It provides one of the most extensive visual and written records of the contemporary, transcultural desire for luxury. An increasingly globalized obsession, "our aspiration to wealth, its connection to our identity and that of the American Dream, and the way we emulate and package and export our notions of it, and the contagious virus that is the addictive culture of consumerism," marks what Greenfield calls in the monograph "a seismic shift" in cultures and values around the globe.¹⁰

In *Generation Wealth*, Greenfield makes a surprising about-face, literally turning her personal story as a woman juggling her career, research passions, and family acrobatics into the main subject of the film. Instead of remaining invisibly off-screen as she did in *Thin* and *Queen of Versailles*, Greenfield places herself squarely in front of the camera's lens. *Generation Wealth* also features a personal voice-over by Greenfield, a first in her oeuvre; neither *Thin* nor *Queen of Versailles* share this reflexive interest in the filmmaker and instead flesh out their characters using a combination of observational techniques and extensive interviews. In this more personal version of feminist vérité Greenfield combines a range of key techniques from the long history of women's documentary filmmaking. As I discuss elsewhere, women's documentary filmmaking has long been committed to working through the relationships and power dynamics between selves and others. In *Generation Wealth*, Greenfield—sometimes with obvious discomfort—places her story at the center of a broad investigation about how capitalism and its voracious appetites implicate each one of us, albeit differently.

Curiously, reviews of *Generation Wealth* were less flattering than her previous films, suggesting that the personal turn ended up turning off critics. Perhaps her most ambitious film because of its twin commitments to our culture of materialism and to her personal journey as its chronicler, *Generation Wealth* has also proven to be Greenfield's least popular documentary. Writing in the *Guardian*, Guy Lodge called it "a frustratingly empty look at late capitalism" and more menacingly criticizes Greenfield's personal approach as falling "into its own narcissistic trap." Other critics have criticized *Generation Wealth* as "unfocused" and "messy."¹¹ One cannot help but detect the sexist undertones of these male reviewer's discomfort with a woman who dares to create a public for her personal story—one shaped by significant success and a resistance to traditional roles for women no less. And in fact, one might

Fig. 11.3 In *Generation Wealth* (2018), Lauren Greenfield makes a literal about-face and turns her personal story into the film's main subject.

also perceive in their unease an ignorance about the history of feminist film aesthetics, for *Generation Wealth* weaves Greenfield's personal story into the narrative in ways that resonate with a cohort of feminist vérité documentaries, which her work both retroactively identifies and exemplifies.

Generation Wealth's opening sequence is characteristic of Greenfield's documentary style, showcasing flashy camera work, close-ups, sly juxtapositions, and segments of interviews. Here, Greenfield focuses on the way money inspires love and admiration, adoration and sacrifice *globally*. The film begins in a language class in China where a privately tutored student learns to properly enunciate brand names: Dolce & Gabbana, Louis Vuitton. In the United States, a white woman evokes *The Federalist Papers* as protection for her right to work herself to the bone, if she so chooses, for the unfettered accumulation of wealth. The opening montage includes interviews with experts and with everyday people about money: money in clubs, money in the market, money as freedom. In sum, a resounding chorus agrees: money indeed makes the world go round, and each of us exists in no small measure in relation to this fact about the transnational reach and saturation of capitalism.

As much as *Generation Wealth* wants to forward a universal claim about our global entrenchment in the machinations of capital and its prescribed desires, however, it also foregrounds Greenfield's deeply particular story as one of capitalism's storytellers and ethnographers. She appears initially in close-up, looking at her own images as her voice—didactic and earnest—takes over the soundtrack: "I've been a photographer for twenty-five years, with my lens focused on wealth and the excesses of our culture," she begins. As she narrates the arc of her career and her own obsession with capitalism's obsessions, Greenfield's visage is juxtaposed with her photographic work: images of breast implants, coiffed poodles, jeweled logos, bodybuilders, plastic surgery for dogs and for celebrities. The effect is twofold. On the one hand, viewers take in the excesses of capitalism; on the other, we come to know Greenfield the filmmaker.

Over the course of the documentary, we hear of Greenfield's longstanding interest in "culture" in the anthropological sense, in photography, and in money. As an undergraduate, Greenfield studied photography and visual anthropology at Harvard. After graduation, she began her career by interning at *National Geographic* magazine. The young photographer's first major project was with her mother, a professor of anthropology, in a Mayan village in Chiapas, Mexico. Professor Greenfield did the writing and her daughter, Lauren, took photographs. Moving and still images from the time show a young Greenfield, who stands out from the Indigenous women who surround her. Her mother stands out, too, but her radiant smile conveys the sense that she is at home and happy in the Mexican village. Images of Greenfield, in contrast, are melancholy. In voice-over, Greenfield explains that it was during this traditional ethnographic assignment that she experienced the conflicts of power and perspective that would shape her later work and pivot her inquiry from ethnographic to autoethnographic. As she contemplated her next career move, she began to realize that the world she had grown up in, Los Angeles, had its own story to tell—a story about gender, youth, capitalism, and culture—that was also her story. Rather than look to "foreign cultures," for photographic and cultural analysis, she began investigating how the culture of excess in 1990s LA was constricting the lives of young people by emphasizing individualism, consumerism, and image.

The woman-next-door narrator she cultivates in the voice-over would shy away from calling out neoliberalism specifically. Yet the analysis Greenfield the filmmaker constructs, especially through her interview with Florian Homm, a repentant capitalist mogul, traces the culture of excess from the 1970s—when deregulation made money cheap and the United States transitioned "from an empire of production to an empire of consumption," in journalist Chris Hedges's terms—effectively to the present, when cheap money brought markets crashing down. Indeed, the documentary deftly winds its way back to the 1970s on two key points: feminism, especially in the film's form and focus on the woman filmmaker, and neoliberalism in terms of its political and temporal framing. Whereas her voice-over tends to oversimplify these matters, Greenfield nonetheless provides illuminating evidence through her editing. In one key sequence of scenes, for example, Homm, who sits on a lavish leather couch in a luxurious European sitting room, explains, "If you give money out at no cost to hundreds of millions worldwide, they're going to do stupid things with it." Greenfield then cuts to an excerpt of Jackie Siegel from *Queen of Versailles* explaining how she and her husband just "happened" to begin building the biggest house in America. One obvious takeaway is that the Siegels' access to free money led them to the "stupid" decision to build an obnoxiously large house (which they risk losing in the 2008 financial crash). Although, as we see here, Greenfield tends to hand the mic over to her interview subjects when she needs analysis and explanation, her editing choices—and this is true throughout her oeuvre—sharply intervene and shape the documentary's overall argument about the perils of unfettered capitalism and the way it requires the exploitation of vulnerable, exploitable subjects, especially along axes of gender and race.

The more personal (and feminist) segments of the documentary include interviews with Greenfield's family, especially her parents and her children. Indeed, stories about mothers—a pillar of both feminist thought and documentary filmmaking—take center stage in *Generation Wealth*. From Greenfield's voice-over as well as interviews with her family members, we learn that she grew up in Venice, California, with her father as the primary caregiver. Her mother's story fits squarely into a narrative about second-wave women's liberation, which Dr. Greenfield evokes when explaining why she moved to Santa Cruz when her children were quite young. After earning her PhD, Dr. Greenfield says she found her career floundering when she had children. Without remorse, she tells her daughter the filmmaker that she took a job in another city to pursue her career, quite certain that her children would remain healthily attached to their mother despite the distance between them.

The influence of seventies feminism is clear on mother and daughter; they are both ambitious intellectual women dedicated to their work. Dr. Greenfield clearly took her cues from some women's liberation rhetoric of the 1970s, especially in the wake of Betty Friedan's *The Feminine Mystique*, which urged middle-class women to get out of the house and into the workforce. Yet, tellingly, Greenfield seems to be operating without a clear reference to contemporary feminism (even of the specious *Lean In* variety) or cognizant of the vicious backlash against feminism that her generation endured. When she asks her mother pointedly if she regrets her choices as a parent, Dr. Greenfield admits only to feeling remorse that she had not known how abandoned her daughter felt. Greenfield, in contrast, often seems troubled by her own inability (unwillingness?) to be both an ideal mother and an ideal professional—a subjective knot that feminists have attempted to unravel for almost fifty years. Greenfield's juxtaposition between her story as a working mother and her mother's story opens the space to analyze the role of feminism in both of their lives, even though the documentary shies away from landing a critique of gendered domesticity explicitly.

In *Generation Wealth*, Greenfield is more interested in exploring subjective ambivalence or contradiction—including her own—than she is in positing solutions to the global problem of neoliberal capital expansion or exploitation. Nonetheless, her work pries open some of feminist documentary's most pressing political questions about the dynamics of power between filmmakers, subjects, and audiences, as well as the troubling tension between neoliberalism and feminism—especially as it shapes the lives of upwardly mobile white women like her. Where critics saw a troubling break with her vérité style, I argue that Greenfield's significance as a documentary auteur is solidified less by her adherence to a singular set of documentary practices (observational filmmaking, for example) and is due instead to her persistent examination of the ideological and material forces of sexism, capitalism and racism that shape the lives of people—especially women—across the spectrum of power around the globe.

Feminist Vérité and Reparative Reading

Greenfield's oeuvre belongs within the category of feminist vérité—a term I use to describe the thematic and aesthetic commitments of a range of women's documentary films, especially those that combine observational techniques with filmed interviews as well as focus on a constellation of issues related to gender politics. This mode of feminist documentary, I argue, has been both dominant and discredited since it took hold in the early 1970s. That is, while women documentary filmmakers, and especially those in search of broad popular audiences, have continued to pursue feminist vérité, likely because of its commitment to lived experience, affective impact, and visions of political collectivity, feminist film scholars have tended to either ignore or deride work in this vein. Without overstating the division between practice and theory, my claim, following the observations made by Diane Waldman and Janet Walker in *Feminism and Documentary*, is that an antirealist and antipopular bent in both feminist scholarship and documentary filmmaking have remained entrenched to the detriment of both. Greenfield's oeuvre, thus, creates an opportunity to revisit the contemporary history of feminist documentary, reconsider habitual modes of dismissal and analysis, and evaluate the pressing questions her work raises about twenty-first-century feminism, especially its relationship to capitalism.

Most reviewers of Greenfield's films single out her vérité style—that is, Greenfield's commitment to a mode of filmmaking in which the camera seems to merely follow subjects through their daily lives, without comment or intervention by the film crew (made so familiar today by the artifice of reality TV). As a burgeoning documentary auteur, Greenfield's place in the history of documentary filmmaking might indeed be sealed by her vérité signature, which puts her in the esteemed company of Direct Cinema pioneers like the Maysles brothers and Frederick Wiseman and pioneering women documentarians such as Barbara Kopple and Laura Poitras. However, rarely noted is Greenfield's persistent inclusion of filmed interviews, which—once upon a time—would have violated a major premise of US vérité conventions, as inaugurated by the Drew Associates in the late 1950s. And though the French tradition of vérité à la Jean Rouch and Edgar Morin, most celebrated in *Chronique d'un été* (1961), also depended heavily on interviews, Greenfield's noticeable absence from her films (prior to *Generation Wealth*) distinguishes her from the participatory practices of French vérité as well. In other words, despite being hailed as a vérité filmmaker, Greenfield's techniques actually exceed the most traditional conventions of either American or French vérité.

In contrast, I argue that her feminist commitments actually connect her to an alternative vérité tradition, legible most productively within the history of women's documentary filmmaking. Greenfield's two feature-length documentaries, *Thin* and *Queen of Versailles*, depend heavily on filmed interviews in ways that differ from either (the American or the French) traditional patriarchal lineage of vérité. *Queen of Versailles*, for example, includes interviews with David and Jackie Siegel, but also the nannies, drivers, and company employees whose labor makes their extravagant lifestyle possible. This interest in hearing directly from ordinary working people, and especially disenfranchised women, connects Greenfield more directly to women documentary filmmakers who began their filmmaking careers in the revolutionary gales of the 1970s, such as the women of San Francisco Newsreel who made *The Woman's Film* (1971), Joyce Chopra and Claudia Weill in *Joyce at 34* (1972), Mirra Bank who made *Yudie* (1974), and so many more. In contrast to the 1960s' trend of Direct Cinema vérité filmmaking, which was a male-dominated enterprise and often featured public celebrities, feminist vérité of the 1970s consistently paired observational footage with filmed interviews, mostly with ordinary women. Consider the interviews with Mrs. Fischer in the Direct Cinema "classic" *Happy Mother's Day*, codirected by Richard Leacock and Joyce Chopra; even here we see hints of the future of feminist vérité, as when Chopra is recorded asking Mrs. Fischer direct questions about her feelings regarding her newborn quintuplets. The same is true for the most observational examples, such as Kopple's masterwork *Harlan County USA* (1974), Midge Mackenzie's neglected *Women Talking* (1970), and the more personal films of Amalie Rothschild, Martha Coolidge, and Caroll Parrot Blue.

This style of filmmaking was occasionally denigrated in shorthand as "vérité" by antirealist feminist film scholars, such as Laura Mulvey and Claire Johnston in the 1970s. Following Alexandra Juhasz and others, however, I read this mode of work as a bold new form of feminist countercinema that was deeply invested in the faces, bodies, and experiences of speaking women.[12] As a term, *feminist vérité* reclaims the notion of vérité, pairs it with feminism, and reignites its complexity for the analysis of contemporary work. Feminist vérité, I argue, has always been as much about listening to its subjects as it has been about making visible new political subjects—mothers, daughters, wives, workers, female intellectuals, third-world revolutionaries—in public life. The deep attention to the everyday lives and struggles of women that characterizes feminist documentary draws its crucial force from commentary and analysis shared in interviews by those very same women. That these radical techniques should find a home in Greenfield's popularized work on women and girls hints at a vital core of feminist documentary, which is the desire to remain attuned and accessible to women across differences in class, race, education, and experience.

As feminist and documentary scholars, our collective inability to engage with popular forms of documentary filmmaking reflects an entrenched methodological myopia, not about vérité or realism uniquely, but rather about the function of critical labor and the nature of worthy objects more generally. As Robyn Wiegman eloquently reminds us, until quite recently, politically engaged academic scholarship privileged "symptomatic" readings, otherwise known simply as "critique," in which uniquely gifted critics claimed to reveal "the hidden contingencies of what things really mean" by enacting either mastery or disdain over their objects.[13] Certainly, feminist and documentary studies, too, have been forcefully shaped by the reading practices of ideological critique and the hermeneutics of suspicion, which seek to reveal nefarious ideological messaging or its challenge in either specious or opaque objects—Hollywood filmmaking and avant-garde film, for example.[14] If the value of critical labor centers primarily on the sharpness of the critique, the academic critic is likely to choose objects worthy of this particular mode of analysis, concomitantly contributing to the formation of a canon that excludes work that calls for other modes of reading, such as feminist vérité, and in this case, the work of Lauren Greenfield.

Analyzing the affective and activist potential of feminist vérité, I argue, calls for what Eve Sedgwick, following psychoanalyst Melanie Klein, terms *reparative reading*. Throughout her later writing on affect, criticism, and queer subjectivity, Sedgwick developed her thoughts about love, ethics, and critical labor in distinction to what she argued was the crushing and habitual "paranoid" stance of the academic. Reparative reading offered the possibility of a new encounter between critics and cultural objects, according to Sedgwick—one less burdened by the need to expose, unveil, and outsmart the object. She writes, "reading from a reparative position is to surrender the knowing, anxious paranoid determination that no horror . . . shall ever take the reader by surprise: to a reparative reader, it can seem realistic and necessary to experience surprise."[15] The surprise, explains Wiegman in her nuanced reconsideration of Sedgwick's work and legacy, is not that the world is plagued by capitalism, racism, sexism, violence, and homophobia—this is something the critic already knows and fears intimately. Rather, the surprise may be that by constructing new relationships with objects, what Heather Love refers to as thinking "with" rather than "against" cultural objects, we might find the sustenance we so desperately need in order to imagine and enact a newly just critical and existential practice.[16]

Returning to feminist film and documentary studies then, we might recast the legacy of the so-called field-shaping "realist debates" not as a struggle over particular formal practices (realism versus experimentalism) but rather as a debate about feminist methodology and its relationship to politics and objects. For what Wiegman draws out of Sedgwick is indeed a claim about how our methodological commitments determine the objects we deem worthy (in this case) of feminist and documentary analysis. Indeed, neither documentary studies nor feminist film studies have tended to read feminist vérité reparatively. Instead, the analytical force of feminist film theory has accrued around its revelatory, paranoid power and its impressive ability to take down the patriarchal habits of narrative cinema. Frankly, is Mulvey's legacy not also a decades-long proliferation of fully paranoid readings of classical Hollywood and by extension most mainstream narrative filmmaking?

With the insight provided by close readings of Greenfield's films, this essay has argued that paranoid readings serve us little in the face of popular feminist documentary filmmaking, which has always ventured to say something true and surprising about the gendered experiences of humans, especially women. The habitual disconnect between objects and methods in part explains the chasm between women's filmmaking and feminist film theory and also helps us understand how popular feminist documentary auteurs like Greenfield, whose work resonates so strongly with the legacy of feminist documentary filmmaking, remain off the academic radar and fail to signal "feminist documentary" in the public realm today.

Notes

1. Kirchdoerffer, "Flash, Cash, and the Ratings Dash," 33.
2. Murray, "I Think We Need a New Name for It," 65–81.
3. Nichols, *Representing Reality*, 3–4.
4. Box Office Mojo, "Queen of Versailles."
5. Kohn, "Sundance Review."
6. Mead, "Housing Crisis."
7. Lamm, "On the Other Side of the Icon."
8. Annenberg Space for Photography, "Voice of the Photographer." Also see Lichter-Marck, "Money Changes Everything."
9. Greenfield, *Generation Wealth*, 10.
10. The first quotation is from Greenfield's artist lecture delivered at the Annenberg Space for Photography ("Lauren Greenfield Iris Nights") in 2017. Greenfield, *Generation Wealth*, 10.
11. The critical response to *Generation Wealth* has been mixed. "Its structure makes for an unfocused thesis," wrote Jeannette Catsoulis in her review in the *New York Times*. Robert Abele agreed in his review in the *Los Angeles Times* that the film is "unwieldy" but also "an achievement—a messy, conspicuous and sporadically absorbing one."
12. Mulvey, "Feminism, Film, and the Avant Garde"; Johnston, "Women's Cinema as Counter Cinema." For reconsiderations of the "realist debates," see Waldman and Walker, *Feminism and Documentary*; Juhasz, "They Said We Were Trying to Show Reality."
13. Wiegman, "Times We're In."
14. Ibid., 6.
15. Sedgwick, "Introduction: Queerer than Fiction." See also Keeling, "Critical Theory and Popular Education."
16. Love, *Feeling Backward*.

References

Abele, Robert. "Review: 'Generation Wealth' Examines Extreme Consumerism with a Self-Probing Eye." *Los Angeles Times*, July 19, 2018.
Adams, Guy, "David and Jackie Siegel: Meet the King and Queen of Versailles." *Independent*, August 15, 2012. http://www.independent.co.uk/news/world/americas/david-and-jackie-siegel-meet-the-king-and-queen-of-versailles-8046797.html.
Annenberg Space for Photography. "Lauren Greenfield Iris Nights: Generation Wealth." YouTube video, May 30, 2017, 19:04. https://www.youtube.com/watch?v=3F1IYbPGv2Y.

———. "04 Voice of the Photographer Lauren Greenfield." YouTube video, July 30, 2009, 03:21. https://www.youtube.com/watch?v=9m5vu2lzygY.

Always. "Always #LikeAGirl." YouTube video, June 26, 2014, 03:18. https://www.youtube.com/watch?v=XjJQBjWYDTs.

B&H Photo Video. "Real Exposures: Lauren Greenfield." YouTube video, April 12, 2013, 29:34. https://www.youtube.com/watch?v=P8UGzlayxeY.

Barnes, Brooks. "Documentary Footage Raises Questions about Lawsuit." *New York Times*, January 20, 2012. https://carpetbagger.blogs.nytimes.com/2012/01/20/documentary-footage-raises-questions-about-lawsuit/.

Box Office Mojo. "The Queen of Versailles." Accessed August 18, 2019. http://www.boxofficemojo.com/movies/?id=queenofversailles.htm.

Catsoulis, Jeannette. "Review: 'Generation Wealth' Examines Toxic Materialism." *New York Times*, July 19, 2018.

DeFore, John. "The Queen of Versailles: Sundance Film Review." *Hollywood Reporter*, January 9, 2012. http://www.hollywoodreporter.com/review/queen-versailles-sundance-film-review-283517.

Greenfield, Lauren. *Generation Wealth*. London: Phaidon Press, 2017.

———. "Generation Wealth.'" Accessed November 25, 2020. http://www.laurengreenfield.com/index.php?p=R215BRG7.

John Adams Institute. "Lauren Greenfield." YouTube video, May 23, 2017, 01:14:16. https://www.youtube.com/watch?v=vFTdusPCcJM&t=2370s.

Johnston, Claire. "Women's Cinema as Counter-Cinema." In *Notes on Women's Cinema* London: Society for Education in Film and Television, 1973.

Juhasz, Alexandra. "'They Said We Were Trying to Show Reality—All I Want to Show Is My Video': The Politics of the Realist Feminist Documentary." *Screen* 35, no. 2 (Summer 1994): 171–190.

Keeling, Kara. "Critical Theory and Popular Education." *Cultural Studies* 28, no. 4 (2014): 676–689.

Kirchdoerffer, Ed. "Flash, Cash, and the Ratings Dash: HBO's Sheila Nevins." *Realscreen* 1 (September 1, 1998). http://realscreen.com/1998/09/01/23169-19980901/.

Kohn, Eric. "Sundance Review: 'Queen of Versailles' Portrays the Deadly Combo of Ego, Wealth and Ego." *IndieWire*, January 20, 2012. http://www.indiewire.com/2012/01/sundance-review-queen-of-versailles-portrays-the-deadly-combo-of-ego-wealth-and-ego-49640/.

Lamm, Kimberly. "On the Other Side of the Icon: Making Images with Mary Harron." Unpublished manuscript, 2017. Microsoft Word file.

Lichter-Marck, Ruth. "Money Changes Everything: An Interview with Lauren Greenfield." *Rookie*, no. 21 (May 23, 2013). https://www.rookiemag.com/2013/05/money-changes-everything-an-interview-with-lauren-greenfield/.

Love, Heather. *Feeling Backward: Loss and the Politics of Queer History*. Cambridge: Harvard University Press, 2007.

Mead, Rebecca. "Housing Crisis." *New Yorker*, July 9, 2012. https://www.newyorker.com/magazine/2012/07/09/housing-crisis.

Mulvey, Laura. "Feminism, Film, and the Avant Garde." *Framework* 10 (Spring 1979): 3–10.

Murray, Susan. "I Think We Need a New Name for It: The Meeting of Documentary and Reality TV." In *Reality TV: Remaking Television Culture*, edited by Laurie Ouellette, 40–56. New York: New York University Press, 2004.

Nichols, Bill. *Representing Reality*. Bloomington: Indiana University Press, 1991.

The Numbers. "All Time Worldwide Box Office for Documentary Movies." Accessed November 7, 2020. httpshttps://www.the-numbers.com/box-office-records/worldwide/all-movies/genres/documentary.

Schwab, Isabel. "The 'Queen of Versailles' Death Mystery: A Fallen Heiress and a Family Under Fire." *Daily Beast*, June 14, 2015. http://www.thedailybeast.com/the-queen-of-versailles-death-mystery-a-fallen-heiress-and-a-family-under-fire.

Sedgwick, Eve Kosofsky. "Introduction: Queerer Than Fiction." *Studies in the Novel* 28, no. 3 (1996): 277–280.

———. *Touching, Feeling: Affect, Pedagogy, Performativity*. Durham, NC: Duke University Press, 2003.

Smaill, Belinda. "Cinema against the Age: Feminism and Contemporary Documentary." *Screening the Past*, August 2012. http://www.screeningthepast.com/2012/08/cinema-against-the-age-feminism-and-contemporary-documentary/.

Thornham, Sue. *What If I Had Been the Hero: Investigating Women's Cinema*. London: Bloomsbury, 2012.

Waldman, Diane, and Janet Walker, eds. *Feminism and Documentary*. Minneapolis: University of Minnesota Press, 1999.

Warren, Shilyh. *Subject to Reality: Women and Documentary*. Champaign: University of Illinois Press, 2019.

Wiegman, Robyn. "The Times We're In: Queer Feminist Criticism and the Reparative 'Turn.'" *Feminist Theory* 15, no. 1 (2014): 4–25.

SHILYH WARREN is Associate Professor of Film and Aesthetic Studies at the University of Texas at Dallas. She is author of *Subject to Reality: Women and Documentary Film*.

12

CITIZENFOUR AND THE ANTIREPRESENTATIONAL TURN
Aesthetics of Failure in the Information Age

S. Topiary Landberg

One of the dominant goals of popular, progressive political documentary since the mid-twentieth century has been to provide a platform for underdogs, minorities, the oppressed, and for aggrieved peoples to become visible and to be heard. But, in thinking about the mainstream of what Thomas Waugh has referred to as "committed" documentaries of the past fifteen years, I want to suggest that a "personal is political" (identity politics) ethos, along with a social-realist relationship to earnest and straightforward representations, is increasingly being challenged by a countervailing interest in the power of obfuscation and the resistance to visual representation. In a wide array of internationally award-winning documentary films, antirepresentational strategies that question beliefs about representation, truth, and evidence have been gaining in popular appeal. These strategies are being used by a wide variety of documentary films, from animated works such as *Persepolis* (2007) and *Waltz with Bashir* (2008) to live action films such as *5 Broken Cameras* (2011), *Standard Operating Procedure* (2008), *The Unknown Known* (2013), *Exit through the Gift Shop* (2010), *Faces Places* (2017), *Zero Days* (2016) and *Citizenfour* (2014). In a number of striking cases, documentary films dramatize representational failures, staging critiques of surveillance regimes and asserting the importance of privacy and anonymity at the level of aesthetics. And while documentary scholar Jonathan Kahana reminds us that the documentary film form has always been "about something more than or other than what it depicts," since 9/11, an increasingly wide range of nonfiction filmmakers are highlighting the power of nonrealist modes of representation and foregrounding techniques of obfuscation.[1]

The idea that we've turned the corner away from a socially progressive reliance in straightforward, earnest truth-telling representational strategies first struck me when I viewed Hito Steyerl's *How Not to Be Seen: A Fucking Didactic Educational .Mov File* (2013), a provocative and ironic video critiquing the ubiquity of digital surveillance.[2] In that video, and in Steyerl's essay "The Spam of the Earth: Withdrawal from Representation," the artist, who describes our age as one of "total overvisibility," provocatively questions whether there might be some correspondence between our ballooning ability to create representations of ourselves and the decreasing amount of agency and political representation that so many in the world face today.[3] Steyerl's suggestion that representational power might be inversely proportional to political power poses a challenge to progressive documentarians who have labored for many decades with the assumption that giving voice and image to disempowered people and experiences is, in and of itself, a form of empowerment. As if to counter these representational assumptions, there is a growing trend among politically engaged media-makers to move away from a personal is political representational ethos that equates representing the world in a straightforward, realist manner with a form of political activism. Instead, documentary filmmakers are increasingly employing representational strategies that highlight and critique the ubiquity of surveillance and digital recording devices in our everyday lives. This antirepresentational turn in documentary media-making twists widely practiced strategies of naturalistic, personal, and embodied representational aesthetics widely practiced by feminist, queer, and postcolonial filmmakers in the middle to late twentieth century, to assert twenty-first-century ideals of privacy and encryption—suggesting that withdrawal from realist representation can also be a form of political empowerment.

Antirepresentationalism and the Aesthetics of Failure

Antirepresentationalism is a term often employed in visual art to refer to the use of abstraction and other alternatives to literal or realist representational techniques. But what could *antirepresentationalism* mean when referring to an ontologically realist form such as documentary film that historically has been defined by the rhetoric of indexicality and evidence? And why would documentary filmmakers choose to turn away from the goal of creating authentic, realist representations, when the form of documentary, as Bill Nichols points out, has been so successful at continually innovating its aesthetic approaches to realism over the course of the twentieth century?[4]

By representing the world authentically; providing truthful representations of people, events, places, and ideas; giving voice to actual people; and documenting their authentic experiences and struggles, documentary film has often been defined as a form or mode of cinematic practice rhetorically distinct from fiction film and one that has a unique potential to influence audiences.[5] For example, Jane Gaines, addressing the question of whether and how documentary films can actually "change the world," credits realism with the power to inspire "political mimesis," defined as the effect of documentaries to physically motivate viewers to join social and political activist movements portrayed on screen, such as the antiwar or civil rights movements.[6] Yet Gaines complicates the idea of political mimesis, questioning whether representations of violence that are used for evidence of injustice can unintentionally inspire more violence by repeating and circulating troubling images of racism, such as the police beating of Rodney King. Gaines concludes her essay by questioning whether documentaries can meaningfully "change the world" in an increasingly apolitical, materialistic cultural moment of the late 1990s in which "the fall of communism" and the rise of neoliberal economic imperatives had seemingly destroyed any last vestiges of the left wing and its passionate defense of the social welfare state.

Coincident with the rise of a neoliberal political and cultural order in the late twentieth century, many scholars noted an increasing popularity of documentary film. Paula Rabinowitz described the renaissance in documentary films as "part of a puzzling contradiction" that occurred in this period of political repression by the New Right and marked by a backlash against gains in civil rights for minorities, women, and gays.[7] Bill Nichols describes the "golden age" of documentary that begins in the 1980s as marked by the development of both a reflexive mode and performative mode that "emphasize the subjective or expressive aspect of the filmmaker's own involvement with a subject."[8] While Paul Arthur, in his essay "Jargons of Authenticity," describes the increasing popularity of documentary, noting "there is currently more popular interest in nonfiction cinema than at any time since the late sixties."[9] Citing popular and provocative autobiographically performative films such as Ross McElwee's *Sherman's March* (1987), Michael Moore's *Roger and Me* (1989), and Errol Morris's *The Thin Blue Line* (1990), Arthur suggests that this "new documentary" features the process of filmmaking along with an inscription of the filmmaker as both subject and antihero and, in so doing mocks, denies, or dismisses traditional documentary notions of authority and verisimilitude. He goes on to suggest that "the prospect for completion of a straightforward documentary project of any stripe may be under interrogation. . . . *Failure* to adequately represent the person, event, or social situation stated as the film's explicit task functions as an inverted guarantee of authenticity."[10]

Arthur defines the idea of a documentary "aesthetics of failure" as films structured around failures to achieve highlighted goals—such as Moore's failure to interview GM's CEO in *Roger and Me* or McElwee's failure to get a date in *Sherman's March*—arguing that these failures function as allegories for larger sociopolitical and economic failures.[11] Yet Arthur critiques the pose of ambivalence on the part of a bumbling antihero filmmaker toward the *technologies of representation* (e.g., Moore highlighting his failure to turn on his tape recorder at a particular time). Arguing that in many cases, the filmmakers' technical failures inadvertently demonstrate inauthenticity rather than the realness that the filmmaker's pose of inadequacy was designed to imply. Arthur concludes the essay by asking whether documentary film—in the face of its increasing embrace of fiction film techniques and the use of irony and disingenuous performance—might still meaningfully be considered a distinct form of filmmaking or whether it is the documentary film itself that has failed to maintain its own identity.

While it could be assumed that reflexive and performative documentaries that rely on staged and disingenuous performance techniques may have risked alienating documentary audiences who expected realism and objective notions of "the truth," it appears that the opposite effect was true. Arthur contextualizes the popularity of postmodern documentary as a reflection of the cultural zeitgeist of mistrust or suspicion of authenticity, truth-claims, and authority in general. But where Arthur viewed documentary's incorporation of fiction film strategies as a kind of failure for documentary, more recent scholarship by Erika Balsom and Hela Peleg argue that postmodern documentary films heralded a rise in hybridization and a loss of relevancy for previously held boundary distinctions.[12]

Failure Aesthetics 2.0

In *The Queer Art of Failure* (2011), Jack Halberstam argues that hybridity is a queer strategy to resist binary essentialisms and refuse participation in systems of reproduction that "do not reflect our values."[13] Toward the beginning of *The Queer Art of Failure*, Halberstam cites the work *Seeing Like a State: How Certain Schemes to Improve the Human Condition Have Failed* (1999) as central to his own thinking about the value of failure.

James C. Scott details the ways the modern state has run roughshod over local, customary, and undisciplined forms of knowledge in order to rationalize and simplify social, agricultural, and political practices that have profit as their primary motivation. In the process, says Scott, certain ways of seeing the world are established as normal or natural, as obvious and necessary, even though they are often entirely counterintuitive and socially engineered.... Scott identifies "legibility" as the favored technique of high modernism for sorting, organizing, and profiting from land and people and for abstracting systems of knowledge from local knowledge practices.[14]

Halberstam extrapolates from Scott the insight that bureaucratic legibility can have negative consequences for various types of subjects, such as undocumented workers, queers, and racialized minorities, who are vulnerable to visibility to and representation by the state.[15] Under these conditions, identity, personal representation, and even subjectivity itself can serve a different function than the ones often intended by documentary filmmakers and journalists who seek to represent "the truth." For vulnerable subjects, empowerment can be defined as the ability to elude representation. Halberstam argues that in these contexts, resistance to representation is a paradoxical form of empowerment that upends the one assumed by an identity politics aesthetic of visibility.[16] Both Halberstam and Steyerl make the point that in the hypervigilant, high-security state we live in today, being invisible, abstracted, masked, or otherwise rendered anonymous can be useful and sometimes safer and more expedient than speaking up and representing one's position (political as well as geospatial).

In this new era, one in which privacy and publicity, truth and doubt, have new and potentially reversed meanings and functions, documentary antirepresentationalism embodies a queer orientation toward the politics of representation. This orientation moves beyond Arthur's concept of failure aesthetics as simply the dramatization or performance of a central protagonist antihero's personal failures. In the twenty-first century, an antirepresentational failure aesthetics can highlight different, even contradictory, representational approaches that prioritize the safety and privacy of subject identities over the needs of the filmmaker to capture images and testimony as evidence. In the post-9/11 context, documentary is turning away from the older poststructuralist critiques of objectivity, to return us forcefully to the relevancy of materiality and lived consequence.[17] Yet this return to truth acknowledges that verisimilitude and authenticity are not sufficient, per se, but are only rhetorical strategies that expose greater underlying truths beyond what can be faithfully represented. In this new era, I see four distinct anti-representational approaches: (1) withdrawal from realism, (2) intentional obfuscation and the dramatization of representational failures, (3) a focus on missing, disappeared, or invisible subjects, and (4) ironic forms of pedagogy (i.e., lying to reveal the "truth").

Withdrawal from Realist Representation

Animation is the most obvious type of antirepresentationalism used in popular documentary film and a technique that has been used in documentary at least since the 1940s. However, the use of animation as a technique to anonymize the identities of precarious subjects has received a good deal of notoriety in recent films such as *Persepolis* (2007), *Waltz with Bashir* (2008), *Last Hijack* (2014), and *Zero Days* (2016). Various forms of visual and aural masking of the identity of vulnerable documentary subjects' identities is not a new strategy for documentary films dealing with subjects facing danger or threat. For example, in *Underground* (1976) members of the terrorist organization the Weather Underground are interviewed in shadow to protect their identities. In *Trembling Before G-d* (2001), the use of shadow to mask the identity of gay Hasidic interviewees who speak while remaining closeted, suggests that "coming out" may not be an act of personal liberation for everyone, as it has been portrayed in canonical gay documentaries such as *Word Is Out* (1977). In a radically different example, *Exit through the Gift Shop* (2010), the artist Banksy's use of visual and aural masking techniques functions as both a protection from the possibility of arrest for the crime of graffiti as well as a performative refusal of personal celebrity constructed by the art world.

Acts of Obfuscation and the Dramatization of Representational Failures

A second mode of antirepresentationalism is the dramatization of acts of obfuscation or intentional representational failures. In the Academy Award–nominated *5 Broken Cameras* (2011), the serial destruction of the central protagonist-filmmaker's video cameras serves as both allegory and an ironic form of evidence of the atrocities and violence of the Israeli occupation of Palestine. The film includes illegible and damaged footage with artifacts and dropouts, presenting footage that repeatedly fails to fully and clearly represent the situations that the filmmaker is attempting to document. This "failed" footage serves as evidence that the documentary act by Palestinians is an inadequate weapon against the power of the Israeli army.

A Focus on Missing, Disappeared, or Invisible Subjects

Instead of a focus on individuals, heroes, survivors, and people who live to tell their tales, in a significant number of important and widely acclaimed international documentaries, there is an increasing focus on those who are no longer present or who cannot speak for themselves. For example, in *Nostalgia for the Light* (dir. Patricio Guzman, 2010), the landscape of the Atacama Desert in Chile serves as a kind of antirepresentation of the invisible and unattainable evidence of Pinochet's murder and disappearance of so many Chilean political prisoners. In Ava Duvernay's Oscar nominated *13th* (2016), the film's focus is on portraying the structural roots, the underlying economics and the enormous scale of the problem of mass incarceration: the institutional disappearance of one-fourth of African American men in the United States.

Ironic Pedagogy: Lying to Reveal the "Truth"

In *The Queer Art of Failure*, Halberstam defines counterpedagogy as a strategy to avoid "scientific" forms of knowing in order to engage in and teach antidisciplinary knowledge invested in "counterintuitive modes of knowing such as failure and stupidity."[18] "Ironic pedagogy" or, the strategic use of lying to expose a greater underlying truth is a strategy in which a film's protagonist asserts one position while clearly meaning the opposite, sometimes while assuming a false identity. In these cases, the sober, straightforward representation of the real is turned on its head and irony functions as an antirepresentational approach to truth telling. This strategy has been increasingly popular with US leftist political activists since the 2000 election, when a street theater group called Billionaires for Bush popularized the strategy of posing as callous, greedy right-wing billionaires who spouted disingenuous positions in order to gain attention on the news and ironically amplify and popularize progressive political positions.[19] The anticorporate activist duo the Yes Men raised the performative strategy of ironically impersonating powerful people to both entertaining and effective results. In *The Yes Men* (2003) documentary and the subsequent films *The Yes Men Fix the World* (2009) and *The Yes Men Are Revolting* (2014), we learn about various Yes Men hoaxes in which they impersonate members of organizations, such as Dow Chemical. A central Yes Men tactic, documented in the first film, was creating a fake press announcement in which seeming corporate officials suddenly take responsibility for previously unacknowledged corporate malfeasance. While the hoaxes are often quickly revealed as fake, the media storm surrounding the claim and the subsequent reveal succeed in bringing worldwide press attention to causes that benefit from renewed public attention and interest.

Michael Moore's *Fahrenheit 9/11* (2004) is another example of a performative documentary that traffics in failure and stupidity. Moore's film is a polemical screed against the Bush administration's war on terror and the mainstream news media that played patsy to the run-up to the Iraq War. The didactic narration drips with sarcasm as Moore points out one irony after another in the press's handling of the many disturbing aspects of the Bush administration's policies and actions. Moore's persona as a working-class everyman is itself somewhat ironic, since Moore, a famous and financially well-off filmmaker with access to the most powerful film distribution machine in Hollywood, marshals the pose of an unassuming, midwestern know-nothing with the pointed intention of appealing to middle Americans in the hopes of swaying the 2004 election. Although the film was widely criticized for manipulating historical facts and did not succeed in helping John Kerry beat the incumbent Bush, popular consensus was overwhelmingly positive: the film took home Europe's biggest film prize, the Cannes Film Festival's *Palme d'Or*, and became the highest-grossing documentary film in history.[20]

Citizenfour

As a film that centers on the straightforward, observational footage of the eight-day long, in-person, on-camera interview with its central character, Edward Snowden, Laura Poitras's *Citizenfour* (2014) may not, at first thought, seem like a good example of an antirepresentational documentary. And yet, despite the important role that straightforward, observational documentary filmmaking plays in the film, *Citizenfour* highlights the importance of withdrawal from representation in interesting and surprising ways.

To begin, *Citizenfour* presents a kind of ironic form of pedagogy: deliberately failing to meet mainstream expectations of what documentaries should do by withholding most important details about the subject from its viewers. It is a film that assumes its viewers already know who Edward Snowden is and, because of him, already know that the American government has been collecting and storing huge amounts of electronic data about all of us, around the world, citizens of the United States or not. Yet, curiously, the film provides no backstory or insights into Snowden's motivations, other than the little bit that Snowden expresses on camera. Watching the film in the theater soon after its October 24, 2014, release felt like experiencing a déjà vu of one of the biggest international news stories of the previous year. In fact, audiences get significantly less information than what has been reported about Snowden in many other venues.

Secondly, as a hybrid "documentary thriller," the strategic use of both representational and antirepresentational strategies is striking. The thriller genre is an apt choice for an antirepresentational film since thrillers are often centered on the cover-up of important information and are designed to deliver experiences of suspense and anxiety to viewers. And because thrillers often involve following a main protagonist as they uncover and then deliver secret, sensitive information while having to elude detection or capture, the real-life story of Edward Snowden fits well into a spy story framework. By dramatizing the effects of the existence of the government's warrantless wiretapping program yet failing to show or explain this technology or how exactly we might take action against the types of government surveillance activities that Snowden reveals, *Citizenfour* provides viewers with a cinematic experience more akin to a fiction film than a standard documentary. Here is a film in which an antirepresentational aesthetic strategy underscores its narrative message: that Snowden's revelations are a spy story with a disturbing, real-life twist: the private security contractor (high-tech government spy) turns rogue in order to reveal the extent to which the US government is revealed to be the real spy, spying on all of us.

The spy story, thriller format is a savvy choice that likely shaped its widespread popular appeal and positive critical reception leading to its 2015 Academy Award for Best Documentary Feature. For example, *New York Times* film critic A. O. Scott described the film as "a tense and frightening thriller that blends the brisk globe-trotting of the "Bourne' movies with the spooky atmospheric effect of a Japanese horror film."[21] From the two-dimensional text animations of email communications between LP and ES to the disembodied long-lensed wide landscape footage of data collection centers and the film's concluding scene of scribbled notes presented to us as a confounding representational failure, *Citizenfour* provides a compelling contemporary example of how representation can, simultaneously, be a means for empowerment and a framework for oppression.

In considering the hybrid nature of *Citizenfour*, it is significant to point out that the film was edited and coproduced by the acclaimed French American feature film editor Mathilde Bonnefoy, widely celebrated for her editing of the formally innovative and internationally acclaimed German thriller *Run Lola Run* (1998). In an interview in *Filmmaker Magazine*, Bonnefoy explains that Poitras was interested in working with a fiction film editor and, because of the politically sensitive nature of the material, sought someone based outside of the United States. The Berlin-based Bonnefoy, who describes herself as having crisscrossed documentary and fiction, notes:

> I mean, it's not like I'm a "fiction editor," but she [Poitras] knew that I had a lot of experience with fiction. And she had this feeling that this film she was working

on—and this was prior to Ed Snowden contacting her—had some thriller potential, that the film would have a narrative pull to it that was similar to what we could find in fiction films. So, she was quite interested in that part of my experience. *Run Lola Run* is a highly kinetic film, and I think she was interested in general by that aspect, the modernity, because of course the film we're dealing with now is highly technical. It speaks to a younger generation.[22]

From reading interviews and articles about the making of the film, what comes across is the important influence that Bonnefoy and producer Dirk Wilutzky had on the approach of *Citizenfour*, particularly in crafting Poitras's role as a character in her own film. In a narrative that is starkly divergent from Poitras's other works, which have been largely observational films in the tradition of Frederick Wiseman, Poitras's role is particularly notable given that *Citizenfour* is framed as the third film in her post-9/11 trilogy with *The Oath* (2010) and *My Country, My Country* (2006) (works not edited by Bonnefoy). Bonnefoy describes the process of getting Poitras to agree to play the role of narrator:

> It was very difficult for her [Poitras] to accept being a part of the film. It's something that goes extremely against her instincts and her desires. She naturally is the person in the background who no one notices, and she seems to like it that way. . . . It took us also a while to fine-tune the way in which she would be present. . . . And suddenly, there was the idea come upon that she could read them. And as soon as she did that, we knew: Okay, that's it. She has a beautiful voice, I think—delicate and precise and very feminine, which does the film extraordinarily well because it's all men. So, suddenly you have this balance of—how can I say—vibrations. And also, there's something about her voice that is extremely strong for narration. Immediately you think you're in a fiction film because it's such a beautiful inner voice.[23]

While most mainstream film reviews, such as A. O. Scott's in the *New York Times*, fail to mention Bonnefoy's influence directly, many reviewers make the point that the documentary is notable for its aesthetic construction as a "thriller" and emphasize the film's fast-paced, entertainment values. In Scott's words: "There are two ways to look at *Citizenfour* . . . The first and most obvious is as a piece of advocacy journalism. . . . The second is as 'a movie, an elegant and intelligent contribution to the flourishing genre of dystopian allegory.'"[24] Yet, despite the thriller aspects of the film, *Citizenfour* isn't content to simply titillate or entertain us. This is a film that seeks to unseat our habitual notions about the politics of representation itself. Rather than focusing on the details of the National Security Agency (NSA) program, or on Snowden's personal biography and character, the film places his act of disclosure and the process of the revelation of his identity center stage. Instead of providing information or new insight into the story, *Citizenfour* hinges on the antirepresentational experiences of disappearance, illegibility, encryption, and exile in order to disrupt our notions about individuality, individual action, identity and citizenship.

Rather than a straightforward accounting of Snowden's act, the film functions as a dramatized backstage view of the making of the Snowden story as an event in the press. The film offers its audience not just a portrait of Snowden and the real-time unfolding of Poitras's experiences with "citizenfour" and her drama of unintended involvement in the Snowden affair. It also repeats experiences of meditation on what the act of Snowden's revelations mean for others. As such, *Citizenfour* continually shifts its attention from the existence of government spying programs to the act of blowing the whistle—attending to the actualities of reporting the story and the impact that this reporting has on the lives of its other main characters—as well as to suggestions of what this story should mean for the rest of us. In so doing, *Citizenfour* repositions our attention, away from Snowden—in some sense restoring his antirepresentational position as a missing or invisible subject—toward a recognition of our own shifting relationships to information, representation, and the concept of citizenship itself.

Nationalisms and the Question of Citizenship

The use of the word *citizen* in the film's title not only simply invokes the centrality of Snowden and his chosen codename but also points to the centrality of the idea of citizenship in general. Using the codename "citizenfour" to denote Snowden, a man who is famous for having been accused of being a traitor to his country and is now stateless (living in Russia), places the concept of citizenship in the foreground of the film's consciousness. In this way, the film presents not simply a forceful critique about the NSA data collection program but also attempts to make legible what these revelations mean for our understanding of national identity, with our foundational American assumptions about the constitutional rights of privacy for all US citizens and for freedom of the press.

Citizenfour also calls attention to borders, not simply the frame within the frame rendered by the camera, but also the geographic frame of national borders. With its self-conscious spy story format predicated on relentless location hopping from Berlin to Brazil to New York to Hong Kong to London, back to Rio, then on to Berlin and finally Moscow, the film foregrounds the global aspects of this story. Documenting the reporting and publication process of this supposedly American story from mainly outside of the United

States, the film carefully attends to the fact that all of its main characters, not simply Snowden, but also Glenn Greenwald and Poitras, are all American citizens who endure, whether by choice or by professional necessity, forms of political exile from the "homeland," placing issues of citizenship, freedom of expression, and personal "liberty" front and center.

Public Privacy and Private Publics

Throughout *Citizenfour*, there is a pervasive sense that publicness and privacy are becoming reversed or untethered from the ways we have conventionally understood these notions. For example, rather than a standard documentary treatment in which various sit-down interviews present different personal perspectives of the subject in direct private address to the viewer, the observational footage of the unfolding of Snowden's and the journalists' private experiences are juxtaposed with the story unfolding in public lectures, press conferences, and television news broadcasts. In this way, *Citizenfour* makes the point that this story about secrecy and privacy is a story about information breaking into the public consciousness. As such, the film emphasizes the tension between publicness and privateness, which is the heart of the story of NSA data collection. Meanwhile, the landscape sequences that supposedly depict government surveillance activities hiding in plain sight show us "evidence" of data collection centers that appear to be regular, nondescript buildings viewed from afar. Those landscape images may be regarded as antirepresentational insofar as they prove nothing about the existence of the data collection activities, which are so enormous as to be unfathomable and potentially impossible to represent cinematographically. A. O. Scott's review alludes to this representational challenge in his review: "Plenty of movies have tried to imagine the contours of state power, but *Citizenfour* stands alone in evoking the modern state as an unseen ubiquitous presence, an abstraction with enormous coercive resources at its disposal."[25]

Rather than deploy standard representational tactics to prove the facts of government surveillance, *Citizenfour* reveals an emergent reversal of how we define public and private. This reversal is expressed aesthetically in the film through the use and juxtaposition of four radically different modes of representation, placing highly subjective sequences in contrast to highly objective modes of cinematography:

The tension between highly subjective and highly objective modes of representation is rendered especially palpable in the sequences of two-dimensional, animated black-and-white text treatments of Snowden and Poitras's

Fig. 12.1 Subjective, intimate, vérité-style portraiture taking place over eight days in Snowden's Hong Kong hotel room.

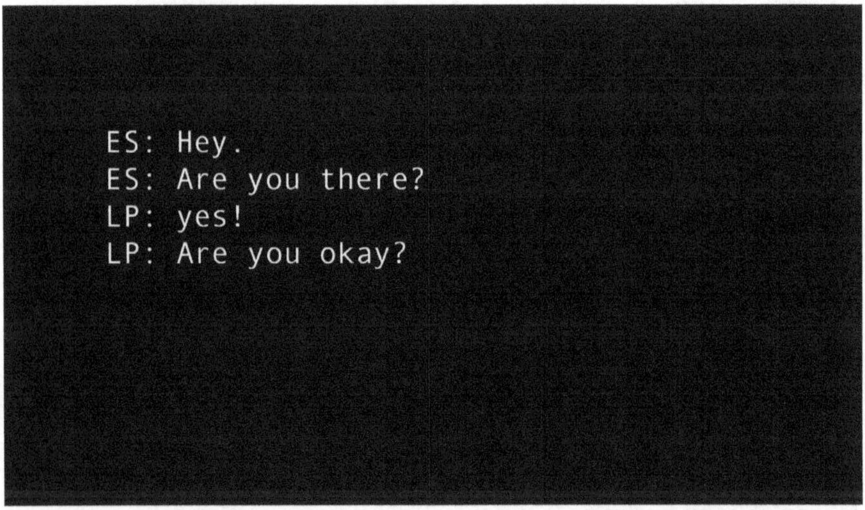

```
ES: Hey.
ES: Are you there?
LP: yes!
LP: Are you okay?
```

Fig. 12.2 Two-dimensional black-and-white text animations of email exchanges between Snowden and Poitras, read aloud in voice-over by Poitras.

Fig. 12.3 Aerial landscapes of government buildings photographed by Trevor Paglen.

Fig. 12.4 Documentation of public presentations, press conferences, and senate hearings.

email exchanges, read to us in the filmmaker's strikingly personal voice-over narration. These sections are at once the film's most intimate expression of (the filmmaker's) subjective, embodied experience, yet one in which we are denied any visual experience of Poitras and instead given the most impersonal of visual treatments as flat white text on a black background. As compared with the insistent realism of the vérité Snowden sections and the objective quality of the landscapes and documentation of the public presentations, these epistolary segments signify an antirepresentational withdrawal from realism and place us squarely within the realm of fiction. Not that the email communications are fictional per se, but as viewers, we never see Poitras's computer or any realist framing device of her email computer program. Instead, the experience of their communication, read aloud to us by the filmmaker-narrator, has a diaristic quality fabricated and dramatized through reenactment. In these sections, the role of the filmmaker as character and central consciousness is foregrounded, in a manner quite unlike the rest of the film.

In *An Accented Cinema: Exilic and Diasporic Filmmaking*, Hamid Naficy suggests that the epistolary film form is an important genre of filmmaking by and about exile. Considering *Citizenfour* as an epistolary film and what Naficy terms an *accented film* that emphasizes the experience of spoken accented languages (e.g., the scene of Greenwald addressing an audience in Brazil speaking in heavily accented Portuguese) allows us to see the important roles that geographic displacement and exile play in the film. Nowhere is the film's critique of nationalism, surveillance, and national security more poignant than in the climactic moment of President Obama declaring Snowden an enemy of the state at a White House news conference, presented in the film as being viewed on a television. It strikes me that this moment, rather than Snowden's disclosures, are the film's "moment of truth" in which Obama's failure to act in accordance with his constitutional duties to protect and defend the Constitution and all US citizens' civil liberties is the film's dramatic apex. Notably, at this point in the film, Snowden himself has all but disappeared, to be rendered again as only ES, the symbolic figure of epistolary exchange with LP. Snowden's sudden appearance and equally sudden disappearance are rendered as antirepresentational counterpresence. Snowden's disappearance is echoed in the near complete visual absence of the filmmaker or narrator (save for the one tiny moment when we glimpse a reflection of Poitras behind the camera in the mirror behind Snowden) in strong contrast to the sense of intimacy created by her voice-over narration.

Invisibility and the Aesthetics of Failure

Poitras's visual absence is mirrored by another conceptual absence—that of the data itself. At one point in the film we are given a quick montage of some of the visual graphics (data) that Snowden has copied and passed off to the journalists. But these, as Greenwald says, are basically incomprehensible to anyone without an in-depth understanding of the arcane workings of the NSA. Incomprehensibility and obfuscation is further emphasized by the last scene of the film, in which we see Snowden, months later, in Moscow, meeting again with Greenwald. In this last scene of the film, which functions as a kind of epilogue, Greenwald discloses information to Snowden about an unnamed second NSA leaker. As a perfect coda to an antirepresentational film about leaking information about data collection, these half-legible handwritten notes that Greenwald silently passes to Snowden are explicitly and maddeningly incomprehensible.

Returning to Halberstam's *Queer Art of Failure*, I want to suggest that *Citizenfour* can be viewed as a queer film offering a contemporary twist on the coming out story. Greenwald, who in the course of the film is revealed to be gay, nods to the film's queerness when he asks Snowden whether and how he wants to "out himself" as the source of the NSA leak. By framing Snowden's disclosure in the language of gay politics, Greenwald demonstrates concern for the ramifications of Snowden's act of disclosure, suggesting that it could be viewed as an act of political and social liberation. Yet in *Citizenfour*, this "outing" leads to Snowden's exile (along with Greenwald's and Poitras's effective temporary exiles) as the opposite of liberation. Another interesting reversal of the more standard contemporary tropes of coming out stories, the film only reveals that Greenwald himself is gay when his boyfriend is detained for many hours in the Rio airport. Greenwald's outing is not presented as a personal revelation that gives us insight into his motivations or character but, rather, as evidence that Greenwald is being surveilled by the government with the suggestion that his boyfriend's detention is collateral damage and proof of governmental retaliation. Thus, the portrayal of Greenwald's gayness (his personal identity) is framed in a deeply political context, a *queer* context in the sense that his gay identity demonstrates not the existence of homophobia but, rather, the existence of a nefarious and extralegal American operation in which personal information can be used against a person for purposes of political intimidation. As a queer documentary, *Citizenfour* inverts the feminist dictum to personalize the political, demonstrating how, in this new world, the political becomes personal.

In conclusion, I return to Halberstam's insight that hybridity can be a queer strategy to resist being confined by binary identities.[26] By taking a queer, hybrid approach to genre, *Citizenfour* successfully eludes the expectations of documentary film; presenting itself ironically as a documentary about data and surveillance that fails to provide any new or actionable information or evidence. As a counterpedagogy, *Citizenfour* provides antidisciplinary knowledge invested in "counterintuitive modes of knowing such as failure and stupidity" particularly in the film's last scene.[27] As we witness Greenwald and Snowden pass scribbled notes back and forth, speaking in a cryptic dialogue about the president of the United States and 1.2 million people being on "the list," it is clear that we, the audience, are intentionally being left out of the conversation. Yet, for me, this moment is when the filmmakers render the "aesthetics of failure" most clearly: a dramatic performance of obfuscation and illegibility in which the current state of government surveillance is rendered in perfect clarity. In effect, the film is telling us that this documentary film is not the medium in which evidence will be revealed. Rather the film can only point us to personal encounters with the effects of this regime of surveillance. In this culminating scene of the film, it is the act of disclosure, not the content of what is being disclosed, that is the subject. By framing the communication of information as one that must necessarily be encrypted, we are left instead with the experience of what we cannot see and are not permitted to know. As an allegory for the way the NSA and our government treat its citizens and the right to access of information, it is *Citizenfour's* antirepresentational approach that provides the key to this film's power and relevance.

Notes

1. Kahana, *Intelligence Work*, 7.
2. In the permanent collection of the Museum of Modern Art.
3. Steyerl, "Spam of the Earth," 171.
4. Nichols, *Introduction*, 32.
5. Nichols writes that "fiction attends to unconscious desires and latent meanings" while "documentary, on the other hand, attends to social issues of which we are consciously aware." See Nichols, *Representing*, 4.
6. Gaines and Renov, *Collecting Visible Evidence*, 90.
7. Rabinowitz, *They Must Be Represented*, 2.
8. Nichols, *Introduction*, 1, 32.
9. Arthur, "Jargons of Authenticity," 126.
10. Ibid., 127.
11. Ibid., 128–129.
12. Balsom and Peleg, *Documentary across Boundaries*, 14.
13. Halberstam, *Queer Art of Failure*, 9.
14. Ibid.

15. Ibid., 10.
16. Ibid., 9.
17. Balsom and Peleg, *Documentary across Boundaries*, 15.
18. Halberstam, *Queer Art of Failure*, 11.
19. Boyd, "Truth Is a Virus."
20. According to Box Office Mojo, *Fahrenheit 9/11* grossed $119,194,771 domestically, significantly higher than any other documentary film in history; see Box Office Mojo, "Fahrenheit 9/11."
21. Scott, "Intent on Defying an All-Seeing Eye."
22. Macaulay, "Positive Trauma."
23. Ibid.
24. Scott, "Intent on Defying an All-Seeing Eye."
25. Ibid.
26. Halberstam, *Queer Art of Failure*, 140.
27. Ibid., 11.

References

Arthur, Paul. "Jargons of Authenticity." *Theorizing Documentary*, edited by Michael Renov, 108–134. New York: Routledge, 1993.

Balsom, Erika, and Hela Peleg. *Documentary across Boundaries*. Cambridge: MIT Press, 2016.

Box Office Mojo. "Fahrenheit 9/11." Accessed November 25, 2020. https://www.boxofficemojo.com/release/rl2672854529/.

Boyd, Andrew. "Truth Is a Virus: Meme Warfare and the Billionaires for Bush (or Gore)." Andrew Boyd: My Many Hats Hang Here. Accessed November 25, 2020. http://andrewboyd.com/truth-is-a-virus-meme-warfare-and-the-billionaires-for-bush-or-gore/. Originally published in *Cultural Resistance Reader*, edited by Steven Duncombe, 369–378. New York: Verso, 2002.

Gaines, Jane, and Michael Renov. *Collecting Visible Evidence*. Minneapolis: University of Minnesota Press, 1999.

Halberstam, Jack. *The Queer Art of Failure*. Durham, NC: Duke University Press, 2011.

Kahana, Jonathan. *Intelligence Work: The Politics of American Documentary*. New York: Columbia University Press, 2008.

Macaulay, Scott. "Positive Trauma: Editor Mathilde Bonnefoy on CITIZENFOUR." *Filmmaker Magazine*, October 20, 2014.

Nichols, Bill. *Introduction to Documentary*. Bloomington: Indiana University Press, 2010.

———. *Representing Reality*. Bloomington: Indiana University Press, 1991.

Rabinowitz, Paula. *They Must Be Represented: The Politics of Documentary*. New York: Verso, 1994.

Scott, A. O. "Intent on Defying an All-Seeing Eye: 'Citizenfour,' a Documentary about Edward J. Snowden." *New York Times*, October 23, 2014.

Steyerl, Hito. "The Spam of the Earth: Withdrawal from Representation." In *The Wretched of the Screen*. Berlin: Sternberg Press, 2012.

S. (SAMUAEL) TOPIARY LANDBERG is an interdisciplinary media artist practitioner and scholar. She received a PhD in film and digital media from the University of California, Santa Cruz.

PART V.
DOCUMENTARY GENRES

This fifth section considers the evolution of several popular documentary genres that operate in relation to established fictional and historical film genres. In "Of Kids and Sharks: Victims, Heroes, and the Politics of Melodrama in Popular Documentary," Christie Milliken explores the melodramatic mode as it runs through contemporary documentary, threading conventions such as moral polarization, inducement to pathos, dramatic hyperbole, and attention to time constraints. Using two apparently quite different films as case studies (one about children at risk in Calcutta's slums, *Born into Brothels* [2004], and another about international shark fishing and finning, *Sharkwater* [2006]), Milliken argues that not only are the conventions of melodrama pervasive across many documentary subgenres but also that the intersecting synergies and concerns of documentary and melodrama studies should be productively considered alongside one another. If we accept—as many scholars have argued—that melodrama is "a system for making sense of experience," Milliken asks why we continue to ignore its pervasiveness as a mode in documentary itself.

In "Strategies of the Popular Music Documentary's Recovery Mode," Landon Palmer takes up the theme of nostalgia in relation to the recent upsurge of retrospective music documentary, or what he calls "recovery" documentary. Situating this recent phenomenon within the larger context of music documentaries as "one of the most popular and lucrative nonfiction genres," Palmer considers the curious upsurge of this recovery documentary subgenre through three recent feature-length films: *Searching for Sugarman* (2012) and *20 Feet from Stardom* (2013), both Academy Award winners, and the lesser-known *A Band Called Death* (2012). Palmer observes the often ambivalent reframing of popular music history that these films offer: simultaneously upholding romantic notions of popular music history and stardom while leveling pointed criticism at the exploitative commercial circuits through which musical fame is generated. By presenting their subjects as "lost" or "forgotten" chapters within a canonized history of popular music, recovery narratives not only expand and interrogate established canons but also reflect emergent, narrowcast models of consumption and connoisseurship. Recovery documentaries, he contends, ultimately use the musical tools of the twenty-first century as a means to rewrite popular music history.

This section concludes with Dylan Nelson's chapter, "Assembling *Nanking*: Archival Filmmaking in the Popular Historic Documentary," an analytical account of the documentary *Nanking* (2007), on which she served as producer. Nelson reflects on critical practices as an "archival filmmaker," particularly the methods, ethics, and decisions in the making of a historical documentary about a subject—the Nanking Massacre in 1937—with only minimal available archival material to draw from. Her critical self-assessment of the editing process allows Nelson to explore broader questions of narration, authority, misrepresentation, and "misillustration" that persistently accrue around archival documentary practice. From a maker's perspective, debates about strategic uses of the archive, appeals to emotion, and the commercial imperative to tell a compelling story are considered through the refreshing perspective of a writer poised at the intersection of theory and practice. The so-called Rape of Nanking by the Japanese army has frequently been referred to as World War II's "forgotten holocaust," a point that motivated directors Bill Guttentag and Dan Sturman to make the film. For her part, Nelson defends the move toward reaching a mainstream audience in this way: "If, as a filmmaker working in the historic mode, I want to reach a broad audience—defined as having worldwide theatrical release, a cross-platform broadcast, and an extensive festival run—I need my documentaries to be entertaining." Nelson's observation encapsulates many of the tensions that inhere in this volume—and this section particularly—reminding us that documentary filmmaking is powerfully implicated in the impulse to tell stories using the strategies of narrative and fiction.

13

OF KIDS AND SHARKS
Victims, Heroes, and the Politics of Melodrama in Popular Documentary

Christie Milliken

In two essays published in 2007, Jane Gaines considers Marxist discourse that has accrued around radical politics and "committed" documentary—one framed around the "production of outrage," the other "documentary radicality" and its vicissitudes—to propose that we read radical documentary film as a species of body genre,[1] which aims to "provoke outrage" and "make us want to do something."[2] As she puts it: "radicality is a pedagogy that *may be* aligned with productive overstatement, that is, with melodrama. The supreme political value of melodramatic hyperbole may be the boost it gives the portrayal of the need for swift change and the possibility and the hope for awe-inspiring reversal."[3] Gaines gestures toward the value—for documentary studies scholars—of rethinking documentary in terms of melodrama. This paper engages Gaines's provocation as a catalyst to explore melodramatic conventions and the melodramatic mode in two thematically different popular, committed[4] documentary case studies: *Born into Brothels* (dir. Zana Briski, Ross Kauffman, 2004) and *Sharkwater* (dir. Rob Stewart, 2006). *Born into Brothels* deals with a small group of vulnerable children in Sonogachi, an infamous, impoverished red-light district in Calcutta; *Sharkwater* is an ecodocumentary that focuses on the rapid demise of the global shark population and inhumane practice of shark finning.

Despite their obvious topical differences, both films rely on the longstanding Griersonian realist legacy of suffering victims ("the tradition of the victim")[5] for their advocacy, a dynamic predicated on the notion that disenfranchised others (respectively, kids and sharks) "must be represented" in the name of social justice and commitment to change or reform. These case studies will be used to consider the ways in which popular (or mainstream) documentaries dramatize (and visualize) the problems they set out to resolve through powerful emotional appeals (pathos), moral polarization, overstatement, dramatic hyperbole, attention to time constraints and deadlines, and other strategies characteristic of melodrama[6] as part of their attempt to politicize and hopefully mobilize viewers. The aspiration to achieve "awe-inspiring reversals" (here, to save children from sexual slavery and to prevent the global collapse of the planet's shark population) is a narrative trope widely deployed in socially committed documentaries by defending "the virtues of beset victims."

The melodramatic elements in both documentaries are abundantly clear to the many cultural critics who have assessed these films. Part of my point, then, is to argue that their use of melodrama and the "mainstream" appeal that this assumes is simultaneously what makes these films "popular" while also, to many critics, undermining them as worthy objects of attention and advocacy. This chapter thus aligns with the broader aspirations of this anthology: offering critical engagement with canon formation and "privileged texts" in documentary studies by highlighting the ways in which certain texts productively underscore the discipline's ongoing and often fraught battle between art, commercialism, and advocacy. Although I'm using only two texts here to support my claims, I paraphrase Thomas Elsaesser from one of the foundational essays on film melodrama, "Tales of Sound and Fury": "it is difficult to see how references to twenty more [documentaries] would make the argument any truer."[7]

Saving Kids

Born into Brothels focuses on British-born, New York–based photojournalist Zana Briski (also a codirector of the film) and her encounter with eight children of sex workers to whom she offers photography lessons during several of her months-long sojourns in the red-light district of Sonagachi. The documentary is framed as an individualist narrative of one white Western woman's aspiration to "make a difference" in the lives of the kids (at the time aged eight to twelve) who participated in her weekly photography class. Through their artistic labor, these children perform something of an autoethnographic project via their candid photographs of life in the district, images of which are woven into the film.[8] *Born into Brothels* alternatively combines elements of expository, performative, and observational documentary modes as well as a sometimes unconventional, nuanced, often poetic view of brothel life in part enabled by the children's photographs. While it includes a clichéd social uplift message by offering visible evidence of childhood empowerment through artistic expression, it also concludes with ambivalence about the fate of the children and the impact of Briski's efforts (and influence). Over the course of the film, her project as teacher to the kids begins to shift as she attaches greater importance to getting them out of the district and into local boarding schools. This imposes a timeline, an urgency to the documentary, as the girls in her photography class approach adolescence and are increasingly at risk of being forced "onto the line," that is, into prostitution.

Born into Brothels was an enormous success for its makers, winning the Academy Award for Best Documentary Feature in 2004, the Sundance Film Festival Grand Jury Prize, and multiple Audience Awards at film festivals across North America. It also received the 2004 Human Rights Watch Nestor Almendros Prize for Courage in Filmmaking. Nevertheless, there is a striking disparity between popular newspaper and press reviews and scholarly criticism of the film. In a generally positive review in the *New York Times*, for example, A. O. Scott states: "[The film] tempers its optimism with realism in a way that is both uplifting and heartbreaking."[9] Other adjectival clichés most frequently used to describe the documentary and quoted on the DVD's cover include "inspiring," "heartwarming," "heartwrenching," "moving," "captivating"—all of which speak to the film's pathos and emotional address. On other fronts, *Born into Brothels* has been dismissed as a conventional narrative documentary addressed to Westerners (as white saviors) and about exoticized others. For example, in an article tellingly entitled "A Missionary Enterprise," Praveen Swami asserts: "If *Born into Brothels* were remade as an adventure-thriller in the tradition of *Indiana Jones and the Last Crusade*, its posters might read: 'New York film-maker Zana Briski sallies forth among the natives to save souls.'"[10]

Early in the documentary, Briski talks about her initial aspiration for moving to Sonagachi—to live in the brothels and photograph the sex workers there, an aspiration foreclosed by suspicions of this white Western "tourist" and her intrusive camera. Many critics read Briski's investment in the children of the sex workers—who were drawn to her outsider status and presence—as another path to the mired ethics of her surveillance gaze. For example, Frann Michel observes the degree to which the children become conduits to the spectacle of the environment in which they live and the film's "paradoxical" reliance on the children for access to the exotic world of Sonogachi, while Briski simultaneously attempts to distance and remove them from that world.[11]

Of course, the benefits of working with children—the emotional pathos they can provoke—was not lost on the filmmakers, the film's critics, and its audience. In a book about the politics of documentary and emotion, Belinda Smaill devotes a chapter to *Born into Brothels*' treatment of children and the complex relation between childhood, emotions, victimization, and politics. Accepting the widely held view that childhood is a notoriously compelling—if difficult—mode of personhood to represent on film, Smaill concentrates on how our cultural projections onto children have become powerfully imbricated with emotions that accrue around innocence, vulnerability, possibility, and purity.[12] As she puts it: "The experience of being a child has been displaced in public culture by the burden of hyperbole and pathos; the 'child' often becomes the discursive screen onto which a society's fears and hopes are projected."[13] In *Born into Brothels*, we root for these engaging, resourceful, strong, sometimes precociously wise and photogenic children even as we bear witness to a Western, touristic gaze. The kids, in Smaill's words, "come to exemplify a vulnerability to exploitation that stands as effectively representative of the lack of safety that is the betrayal of globalism."[14]

That discourse—positive and critical—about the film persistently points to its emotional impact, its pathos, and our identification with the child-victims underscores the degree to which *Born into Brothels* can be read in relation to the melodramatic mode. Hyperbole, pathos, innocence, victimization, villainy: this is the language and ethos of melodrama. For Peter Brooks, the historical development of melodrama reflects the transformation of social and political life connected to the "liquidation" of the traditional Sacred and its representative institutions of Church and Monarch. While it represents a profound ideological shift, the melodramatic mode is nevertheless still fueled by a need to forge some semblance of truth and morality. *The melodramatic imagination* is thus a product of modernity, the expansion of capitalism and the explosion of socioeconomic and technological development that characterizes a shift to cultural, intellectual (and industrial) models of instrumental rationality. Brooks is pointedly less concerned with defining melodrama as a genre or set of themes than with exploring its persistence as "a fictional system for making sense of experience."[15]

Film studies scholars have applied Brooks's model to read film melodrama as an epistemological mode distinct from, but related to, realism. In the introduction to her path-breaking anthology on film melodrama, *Home Is Where the Heart Is*, Christine Gledhill offers a history of its theatrical origins onto the silent screen and beyond. Advancing a position aligned with Brooks, Gledhill sees melodrama as a complex cross-cultural form: "As a mode melodrama both overlaps and competes with realism and tragedy, maintaining complex historical relations with them. It refers not only to a type of aesthetic practice, but also to a way of viewing the world."[16] While she attends to the concepts of high emotionalism, pathos, and excess, Gledhill reads melodrama as grounded in the conflicts and problems of everyday reality, albeit via different strategies, modes of address, and forms of engagement and identification. As she argues: "Melodrama must conform to realism's ever shifting criteria for relevance and credibility, for it has power only on the premise of a recognizable, socially constructed world."[17]

Revisiting the terms of the debate established by Gledhill, Elsaesser, and others, Linda Williams makes the case for melodrama as the bedrock of American film and American culture much more broadly.[18] Williams pursues the "moral legibility," of melodrama as a way of making sense of experience less from the standpoint of rational logic than emotional affect: "We go to the movies not to think but to be moved. In a postsacred world, melodrama represents one of the most significant, and deeply symptomatic, ways we negotiate moral feeling."[19] Williams sees melodrama as a crucial way in which we interpret—not just literary, theatrical, or filmic texts—but public discourse more broadly. In her view, melodrama is crucially implicated in how we dramatize and understand the injustices and afflictions of our world.

Although this might appear to counter the rational, epistemological claims so often made about documentary as a fundamentally sober epistephilic mode,[20] many documentary theorists have considered issues of affect and emotion in that "genre" from its inception.[21] Smaill's book focuses precisely on emotion and politics in documentary, though the connection to melodrama remains unexplored. The oft-maligned status of popular (Oscar-winning, crowd-pleasing, festival-audience-award-winning) documentaries with their slick appeal to emotion, sensation, moral polarization, and excess, against more sober, rational, intellectually and formally challenging work might account for part of the reason why the connection between documentary and melodrama is relatively underdeveloped (and sometimes maligned). Yet the social and cultural reach of many popular, mainstream documentaries is reason enough to consider their rhetorical mode and methods, however problematic, sensational, or heavy-handed they may be.

As "a fiction unlike any other," documentary attempts to make sense of *the* world.[22] More often than we perhaps acknowledge, representations of *the* world in documentary are often framed through moralistic, narrativized appeals to our sense of justice. Insofar as melodrama figures the social whole "from the vantage point of suffering,"[23] documentary and melodrama have much in common. Committed documentary—like melodrama—may be said to offer a vision of the world that expresses itself through moral absolutes by drawing sharp, polarizing distinctions between opposing forces, often marked as good and evil. Committed documentaries nurture moral outrage, as Gaines suggests, generating sympathy for victims, appealing to emotion, and trafficking in pathos and affect. This is the crux of the celebration *and* critique of *Born into Brothels*. Briski's project—which morphs from photography lessons to a deadline-driven, seemingly heroic effort to remove the children from an inevitable life of prostitution by placing them in boarding schools—can be easily construed as humanitarian engagement (however misguided, *un*heroic and problematic her actual conduct may be). And, as with almost any humanitarian documentary dealing with children, these are worthy victims.

For many critics, the problem lies in what is omitted and who gets villainized in Briski's moral framework. Among a coterie of potential villains from anonymized lurking pimps, johns, and pedophiles to useless and incompetent government bureaucrats, it is the families, often the parents of the children who are arguably most cruelly depicted as uncaring, abusive, drug-addicted, ineffectual, or absent. Unlike the children who are granted talking-head testimony throughout the documentary, many of their parents—mothers in particular—are either visualized negatively, often shown as dismissive, sometimes even violently toward the children. Richard Schickel's review in *Time Magazine* illustrates a common response to such a moralizing frame. Tellingly entitled: "The Sins of the Mothers," the review asserts: "they [the mothers in *Born into Brothels*] seem to believe that this brutal, poverty-stricken life is all their offspring deserve. In the end, only about half the children get out. The rest have apparently sunk back into hopelessness. For her part, Briski keeps trying. She has a foundation. She has her passion for righteousness. And now she has this very moving film, which at the least must awaken our compassion and perhaps, our donations. The question is, Can it awaken the imagination of the mothers of these children, encourage them to let them go, let them grow?"[24] Schickel's response elucidates one of the most sustained criticisms that gets lodged against melodrama: its tendency to personalize problems and deflect attention from larger structural and systemic issues. Here bad mothering is largely to blame for the plight of the children rather than systemic social inequality, poverty, racism, sexism, misogyny, and global capitalism.

Schickel's emotive, moralizing response underscores a representational trend that Susan Moeller sees in media coverage more broadly. In "A Hierarchy of Innocence," Moeller argues that in the last decades of the twentieth century, children have become "a moral referent. . . . a motive for action," replacing women as "public emblems of goodness and purity." Children, she maintains, "are a synecdoche for a country's future, for the political and social well-being of a culture. Stories about children are sentimental. They employ the emotional hooks that 'tearjerker' movies do. Stories about children goad adults into a response."[25] In her framework, Moeller invokes here the conventions of pathos and action foundational to melodrama. By highlighting the victimization of children against a culture of neglect (and sometimes unequivocal abuse), *Born into Brothels* dramatizes and visualizes a moral legibility fundamental to the melodramatic mode. It *makes sense of experience* by blaming bad parenting and neglect for the plight of these children at risk, thus personalizing and individualizing problems that extend far beyond their individual plight and that of their parents.

By installing herself as white savior to these brown children, Briski and Kauffman create a grossly oversimplified picture of the social and economic complexities of their lives and their futures in Sonagachi. The film thus perpetuates a widespread and long-standing stigma about sex workers, polarizing a multifaceted situation in order to unite viewers: provoking outrage at the injustices perpetrated on innocent victims and presuming that poverty—among other things—is synonymous with familial neglect. That the mothers of the children documented in *Born into Brothels* generally refused to be interviewed or to actively participate in the documentary is hardly surprising, given the disparaged and precarious status of their sex work. By redirecting attention from her original project to the children, Briski is better able to justify her voyeuristic encounter as a humanitarian one.

The opening sequence of the film underscores its use of melodramatic formal devices, illustrating what Elsaesser describes as melodrama's "transcendent, wordless commentary" to give abstract emotion its "spectacular form." From an arresting, portentous image of moths circling a solitary luminous light bulb, a musical score begins, slowly at first, punctuating a series of images that juxtapose artfully composed extreme close-ups of children's eyes with what appear to be surreptitiously obtained, slow-motion images of brothel life captured in half-light, from chest level, oftentimes precariously angled, out of balance and focus. The stasis of the children (who slowly look left and right) is contrasted with the action and mobility portrayed both within the mise-en-scène of the brothel imagery and often through the camera's roving movement itself, which gradually gathers momentum (from slow motion to regular speed) as the musical rhythm increases. The shift in speed is initiated by an image in which one of the children—Kochi—looks directly into

Fig. 13.1 Layering of pathos as Gour contemplates the imprisonment and victimization of zoo animals in *Born into Brothels* (2004).

the camera. This opening musical sequence dramatizes the polarization that will be the film's focus: children in peril in a perilous world of exploitation and corruption, conforming to Elsaesser's observation about the proximity between style, technique, and theme in melodrama.

After this pretitle sequence it is Kochi's voice we first hear: "The men who enter the building are not good. They are drunk. They come inside and shout and swear. The women ask me 'when are you going to join the line?' They say it won't be long." This articulates what the opening montage sequence has just wordlessly revealed through music and image. Kochi's statement establishes a deadline; the need for imminent action to rescue the children from the looming grip of generational sex traffic. We later learn that Kochi has lost her mother, was almost sold by her biological father, and was subsequently saved from this fate by an older sister whose current ability to protect her remains precarious.

For the three boys who participate in Briski's photography class, the threat of sexual slavery is never overtly discussed, though the fact of their poverty and risk of entry into a criminal underworld is certainly implied. On a photography excursion to the Calcutta Zoo, one of the boys, Gour, is shown watching and commenting on the fate of the animals. The overt emotional appeal of such a sequence is evident both in the delight it clearly offers to the children and the metaphoric commentary on their own lives that images of caged animals invoke. Gour's voice-over comments as we see images of monkeys, giraffes, a peacock, leopard, camels: "The animals in the zoo are shut in their cages. They are fed only once a day and that's too little. . . . People feed them plastic bags. The animals don't know. They think it's food and eat it up . . . which is harmful to their health." Through the exchange of gazes between the children and the animals, the repeated images of bars, cages and chain link fence, the symbolism of the sequence is hardly subtle, yet highly evocative in underscoring the parallel between the victimization of the children and the animals, even as Gour himself makes no such connection.

Saving Sharks

Kids, giraffes, sharks: from charming, photogenic vulnerable kids to captive, charismatic megafauna to apex predators with a global reputation as relentless killing machines might appear to be a stretch. *Sharkwater*, however, leverages the tactics of melodrama to remarkably similar effect. The film—like *Born into Brothels*—was a resounding success on the film festival circuit, picking up over twenty awards and delivering the biggest theatrical distribution and box office of a Canadian-made documentary in that country's history.[26] What initially began as a project to visualize and salvage the reputation of sharks—typecast by Hollywood as unequivocally villainous from *Jaws* (dir. Steven Spielberg, 1975) and *Deep Blue Sea* (dir. Renny Harlin, 1999) to more parodic, excessive, and camp iterations beginning with *Sharknado* (dir. Anthony Ferrante, 2013) and its sequels—morphed into an activist bid to save the species as its director and principle photographer, Rob Stewart, became aware of the market in shark finning and the devastation of the world shark population, which we learn has decreased by 90 percent over the past thirty years.

The documentary begins by introducing Stewart as he walks along a beach, nostalgically recounting his love of sharks from early childhood. Credits interspersed with mesmerizing colorful images of underwater flora and fauna, black-and-white footage from old shark documentaries, and Stewart's voice-over are woven together by a soothing, symphonic musical score. Footage shows Stewart as a young boy fishing and building his personal connection to the water and then as an adult scuba diver amid a cluster of images showing multiple sharks against the azure blue waters. In a striking sequence immediately preceding the title image for the film, Stewart is shown kneeling on the ocean floor holding and stroking one. This image, captured first frontally (as a two-shot of man and shark) and then from the side (for maximum visibility) as he massages the creature's belly, is punctuated by wistful, elegiac, decelerated music. About fifteen seconds into this arresting sequence, Stewart's voice-over intones: "You're told your whole life—since you're a kid—sharks are dangerous. You're warned about venturing too far into the ocean, but then finally you're under water and you see the thing that you were taught your whole life to fear and it's perfect. And it doesn't want to hurt you. And it's the most beautiful thing you've ever seen. And your whole world changes." From this simultaneously captivating, startling, and somewhat hyperbolic introduction, *Sharkwater* chronicles Stewart's discovery of the magnitude of shark finning and long-lining[27] on a trip that initially began as an effort to capture footage of hammerhead sharks in a protected marine reserve near the Galapogos Islands. The connection between long-lining and the global—sometimes illegal—practice of shark finning to support the Chinese market for shark fins mobilizes Stewart to embrace his cause with greater urgency via his collaboration with conservation activist Paul Watson, whom he joins on a journey to Costa Rica's Cocos Island. Watson, one of the original co-founders of Greenpeace, runs the Sea Shepherd Conservation Society[28] and is commissioned by the Costa Rican government to patrol the waters for shark finners. As Stewart learns more about the practice from Watson, the crew finds and interrupts an illegal fishing boat—the *Veradero*—in Costa Rican waters. Images of Watson's Sea Shepherd—first water bombing and then ramming the fishing vessel—ensue in what becomes a dramatic, aggressive showdown. After the *Veradero* surrenders and is escorted to port, Stewart and the rest of Watson's crew are charged with attempted murder and other crimes, heightening the drama of the high-seas intrigue. Here the injustice of the Costa Rican government's about-face—they had hired the Sea Shephard to do precisely this job—is revealed to have a much broader geopolitical backstory. The Costa Rican government is being paid off by the "Shark Fin Mafia." This group, Stewart tells us, is run by Taiwanese mobsters who operate illegal shark fin processing plants in Costa Rica and collude with the government to enrich its coffers. Stewart then goes on a dangerous mission to surreptitiously find and film the illegal processing plants.

The connections between *Sharkwater* and the thriller format must certainly be in evidence from this summary and were not lost on many critics. Neither is the film's melodramatic underpinning: its effort to villainize an alleged organized crime operation in its effort to rescue wrongly and unjustly vilified sharks. In a review in the New York Times, Matt Seitz surmises: "Mr. Stewart's movie audaciously characterizes the pillaging of the oceans—and the world's indifference to it—as a moral blot on human history equal to that of the slave trade. It builds its case with quotations from sympathetic conservationists (including Mr. Watson) and mournful sequences depicting the capture, butchery and abandonment of sharks, shot and edited to evoke the horrors of the Middle Passage. Brazenly melodramatic and furiously angry, Sharkwater aims to be nothing less than the Uncle Tom's Cabin of aquatic conservation: propaganda with teeth."[29] Similarly, a Sight and Sound review of the film pejoratively invokes the critical vocabulary of melodrama and excess when describing the high-seas chase: "As Watson and his crew attempt to scuttle the wrong-doers with high-powered jets of water, the excitement is obvious, so the choppy editing and swooping camera seem hysterical over-compensations for what is in fact a largely stationary head-to-head."[30]

To be clear, Stewart is careful not to equate all fishing with such dubious practices, nor does he cast aspersion on many of the local fishermen, who he knows to be poor, underemployed laborers in this immoral market. When, for example, the Sea Shepherd comes upon a stalled fishing vessel housing a sick diver, Stewart remarks on the gravity of the man's affliction—the bends (decompression syndrome)—and his probable expendability to his employers. Nevertheless, the use of music, visual effects, moral polarization and dramatic hyperbole in Sharkwater underscores the victimization accorded principally to sharks by engaging a dialectic of pathos and action. The images of shark finning operations show a scale and magnitude of slaughter that speaks for itself. Gruesome images of sharks being finned and then thrown into the water (still alive) are also captured from both above and under the water, which begs the question of access, interference, complicity, and ethics in the shooting of such footage.

One of the most striking, counterintuitive images and the one offered up in trailers for the documentary as a form of "money shot," however, remains the images showing Stewart quite literally embracing a shark. Not only is this scene mentioned in almost every review, but it also inspires Helen Hughes's explicit focus in her ecocritical assessment of the film. Framing Sharkwater in a long tradition of wildlife documentary, Hughes reads the unusual inclusion of man and shark in the same frame here less as "petishism," or anthropomorphism, than as a persuasive strategy to ask viewers to rethink their own understanding of the shared planet—to think less with fear and more with a shark's point of view.[31] Against ecocritics like Sean Cubitt who argue for the exclusion of human beings in ecological representations of the oceans,[32]

Fig. 13.2 Stewart's embrace and the spectacle of empathy in *Sharkwater* (2006).

Hughes defends *Sharkwater* for its activist effort to "make visible the necessity for human cooperation in the protection of endangered species."[33] The shark hug, in this case, can be said to solicit what Lori Gruen calls "entangled empathy"—a type of caring perception in which we are called on to be "responsive and responsible" in our relationships with others.[34] As with *Born into Brothels*, which gestures—however problematically—toward seeing life in Calcutta through the eyes of the children, *Sharkwater* asks us to consider the shark's point of view, albeit from a different frame than the sentient anthropomorphization dramatized so emotively in *The Cove* (Louie Psihoyos, 2009) and *Blackfish* (Gabriela Cowperthwaite, 2013), documentaries which enjoy the advantage of being about culturally beloved mammals—dolphins and orcas, respectively—less in need of a reputational makeover and thus easier to envision as victims.

Assuming that *Sharkwater* persuasively makes its case, the awkward and sometimes over-earnest performance of Rob Stewart notwithstanding,[35] what is the value of framing these two films within the melodramatic mode? What is gained from reading these mainstream, somewhat predictable social and ecological justice documentaries in relation to this pervasive, fictional mode? Social melodrama, the kind that engages social and cultural issues, has always maintained a kinship with the real world, no matter how overblown, obvious, excessive, ironic, or sophisticated the aesthetic and narrative mechanics of the film might be. Documentary, particularly social and politically committed documentary of many stripes, engages the tactics of social melodrama as it dramatizes and invites pathos and action through strikingly similar uses of realism, sentiment, and spectacle. What is so often used as the justification for melodrama's dismissal—its tendency to personalize the political, to deflect attention from larger systemic issues, to draw sharp distinctions between opposing forces by expressing itself through moral absolutes—is precisely the criticism that gets lodged against many popular documentaries such as these. But—like melodrama—*Born into Brothels* and *Sharkwater* reveal multiple contradictions even as they present their forceful cases. Their ideological contradictions are not merely the domain of astute critics and theorists.

In an essay on melodrama and the women's film, Pam Cook considers the "foreclosure" of female desire that so frequently gets dramatized in films addressed to women as they negotiate a "matrix of contradictory determining factors: economic, social, historical, ideological and industrial." Her point is that melodrama is notorious for "posing problems for itself that it can scarcely contain."[36] In a similar vein, Laura Mulvey argues: "Ideological contradiction is the overt mainspring and specific content of melodrama, not a hidden, unconscious thread to be picked up only by special critical processes." For Mulvey, "the strength of the melodramatic form lies in the amount of dust the story raises along the road, a cloud of over-determined irreconcilables which put up resistance to being neatly settled in the last five minutes."[37]

While it may or may not be read as a feminist text, *Born into Brothels* is substantially less polarizing and more contradictory than its melodramatic tactics would suggest. In the film's coda, updating the lives of the children a year after filming was completed, we learn that several chose to leave the boarding schools in which they were placed, suggesting that on some level, life away from the brothels was not what they had hoped it would be. Perhaps their home life is less squalid and unloving than Briski would have us believe? Their placement in the schools, the argument for their removal from their families as their "only hope" is fraught with a racist colonial legacy of extracting children from their families (and culture) in the interests of empire-building via pedagogization. This gesture, in fact, alienates Briski from many viewers of the film who are otherwise compelled by the children themselves but read her motives and representational choices as self-aggrandizing and duplicitous. Frann Michel argues that—contrary to Briski's claim in the film—several boarding schools in Calcutta are *explicitly* geared toward placing children of sex workers, thus the relentless stigmatization that Briski claims to be battling on behalf of the children is more than disingenuous. Moreover, while she portrays herself as their solitary savior, it's impossible to ignore that Briski relies on multiple community supports in the film, including translators for virtually all of her non-English communication in the film (including with the kids!). The consequence of reading Briski as decidedly *unheroic* and morally compromised, reveals the "moral polarization" as more complex, contradictory, and deliberative than our dismissive critical impulses often allow. Finally, the issue of the prostitutes themselves becomes another way in which the narrative mechanics of melodrama underscores but also undermines critical engagement with the film. The virtue and vulnerability accorded to children, and the lack of any such compassionate allowance to their mothers (never mind to the broader socioeconomic conditions in which they live) is no doubt a crucial reason for the many objections raised to this film project. Indeed, it may well be that because *Born into Brothels* traffics in such well-worn melodramatic clichés that there is so much critical ambivalence and even hostility toward the project.

In *Sharkwater*, Stewart similarly kicks up a dust of overdetermined irreconcilables. His somewhat narcissistic self-representation—especially when he is hospitalized with a flesh-eating disease in Costa Rica and pines to be back in the ocean saving sharks—actually functions more as a distancing device that undermines his heroism and sharpens our critical faculties. After another ruminative foray into the Costa Rican waters, Stewart returns to that country to find that the attention attracted by his legal battle and activism has miraculously mobilized members of the local community to rally around his proshark, antifinning cause. This plays like so many "false happy endings" and "awe-inspiring reversals" tacked onto countless melodramas and, again, can be read as hyperbolic and unpersuasive in relation to the many problems opened up by the preceding ninety minutes of the film.

Beyond these two case studies, I hope to have shown that the relationship between melodrama and documentary is far more pervasive than often acknowledged as well as that melodrama can productively reconfigure patterns of identification and generate new topics of debate around specific sociopolitical issues to be sure, but also around documentary specifically. Rather than merely dismissing melodrama for being too simplified or polarizing as a rhetorical frame, understanding its mechanics might enable readers to more complexly understand how and toward what ends it can simplify or complicate a specific situation. While it may often invoke a polarizing frame that appears to reinforce sharp delineations between right and wrong, our familiarity with and skepticism toward the clichés of melodrama often sharpens our moral reflexes and critical responses. But it can also inspire, provoke, move us, and—hopefully—mobilize us to take action around a cause. As

Michael Renov reminds us, "pathos is more persuasive than logic."[38] Melodrama may be a less productive frame when controversies are well-defined (for example, the sexual slavery of children is universally condemned), but it can also transform local issues into broader regional, national, or global geopolitical concerns, like saving the global shark population and thus the ocean's ecosystem. Mindful of the degree to which its critics read melodrama for its facile, excesses, and reification of controversies, I argue that attention to its ubiquity across popular documentary is a crucial way in which we can begin to negotiate (if not reconcile) the ongoing battle between art, advocacy and entertainment. As a mode operative across so much of the documentary genre, we would do well to reconsider the ways in which melodrama might function as a strength in some situations, a weakness in others. Rather than dismiss it for its reductive simplicity, or rehabilitate it for its recuperative complexity, perhaps the more important question might be how melodrama simplifies and complicates specific documentary scenarios and the transformative effect this might have. Read in this way, melodrama and documentary, this deliberative conjunction of the fictive and the real, may be better understood as a pervasive—sometimes persuasive—but no less formative way in which committed documentary tries to make sense of experience.

Notes

1. Gaines borrows the concept of *body genre* from Linda Williams's oft-cited article "Film Bodies," 4.
2. Gaines, "Production of Outrage," 49.
3. Gaines, "Documentary Radicality," 18.
4. I borrow this term from Tom Waugh's canonical anthology, *Show Us Life: Toward a History and Aesthetics of the Committed Documentary*, in which he defines as committed those documentaries made and distributed with the goal of altering social and political realities; made as specific ideological undertakings with the goal of "radical socio-political transformation" (xiv).
5. Winston, "Tradition of the Victim," 763–775.
6. The film studies scholarship that forms the basis for the characteristics I enumerate here includes Christine Gledhill's edited collection *Home Is Where the Heart Is*; Landy, *Imitations of Life*; Singer, *Melodrama and Modernity*; and Klinger, *Melodrama and Meaning*.
7. Elsaesser, "Tales of Sound and Fury," 43.
8. For a provocative analysis on the political economy of the film through its use of the children's photographs, see Rangan, "Immaterial Child Labor."
9. Scott, "Nurturing the Talents."
10. Swami, "Missionary Enterprise."
11. Michel, "From 'Their Eyes' to 'New Eyes,'" 53.
12. See also, MacDougall, *Corporeal Image*.

13. Smaill, *Documentary*, 139.
14. Ibid., 158.
15. Brooks, *Melodramatic Imagination*, xvii.
16. Gledhill, "Melodramatic Field," 37.
17. Ibid.
18. For a journalistic argument about the pervasive influence of melodrama in post-9/11 popular culture, see Mendelsohn, "Melodramatic Moment." For a more recent account of melodrama in relation to American politics see Anker, *Orgies of Feelings*, and Gorin, "Politics and Popular Culture."
19. Williams, "Melodrama Revised," 61.
20. See Nichols, *Representing Reality*.
21. Nichols's concept of "discursive sobriety" is the foundation for many debates about the art and poetics of documentary in much the same way that Mulvey's "Visual Pleasure" is the touchstone for film theory debates about gender and gaze theory. To name just one example, see Renov, "Toward a Poetics of Documentary."
22. Nichols marks a useful distinction between fiction and nonfiction by arguing that fiction presents *a* world, while documentary offers access to *the* world. See *Representing Reality*, 109.
23. Zarzosa, *Refiguring Melodrama*, 145.
24. Schickel, "Sins of the Mothers," 77.
25. Moeller, "Hierarchy of Innocence," 38–39.
26. Livingston, "Great White Hope," 34.
27. Long-lining is a fishing equivalent to clear-cut logging that consists of illegally trailing monofilament lines up to one hundred miles in length with up to eight thousand baited hooks set on each line. See Bahnsen, "War on Sharks," 14.
28. The Sea Shepherd Conservation Society, formally incorporated in the United States in 1981 in Oregon, was formed by Canadian Captain Paul Watson who founded the Earth Force Society in 1977 in Vancouver, British Columbia. The original mandate of both organizations was marine mammal protection and conservation with an immediate goal of shutting down illegal whaling and sealing operations. Sea Shepherd has since expanded its mission to include all marine wildlife.
29. Seitz, "Cut the Scary Music," E12(L).
30. Wigley, review of *Sharkwater*, 78.
31. Hughes is borrowing the term *petishism* from Laura Marks, who defines it "as an inappropriate human identification with animals that comes from the fear that we may be more like animals than we choose to admit." See Marks, *Touch*, 24–27. This is summarized in Hughes, "Humans, Sharks," 738.
32. See, in particular, Cubitt's discussion of the BBC's *Blue Planet* in *EcoMedia*.
33. Hughes, "Humans, Sharks," 735.
34. See Gruen, *Entangled Empathy*.
35. Many reviews take Stewart to task, sometimes very cleverly, to wit: "The scenes of this near amphibious activist beached up in a hospital with a 'flesh-eating disease' are so insistent on his saintly return to the fray that they verge on the narcissistic" (Wigley, review of *Sharkwater*, 80). And this: "Stewart's Abercrombie & Fitch surfer-dude look works fine on camera and, yes, he looks hot in a Speedo swimming with sharks. But with his droning monotone, his often prosaic observations and tendency toward self-aggrandizement (every second sentence of the narration starts with "I"), he's an irritating distraction from the main attraction." See Rooney, review of *Sharkwater*.
36. Cook, "Melodrama and the Woman's Picture," 249.

37. See Mulvey, "Notes on Sirk," 75–76.
38. Renov, "New Documentary Horizons."

References

Anker, Elisabeth R. *Orgies of Feelings: Melodrama and the Politics of Freedom*. Durham, NC: Duke University Press, 2014.

Bahnsen, C. J. "The War on Sharks." *E Magazine* 18, no. 6 (November–December 2007): 14–17.

Brooks, Peter. *The Melodramatic Imagination: Balzac, Henry James, Melodrama, and the Mode of Excess*. New Haven, CT: Yale University Press, 1995.

Cook, Pam. "Melodrama and the Woman's Picture." In *Imitations of Life: A Reader on Film and Television*, edited by Marcia Landy, 248–262. Detroit: Wayne State University Press, 1991.

Cubitt, Sean. *EcoMedia*. Amsterdam: Rodopi, 2005.

Elsaesser, Thomas. "Tales of Sound and Fury: Observations on the Family Melodrama." In *Home Is Where the Heart Is*, edited by Christine Gledhill, 43–69. London: BFI, 1988.

Gaines, Jane. "Documentary Radicality." *Canadian Journal of Film Studies* 16, no. 1 (Spring 2007): 5–24.

———. "The Melos in Marxist Theory." In *The Hidden Foundation: Cinema and the Question of Class*, edited by David E. James and Rick Berg, 56–71. Minneapolis: University of Minnesota Press, 1996.

———. "The Production of Outrage: The Iraq War and the Radical Documentary Tradition." *Framework* 48, no. 2 (Fall 2007): 36–55.

Gledhill, Christine. "The Melodramatic Field: An Investigation." In *Home Is Where the Heart Is*, 5–42. London: BFI, 1988.

Gorin, Lilly J. "Politics and Popular Culture." *Society* 53, no. 5 (2016): 482–486.

Gruen, Lori. *Entangled Empathy: An Alternative Ethic for Our Relationship with Animals*. Brooklyn: Lantern Books, 2015.

Hughes, Helen. "Humans, Sharks and the Shared Environment in Contemporary Eco-Doc." *Environmental Education Research* 17, no. 6 (December 2011): 735–749.

Klinger, Barbara. *Melodrama and Meaning: History, Culture and the Films of Douglas Sirk*. Bloomington: Indiana University Press, 1994.

Landy, Marcia, ed. *Imitations of Life: A Reader on Film and Television*. Detroit: Wayne State University Press, 1991.

Livingston, Catharine. "Great White Hope: An Eco-filmmaker Dives Deep to Keep Sharks Off the Menu." *National Geographic Adventure* 10, no. 2 (March 2008): 34.

MacDougall, David. *The Corporeal Image: Film, Ethnography, and the Senses*. Princeton, NJ: Princeton University Press, 2006.

Marks, Laura. *Touch: Sensuous Theory and Multisensory Media*. Minneapolis: University of Minnesota Press, 2000.

Mendelsohn, Daniel. "The Melodramatic Moment." *New York Times*, March 23, 2003.

Michel, Frann. "From 'Their Eyes' to 'New Eyes': Suffering Victims and Cultivated Aesthetics in *Born into Brothels*." *Post Script* 26, no. 3 (Summer 2007): 53–61.

Moeller, Susan D. "A Hierarchy of Innocence: The Media's Use of Children in the Telling of International News." *Press/Politics* 7, no. 1 (2002): 36–56.

Mulvey, Laura. "Notes on Sirk and Melodrama." In *Home Is Where the Heart Is*, edited by Christine Gledhill, 75–82. London: BFI, 1988.

Nichols, Bill. *Representing Reality*. Bloomington: Indiana University Press, 1991.

Rangan, Pooja. "Immaterial Child Labor: Media Advocacy, Autoethnography, and the Case of *Born into Brothels.*" *Camera Obscura* 25, no. 3 (2011): 143–178.

Renov, Michael. "New Documentary Horizons." Paper presented at the Society for Cinema and Media Studies Conference, Toronto, Ontario, March 2018.

———. "Toward a Poetics of Documentary." In *Theorizing Documentary*, edited by Michael Renov, 12–36. New York: Routledge, 1993.

Rooney, David. Review of *Sharkwater. Variety*, October 16, 2006.

Schickel, Richard. "The Sins of the Mothers." *Time* 165, no. 6 (February 7, 2005): 77.

Scott, A. O. "Nurturing the Talents of Children." *New York Times*, December 8, 2004.

Seitz, Matt Zoller. "Cut the Scary Music: Here Sharks Are More Endangered Than Dangerous." *New York Times*, November 2, 2007, E12(L).

Singer, Ben. *Melodrama and Modernity: Early Sensational Cinema and Its Contexts.* New York: Columbia University Press, 2001.

Smaill, Belinda. *The Documentary: Politics, Emotion, Culture.* London: Palgrave MacMillan, 2010.

Swami, Praveen. "A Missionary Enterprise." *Frontline: India's National Magazine* 22, no. 8 (April 22, 2005). https://frontline.thehindu.com/arts-and-culture/cinema/article30204258.ece.

Wigley, Samuel. Review of *Sharkwater. Sight and Sound* 18, no. 3 (March 2008): 78–80.

Williams, Linda. "Film Bodies: Gender, Genre, Excess." *Film Quarterly* 44, no. 4 (Summer 1991): 2–13.

———. "Melodrama Revised." In *Reconfiguring American Film Genres*, edited by Nick Browne, 42–88. Berkeley: University of California Press, 1998.

———. *Playing the Race Card: Melodramas of Black and White from Uncle Tom to O.J. Simpson.* Princeton, NJ: Princeton University Press, 2001.

Waugh, Thomas. *Show Us Life: Toward a History and Aesthetic of the Committed Documentary.* Metuchen, NJ: Scarecrow Press, 1984.

Winston, Brian. "The Tradition of the Victim in Griersonian Documentary." In *The Documentary Film Reader*, edited by Jonathan Kahana, 773–775. New York: Oxford University Press, 2016.

Zarzosa, Agustin. *Refiguring Melodrama in Film and Television.* New York: Lexington Books, 2013.

CHRISTIE MILLIKEN is Associate Professor in the Department of Communication, Popular Culture and Film at Brock University. She is author of journal articles and book chapters on sex education film and video, 1960s cinema, and AIDS video activism.

14

STRATEGIES OF THE POPULAR MUSIC DOCUMENTARY'S RECOVERY MODE

Landon Palmer

After the theatrical release of *Amy* (dir. Asif Kapadia, 2015), an archival portrait of Amy Winehouse's fame, substance abuse, and death, Universal Music Group CEO Lucian Grainge stated in an interview that, "Increasing our presence in film, television and short-form video is critical to our strategy. . . . These projects can open a whole new world of opportunities for our artists, and underscore their massive appeal beyond recorded music."[1] For decades, music documentaries have not only constituted one of the most popular and lucrative nonfiction genres but also have long functioned as a moving image extension of the recording industry.[2] From concert films to biographical portraits, music documentaries have proven to be a rich and continually revisited site for shaping star images, offering moving image records of live performances, promoting the anniversaries of classic albums and events, and contributing to the narratives of popular musicians, genres, and histories.

Recently, a subgenre of recovery documentaries has emerged as one of the most revisited modes of the popular music documentary. In contrast to biographies of well-known artists or concert films, recovery documentaries operate on the premise of the audience's lack of knowledge about the film's subject, and the mission of the film is to emplace said subject within their seemingly rightful role in music history. Two of the most prominent examples of this mode—*Searching for Sugar Man* (Malik Bendjelloul, 2012) and *20 Feet from Stardom* (Morgan Neville, 2013)—successively won the Best Documentary Academy Award and were among the highest-grossing theatrically released documentary features of their respective years. But the recovery mode persists well beyond its most high-profile examples, and recent years have seen a glut of such films focusing on various figures of the music industry, including underrated musicians and bands, backup singers, near-forgotten music cultures, and influential behind-the-scenes moguls. The recovery mode of the popular music documentary does not deserve scholarly attention simply because of its pervasiveness; it warrants analysis due to what these films' generic tropes say about the music industry with which they so thoroughly represent and interact, particularly regarding power and identity. Through a comparative examination of three artist-focused recovery films that focus on subjects whose careers were limited by industrial marginalization on the basis of race—*Searching for Sugar Man*, *20 Feet from Stardom*, and *A Band Called Death* (dir. Mark Covino and Jeff Howlett, 2012)—all of which were released theatrically in the United States across eleven months between 2012 and 2013, this chapter demonstrates how recovery documentaries often manifest an ambivalent reframing of popular music history. Contemporary recovery documentaries deploy familiar romantic notions of popular music history and stardom while also leveling critiques of the commercial circuits through which musical fame has been produced. These three films reiterate the music industry's narrative of pop fame as indicator of artistic merit by marshalling as talking heads renowned and established music industry figures who are meant to lend legitimacy to the film's overlooked subject; at the same time, these recovery films explore the limits within which such fame is granted by highlighting the music industry's practices of structural exclusion and exploitation of persons of color. Recovery films invoke the authority of the popular music canon while also critiquing its barriers.

The recovery mode and its narrative and promotional strategies have particular implications for the industrial structure of contemporary music documentaries. These films' revivals of lost music personalities are often enabled by web-based global circuits for the circulation of media and culture as well as specialty repertory labels that were unavailable during their subjects' initial career pursuits. Recovery films thereby read popular music's past through the omnivorous, narrowcast consumption practices of popular music's present.[3] The subjects of these documentaries are then recirculated through these consumption practices towards both promotional and paratextual ends, as festival and commercial releases of recovery films often run concurrently with their subjects' revival tours and reissued albums. Thus, rather than utilize the documentary as a means for a recording company to further profit from and extend the image of an established artist, as the Universal Music quote indicates, recovery films seek to revive commercial and cultural interest in a marginalized subject. In both filmic text and extracinematic context, recovery documentaries use the musical tools of the twenty-first century as a means for rewriting popular music's history.

However, such tellings of history are often manifested within conventional parameters with respect to the recording industry. Recovery films frequently (1) reiterate the presumed authority of the canon by using established music figures as the principal frame of reference for musical "greatness" and (2) suggest that the contemporary revival of the documentary subject, in which the film not only represents but also participates and augments, offers a corrective for the historical injustices leveled by the music industry. Many recovery documentaries aim to expand the notion of *who* is allowed to be a popular music star; the three films of this study directly challenge industrial tokening practices as well as the general white paradigm that acutely defined much of twentieth-century popular music stardom. But in so doing, these films seek to place their subjects alongside established artists rather than deploy their critiques to deconstruct the meritocratic myths of musical fame and the attendant industrial practices that have provided a platform for some artists while exploiting and marginalizing others. In excavating these tropes across three films, the following pages offer a genre and industrial analysis of the music documentary's recovery mode in order to demonstrate how its strategies of critique and promotion operate through commercial aims shared across contemporary popular music and nonfiction practices.

Music Documentaries and Media Industries

In film and media studies, the subfield of media industries studies has flourished in recent years as a discipline wherein scholars have focused on individuals, organizations, histories, and practices located at various tiers of production and media labor, considering these phenomena within the larger structures in which they operate.[4] While the historical practices of film studios have had a substantial legacy within film studies,[5] recent contributions to media industries studies have made way for less centralized or overtly commercial examples of production cultures, demonstrating how marginal moving image media work also entails tailored promotional efforts and other commercial strategies.[6] This chapter, in part, seeks to make the recording industry a component of the academic conversation about popular music documentaries. Understanding the relationships that music documentaries have to their industrial contexts can illuminate why particular documentary modes are more befitting for certain subjects, contexts, and commercial aims.[7]

While music documentaries have received increased scholarly attention in recent years, relatively little attention has been given to their industrial functions.[8] Due to their prominence within the commercial history of nonfiction features, music documentaries warrant analysis from the vantage point of industry and political economy in order to evaluate the relations between nonfiction filmmaking and the music business. From concerts to biographies to recovery projects, popular music documentary modes not only take on aesthetic, narrative, and generic functions; rather, such modes speak to their very usefulness for the music industries from which they emerge, even if the film in question overtly critiques said industry. The recovery mode presents a rich area for a media industries approach to the popular music documentary because it evinces the adaptability of the music documentary as an extension of the recording industry and vice versa. During a continued conversation that has echoed across numerous facets of entertainment culture regarding who has been, and continues to be, excluded from representation and power within media industries, some recovery documentaries have offered an instructive means for challenging the industrial norms that have determined visibility and exploitation. Recovery films, at their most urgent, ostensibly critique the canon and potentially begin to construct a new, more inclusive history of popular music. However, the extent to which these films challenge persistent myths about meritocracy and "greatness" within the music industry are worth note. The recovery mode's tendency to add to the canon without dismantling it speaks to why such films are useful for the recording industry now, and why the music business can sustain such critiques.

As observed by Alison Huber, a major project of music documentaries has been the production of "official" histories of popular music, a prominent mode since at least the initial airing of the television documentary *All You Need Is Love* (dir. Tony Palmer, 1975). Huber argues that documentaries seeking to canonize popular music history "present themselves as authoritative public texts that circulate understandings about popular music's past."[9] The more recent recovery mode offers an intervention into such established understandings of popular music's past, presenting smaller-scale but, potentially, critically rich rejoinders to official narratives. But what are the terms of recovery? The following comparative analysis is not meant to taxonomize a set of tenets ubiquitously applicable across recovery music documentaries; rather, I seek to illuminate the comparable relationship to the music industry expressed by these films and indicated by their contexts that exceeds the unique aspects of each subject.

Searching for Sugar Man

Searching for Sugar Man examines the career revitalization of Sixto Rodriguez (who goes by the stage name Rodriguez), a Detroit-based folk-rock musician who released two albums in the early 1970s before seemingly vanishing into obscurity. In telling Rodriguez's story, the film largely assumes the perspective of his fan base in South Africa, where Rodriguez's first album, *Cold Fact* (1970), became a soundtrack for the white antiapartheid youth movement and rock scene. As Rodriguez enthusiast Stephen "Sugar" Segerman states, in South Africa *Cold Fact* was an anticipated part of any "white, liberal household" music library alongside the Beatles' *Abbey Road* (1969) and Simon and Garfunkel's *Bridge over Troubled Water* (1970). For the South African Rodriguez fans depicted in the film, the former apartheid government's rigid control of the country's culture meant that they did not have access to Rodriguez himself as a live musician and, more importantly, did not know that his large South African fan base was a notable exception to Rodriguez's relative obscurity over the world, especially in his native United States.

Searching for Sugar Man's first half divides its narrative between the South African reception of Rodriguez's music and an account of Rodriguez's brief music career in Detroit. In both respects, the film constructs an aura of mystery around the performer. For example, in recalling their first instance of seeing Rodriguez perform live, producers Mike Theodore and Dennis Coffey detail their long journey into an impoverished neighborhood of Detroit, recount the haze of smoke enveloping the club, and describe Rodriguez's unusual performance stance with his back to the audience. Such description supports the first act's mythical account of Rodriguez's obscurity, lending weight to theories about his dramatic death circulating among his South African fan base. In juxtaposing Rodriguez's music career in Detroit with his reception in South Africa, *Searching for Sugar Man* utilizes his South African following as a lens into an alternative history wherein the musician received the celebratory reception that the film and its talking heads argue he justly deserved.

Key to *Searching for Sugar Man*'s recovery of Rodriguez is the emerging global digital communication landscape of the 1990s. Similar to the lore outlined by South African fans surrounding *Cold Fact*'s grassroots importation from the United States—as a record brought in from abroad that was shared and copied into oblivion—South Africa's revitalization of Rodriguez's career is depicted as the work of fans. Segerman and music journalist Craig Bathrolomew-Strydom collaborated on a website dedicated to the "Great Rodriguez Hunt" after Segerman read Bathrolomew-Strydom's CD liner notes on a Rodriguez release that asks if there are "any musicologist-detectives out there" who can help find the musician. From here, *Searching for Sugar Man* tracks a circuit of "musicologist-detectives" until, in 1997, Rodriguez's daughter, Eva Rodriguez, made contact with them. Forty-eight minutes into *Searching for Sugar Man* (approximately halfway into its runtime), Rodriguez is finally introduced to Bendjelloul's camera, thereby reproducing for the viewer a sense of "discovering" the elusive musician. This reveal transitions the focus of the film's second half to Rodriguez's South African tour and belated encounter with his most fervent fan base, complete with footage from a 1998 Cape Town concert in a stadium with several thousand attendees.

Although the marketing materials for *Searching for Sugar Man*'s US commercial release reveal that he is, in fact, alive, thereby potentially diminishing this element of surprise, the film's strategy of foregrounding Rodriguez's career and reception before introducing the performer himself to the camera invites the audience to participate in righting the injustice against this overlooked artist. Not only is there a back catalog of music available whose songs have been heaped with praise throughout the film's run time, but such music is contextualized with an inspiring story of a musician still around to witness his belated appreciation. Indeed, *Searching for Sugar Man*'s narrative structure reveals its assumptions regarding the audience's base of musical knowledge: that they had likely heard little of this artist before the film's making but can be convinced of his greatness by the history of his reception, most notably via points of comparison made by his fans and producers. Beyond Segerman's statement of *Cold Fact*'s place alongside other countercultural-era rock records, several of the film's supporting figures make direct comparisons between Rodriguez and Bob Dylan, such as when Coffey observes, "The only writer that I had heard of, of that time period, was maybe Bob Dylan—that was writing that well." Clarence Avant, owner of Sussex Records, the label to which Rodriguez's first two albums were initially released, asserts, "Bob Dylan was mild to this guy." That Rodriguez's songwriting is a site of fascination for the film's fans—Segerman discusses attempting to find Rodriguez through geographical clues in his song lyrics—reinforces this comparison.

The authority necessary for these industry figures to make this comparison is established by professional affiliations listed on-screen. When Coffey is introduced as a talking head, a graphic appears on the left side of the screen that lists the artists with whom he has worked, including Marvin Gaye, Stevie Wonder, and The Temptations. When the film introduces Steve Rowland, producer of Rodriguez's second album, *Coming from Reality* (1971), similar

Fig. 14.1 *Searching for Sugar Man* (2012) establishes the credentials of Rodriguez producer Dennis Coffey.

credits are displayed. However, Rowland's roots in the entertainment industry are covered in more biographical depth, such as when he shows the camera a picture of himself with James Dean. Thus, Rowland's firsthand history in the entertainment business is established before he effectively delivers the film's thesis: "He's my most memorable artist . . . This guy deserves recognition. Nobody in America had even heard of him. Nobody was even interested in listening to him. How can that be? How can that be, a guy who writes like this?" Rowland articulates the interminable gap between Rodriguez's talents and his lack of fame, a gap for which the film being viewed serves as a corrective. If Rodriguez is "like" Bob Dylan, then why wasn't Rodriguez similarly famous to Dylan, at least in the United States?

The music industry's lack of an established marketing language for a folk-rock musician of Mexican heritage is introduced as a contributing factor to Rodriguez's lack of fame when Avant states that Rodriguez was a difficult sell because he has "a Spanish name, a Latin name. Latin music was not happening then." A more pointed explanation suggested by the film is Avant's possible exploitation of Rodriguez, namely its insinuation that Avant pocketed Rodriguez's overseas sales, thus rendering the musician oblivious to his fame abroad. The film's principal piece of evidence for this is a contentious interview with Avant in which he shuts down questions about the income gained from Rodriguez's South African album sales with "Rodriguez never happened as far as I'm concerned. Period." In exploring the knowledge gap between Rodriguez's South African renown and American obscurity, Avant is heavily suggested to be the source of that gap, implicitly building on histories of artist exploitation at the hands of record executives. *Searching for Sugar Man*'s cultural influence and afterlife took part in the project of bringing "justice" to Rodriguez's career when Harry Balk, the producer who first signed Rodriguez, brought a lawsuit against Avant for "copyright infringement, fraud and tortious interference."[10] That Rodriguez himself was not party to this case speaks to the functions of these documentaries and their prospective influence as working seemingly on behalf of the artist.

Searching for Sugar Man's situating of Rodriguez's fame through a bifurcated geographic lens places the film in an ambivalent position regarding its evaluation of rock fame and renown. The film uses established American names as a barometer for artistry, fame, and industrial legitimacy yet, at the same time, decenters the United States as the defining measure for rock fame by focusing on Rodriguez's success in South Africa, with Rodriguez's tour of the country serving as its climax. In seeking to correct Rodriguez's obscurity outside of South Africa, *Searching for Sugar Man* utilizes US-centric terms for achievement in countercultural rock music in order to celebrate a musician's realization of his own renown outside this central global circuit of media fame.

While *Searching for Sugar Man* found undeniable success in its critical and commercial reception—and was a major contributor to the revitalization of Rodriguez's career in the US—it came under notable scrutiny for this bifurcated structure. The film was accused of mythmaking by simplifying the scope of Rodriguez's international career, particularly in leaving out his Australian tours.[11] Regarding the film's place within the larger context of Rodriguez's career revitalization, *Searching for Sugar Man* might be more accurately seen as an apotheosis of, rather than an engine for, such efforts. The film's 2012 release followed a 2008–2009 reissuing of Rodriguez's first two albums from Light in the Attic Records, an indie label that, as its name suggests, specializes in releasing overlooked music. Light in the Attic also released the film's soundtrack, thus demonstrating the reciprocal relationship between independent music distribution and independent filmmaking in recovery projects. Although *Searching for Sugar Man*'s narrative posits the finding of Rodriguez as an immediate, surprising reveal, recovery films such as this can often be part of a greater cultural reinvestment in a subject based on their renewed value within a narrowcast media context.

20 Feet from Stardom

While *Searching for Sugar Man* suggests that its subject's lack of knowledge of his own success can be located in his potential exploitation by one record executive, *20 Feet from Stardom* explores larger structural reasons for the gaps between musicians' evident talents and their degree of fame. With its title serving to reference the space across the stage (or the studio) between a star vocalist and their backup singers, *20 Feet from Stardom* explores the labor and history of backup singing, focusing in particular on the hardships in making the transition from the back to the front of the stage. The film's subjects consist primarily of female singers of color who frankly discuss the difficulties of finding work, success, and stardom within a music industry that has a history of exploiting their talents. *20 Feet from Stardom*'s principal cast features four singers listed in the opening credits—Darlene Love, Merry Clayton, Lisa Fischer, and Judith Hill—although the film incorporates the stories, voices, and testimonies of several others. One instructive device in the film's goal to refocus the audience's perspective beyond the front of the stage is its reorientation of the audience's focus on existing concert documentaries. Excerpts from *The Concert for Bangladesh* (dir. Saul Swimmer, 1972) and *Stop Making Sense* (dir. Jonathan Demme, 1984) that prominently feature backup singers are integrated into the film, prompting the viewer to reinterpret the moving image record of established concerts by highlighting the work of background figures that did not initially constitute these documentaries' principal subjects.

Love's professional history provides illuminating evidence for the exploitation experienced by backup singers. This is illustrated by her account of her experience with producer Phil Spector, who convinced the singer to adopt her stage name from Darlene Wright and then had her, in backup singer Patti Austin's words, "ghosting for records that had other peoples' names on them." Even in the production of a stage name, a key step in the process of star making, this type of labor can be rendered invisible, and Love's eventual, fraught falling out with Spector cemented her realization that she needed a solo career to maintain artistic integrity and personal self-worth. *20 Feet from Stardom* explores a system of push and pull in the music industry between opportunity and marginalization, work and exploitation. Spector's extensive work with African American singers and his "wall of sound" approach to producing helped to establish backup singing as an important component of popular music recording and performance. Moreover, the desire by various rock groups of the British invasion to—in Love's words—"sound Black" cemented a place for Black female backup singers on stage and in the studio.

Fig. 14.2 *20 Feet from Stardom* (2013) resituates *Stop Making Sense* (1984) to focus on the Talking Heads' backup singers.

Although such music practices made careers out of backup singing, they did not open a pathway for solo success for even the most consequential of backup vocalists on 1960s and 1970s recordings. While Love's solo (and backup) career was limited by the fact that she refused continued subjection to Spector's treatment, Clayton's powerful debut as a solo artist faltered due to racially exclusive and typifying star-genre practices. As stated by backup singer Gloria Jones, "there's only one Aretha [Franklin], . . . and that's the way they felt in those days. There could only be Aretha and there could only be Diana Ross."

In explaining why the gap from the back of the stage to the front has been so complex for backup singers, *20 Feet from Stardom* combines accounts of adversity with observations about the relationship between temperament and stardom. Through chronicling Fischer's career, the film's subjects contend that personal characteristics beyond musical talent and skill contribute to success within the music industry. As Fischer summarizes, "I think there is a psychology behind [stardom]. I think most background singers will agree that we're not really good self-promoters. The industry is for those who put themselves on display and are willing to play the game, and some people aren't." *20 Feet from Stardom*'s shared focus on both structural and personality-based obstacles to solo stardom offers a multifaceted picture of what musical success means in industrial terms, complicating the mythologies around famous artists that suggest renown to be a barometer of talent. The film thereby imagines a popular music history from the 1960s onward that might have been had structural barriers not existed, had circumstances occurred differently, had the recording industry been able to accommodate less aspirational personalities or had success been an objective measure of musical ability.

20 Feet from Stardom frames its principal subjects' testimonies with accounts and commentary by recognizable singers whose presence was key to the film's promotion, including Bruce Springsteen, Mick Jagger, Sting, and Stevie Wonder. In portraying all of its talking heads as workers with insight into the music industry, these famous figures are presented similarly to the film's principal subjects in terms of the authority of their perspective. However, these established voices are also meant to lend weight to the testimonies delivered by the film's principal subjects. Springsteen's is the first voice heard in the film, which emerges with a statement about the distance between the back and front of the stage: "that walk to the front is, is complicated. . . . Singing background remains a somewhat unheralded position, y'know. . . . It's a conceptual leap." This statement functions alongside the film's title toward establishing its perspective on the relationship between backup singing and solo vocal stardom. Established stars largely express sympathetic and somewhat distinct views of backup singers' labor and the difficulties they face, but they are also situated by the film to serve as the audience's means of access to less famous figures. In this respect, *20 Feet from Stardom* reinforces the appeal of established singers in order to tell a story about marginalized singers. Darlene Love is not only important due to her talents and what her history says about the difficult working conditions of the music business; she is important because Bruce Springsteen says so.

Perhaps unsurprisingly, the film's established voices more readily emphasize the relationship between stardom and temperament rather than discuss structural issues faced by female singers of color. Springsteen states in the film's opening, "I know tremendous background singers who just aren't comfortable in that position. You got to have that narcissism, you got to have that ego. It can be a pretty long walk." However, Springsteen also credits stardom to circumstance when he observes, "Many of these singers came out of the music business at a time when the singer depended on [a] songwriter, somebody who knew how to feature their voice, somebody who knew how to create a hit arrangement. Those are a lot of things to be dependent upon, you know?" Sting is more ambivalent about what explains the gap between stars and backup singers but does not consider professional music to be a meritocratic vacuum: "It's not a level playing field. It never is a level playing field . . . It's circumstance, it's luck, it's destiny. I don't know what it is." Yet even this acknowledgment transitions to a question of temperament when he concludes, "But the best people deal with that." By contrast, the backup singers discuss how the myth of a meritocratic music industry was put into stark relief by their personal experience, as when Clayton observes, "I felt like if I just gave my heart to what I was doing, I would automatically be a star." Composer Chris Darrow presents the film's most direct comment on the arbitrary nature of fame when he states late in the film, "There are machines that make people stars that don't have talent." *20 Feet from Stardom* overtly deconstructs the notion of fame. However, by utilizing the aura of famous singers in order to lend its narrative authority, the observations about fame from singers occupying various tiers of the music industry become part of a polyphony of voices measuring the path to renown based on an indeterminate balance of talent, temperament, and circumstance.

Yet the lesser-known voices remain resonant by the film's end, such as backup singer Dr. Mable John's powerful contextualization of the stakes of recognition within the history of African American female labor going ignored: "We in the music industry, especially African American people, need to know our worth. We need to know, as women, that we are important. And I think the breakdown is when a woman doesn't know who she is, and she settle[s] for less. Check out your worth, because you're worth more than that." Claims to the worth of *20 Feet from Stardom*'s four central subjects were echoed during the film's promotion as part of a greater publicity campaign that highlighted these otherwise overlooked careers.[12] However, the aim of *20 Feet from Stardom* was not simply to turn backup singers into stars but also to make previously invisible labor both visible and celebrated.

A Band Called Death

Commercially released two weeks after *20 Feet from Stardom*, *A Band Called Death* received only a fraction of its theatrical returns. However, this comparably minor work about a marginal musical act speaks to certain continuities shared across numerous documentaries in the recovery mode. More importantly, *A Band Called Death* illustrates how the terms for a musical acts' larger recovery within cultural discourse informs the characterization of that recovery in popular documentary cinema, as the film's argument about its subject's importance extends from the recovery of that subject via culture writing, record labels, and collectors.

Death was a rock group that formed in the early 1970s in Detroit between three African American siblings—David, Bobby, and Dannis Hackney—who were inspired by The Who to form a sound based in loudness and speed.

A Band Called Death examines the Hackney brothers' protracted pursuit of a recording contract, subsequent family and musical history throughout the formation of other groups, and revitalization through the twenty-first-century circulation of their music. Death has been characterized as an all-Black "proto-punk" band, and the reason for Death's unique appeal as a lost chapter in rock history also provides a key critical framework for the film's evaluation of their windy path to recognition. Despite rock's roots in African American popular music styles, by the early 1970s rock had come to be regarded by musicians, producers, critics, and consumers as a largely "white" genre, especially concurrent to the emergence of soul, funk, and disco.[13] Death's surviving members (Bobby and Dannis Hackney) explain the difficulties of performing rock while Black in both personal and industrial terms. The siblings detail how the passion in their music emerged from a desire make noisy "white boy music" in an act of rebellion against the neighbors of their predominately Black neighborhood. Once they attempted to climb the ladder of industrial legitimacy, they similarly faced, in Bobby's words, "rejection for the fact that we were Black and playing rock 'n' roll."

A Band Called Death spends much of its runtime explaining how the group's name halted their musical careers. As elucidated by his surviving brothers, David Hackney approached Death as a positive concept for the band—"the ultimate trip" as Dannis Hackney explains. However, music industry figures protested that "Death" could not be readily incorporated into the marketing and publicity machine requisite for a recording contract. After Death recorded their first demo in Detroit's United Sound, studio supervisor Brian Spears enthusiastically shared the music with Don Davis, owner of the studio and Groovesville Records, who recounts in the film to have responded with, "Brian, have you lost your mind? Nobody is going to buy a song by a group called D-E-A-T-H." Famed record producer Clive Davis reportedly concurred, offering Death a recording contract on the condition that the band change their name. Due to David Hackney's commitment to the band's concept, Death was never signed. Problems presented by the band's name were later expressed in more overtly racist terms. After the Hackneys moved to Vermont and attempted to publicize Death by distributing fliers around their town, a police officer visited their residence and stated the he did not want to see any "gangs" around. Such problems extended to Death's attempt at generic reinvention. The brothers' formation of a rock-gospel group named The 4th Dimension was cut short when a college newspaper review praised their music but critiqued its religious undertones. The Hackneys only found relative contemporaneous success when Bobby and Dannis formed the reggae band Lambsbread. As depicted in *A Band Called Death*, the Hackneys' potential music careers were determined by racial categorization of popular music genres in both overt and implicit ways.

As with *Searching for Sugar Man*, the final act of *A Band Called Death* tracks its subject's revitalization through web-based music circulation and the work of grassroots music communities. Death's resurgence is chronicled through two parallel stories. In the first, a network of rare music collectors and musicians explain their encounter with a highly valued, "super hard-to-find" 45 rpm single by "an all-Black punk band from Detroit." Concurrently, Bobby's son, Julian Hackney, recounts an extraordinary coincidence during college when a friend heard and shared with him music by a band called "Death" at an underground music party, and Julian immediately recognized his father's voice. With their father seemingly unaware of the significance of their music to contemporary acolytes of punk rock, the younger generation of Hackneys discuss for the camera their revelatory experience of first hearing Death and knowing that they had discovered something significant that the rest of the music world knew little about. This sequence culminates in Death's music attracting the attention of independent record label Drag City, who released Death's first two albums in 2009 and 2011 based on the masters preserved in Bobby Hackney's attic. Illustrating the logic of record hunting, this sequence depicts a network of appreciation that pursues obscure artifacts in the hope of finding overlooked pieces of music history, a community fostered through a digital network of information-sharing and driven by an assumption that such practices can, like the recovery mode itself, fill in gaps of musical knowledge.

With the support of specialty labels, acts such as Death and Rodriguez are given a means for appreciation and listener access that was unavailable in the corporate music structure of the 1970s through which these artists initially pursued careers. Thus, independent music labels and recovery films work in harmony to make previously obscure music commercially accessible. Indeed, these labels and films do much more than bring to the fore a previously obscure, marginal act; they produce a historical intervention in doing so, emplacing these musicians within a distinct interpretation of the music industry's larger history. Drag City's promotion of Death described the band in similar terms indicated by the third act of *A Band Called Death*: as an important, heretofore untold chapter in the early history of punk rock, one that should compel anyone invested in punk to rethink its legacy in the United States.[14] Such a narrative, particularly in regards to the band's status as Black progenitors of punk, was emphasized in a 2009 profile of Death in the

New York Times that described the band as "punk before punk was punk."[15] In *A Band Called Death*, this narrative is emphasized by established musicians who serve to legitimate Death's punk bona fides, such as Henry Rollins, Mickey Leigh, and Mick Collins. Several celebrity appearances are used to offer brief statements about how extraordinary the band's story is, while others serve to emphasize Death's unsung historical significance, as when Questlove reflects, "The Ramones got all the glory. This is pretty much The Ramones, but two years earlier." This discursive historical emplacement of Death was reinforced in Drag City and the Hackney family's promotion of the band on tour: the younger generation of Hackneys formed a band to tour alongside, cover, and promote Death, effectively combining recovery with legacy production. In making Death available to the general public for the first time, music discourse, Drag City Records, the Hackney family, and, finally, *A Band Called Death* cohered in articulating a historical claim to the band's significance.[16]

Conclusion

In presenting his justification for researching lesser-known composers, musicologist Phil Ford writes, "The reason to contemplate a minor album by a minor composer is not only to imagine such alternative histories and listening practices but thereby to question the history that is not alternative but given."[17] The recovery mode of the music documentary exhibits such possibilities by presenting "minor" histories that not only compel the imagination of filmmakers and viewers to consider what could have been but also challenge the terms that have been accepted for the known, "major" history. Recovery films have presented compelling appeals to this former aspect of minor history, displaying the lives of subjects whose contributions can inspire a more inclusive canon and whose histories speak to the strict gatekeeping practices of creative industries. However, this latter possibility—"question[ing] the history that is not alternative but given"—requires a more radical view of music figures who are not in need of recovery alongside the industry that reinforces their myth. The recovery mode has produced several repeated (and, at times, limited) strategies that locate the music industry's problems in past injustices that the documentary itself serves to correct by adding to, rather than deconstructing, popular music's cast of heroes. However, as perhaps the first mainstream tradition of the music documentary that regularly examines popular music's industrial history with an overt critical lens, the popularity of the recovery mode presents a timely potential to illuminate the invisible work of music and challenge a music world that sets the terms for visibility and compensation. Or, as Dr. Mable John puts it, these movies present the possibility for marginalized musicians to see their worth finally checked.

Notes

1. Sakoui, "Why the World's Largest."
2. Malitsky places the music documentary among "the most commercially successful documentary genres" ("Knowing Sports," 206).
3. See Baker, "Notes on the Rockumentary Renaissance," 7.
4. Among the many contributions to this field, foundational works include Caldwell, *Production Culture*; Mayer, Banks, and Caldwell, *Production Studies*; and Holt and Perren, *Media Industries*.
5. See, for example, Schatz, *Genius of the System*.
6. The open-access *Media Industries Journal* has been particularly useful in this respect. See, for example, Mann, "Welcome to the Unregulated Wild, Wild, Digital West," and Wyatt, "Donald Rugoff, Cinema V, and Commercial Strategies of the 1960s–70s Art Cinema."
7. Hogarth examines the global market context for documentary production in *Realer Than Reel*, 19–40. For more recent developments in industrial studies of documentary, see Zoellner, "Professional Ideology and Programme Conventions"; Winton, "Good for the Heart and Soul, Good for Business"; and Vallejo, "Of Calendars and Industries."
8. For examples of relevant critical engagement with music documentaries see Beattie, *D. A. Pennebaker*; Beattie, *Documentary Display*; Kahana, *Intelligence Work*; Wright, "The Good, The Bad, and The Ugly '60s"; and Baker, "Notes on the Rockumentary Renaissance."
9. Huber, "Remembering Popular Music," 514.
10. Sisario, "Now That 'Sugar Man' Is Found."
11. See Byrnes, "Rodriguez Found."
12. See Barnes, "Voice behind Mick"; Feinberg, "Grammys Week"; and Brown, "20 Feet from Stardom."
13. Hamilton analyzes and complicates this narrative in *Just around Midnight*.
14. Drag City Records, "Death."
15. Rubin, "This Band Was Punk."
16. The promotion of Death as proto-punk obscured the other genres in their catalog. Far from lifelong pioneers of punk, the Hackneys were versatile musicians who worked convincingly across a variety of styles (Heller, "Death III").
17. Ford, *Dig*, 185. Ford's concept of minor histories is informed by Gilles Deleuze and Felix Guattari.

References

Baker, Michael Brendan. "Notes on the Rockumentary Renaissance." *Cinephile* 10, no. 1 (Summer 2014): 5–10.
Barnes, Brooks. "The Voice behind Mick (and Others)." *New York Times*, June 7, 2013. http://www.nytimes.com/2013/06/09/movies/the-voice-behind-mick-and-others.html?pagewanted=all&_r=0.
Beattie, Keith. *D. A. Pennebaker*. Champaign: University of Illinois Press, 2011.

———. *Documentary Display*. New York: Wallflower Press, an imprint of Columbia University Press, 2008.
Brown, Mick. "20 Feet from Stardom: Exclusive Interviews with the Stars," *Telegraph*, March 4, 2014. http://www.telegraph.co.uk/culture/film/oscars/10673715/20-Feet-From-Stardom-exclusive-interviews-with-the-stars.html.
Byrnes, Paul. "Rodriguez Found, but Take This Sweet Story with a Grain of Salt." *Sydney Morning Herald*, October 4, 2012. http://www.smh.com.au/entertainment/movies/rodriguez-found-but-take-this-sweet-story-with-a-grain-of-salt-20121003-26znp.html.
Caldwell, John Thornton. *Production Culture: Industrial Reflexivity and Critical Practice in Film and Television*. Durham: Duke University Press, 2008.
Drag City Records. "Death, . . . For the Whole World to See." DragCity.com. Accessed October 20, 2020. http://www.dragcity.com/products/for-the-whole-world-to-see.
Feinberg, Scott. "Grammys Week Offers Well-Timed Showcases for 'Twenty Feet from Stardom' Singers." *Hollywood Reporter*, January 24, 2014. http://www.hollywoodreporter.com/race/grammys-week-offers-well-timed-673851.
Ford, Phil. *Dig: Sound and Music in Hip Culture*. New York: Oxford University Press, 2013.
Hamilton, Jack. *Just around Midnight: Rock and Roll and the Racial Imagination*. Cambridge, MA: Harvard University Press, 2017.
Heller, Jason. "Death III." Pitchfork, April 22, 2014. https://pitchfork.com/reviews/albums/19228-death-iii/.
Hogarth, David. *Realer Than Reel: Global Directions in Documentary*. Austin: University of Texas Press, 2006.
Holt, Jennifer, and Alisa Perren. *Media Industries: History, Theory, and Method*. Malden: Wiley-Blackwell, 2009.
Huber, Alison. "Remembering Popular Music, Documentary Style: Tony Palmer's History in *All You Need Is Love*." *Television and New Media* 12, no. 6 (2011): 513–530.
Hynes, Eric. "Make It Real: Video Revives the Radio Star." *Film Comment*, December 4, 2015. https://www.filmcomment.com/blog/make-it-real-video-revives-the-radio-star/.
Kahana, Jonathan. *Intelligence Work: The Politics of American Documentary*. New York: Columbia University Press, 2008.
Malitsky, Joshua. "Knowing Sports: The Logic of the Contemporary Sports Documentary." *Journal of Sport History* 41, no. 2 (Summer 2014): 205–214.
Mann, Denise. "Welcome to the Unregulated Wild, Wild, Digital West." *Media Industries Journal* 1, no. 2 (2014): 30–35.
Mayer, Vicki, Miranda J. Banks, and John Thornton Caldwell, eds. *Production Studies: Cultural Studies of Media Industries*. New York: Routledge, 2009.
Rubin, Mike. "This Band Was Punk before Punk Was Punk." *New York Times*, March 12, 2009. http://www.nytimes.com/2009/03/15/arts/music/15rubi.html.
Sakoui, Anousha. "Why the World's Largest Record Label Wants to Be a Movie Studio." *Japan Times*, August 5, 2015. https://www.japantimes.co.jp/culture/2015/08/05/music/worlds-largest-record-label-wants-movie-studio/#.WeUUbxR3g7c.
Schatz, Thomas. *The Genius of the System: Hollywood Filmmaking in the Studio Era*. New York: Pantheon Books, 1988.
Sisario, Ben. "Now That 'Sugar Man' Is Found, Lawsuit Focuses on Missing Royalties." *New York Times*, May 2, 2014. https://www.nytimes.com/2014/05/03/business/media/now-that-sugar-man-is-found-lawsuit-focuses-on-missing-royalties.html?_r=0.
Vallejo, Aida. "Of Calendars and Industries: IDFA and CPH:DOX." *Necsus: European Journal of Media Studies* 9 (Spring 2016). https://necsus-ejms.org/calendars-industries-idfa-cphdox/.

Winton, Ezra. "Good for the Heart and Soul, Good for Business: The Cultural Politics of Documentary at the Hot Docs Film Festival." PhD diss., Carleton University, 2013.

Wright, Julie. "The Good, The Bad, and The Ugly '60s: The Opposing Gazes of *Woodstock* and *Gimme Shelter*." In *The Music Documentary: Acid Rock to Electropop*, edited by Robert Edgar, Kristy Fairclough-Isaacs, and Benjamin Halligan, 89–104. New York: Routledge, 2013.

Wyatt, Justin. "Donald Rugoff, Cinema V, and Commercial Strategies of the 1960s–70s Art Cinema." *Media Industries Journal* 4, no. 1 (2017): 1–20.

Zoellner, Anna. "Professional Ideology and Programme Conventions: Documentary Development in Independent British Television Production." *Mass Communication and Society* 12, no. 4 (2009): 503–536.

LANDON PALMER is Assistant Professor in the Department of Journalism and Creative Media at the University of Alabama. He is the author of *Rock Star/Movie Star: Power and Performance in Cinematic Rock Stardom*.

15

ASSEMBLING *NANKING*
Archival Filmmaking in the Popular Historical Documentary

Dylan Nelson

Documentary film "contributes to the formation of popular memory," as Bill Nichols puts it, in part by bringing lesser-known episodes of history to life for a wide audience.[1] The historical documentary re-creates the past in the present, choosing certain narratives over others and, in the process, determining which events can be popularly attended to and how those events might be known. Focusing on the 2007 documentary feature *Nanking* (dir. Bill Guttentag, Dan Sturman), on which I served as a producer and researcher, this chapter considers questions of creativity, selection, verisimilitude, and entertainment in the popular historical documentary. I analyze the rhetoric of selected sources in the film; discuss the provenance and circulation of some images and the contexts in which they have been used over time; and outline the creative rationale behind their inclusion in *Nanking*. Finally, I address what Nichols calls the "fraught area of debate" around responsible use of archival materials in documentary film.[2]

What makes a documentary "popular"? Its content? Its style? The number of people who see it? By one measure, theatrical box office, a review of the top one hundred highest-grossing American documentaries since 1982 suggests that if you're making a popular documentary, you're making a film about an animal or a pop singer—or you're Michael Moore.[3] Four of the top twenty are by Moore, including the top spot for *Fahrenheit 9/11*, which, with an astounding $119 million in domestic box office, is $42 million ahead of its closest competitor, *March of the Penguins*. Moore's secret for reaching a broad audience? "The first rule of documentaries is: Don't make a documentary—make a MOVIE."[4] Among Moore's precepts: Art first, politics second. Use humor. Make it new. And think of the audience: "The audience, the people who've worked hard all week—it's Friday night, and they want to go to the movies. They want the lights to go down and be taken somewhere.... They want to be entertained. And there, I said it—the big dirty word of documentary filmmaking. Entertained."[5]

The 1937 Rape of Nanking has been called World War II's "forgotten holocaust."[6] In their application for a News and Documentary Emmy Award, directors Bill Guttentag and Dan Sturman wrote that they made their documentary feature about these events, *Nanking*, because they believe "the words 'forgotten' and 'holocaust' should never be in the same sentence."[7] This statement gestures toward the popular in declaring, simply, *more people must know*. And if, as a filmmaker working in the historical mode, I want to reach a broad audience—defined as having a worldwide theatrical release, cross-platform broadcasts, and an extensive festival run—I need my documentaries to be entertaining. "Entertaining" does not mean funny, or fluffy, or drawing on already mainstream subject matter. For me, an entertaining film engages an audience's intellectual and emotive faculties. An entertaining documentary makes viewers *feel*, even as it helps them learn.

But a documentary about the past must not solely entertain. It must draw on the historical record in order to provide a clear and accurate depiction of events. If documentary is, as Nichols says, "an expressive art... more an art than a news report,"[8] then of course creativity must be part of documentary treatment, including narrative strategies drawn as much from Hollywood as from journalism.[9] Given that documentary filmmakers engage in a fluid creative practice that implies credibility or even "truth," how creative should historical documentary get? Unlike journalists, who are expected to adhere to an accepted code, documentary filmmakers have no mutually agreed-on set of standards and practices. In a 2009 study by the Center for Social Media, "Honest Truths: Documentary Filmmakers on Ethical Challenges in Their Work," filmmakers articulated three general principles: "Do no harm. Protect the vulnerable. Honor the viewers' trust."[10] These guidelines give little insight into issues of creative license or to what degree we, as nonfiction filmmakers, are responsible to "the truth." What truth? Whose truth?

All film, including documentary, requires subjectivity, elision, and thousands of selective choices. How, then, might filmmakers attempt authoritatively to narrate historic events—especially events that remain disputed and controversial? *Nanking* traverses such domain by telling the story of the Japanese invasion of Nanking, China, in 1937, also known as the "Rape of Nanking" or the "Nanking Massacre," an event that has strained Sino-Japanese relations for more than eighty years and remains polarizing to this day.

Specifically, the Chinese claim that in Nanking between December 1937 and February 1938, Japanese troops murdered at least three hundred thousand Chinese and raped eighty thousand women.[11] Historian David Askew goes so far as to call this claim "a fundamental keystone in the construction of the modern Chinese national identity."[12] Japan has never apologized for the atrocity, and a small but vociferous group of ultra-right-wingers in Japan minimizes or denies the events.[13] Askew argues that the relative positions of both the Chinese government and the denialist elements in Japan have become so entrenched that challenges to either orthodoxy risk being perceived as attacks on either country's national character. He notes, "In this environment, the historian's struggle to maintain objectivity can quickly fall victim to the demands of contemporary politics."[14]

In his book about the historiography of the Nanking Massacre, historian Joshua Fogel assures us that based on all evidence, a "great massacre" did indeed occur in Nanking, but he warns that far more important than granting the atrocity's existence "is a consideration of how the Nanking Massacre has been used both by those who aver and by those who deny it—that is, how it has been appropriated as an ideological tool or for nationalist mobilization."[15] How could we filmmakers, Westerners without a political agenda, navigate this minefield and escape being used as an "ideological tool"?[16] In some ways, our Western positionality is appropriate to the narrative: *Nanking* focuses on the story of the "Safety Zone," a neutral zone for the protection of Chinese civilians, created and defended via the diplomatic efforts of a group of expatriate Westerners who refused to evacuate the city during the invasion. These Westerners documented the atrocities as they happened in their diaries, in letters, and via direct eyewitness interviews that became "incident reports" submitted to Japanese officials alongside pleas to stop the carnage. These on-the-scene records form the narrative core of our film and remain one of the richest sources of documentary evidence about the massacre.

From its earliest moments, then, Westerners were central to efforts not only to intercede in the massacre but also to document and narrate it. Still, it would be disingenuous to suggest that *Nanking* is a project *about* Westerners. The essence of the conflict lies between China and Japan, and we, as filmmakers—like the German businessmen and American missionary eyewitnesses whose words in part make up our film—are only the conduits for this story. We did not want to position ourselves otherwise, nor did we wish to become entangled in the political debates around the massacre. We decided to steer clear of analysis by taking a purely primary source approach to the story of *Nanking*. We would use no historians, no commentators, simply present direct eyewitness testimonies accompanied by primary source archival imagery. Our goal was to create a visceral, immersive account of the Nanking Massacre—that is, to harness historical accuracy to an *audience experience* that was first and foremost emotional.

It is worthwhile, here, to acknowledge the ethics of attempting to represent historical atrocity, particularly within a documentary aimed at creating an empathetic experience of traumatic events for a broad audience. To what extent does showing violent, disturbing images risk reinscribing that violence, thus contravening the previously stated precept "do no harm"? Do such images sensationalize or fetishize violence—or, worse, trivialize the suffering of those who experienced violence? Do the images themselves inflict violence on the subject or on the viewer?

Perhaps most relevant in applying these questions to *Nanking* are the debates around representations of the Holocaust, articulated by filmmakers Claude Lanzmann and Jean-Luc Godard and by numerous philosophers and critics, including Siegfried Kracauer, Jacques Rancière, Jean-Luc Nancy, and Jean-François Lyotard, among others. Documentarian Claude Lanzmann dismissed archival photos and footage as "images without imagination" that "petrify thought and stifle all evocative power."[17] He therefore used no archival imagery from the Holocaust in his monumental film *Shoah*, instead relying on direct witness testimonies. Further, Lanzmann famously stated that even if he had found film showing mass executions within the gas chambers, he would not merely have declined to use the footage. He would have destroyed it.[18] For Lanzmann, to use archival imagery is to reduce the question of the Shoah to one of mere evidence. An image can only incite doubt, only invite further requests for "proof."[19]

Michael S. Roth discusses arguments that support Lanzmann's negation of the archival image: use of image is "identification," an attempt to make spectacle from and to essentialize a trauma so vast it can never be represented, much less known—and in fact *should* not be represented, because such representation is an abomination. Or image is "consolation," providing a false sense of understanding something that cannot be understood.[20] As Gérard Wajcman writes, "Every image of horror is a veil over horror; every image, because it is an image, protects us from horror . . . the image turns us away from that which it makes us see."[21]

But though images are inadequate and inexact, though they are traces, though they are metonyms that can never depict the entirety of an event, must they necessarily be reduced to meaninglessness? Libby Saxton, in her discussion of "discourses of 'unrepresentability'" around the Holocaust, notes that these discourses have fallen into question in recent scholarship.[22] For Roth, art historian Georges Didi-Hubermann offers a viable alternative to the discourse of unrepresentability: that of "possibility."[23] Didi-Hubermann, whose analysis of four photographs from Auschwitz was challenged and maligned by Lanzmann, Wajcman, and others, insists, "In order to know, we must imagine for ourselves. We must attempt to imagine the hell that Auschwitz was in the summer of 1944. Let us not invoke the unimaginable. Let us not shelter ourselves by saying that we cannot, that we could not by any means, imagine it to the very end. *We are obliged* to that oppressive imaginable."[24] For Didi-Hubermann, images do not stifle imagination so much as invoke it, and this kind of imagination is a moral imperative. He notes, "The imaginable certainly does not make radical evil 'present' and in no way masters it on a practical level: what it does do is bring us closer to its *possibility*."[25] He offers the phrase "in spite of all" to gesture toward the value of images in approaching some possibility of understanding, some possibility, as Roth puts it, of "redemption without consolation."[26] Didi-Hubermann writes, "We must know how to look into images to see that of which they are survivors. So that history, liberated from the pure past (that absolute, that abstraction) might help us *to open the present of time*."[27]

In our team's approach to the terrible events at Nanking, we hew more closely to Didi-Hubermann's view than to Lanzmann's. For us, visible evidence is not "mere." Despite the inherent unreliability of archival images, discussed further in this chapter, we believe these images' evidentiary value outweighs the potential harm done by their reproduction. Archival images are fragments—but fragments are all we have, and we should use them, albeit with humility and self-awareness, in spite of all.

A major part of *Nanking*'s claim to authority was our extensive worldwide search for these fragments—for primary source material.[28] In addition to numerous texts, we assembled contemporary newsreels; family and missionary films; footage of the attack on Nanking filmed by the Japanese army and retained in US archives as "foreign records seized"; atrocity photos taken by Japanese soldiers as souvenirs; American and Japanese war propaganda films; and, notably, the "Magee Film," amateur 16 mm footage of the atrocities smuggled out of the occupied city. Our goal was to use text and images drawn only, as much as we could determine, from the time and place, and of the events, we sought to depict.[29] In other words, we sought to gesture as closely as possible toward the indexical bond between archival object and historical actuality.

Jaimie Baron confirms the powerful impact of the primary source when she writes that archival images "seem to bring us into 'contact' with the past.... They offer us an *experience* of pastness, an experience that no written word can quite match."[30] Such images, which bear a strong indexical relationship to the historical world, are nevertheless "unruly." Archival images "seem 'closer' to the past they represent and are potentially seductive in their seeming transparent textuality; and although every trace—written or otherwise—is open to interpretation, indexical audiovisual recordings are especially resistant to full comprehension or interpretation."[31] In his seminal 1964 work *Films Beget Films*, Jay Leyda describes newsreel footage as having a "double content": the information it contains and its formal attributes.[32] Even when viewers may agree on both the content and form of a given image, the image's received *meaning*, as Michael Renov and others have shown, depends on how it is framed within narrative.[33] Facts, including those signified by the content of images, gain "evidential status" only once they are bound into discourse.[34]

Does footage actually show the recorded event it purports to describe? How exhaustively—in an editorial process invariably subject to deadlines and cost pressures—must a filmmaker interrogate archival sources? Leyda describes what Baron calls "archival anxieties":[35] problems of cataloging and misnaming within archives; problems of "accidental forgery," in which staged materials enter the archive as genuine; and problems of authenticity within films that compile archival materials.[36] Besides the dangers of inaccuracy in the record itself, what can be told depends on what archives preserve. That is, issues of power and control, of who deems what to be important, often determine the content of the historical record.[37]

Due to what impulse do archival materials originate? Why do they enter the archive? Who can access archival materials, and how? Such questions of power extend to films that draw upon archival images. In *Nanking*, many major texts relate to the problematic "civilizing project" of Western missionaries in China, preserved in the Divinity School Library at Yale University, which has ties to China going back to 1835.[38] Another crucial source is the numerous Japanese newsreels seized by American troops in World War II; we would never have been able to access such detailed and visceral images of Japanese military operations if our own military had not confiscated the records as spoils of war. Finally, the ability to use an archival object is often determined by cost. Only because we were able to pay for rights to access, duplicate, and license footage and some texts were we able to make our film.

Once a filmmaker has an archival object in hand, what responsibilities does she have in using it—that is, in revealing its meaning through discourse? Is there such a thing as a "greater truth" or an "emotional truth" that takes precedence over the literal? How does one balance verisimilitude and accuracy with dramatic impact? Broadly, we may take as our guide what filmmaker Jon Else describes as a first principle of archival ethics: "Does the audience know what it's getting?"[39] Put another way, what claim does the footage (in the film) make about itself (in the world), and can the audience understand that claim?

Audience research is an inexact science. Even so, day-to-day practice and shot-by-shot analysis help filmmakers identify our own narratives' claims. As director Stanley Nelson says, "You go over your film, you go over scenes, over and over and over again. You know what your film is saying and what it's implying. And if it's not true, then I think there's a problem."[40] Jon Else articulates the truth imperative by putting himself in the position of the audience: "If I think it's a picture of Malcolm X on the screen, it has to be Malcolm X. It's as simple as that."[41]

Is it? *Nanking*'s opening declares its allegiance to the real yet simultaneously effects a creative transformation via reenactment. After the main title, we cut to a Hollywood sound stage. Actors convene. Two expository cards fade in: "The actors in this film portray real people. The words they speak are taken from letters, diaries, and other sources." The actors find seats in a circle of chairs. Veteran character actor John Getz begins to read: "George Fitch. Christmas Eve. Nanking, China, 1937. What I am about to relate is a story which I feel must be told, even if it is seen by only a few. I cannot rest until I have told it and, perhaps fortunately, I am one of a very few who are in a position to tell it. It is not complete—only a part of the whole—and God alone knows when it will be finished. . . . I believe it has no parallel in modern history."[42] As Getz speaks, the film juxtaposes his image with a photograph of the real George Fitch and the identifier "George Fitch, Missionary." According to Nichols, reenactments create "resurrected ghosts that both haunt and endow the present with psychic intensity."[43] We have, in effect, raised George Fitch from the dead. Fitch and Getz look alike, so the audience feels an uncanny echo of the past.

The words Getz speaks are drawn from Fitch's diary of the atrocity, and we filmmakers ventriloquize these words to stand for our own claim to narrative authority: that although the story *our film* can tell is "only part of the whole," the film's urgent purpose is to tell a story that "must be told." That is, we seek "to record, reveal, or preserve," which Renov describes as one of four

Fig. 15.1 Actor John Getz quotes George Fitch and ventriloquizes the film's implicit claims in *Nanking* (2007).

fundamental tendencies of documentary practice.[44] We also seek to disarm the viewer by showing the strings of the staged reading, thereby persuading the audience we are transparent and, therefore, trustworthy. Our truth claim (that we "record, reveal, or preserve") is fundamentally a rhetorical device used to persuade the audience: yes, this happened.

Following Getz as Fitch, actor Woody Harrelson speaks as surgeon Robert Wilson. "I was born and grew up here in China . . . Nanking is my home." Chinese street scenes play. The narrative implies these scenes are from pre-1937 Nanking, and indeed, we sourced the footage from a film called *Our Capital* found in the China Film Archives.[45] During the final finishing phase, however, director Dan Sturman observed of one shot, "That doesn't look like a car from the 1930s." Further research revealed it was a 1940s model. Should we look for a replacement? "Do no harm." Strained by a strict deadline, we decided no one was harmed by this shot's inclusion. In this case, accuracy of place was more important than accuracy in time. The words are "Nanking is my home" and the image shown is Nanking. Our use fit the film's claim, at least as closely as we could make it do so.

After Harrelson, Mariel Hemingway introduces her character: "Minnie Vautrin, dean of Ginling Women's College in Nanking." We cut to a black-and-white banner that reads, "Ginling" and then a shot of an older white woman shaking hands with a young Chinese girl that next pans to a group of young Chinese girls waving happily. This footage was taken at Ginling

College prior to 1937, but the woman shown in the clip is not Minnie Vautrin. She is Matilda Calder Thurston, founder of Ginling College.[46] The film's context does not, precisely, *claim* the woman is Vautrin, but it certainly implies so. We fail Else's Malcolm X test.

In this case, we justified the clip's inclusion via a different ethical calculus. Our search had yielded almost no verifiable moving images of Vautrin, save a clip in which she is (somewhat bizarrely) doing a jig. This actual image of the real Minnie Vautrin did not fit the film's stated context: to depict Vautrin as "dean of Ginling Women's College." The Thurston clip did. The women were of similar age, appearance, and status as administrators at Ginling. The footage was filmed at Ginling. Most important, the image of the smiling woman and joyous girls helped us advance our larger aesthetic and narrative goal of creating a sense of prewar utopia soon to be shattered. We could have substituted a still photo of Vautrin, but we generally prefer moving images for their ability to re-create an experience of living "pastness" for the viewer. We decided the crucial element was "white female administrator at prewar Ginling College" and which administrator it was did not strictly matter. Better a powerful film clip that was close enough.

Representationally, is there such a thing as "close enough"? We can never achieve true indexicality. The signifier will never become the signified. Leyda writes, "Won't any skyscraper do to represent Wall Street? Won't one plough do as well as another? (Who will appreciate your search for the *right* plough shot?)"[47] In *Nanking*, we sought both the "*right* plough shot" and the plough shot that best served the story in a given moment. Our greatest allegiance in the Vautrin/Thurston decision was to the dramatic requirements of our storytelling and, ultimately, the emotional sensibilities of our audience. We may have created a small historical distortion, but we accepted this distortion as necessary to the emotional truth of the larger film.

Elsewhere, we erred on the side of strict accuracy. One of our visual sources for *Nanking* was *The Battle of China*, made in 1944 as part of the "Why We Fight" series directed by Frank Capra for the US Signal Corps. *The Battle of China* is a propaganda film, designed to boost troop and public morale and to persuade both to keep fighting World War II. It is a secondary source that includes a great deal of powerful primary source footage, which the film explicitly describes as genuine in an end title card: "All film used in this picture comes from Chinese sources, American and British Army Photographic Services, Missionaries, Newsreels, and Captured Japanese films."[48] By gesturing toward the primary, Capra makes his truth claim about *The Battle of China* using the same rhetorical device we did in *Nanking* ("The actors in

Fig. 15.2 Cropped frame of a street execution in *The Battle of China* (1944).

this film portray real people"). But his next card includes some important fine print: "Certain non-combat stock scenes were used from historical pictures." A review of the film's footage log shows that by "historical pictures" Capra means Hollywood movies and other American-sourced footage, including the famed 1938 Pare Lorentz documentary about the Mississippi, *The River* (1938), an MGM fictional short entitled "The Rainbow Pass" (1937), and the 1937 MGM blockbuster adaptation of Pearl S. Buck's China-set novel *The Good Earth*.[49]

In the course of editing *Nanking*, we created a visual sequence of horrors carried out by Japanese soldiers. This sequence built to a disturbing climax with a clip of a street execution taken from Capra's film. In the source clip, *The Battle of China*'s narrator intones, "In their occupation of Nanking, the Japs [sic] again outdid themselves in barbarism. . . . They raped and tortured. They killed and butchered." Two rifles fire, the Japanese perpetrators offscreen. Two Chinese slump to the ground, dead.

We did our due diligence to verify the clip's source. The film's log listed the shot as "Executing Chinese—shooting them in back of head" and the source as "Pathé News Reel #4." Unfortunately, "#4" seemed to be a cataloguing code internal to Capra's production, and a search for Pathé newsreels yielded no clear match. We were, of course, aware that some newsreels, including Pathé, staged events, particularly early in the form's development,[50] but the execution clip shared the visual profile of the other contemporaneous news footage we had assembled from confirmed sources. We decided to believe the clip actually showed what it purported to depict: a Japanese atrocity.

The climactic execution sequence made it quite far in the edit of the film. In fact, we were just locking our cut when, at a newly reopened video archive way out in the San Fernando Valley, I found a copy of the original Pathé newsreel.[51] In this original, the execution clips were uncropped, the perpetrators clearly visible.[52] I will not repeat the blue words I heard when I brought this clip into the edit room. The problem? The uniforms on the soldiers didn't look Japanese. We began another search, for experts who could identify the uniforms.[53] We ultimately determined the uniforms were of Chinese military police, not Japanese soldiers. This very real newsreel footage depicted a street execution of Chinese by Chinese police, an event entirely different from the event Capra used it to depict.

Archival footage, bound by narrative, in my view may claim either to *represent* or to *illustrate* an event. When filmmakers claim to *represent*, we create as close to a one-to-one relationship as possible between the image's historic actuality and its meaning-as-created by the film. In other words, we try to reflect the indexical bond between image and past occurrence. We ask ourselves, "What claim does the footage (in the film) make about itself (in the world)?" If the two do not match, we must ask, "To what *degree* does the new use (in the film) change the footage's meaning (in the world)?" The meaning-as-created of the Chinese execution clip is, in Capra's film, "Japanese soldiers kill Chinese prisoners." Its historic actuality: "Chinese police kill Chinese prisoners." These two meanings are strongly divergent. Did, in Nanking, the Japanese kill civilians in the street, execution style? Yes. Documents, letters, and eyewitness accounts all testify they did. Perhaps this was the justification Capra made for cropping the image in the first place; even if the image itself didn't include Japanese soldiers, he used the image to *illustrate* acts Japanese soldiers actually did commit.

However, the clip in our film claimed to *represent*, as evidence, what happened in Nanking in 1937. This wasn't a relatively minor matter of switching administrators or of substituting 1940s footage for 1930s. Capra purposely misrepresented murder. We didn't want to do the same. We were also keenly aware that, as Leyda and Baron have shown, films are themselves archives. Someday, other filmmakers might use *Nanking* as a source for their own

288 | Reclaiming Popular Documentary

Fig. 15.3 Uncropped frame of a street execution from Pathé Newsreel.

"indexical" images. The scale of the potential distortion, amplified into the future, was untenable to us. We pulled the shot from the film and reedited the sequence without it.

"Does the audience know what it is getting?" In addition to using archival images to represent events, filmmakers deploy historical footage in a more generalized manner I call "illustrative." One of our film's most useful visual sources was a 1938 Japanese propaganda film, also called *Nanking*.[54] This film, shot by a Japanese crew immediately after the capital's fall, showcases numerous purportedly benevolent acts by Japanese soldiers. In one sequence, the narration describes "how happy the real refugees were. . . . They hoisted the homemade Rising Sun banners and made friends with Japanese soldiers." A high-angle shot shows a young Chinese girl seated at the opening of a refugee tent. She looks up, directly at the camera. Her expression is at best neutral (I might describe it as "anxious"), but her image *illustrates*, in the meaning-as-created by the Japanese film, the concept "gladness about the occupation." In our film, we use the same shot over a Chinese survivor's testimony about mass rape. "[Japanese soldiers] would capture dozens of young girls and

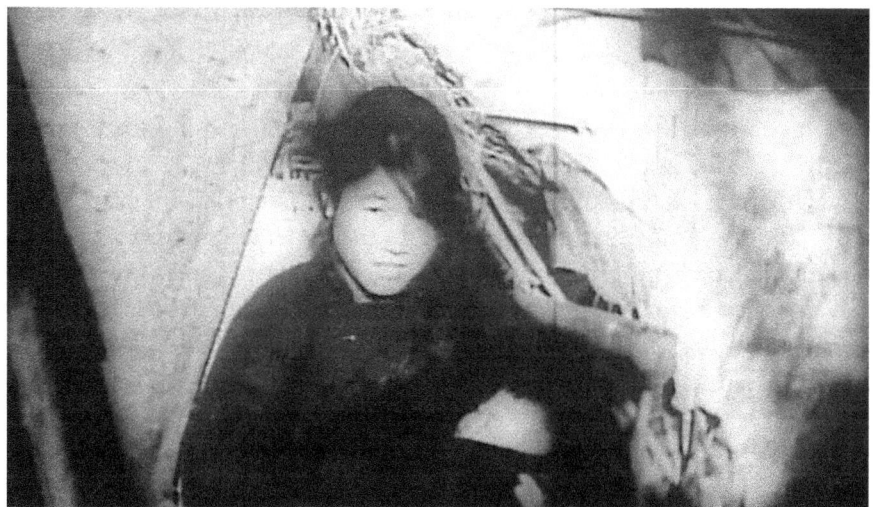

Fig. 15.4 An archival image illustrates oppositional meanings in two films about Nanking.

round them up, and they would choose the pretty ones." The same girl looks up at the same camera—but our film's implication is not that she is "happy" but that she could have been raped.

In both cases, the films illustrate an idea rather than representing a fact. Neither use represents the "actuality" of the girl's situation. It is unlikely the actual girl was glad about the occupation. We also don't know whether she was targeted for rape (though our film doesn't *claim* she was; it only suggests she is pretty). In fact, we don't know anything about this girl, other than that she appears to be a refugee in Nanking. This shot could have originated from another location in China. It could show a Japanese actress posing as a refugee. Here we return to the unruliness of archival or "found" images. Baron writes, "At issue is the belief that documents that read as found . . . can ever be trusted as evidence about the historical past"[55] and concludes that, ultimately, the "matter of historical proof is one of corroboration."[56] The young girl in the shot had a visual profile consonant with Nanking refugee footage we accumulated from other sources. Much other footage in the 1938 film *Nanking* (the walls, the entry by Japanese troops, various identifiable streets and gates, etc.) was clearly filmed in the fallen city. We chose to believe the 1938 film's claim that the woman in the shot *was* a refugee in Nanking, and we therefore chose this shot—to paraphrase Leyda, the right female refugee shot—again because we sought as much fidelity as possible to the place and time of the Nanking occupation.

Another sequence from this 1938 Japanese film demonstrates the various uses to which identical footage can be put. A group of Chinese children plays with fireworks. Some laugh, some duck, some simply watch. This sequence is framed with a title reading "Happy New Year . . . Hurrah for the Japanese Army!" As used in the 1938 film, footage is evidence of peace truly restored. Our film, framing the same clip as part of the pro-Japanese propaganda machine, claims, "This situation was staged for the camera." Finally, a 2007 Japanese denialist TV program used this same exact clip in order to prove that "no massacre occurred," the argument being that children with happy expressions could not possibly have experienced atrocities. One commentator says, "They [the children] really enjoyed playing with it [sic]. Everyone can see whether they are scared or forced to do it or not."[57] Another declares, "It is impossible to imagine plunder, rape, or murder in a place where we can see residents with such natural facial expressions."[58] Here, the revisionists go beyond the original propaganda source and use a specific sequence to claim not merely that "peace has been restored" but that "peace was never disrupted at all."

As in the previous example, *Nanking* sometimes holds up historical imagery itself as an object of examination. The most important footage-object in *Nanking* is the "Magee Film," a remarkable record of the Nanking Massacre and the only moving images drawn from the carnage. During the occupation of Nanking, American missionary John Magee secretly documented Japanese atrocities via eight reels of 16 mm film negative, which fellow American George Fitch smuggled out of the besieged city in the lining of his coat. Our research located four different segments of this crucial film in different archives, including the personal collections of the Fitch and Magee families, and thus pieced together what we believe to be all Magee footage that survives.[59] Near the end of *Nanking*, we show several excerpts from this film, introduced by "George Fitch," who describes them as "so terrible they had to be seen to be believed."[60]

Once again, Fitch's words evoke our film's overarching purpose: to create an experience of images that *would be* seen and believed. This sequence is the evidentiary climax of our film, and we let it speak for itself. The footage unspools: no musical punctuation, no sound save the whirring of a projector, a silent litany of horrors. We see victims (including children) of beating, rape, burning, and mutilation, accompanied by contemporaneous intertitles that soberly describe their injuries.[61] (One example: "Pregnant with her first child, this 19-year old woman was bayoneted when she sought to resist raping at the hands of a Japanese soldier. When admitted to a refugee hospital she was found to have no less than 29 wounds.") The sequence ends with footage of a woman who suffered an attempted beheading: she sits upright, a triangle of flesh hacked from her neck, head only half attached to her body. This clip yields audible gasps whenever *Nanking* is publicly screened and forms the apotheosis of our film's visible evidence.[62] When faced with this image, doubt about the fundamental truth of our narrative becomes impossible.

The irony is that while, for present-day audiences, seeing these images incites and underscores belief, for 1937 audiences less acclimated to graphic images,[63] the images were actually *too* terrible to be believed. Fitch succeeded in getting the film to Shanghai and then to the United States. He attempted a speaking tour, but audiences resisted his story: "My films caused something of a sensation, even illness, on the part of a couple of the audience. And following the meeting, a Japanese gentleman approached me and said that my statements about the atrocities in Nanking were not true—they could not be true—for Japanese were incapable of such acts."[64]

"Truth" again. *Nanking* premiered in competition at the Sundance Film Festival in 2007. Immediately in response to our Sundance premiere, Japanese nationalist filmmaker Satoru Mizushima called our film "a setup by China to control intelligence" and claimed it was a fabrication. He felt "obliged to counter that film by making a film of his own," which "w[ould] tell the world what really happened" by telling "the facts as they are."[65] The resulting film, *The Truth about Nanjing*, focused on defending the heroism of Japan's wartime actions.[66] When *The Truth about Nanjing* was released, our financier and producer, Ted Leonsis, commented: "I know about the... controversy in Japan. So we hired 38 people who spent 18 months all over the world doing research. Our conclusion was that we should have no point of view, to just document what happened."[67]

Of course it is fundamentally false that our film has "no point of view." We set out to create an emotional experience of witness, not an absolute reckoning. Our film is about the Nanking Massacre, but it also invokes the horror of all wars and, as our press materials put it, "the heartbreaking toll war takes on the innocent."[68] Yet Leonsis reiterated our film's "truth claim" using the same rhetoric as Japanese nationalist Mazushima. "What really happened," "facts as they are," "just document what happened": using similar absolutist terms, both those who aver the atrocity and those who deny it simplify the complex interactions between occurrence, image, and narrative that constitute the historical documentary film and that can gesture toward, but never duplicate, the past.

Did we "succeed" in our goal of narrating a past event, inasmuch as is possible, authoritatively? Despite our best efforts, the film did not escape being ensnared in debate and used as an "ideological tool" by elements in both China and Japan. In 2007, *Nanking* had its theatrical release in China, where it became what was then the highest-grossing documentary in Chinese history. It won numerous accolades in the United States, including two Emmy Awards and the George Foster Peabody Award. It has never screened publicly in Japan.

I have attempted, in this chapter, to describe some of the elisions, ethical gradations, and creative compromises that determine the fictive nature of even the most supposedly transparent and authoritatively documented nonfiction films. I have also tried to show how questions of sourcing, implication, and accuracy related to the unruliness of archival images can play out in the making of historical documentaries. In creating *Nanking*, we made our archival choices on a case-by-case basis, each decision carefully weighed in an attempt to balance historical accuracy with dramatic efficacy. Whether using archival footage to represent or to illustrate, in practice I remain keenly aware of the anxieties of the archive. I urge all filmmakers to vet and to deploy their sources with care and with a deep sense of responsibility. It does matter, even if one can never truly capture "the truth."

"God alone knows when it may be finished," George Fitch wrote (and says in our film) of the terror in Nanking. Renov suggests that documentary can perform the "work of mourning"—not for the film subject who relates a harrowing story, or for the filmmaker who documents it, but for an audience whose own experience is sufficiently distant from the event.[69] Although a full reckoning of the Nanking Massacre seems to elude historians, governments, and nations, perhaps the seventy-year gap between 1937 and 2007 created the distance that makes mourning the Nanking Massacre—through our film, and others—possible.[70] During production on *Nanking*, we interviewed, via simultaneous translation, many survivors of the massacre in China. As these survivors told their stories, our translators at times wept so uncontrollably the interviews could not continue. The translators were, in a sense, the film's first audience. For them, the story's particulars were new—but also old, from a faraway past—and thus the story delivered what Baron calls the "evidentiary revelation" promised by the archive. "Paradoxically, something 'old' gains part of its power by also promising something 'new,' something we did not know or had not seen before."[71] Baron's words evoke Michael Moore's challenge to documentary filmmakers: "Take [the audience] someplace they haven't been. Show them something they've never seen."[72] In our case: tether fact to emotion in order to pierce the audience and thereby revitalize—and reclaim—history. Make a *movie*.

Notes

1. Nichols, *Representing Reality*, ix.
2. Nichols, "What to Do."
3. Box Office Mojo, "Documentary Genre."
4. Moore, "Michael Moore's 13 Rules for Making Documentary Films." The article reprints Moore's keynote speech at the 2014 Documentary Conference of the Toronto Film Festival.
5. Ibid.
6. Chang, *Rape of Nanking: WWII's Forgotten Holocaust*; the term *forgotten holocaust* is in the book's title.
7. Guttentag and Sturman, "Application to the News and Documentary Awards."
8. Nichols, "What to Do."
9. Much has, of course, been written about the creative elements of documentary, from Grierson's famous definition of the form as the "creative treatment of actuality" to Rotha's "dramatic statement of facts" to Renov's "fictive" forms that "narrativize the real." See Grierson, "First Principles of Documentary," 147; Rotha, *Documentary Film*, 269; Renov, "Introduction," 6–7.
10. Aufderheide, Jaszi, and Chandra, "Honest Truths," 1.
11. This is the official government position and also the numbers claimed at the Nanking Massacre Memorial in Nanjing (formerly Nanking). See Wakabayashi, "Messiness of Historical Reality," 3–8.
12. Askew, "Nanjing Incident."
13. Yoshida, "Battle over History," 87.
14. Askew, "Nanjing Incident."
15. Fogel, *Nanjing Massacre*, 5–6.
16. Both Chinese and Japanese producer-researchers were central to our production, but the originating producer, Ted Leonsis, and our directing team were all Americans.
17. Lanzmann, "Monument contre l'archive?," 274.
18. Lanzmann, "Parler pour les morts," 15.
19. As example, in a 2011 interview, Lanzmann describes a recent trip to Iran: "Ahmadinejad doesn't believe there was a Holocaust. The Iranians wanted me to prove to them on television that there was. They wanted to see the corpses" (Jeffries, "Claude Lanzmann on Why Holocaust Documentary *Shoah* Still Matters").
20. Roth, *Memory, Trauma, and History*, 192–195.
21. Wajcman, "De la croyance photographique," 69.
22. Saxton, *Haunted Images*, 6–11.
23. Roth, *Memory, Trauma, and History*, 195.
24. Didi-Hubermann, *Images in Spite of All*, 3. Emphasis in original.
25. Ibid., 155. Emphasis in original.
26. Roth, *Memory, Trauma, and History*, 196.
27. Didi-Hubermann, *Images in Spite of All*, 182. Emphasis in original.
28. Purple Mountain Productions, "About the Production."
29. This quest for verisimilitude extended to sound; we hired a sound designer who specializes in World War II battle sounds in an attempt to make our battle sequences model-accurate.

30. Baron, *Archive Effect*, 1.
31. Ibid., 3–4.
32. Leyda, *Films Beget Films*, 22.
33. Renov, "Introduction." See also Nichols, *Speaking Truths with Film*; Baron, *Archive Effect*.
34. Nichols, *Speaking Truths with Film*, 99.
35. Baron, *Archive Effect*, 49.
36. Leyda, *Films Beget Films*, 124–132.
37. Baron, *Archive Effect*, 2–3.
38. Yale University, "Yale and China."
39. Cited in Aufderheide, Jaszi, and Chandra, "Honest Truths," 19.
40. Bernard and Rabin, "Ethical Considerations," 144–145.
41. Ibid., 148.
42. Fitch, "Nanking Diary," 80. Cited in Guttentag and Sturman, *Nanking*.
43. Nichols, *Speaking Truths with Film*, 50.
44. Renov, "Toward a Poetics," 21.
45. "Entire Film Footage Photo Log," Purple Mountain Productions, internal files.
46. Yale Divinity School, "Matilda S. Calder Thurston."
47. Leyda, *Films Beget Films*, 109.
48. Capra, *Why We Fight*.
49. "*The Battle of China*: US War Department Information Film Source Sheets," Record Group 111.8, National Archives.
50. An online history of the British Pathé newsreel describes the period 1933–1958 as the "golden age" of Pathé but admits that for "much" of Pathé's earlier footage, "cataloguing is not helped by a lack of clarity over which events have been captured as they occurred and which are staged" (British Pathé, "History of British Pathé").
51. The Sherman Grinberg Film Library; I owe a debt to its chief archivist, Bill Brewington.
52. Only after *Nanking* was released did we discover this clip had also been included contemporaneously—uncropped—in a National Film Board of Canada anti-Japanese propaganda film, *Mask of Nippon* (1942), which mixes actuality and staged footage to create a despicably racist portrayal of Japanese troops.
53. When we sought references from the National WWII Museum in New Orleans, they told us they been showing the now-contested Capra clip in their orientation film as evidence of Japanese atrocities, for years. This film played in the museum's orientation hall until May 2016, and staff still refer teachers to the film, *The Road to War*, on a site called TeacherTube. In August 2016, a representative of the museum said the misleading shot was "too minor an issue to make too major an issue out of."
54. Akimoto, *Nanking*.
55. Baron, *Archive Effect*, 63.
56. Ibid., 66.
57. Satoru Mizushima, cited in Mizushima, Higashinakano, and Tomizawa, "Perspectives on the Film 'Nanking.'"
58. Shudo Higashinakano, cited in Mizushima, Higashinakano, and Tomizawa, "Perspectives on the Film 'Nanking.'"
59. Four copies of the original film were made and scattered around the world. One was lost when Nazi businessman John Rabe sent a copy to Hitler, in hopes the Führer would be outraged by the atrocities and intervene to help the Chinese.
60. Fitch, "Nanking Diary," 42. Cited in Guttentag and Sturman, *Nanking*.

61. It is worth noting that these images show only the aftermath of atrocity, not the act of atrocity itself; yet their accumulation, their extremity, and their "closeness" to the indexical event bear convincing witness.
62. We worked to calibrate the horror in the film via careful choice and placement of stories and imagery. In many cases, we excluded images or testimony we felt was too graphic.
63. Evans, "Nanking Atrocity," 51.
64. Fitch, "Nanking Diary," 43–44. Cited in Guttentag and Sturman, *Nanking*.
65. Hongo, "Filmmaker to Paint Japan Slaughter as Just Myth."
66. Mizoshima, *Truth about Nanjing*.
67. Ted Leonsis, quoted in Neill, "Look Back in Anger."
68. Purple Mountain Productions, "Film Synopsis."
69. Renov, "Filling Up the Hole," 120.
70. Indeed, perhaps the temporal disparity between "then" and "now" has stimulated the flurry of other filmic interpretations that have appeared since our film premiered.
71. Baron, *Archive Effect*, 6.
72. Moore, "Michael Moore's 13 Rules."

References

Akimoto, Ken, dir. *Nanking*. Tokyo: Toho Films, 1938. Japanese War Department, Military Intelligence Division. Collection of Foreign Records Seized. National Archives, Washington, DC.

Askew, David. "The Nanjing Incident: Recent Research and Trends." *Electronic Journal of Contemporary Japanese Studies*, April 4, 2002. http://www.japanesestudies.org.uk/articles/Askew.html#_edn1.

Aufderheide, Pat, Peter Jaszi, and Mridu Chandra, "Honest Truths: Documentary Filmmakers on Ethical Challenges in Their Work." Washington, DC: Center for Media and Social Impact, 2009.

Baron, Jaimie. *The Archive Effect: Found Footage and the Audiovisual Experience of History*. New York: Routledge, 2014.

"*The Battle of China*: US War Department Information Film Source Sheets." Record Group 111.8. National Archives, Washington, DC.

Bernard, Sheila Curran, and Kenn Rabin. "Ethical Considerations: A Roundtable Discussion with Claire Aguilar, Jon Else, Stanley Nelson, Bill Nichols, and Rick Prelinger." In *Archival Storytelling: A Filmmaker's Guide to Finding, Using, and Licensing Third-Party Visuals and Music*, 141–156. Burlington: Focal Press, 2009.

Box Office Mojo. "Documentary Genre." Accessed January 1, 2018. http://www.boxofficemojo.com/genres/chart/?id=documentary.htm.

British Pathé. "History of British Pathé." Accessed December 12, 2017. https://www.britishpathe.com/pages/history/.

Capra, Frank, dir. *Why We Fight: The Battle of China*. USA: US Army Signal Corps, 1944.

Chang, Iris. *The Rape of Nanking: WWII's Forgotten Holocaust*. New York: Basic Books, 1997.

Didi-Hubermann, Georges. *Images in Spite of All*. Translated by Shane B. Ellis. Chicago: University of Chicago Press, 2008.

Evans, Gary. "The Nanking Atrocity: Still and Moving Images 1937–1944." *Media and Communication* 2, no. 2 (2014): 55–71.

Fitch, George. "Nanking Diary." In *American Missionary Eyewitnesses to the Nanking Massacre, 1937–1938*, edited by Martha Lund Smalley. New Haven: Yale Divinity School Occasional Publication No. 9, 1997.

Fogel, Joshua, ed. *The Nanjing Massacre in History and Historiography*. Berkeley: University of California Press, 2000.

Grierson, John. "The First Principles of Documentary." In *Grierson on Documentary*, edited by Forsyth Hardy, 145–156. London: Faber and Faber, 1966.

Guttentag, Bill, and Dan Sturman. "Application to the News and Documentary Awards." 2008. Purple Mountain Productions LLC internal files.

———, dirs. *Nanking*. Los Angeles: Purple Mountain Productions, 2007.

Hongo, Jun. "Filmmaker to Paint Japan Slaughter as Just Myth." *Japan Times*, January 25, 2007.

Jeffries, Stuart. "Claude Lanzmann on Why Holocaust Documentary Shoah Still Matters." *Guardian*, June 9, 2011. https://www.theguardian.com/film/2011/jun/09/claude-lanzmann-shoah-holocaust-documentary.

Lanzmann, Claude. "Le monument contre l'archive?" *Les Cahiers de Médiologie*, no. 11 (2001): 271–279.

———. "Parler pour les morts." *Le Monde des Débats*, May 2000.

Leyda, Jay. *Films Beget Films: A Study of the Compilation Film*. New York: Hill and Wang, 1964.

"Magee Film." Variously called the "Fitch Film," the "Ghost Films," or "China Invaded." Compiled by Purple Mountain Productions from private sources (David Magee, Tanya Caligiuri), Visual Communications, and the Harmon Foundation Collection. Record Group 200. National Archives, Washington, DC.

Mizushima, Satoru, Shudo Higashinakano, and Shigenobu Tomizawa. "Perspectives on the Film 'Nanking.'" Channel Sakura, Tokyo, March 31, 2007. http://www.truthofnanking.com/tv_program.pdf.

Mizushima, Satoru, dir. *The Truth about Nanjing*. Tokyo: Channel Sakura, 2007.

Moore, Michael. "Michael Moore's 13 Rules for Making Documentary Films." *Indiewire*, September 10, 2014. http://www.indiewire.com/2014/09/michael-moores-13-rules-for-making-documentary-films-22384.

Neill, David. "Look Back in Anger." *Asia-Pacific Journal*, December 1, 2007. http://apjjf.org/-David-McNeill/2599/article.html.

Nichols, Bill. *Representing Reality*. Bloomington: Indiana University Press, 1991.

———. *Speaking Truths with Film: Evidence, Ethics, Politics in Documentary*. Oakland: University of California Press, 2016.

———. "What to Do About Documentary Distortion? Toward a Code of Ethics." *Documentary Magazine*. Accessed December 12, 2017. https://www.documentary.org/content/what-do-about-documentary-distortion-toward-code-ethics-0.

Purple Mountain Productions. "About the Production." Accessed December 1, 2017. http://www.nankingthefilm.com/about.aspx.

———. "Entire Film Footage Photo Log." Washington, DC: Internal production archive.

———. "Film Synopsis." Nanking the Film website. Accessed December 1, 2017, http://www.nankingthefilm.com/synopsis.aspx.

Renov, Michael. "Filling Up the Hole with the Real: Death and Mourning in Contemporary Documentary Film and Video." In *The Subject of Documentary*, 120–129. Minneapolis: University of Minnesota Press, 2004.

———. "Introduction: The Truth about Nonfiction." In *Theorizing Documentary*, edited by Michael Renov, 1–11. New York: Routledge, 1993.

———. "Toward a Poetics of Documentary." In *Theorizing Documentary*, edited by Michael Renov, 12–36. New York: Routledge, 1993.

Roth, Michael S. *Memory, Trauma, and History: Essays on Living with the Past*. New York: Columbia University Press, 2011.
Rotha, Paul. *Documentary Film*. New York: Norton, 1939.
Saxton, Libby. *Haunted Images: Film, Ethics, Testimony, and the Holocaust*. New York: Wallflower Press, an imprint of Columbia University Press, 2008.
Wajcman, Gérard. "De la croyance photographique." *Les Temps Modernes* 56, no. 613 (2001): 47–83.
Wakabayashi, Bob Tadashi. "The Messiness of Historical Reality." In *The Nanking Atrocity, 1937–1938: Complicating the Picture*, edited by Bob Tadashi Wakabayashi, 3–28. New York: Berghan Books, 2007.
Yale Divinity School. "Matilda S. Calder Thurston." American Context of China's Christian Colleges and Schools. Accessed December 5, 2017. http://divinity-adhoc.library.yale.edu/ChinaCollegesProject/MtHolyoke/biographies/Thurston.htm.
Yale University. "Yale and China: A Centuries-old Partnership." Yale and the World. Accessed November 6, 2020. https://world.yale.edu/news/yale-and-china-centuries-old-partnership.
Yoshida, Takashi. "A Battle over History in Japan." In *The Nanjing Massacre in History and Historiography*, edited by Joshua Fogel, 70–132. Berkeley: University of California Press, 2000.

DYLAN NELSON is Associate Professor of Film and Media Studies at Colorado College. She has worked as a producer of, among other films, the documentary features *Groomed* (2021), *Merchants of Doubt* (2014), *The Hollywood Complex* (2011), *Soundtrack for a Revolution* (2009), and *Nanking* (2007).

PART VI.
ENGAGING AUDIENCES

In this sixth and final section of the book, titled "Engaging Audiences," we present four diverse strategies and responses to the allure of the popular. In "Virality Is Virility: Viral Media, Popularity, and Violence," Alexandra Juhasz reflects on a series of text-based provocations she wrote and distributed on social media during the first one hundred days of the Trump presidency. The unconventional structure of this chapter, which consists of a series of reflections on the contested status of truth claims on social media, mirrors the laconic vernacular of platforms such as Twitter and Facebook, supporting Juhasz's ironic critique of popularity-driven, corporate-dominated online communities. Viewed in relation to Juhasz's long-standing commitment to experimentation with pedagogy, mediated presentation, and electronic publishing, this chapter represents a culmination of multifaceted reflections on the logics of virality and the potentials for social engagement online. Framing her argument as a "listicle" presenting the first ten out of one hundred "super hard truths"—resulting in the acerbic portmanteau "SHiTsticle"—Juhasz slams the culture and complacency of the internet while also recognizing its power and potentials. Finally, Juhasz's chapter represents a gesture of defiance against both the virality for which social media was architected and the global dissemination that it affords to even the most repugnant and violent forms of speech and disinformation. Juhasz's chapter is a thoughtful, angry response to a cultural moment when the fetishizing of popularity and virality too readily take the place of mindful engagement with issues of social import and community engagement.

In the next chapter, renowned archivist and ephemeral film collector Rick Prelinger discusses his ongoing Urban History Commons project in "Populism, Participation, and Perpetual Incompletion: Performing an Urban History Commons." Prelinger describes his work for more than a decade creating "film events"—as distinct from film objects or even film screenings—in which audience members collaboratively contribute a live, improvised "soundtrack" for the film in the form of questions, observations, and recollections voiced in real time while the film is being projected. As such, each screening is community-based and distinct, with a viewing experience that varies widely depending on the life experience, engagement, and chance connections among members of the audience. Prelinger's contribution to this book thus functions not merely as a reflective document or "artist's statement" intended to bring extratextual insight about his work but moreover as an extension of the historiographical project that is at the core of Prelinger's work. As an archivist, best known for his voluminous collection of industrial and amateur film that was acquired by the US Library of Congress in 2002, Prelinger has long been devoted to the practice of filmmaking to promote the accessibility of films that are otherwise neglected. Prelinger's *Lost Landscapes* series, then, is perhaps the most literally "popular" work included in this volume—yet also the most obscure. Although Prelinger has staged dozens of events in cities around the country, the number of viewers who are able to attend these live "film events" remains limited, underscoring, in part, the aim of this volume to redefine and reclaim the popular.

George S. Larke-Walsh explores the ongoing popularity of true crime documentaries, concentrating on the subgenre of true crime that deals specifically with criminal *in*justice. Larke-Walsh settles on the hugely popular Netflix series *Making a Murderer* (2015), considering the moral tenor of this subgenre, particularly the degree to which these nonfiction texts elicit moral and intellectual superiority in viewers (defined as "armchair jurors"), who are invited to reflect on the injustices of the American judicial system in sometimes counterproductive and contradictory ways. Blending theories of affect from Brian Massumi and Alison Young, Larke-Walsh recognizes the importance of emotion and affect (as an impulse or intensity that precedes emotion) as crucial components of the spectatorial experience with true crime, where the investigation of injustice encourages a complex blend of dissonant emotions: curiosity, disgust, frustration, and outrage.

This overview of strategies for engagement concludes with Steve F. Anderson's exploration of immersive documentary through the lenses of consumer-grade VR technology. Reading skeptically the hype-cycle surrounding the production and consumption of virtual reality as an "empathy machine," Anderson argues that the current generation of VR poses a far greater challenge to documentary form and practice than the crisis of representation that accompanied the rise of digital imaging in the previous century. Writing against the grain of industry discourse promoting the sensory immersion of spherical video viewing, Anderson considers the many ways that documentary VR can be misappropriated to undermine the traditional power imbalance between viewer and viewed. The choice that is afforded to viewers of a total visual field, he points out, can be equally used to undermine the privileged position of spectatorial omniscience in which viewers exercise total control over the visual field. VR documentaries, while far from popular in terms of audience size, are nonetheless aligned with a "low culture" appeal to the body—addressing feeling over intellect. Anderson highlights that far from being a deterministic experience, this technology creates opportunities for distinctly popular modes of resistant, subjective, and alternative viewing.

16

VIRALITY IS VIRILITY
Viral Media, Popularity, and Violence

Alexandra Juhasz

This chapter is constructed from reworked snippets of writing culled from four discrete albeit conceptually linked publications about online video, social media, and critical internet studies from the past ten years.[1] It builds from a much longer career devoted to thinking about, making, and teaching activist media that usually takes the form of documentary. Most recently this has transformed into a project experimenting with radical digital media literacy, one that engages both within and about social media.[2] Given the compulsions of the current presidential regime, I have become particularly committed to better understanding the uses and abuses of media that are at once seemingly—while also uncertainly—peddling in mimetic-based truth claims. All the while, I have been a consistent critic of the dastardly functions of popularity within online video and culture, again, particularly as this relates to the movement, power, and abuse of ideas and images made about history, identity, and truth while making use of reality-based records.

I attest that I come to my own scholarly and production work (often about deception and fakes) honestly, through my many engagements with activist media around a changing set of political concerns, connected to differing social movements and activist communities, and making use of shifting technologies and formats.[3] I have called this my "media praxis," an integration of theory, practice, politics, and teaching, that

> theorizes and makes media towards stated projects of world and self-changing. This ongoing project, as old as cinema itself, links culture, theory, and politics, in the 20th century, through mediation technologies and indebted to Marxist theories. . . . Unlike [media projects] that might focus upon cinema aesthetics or narrative [here, on mediapraxis.org] analyses of realism, documentary, and

truth are primary. I have found that most theory-writing producers attempt to prove that realist or documentary cinema is the ideal medium for this work and that the artist/intellectual is the worker best suited for this labor towards the struggle ... how do ideas exist in action, and how is this related to the project of radical pedagogy?[4]

My work—like and connected to that held in my website mediapraxis.org quoted here—theorizes, teaches about, and makes media bent on making radical change for people with AIDS, feminists, African American lesbians, prisoners, antiwar activists, women, people of color, and queer and trans people online. While all of my own work has focused on and uses documentary (or fake documentary), my praxis has developed to understand and make best use of reality-based media in light of the stunning affordances of access to production and distribution most recently allowed by digital tools and the corporate internet. I initially moved from activist video to the internet, as did many radical media practitioners, with the advent of YouTube. I went there (accompanied by several years of students taking my class Learning from YouTube) to better understand how or if the corporate internet's "free" platforms could be useful to everyday people and in particular those involved with the radical media praxis tradition to which I was and am devoted.[5] When working on and in YouTube with others, I very much wanted to consider why, when access to media production and distribution were becoming more democratic, more free, and more accessible, the revolution many of us had anticipated did not occur.[6] An early theorist of and interloper within YouTube, and later of social media production and experience more generally, I was deeply suspicious about popularity and virality as logics antithetical to many of the queer and feminist activist goals of critical importance to me: context, solidarity, local experience, embodied theory, enduring commitment.[7] While watching videos of all sorts on YouTube, nearly all made in the form of ironic fakes and thus nearly all trading in some relation to documentary or realism, I also needed to make sense of my earlier commitments to fake documentary (in my linked projects the fake documentary *The Watermelon Woman* [dir. Cheryl Dunye, 1996] and scholarly anthology, edited with Jesse Lerner, *F Is for Phony: Fake Documentary and Truth's Undoing*[8]). In the 1990s, I thought of fake documentary as a productive site for the interrogation of truth, history, and identity. With the dawning of YouTube, I saw that this form was being radically distorted through a corporate (and later governmental) manipulation of people's love of play, uncertainty, and unknowing, turning these pleasures into new modes of capture and control, albeit ones that we all made, wanted, and enjoyed together (online).[9]

Thus, my current work on internet and social media is not about documentary per se, even as it depends on my evolving thinking about and deploying of reality-based, once-indexical media. Across my extensive body of work—from *AIDS TV* to mediapraxis.org, from *F Is for Phony* to *Learning from YouTube*—I have looked to documentary theory, history, and practice to understand the good uses, and many abuses, of truth claims buttressed by mimetic practices seeking to stand and move as evidence, authority, and power. In one of my recent online works (ev-ent-anglement.com), I think about and try to produce justice for the reality-based fragments we now so readily give, willy-nilly, to the man so that he can use these pieces of ourselves to sell us to others and then also to sell us products we have never wanted and needed, including the corporate internet's versions of ourselves.[10]

In this piece, I demonstrate how my earlier, more benign but already deeply suspicious, critique of the dangers of popularity on YouTube built toward what I now see as our deeply unethical and delightfully questionable reality-based popularity practices and now-defunct president, unscrupulous outcomes that ultimately (and continually) culminate in violence. Attempting to produce these interventions within usually invisibilized online logics, I write about, with, and in the vernaculars of the internet, naming them as I go. Hence, I begin this chapter with ten "superhardtruths" (SHiTs) in the form of a listicle originally written on my blog as one citizen's intercession—engaging and connecting with many online others also participating in their own related projects—during the first one hundred days of the Trump administration. There I was focusing on uses, abuses, and remedies to fake news, an exceedingly popular preoccupation and practice of that moment. Here, I grapple with alternative viewing ethics and practices that might occur along and outside of virality, virility, and popularity.

>SHiTsticle[11]
>- Superhardtruth #1: the corporate-state-media muscle of the internet hides in plain sight below a sea of participatory good-'n'-plenty only to manifest as real power, violence, and control on demand.
>- Superhardtruth #2: clown time is over.
>- Superhardtruth #3: short, fast, and fun will be the death of us, or at least some of us.
>- Superhardtruth #4: virality is virility.
>- Superhardtruth #5: our tiny contributions cascade into the mother of all bombs.
>- Superhardtruth #6: #fakenews r us.
>- Superhardtruth #7: internet self-reflexivity leads to corrosive mimicry.

- Superhardtruth #8: people need time to ponder so they can be truly ethical and thoughtful.
- Superhardtruth #9: people need people.
- Superhardtruth #10: people need art and complexity.
- Superhardconclusion: people make the internet. and bombs. and #fakenews. and poetry and song and community. Only we have the power to know and do better.

Virality Is Virility

With Superhardtruth (SHiT) #4, I voice in twenty characters the brutal, self-evident outcome of the not-so-innocent logics of popular digital media and their internet home. While this anthology may make good use of its academic muscle to better understand and value the popular reality-based media that regular people like, watch, and share in great number, I will use my contribution to consider how the flurry, fun, or tomfoolery of our engagements with texts that seek and find approval also make it easier to overlook the lived destruction that these popular products can propel when linked with the institutional power of governments, corporations, and their macho front men: "clown time is over" (SHiT #2). As we consume the many cynical viral falsities that effervescently move across our screens—fake news, fake Freds,[12] tricky witty aphorisms—we also enjoy how for many things on the internet a statement and its opposite can both be true (and false): clown time is our time. Here, I attempt to unearth the connections between popular clowns, distortions of truth, state-sanctioned violence, and our favorite internet pastimes.

As is true of much on the internet, my pithy adages in the form of SHiTs use compression and doublespeak to shine a light on complicated, weighty, worldly concerns with real consequences well beyond any clever wordplay and its social recognition and digital relay. I wrote "virality is virility" on April 17, 2017, as part of the cascade of private shitty contributions referenced previously and reused throughout this effort. On that day, I was responding in kind to Donald Trump who had also preened on Twitter[13]—albeit displaying his signature manly chest-beating—about unleashing the "mother of all bombs" in Syria.[14] At that earlier date, writing the SHiT "virality is virility" felt like my own smart-ass comeback, respectfully played out by me taking up the rules of his game. In a dense alliteration, I expressed at once my dismay and also my larger analysis as a citizen and a feminist scholar of the internet who was trying to make sense of the crisis of fake news in the real time of its (re)invention, deployment, escalating popular attention, and mounting power. But nothing so important, so brutal, so damaging should or can be explained

Virality Is Virility | *307*

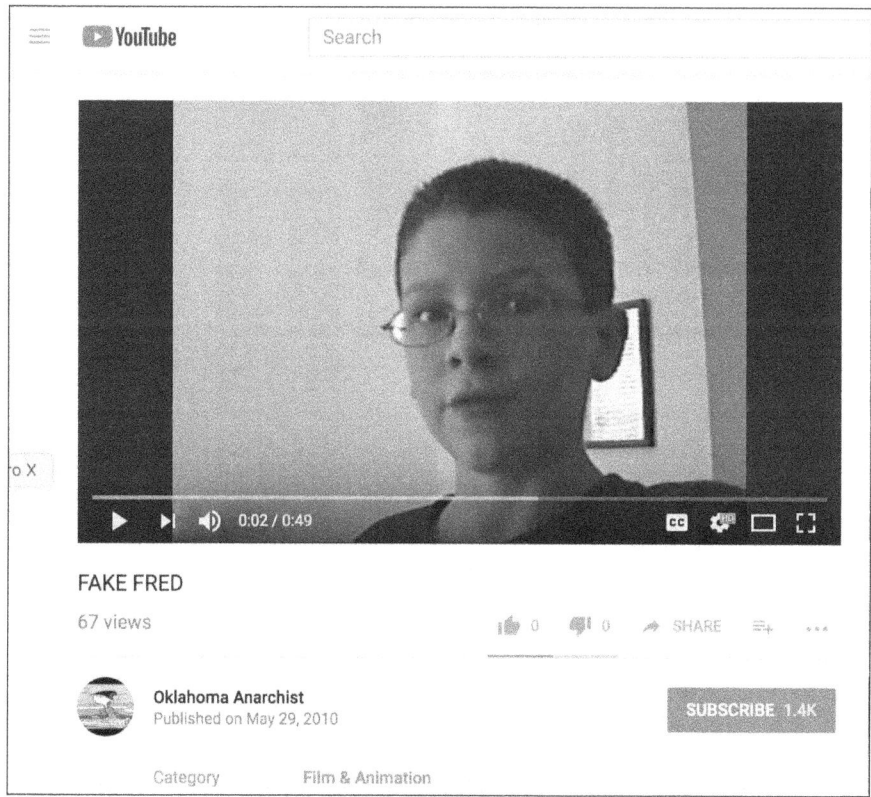

Fig. 16.1 YouTube screenshot: one Fake Fred, "Oklahoma Anarchist," among so many.

in any tweet-seeking retweets, including any of my SHiTs. For, "internet self-reflexivity leads to corrosive mimicry" (SHiT #7). We join in this game to our moral decay. Whenever we unpack, condemn, or inoculate against fake news or self-aggrandizing tweets—politics by any memes necessary—we are lowered accordingly, becoming part and parcel of these processes and their outcomes: "#fake news r us" (SHiT #6).

For instance, on August 8, 2017, our president said, "North Korea best not make any more threats to the United States. They will be met with fire and fury like the world has never seen."[15] Trump's saber-rattling may have reflected his gonzo belief that nuclear weapons can be used to solve regional conflicts, or perhaps it was just another puffed-up effort to deflect attention from his plummeting political support. But whether his threats are authentic, spontaneous, or ruse is really of no matter. In the time of fake news, small manifestations of viral internet-backed expression can produce volumes of

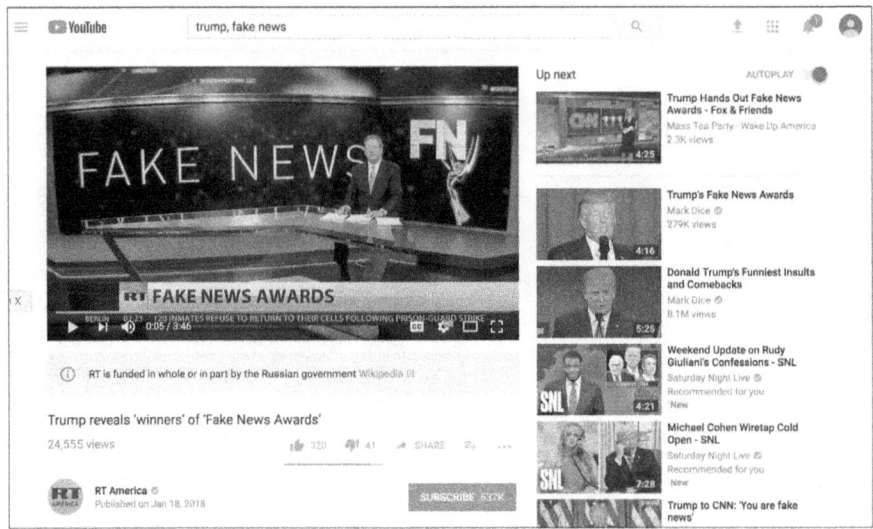

Fig. 16.2 YouTube screenshot: fake news site funded in whole or in part by the Russian government.

attention, fear, and also very real-world results. "Whether that message was mainly a bluff or an authentic expression of intent," wrote Peter Baker and Choe Sang-Hun in the *New York Times* about that latest round of presidential bombast, "it instantly scrambled the diplomatic equation in one of the world's most perilous regions."[16]

How can something so small, a few words, produce something so big, the scrambled relations of a highly militarized zone? How can one man so insecure fabricate results so substantial? With the pairing of our president and social media, we witness how the rules of sexism, networked technologies, pursuit of approval, and state violence align. Bombs and brutality are the logical outcome of gendered formats of heightened digital attention. As we have seen, this internet-fueled aggression can and has been aimed at immigrants,[17] Dreamers,[18] civil rights protesters and champions,[19] the nation of North Korea,[20] and the people of Syria.[21] This definitive mix of internet-fueled numbers, masculine grandiosity, and real-world hostility is what I mean by "virality is virility." Trump's nuclear threats or racist tweets enact a macho posturing central to his political persona and operations—virility[22]—rooted in sanctioned if often despicable forms of male aggression. However, his word choices are inspired by another familiar logic, that of the internet and social media—virality[23]—and its blind faith in power built from attention that grows through networked technologies.

Virality Is Virility | 309

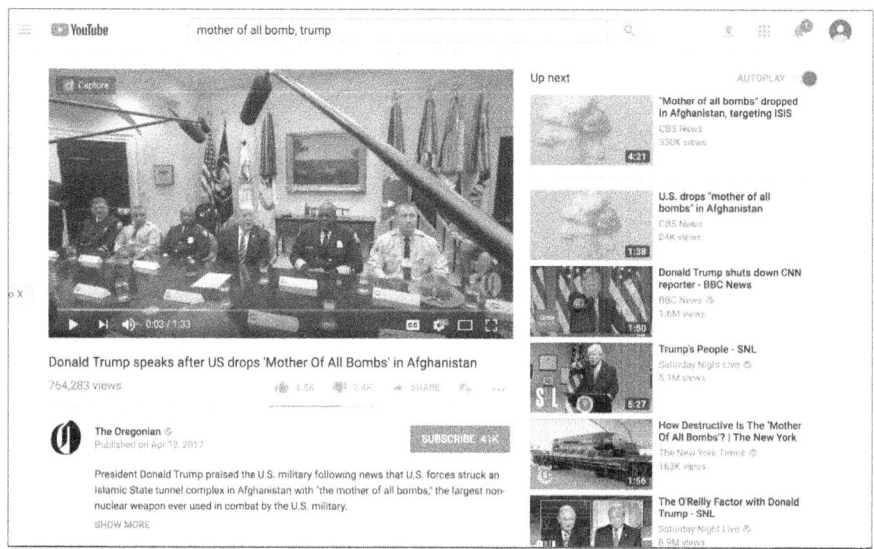

Fig. 16.3 YouTube screenshot: together we build support for and drop the mother of all bombs.

Let me spell this out. Popularity contests (virality), rooted in self-esteem and optics, aggrandized through feeling, accruing capital for some while building might for others, are inevitably patriarchal and thus phallic (virility)²⁴ and, ultimately, necessarily weaponized. Brutally, the results do not stay online but become material in the form of violence.²⁵ While I would never argue that every massively popular video on YouTube, insanely trending tweet on Twitter, or immensely likable picture on Instagram is itself an act of war or even aggression, I do contend that they support and fuel a logical progression from popularity to physical force by way of the phallus.²⁶ This is a definitive, structural cycle into which we are all pulled in, albeit as bit players: "#fake news r us." When we stop and look, when we consider and share, we contribute to a particular, definitive breed of chauvinist escalation rising from a male gaze built for and by today's technologies.²⁷ When we choose to produce in our own right (as I do here and as I did there), "our tiny contributions cascade into the mother of all bombs" (SHiT #5).

In 2007, I was just beginning to seriously study YouTube, still in its adolescence.²⁸ For my class and related "video-book," *Learning from YouTube*, my students and I produced volumes of videos and linked writing (sometimes getting viral attention of our own.)²⁹ There, I goofily maligned popularity as the organizing structure for YouTube's promotion of the hegemonic under the guise of the democratic.³⁰ These early YouTube-based interventions were

310 | *Reclaiming Popular Documentary*

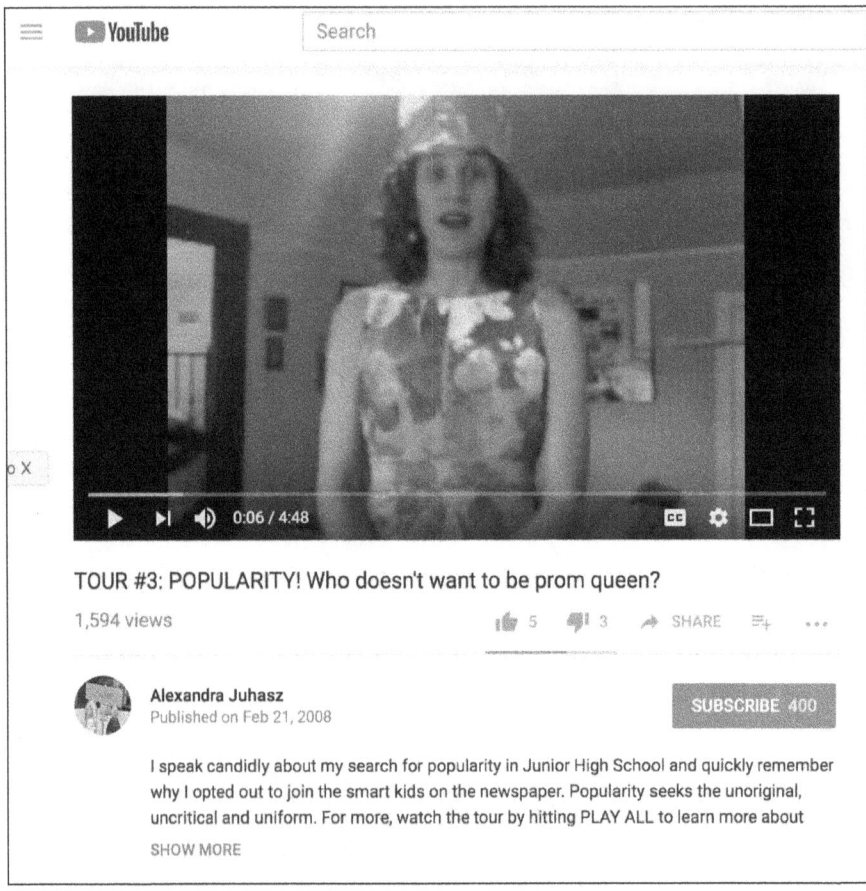

Fig. 16.4 YouTube screenshot: Popularity seeks the unoriginal, uncritical, and uniform.

wry but sweet send-ups that now seem to serve as a setup for the decline into madness that quickly would follow: "Like high school cheerleaders, the popular on YouTube do what we already like, in ways we already know: they are interchangeable and indistinguishable. Entertaining but not threatening, popular YouTube videos speak to a middle-of-the-road sensibility in and about the forms of mainstream culture and media . . . While we can all attest to whether popularity (or its reverse) worked for us in high school, I'll end by suggesting the obvious: It is not the best way to run a forum of knowledge/culture/art production and distribution."[31]

As a critic of digital culture, how did I, in such a short time, go from making sarcastic digs whose humor was situated in the hallways of junior high to dire warnings about global annihilation, that is, SHiT #4, "short, fast, and fun will be the death of us, or at least some of us"? As users of social media, how did we get from playfully or perhaps selfishly choosing the things we prefer over others—popularity—to the potential demise of much of what we most admire in our democracy (immigration, ecological health, reproductive and press freedoms, the fourth estate)?[32]

Let's start with popularity contests. While certainly fun, this juvenile system is best suited for pastimes like picking top models, chefs, or bachelors. But engorging numbers based on up- or downvotes are inadequate to determine a good many of the truly critical decisions in our culture. When we vote quickly with little to guide us but superficial traits or artificial challenges, dominant systems of value override other concerns or qualities, thereby perpetuating familiar beliefs and obvious winners.[33] The overt sexism, racism, and homophobia underwriting the contests referred to earlier are examples of just some of the comfortable viewpoints that fuel and are fueled by today's winner-take-all celebrity matches. A quick vote effectively silences those who have other points of view. Sure nay-sayers can and will continue their gripes on other internet forums. However, critics sidelined, the victor propels forward and the contest continues building momentum and visibility. Contrary contributions, necessary for the robust, informative conversations we need to circulate around the world's most pressing problems, are moved off-screen and efficiently delegitimized like so many (millions on millions) of pussy hats.[34]

Popularity contests, because of their speed and simple organization must be rooted in optics. How something or someone *looks* is an easily manipulated and often false indication of what that thing or person is, believes, does, or will do.[35] And looking itself becomes an increasingly difficult ethical project in a visual regime dominated by viral media.[36] We typically come upon popular media content as part of a larger onslaught experienced alone while engaging in acts of momentary and innocent pleasure, boredom, or curiosity. But when we look with interest at spreadable media,[37] we also engage in much deeper and less pleasurable unseen regimes: complex networks of power, ownership, and access that frame our viewing, knowing, and doing.[38] This nexus of personal vision and systems of power is what I describe in SHiT #1: "the corporate-state-media muscle of the internet hides in plain sight below a sea of participatory good 'n' plenty only to manifest as real power, violence, and control on demand." Accounting for our place in the face of viral videos of cats, top chefs, police brutality, email caches, or threats of nuclear attack—as well as the place of those who make and use viral media to enact or build to destruction—is one within a constellation of necessary ethical and political acts called forth by the real-word weight of social media.

Ethical Looks at Masculinist Video Violence

Considering our ethical stake in making, sharing, and looking at popular media is particularly important at this moment in history because it often feels like our current condition of visual onslaught and abundance allows us no alternatives. Our "choice" to look or not at any viral video is both paradoxical and imperative. Much of my career as a media scholar and activist has been in service of a commonsense "politics of visibility," where showing and seeing the experiences of underrepresented people and points of view is the obvious goal.[39] Recently, the personal and political ramifications of visibility have proven more nuanced. We find that the gaining of familiarity comes with its own, often irrevocable and irrational consequences.[40] For instance, there is an abundant and significant body of critical race scholarship currently developing about the psychic and political ramifications of seeing and sharing viral images of Black death.[41] In a recent editorial, Sherri Williams sums up this body of thinking: "As a Black scholar I want the injustices against Black people to be recorded and shared in the interest of justice and history. But as a Black woman I'm also worried about the mental and emotional health of my people as we continue to consume these videos. I'm equally concerned about the system that creates the violence that leads to these images."[42] As a white scholar and viewer of contemporary internet culture, I support and supplement these concerns from my standpoint in this visual economy: privileged while horrified witness to injustice against Black friends, family, and fellow citizens. But following Susan Sontag, we need to consider not only the pain we might be personally subjected to by witnessing viral brutality but also its possible impending opposite: the deadening effects of overexposure to images that were meant to move or at least enrage us.[43]

One way to "stay woke" when we watch is to look askance. "Images of war have always had an irresistible allure for the camera," writes Alisa Lebow in her essay about what she calls the "unwar film."[44] When any video, tweet, or photograph goes viral, this is in part because it is generically competent, satisfying familiar rules of production and reception inherited from cinema or other traditions while introducing noteworthy content. Given that we are comfortable, as well as titillated, with the pacing, tropes, and thrills of war cinema, Lebow looks to cinematic strategies that help to rupture "the generic spell that binds us" to such images: "we need to look to films that look awry,

Virality Is Virility | 313

Fig. 16.5 YouTube screenshot: Philando Castile? Look askance.

in the Zizekian sense of looking askance or even away from the action, as it were, to that which is happening just outside its purview."[45]

A looking awry from viral video would not be a closing of one's eyes to the actual and ongoing brutality against Black people in our society—and the many others now subject to sanctioned state violence—and its ever-increasing digital record. Rather this would entail looking carefully away from documents of the act of violence. Then we would aim to focus our attention on what Marta Zarzycka names as the critically unseen in war photography— "causality, responsibility, and impact"[46]—even as (or so that) violence is made increasingly visible and spreadable. In her book on the history of filmic representation of death, *Dying in Full Detail*, Jennifer Malkowski argues that only a small number of the internet's overabundant images of death actually go viral. In her analysis of two online activist videos of death (Oscar Grant's murder at the hands of Oakland transit police and Neda Agha-Soltan's shooting by Iranian government-allied Basij militia), Malkowski asks, "How did the Agha-Soltan videos from Iran generate such broad interest among the Western public while the Grant videos remained more nationally, and even regionally, bound?"[47] She details how both political and aesthetic dimensions allow some pieces of activist raw footage to gain and sustain popular appeal: "multiple angles, dramatic blood flow, immersive audio, and the subject's appearance."[48] In a similar vein, Jennifer Terry studies how some of the vast body of footage of war shot by American soldiers and shared on YouTube goes

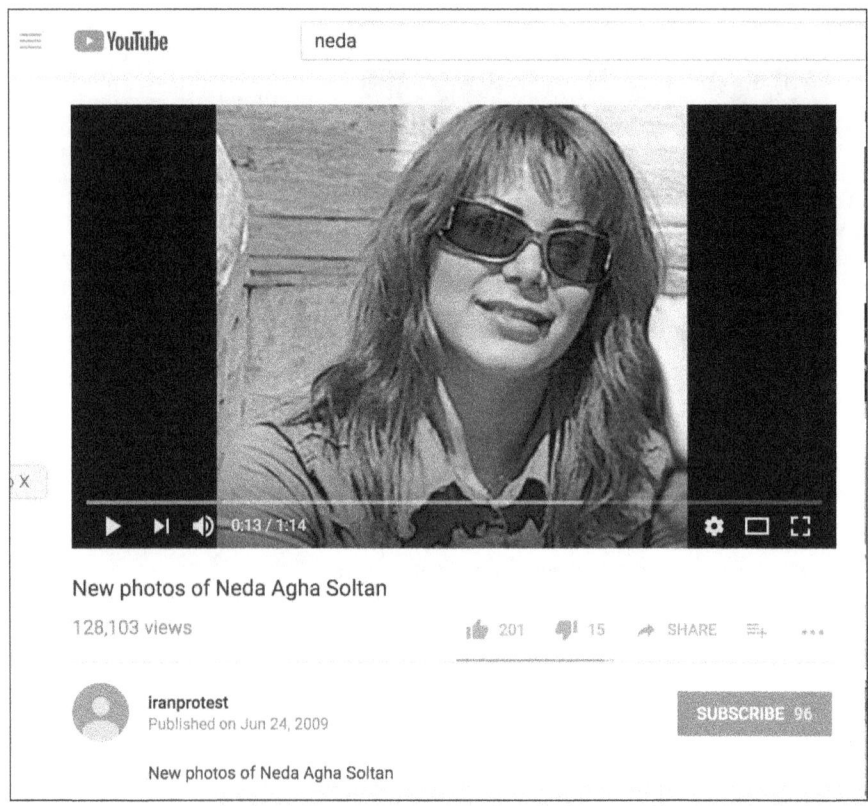

Fig. 16.6 YouTube screenshot: Neda? Look again.

viral. She argues that raw footage that takes on a first-person shooter logic of video games often "succeeds," at least if your rubric is audiences, rankings, and numbers.[49]

Accounts of Diamond Reynold's video of her boyfriend Philando Castile's murder suggest that it is the uncanny professionalism of her raw, unedited video, dramatically aligning with its record of the cruel force of police brutality, that produces its particular poignancy.[50] This explains some of the power and popularity of Reynold's video: it looks at, and away; it shows both violence and its contexts; and it does so in what is at once a new and also a familiar form (viral live feed video). Conventional genre expectations laced onto new uses of technology and critical content produce the contours of our current looking system.

In my own early writing on the Neda YouTube phenomenon in *Learning from YouTube*,[51] I worry that what I have also there called the "video slogans" of YouTube—"pithy, precise, rousing calls to action or consumption, or action as consumption"[52]—can function to produce quick and even strong affective responses, but may be counterproductive to the larger ethical and political needs of movements for social justice: for data, history, connections, and strategies.[53] Slogans, like images, bypass contemplation and rationality and get to us through emotion. The president's power, like much else on the internet, crescendos from bite-sized evocative morsels bearing high-impact feelings. But things whose best or only tendency is growth (like capitalism) are by definition single-minded, totalizing, and ruthless, even if or because they are emotionally resonant.

Why ruthless? Isn't our attention of this sort supportive and connecting? Not a one of us is above the yummy buzz felt from a whole bunch of metaphoric thumbs up. We feel momentarily seen and even liked, even as we anticipate the inevitable fast fall from digital attention and a linked search for more.[54] Our feelings aside, virality's primary function is something else entirely: the always-growing production, circulation, and attention to internet content monetized via eyeballs, clicks, and cookies.[55] The real value of our likes and all internet popularity is dollars for the select, monopolized corporate owners of our content and data. Today's internet has been built by successfully masking its true commitments to a fierce capitalism. A few corporations profit from the volumes of content that we produce and the endless trails we wend through it.

Our rather easy, routinized pastimes—posting pictures, sharing tweets, writing blog posts—are pasted over with the thinnest veneer of entertainment and mock democracy, itself a form of simulation that hides cold-blooded underlying structures. Our images and verbiage get eyeballs to a designated figurehead (pussy hats, Trump, no matter) and the corporations or governments for which they unintentionally or intentionally shill. But, as of yet—against our best efforts over decades of good work, unrest, and decent feminist living—the forces that gain most remain patriarchal. The media, government, corporations, police, and military are dominated by men or male points of view or practices of power.[56]

I want to be clear: when I discuss the *patriarchal* or *male* I am not talking about specific humans (men or those like them) or their personal, embodied choices about gender, sexuality, or sex. Many individual men are great; many women prop up patriarchy. Thus, the word *phallic* is key: a symbolic totem of male power, an icon that can be momentarily claimed and used by any person or institution driven to follow a cruel logic of supremacy buttressed by overt muscle or aggrandized size.[57] This unearned dominance is volatile because it is rooted in binary difference (male/female, white/Black, straight/gay) and maintained through fear and sometimes violence. Ancient in their roots and traditions, adaptive, refined, and always buttressed by privilege, behaviors of patriarchal conquest are also, not in the least coincidently, sexualized and gendered. But masculinity propped up by artifice is always under threat. It needs to be continually, repetitively reexpressed, actualized in social structures and institutions, and operationalized in language and behavior: "I grab [women] by the pussy."[58]

But no one man—person as he is, president as he may be—can maintain the myth of patriarchal virility on his own. He needs sanctions and structures, clubs and schools, images and tweets, as well as money, to buttress his undeserved might. And even so, his virility remains open to challenge, as it should be, given that it is based on nothing more than unthinking biology (parts and bits and hormones with no real rationale other than to replicate a species).[59] And so, inevitably, historically, tragically, calls for a weapon will be the final addition to this nervous mess. Arms are requested to reinsure yet again his might, never big enough even with all the likes and associated ad revenues, the billions earned or stolen via internet viral sales. A bomb is needed, too. Popularity does not only reside online. It becomes material in the form of violence.

Better SHiTs: People/Ponder/Platforms

In my work on YouTube and the feminist internet, I have suggested that the technologies we have been "given for free," like Facebook Live, YouTube, Instagram, or Twitter, come with real albeit veiled structures and hidden costs.[60] People-made-media is relayed to us through corporate-owned platforms that frame our images within their own ethical and political concerns.[61] Corporate media function best for their owners via censorship, profit, ease, and pleasure of use, and other powerful forms of political and algorithmic control.[62] Thus, ethical viewing must be based not just in taking account of our own views of popular media but in looking at the broader political-economic and technological structures that produce, hold, and frame the images and words that we see and share.[63]

Looking at platforms not just content, looking at our use and needs within and from them, looking at how we sustain them, becomes one very necessary part of an ethical consumption of popular digital culture. And this work isn't easy or quick, cute or funny, even if it may start out as pleasing or popular. To look newly we need time and new spaces. We need to do

Fig. 16.7 Screenshot: #SayHerName campaign, The African American Policy Forum. http://aapf.org/sayhernamereport

so in community, in the places that we live and work, and in forums and formats organized outside the cruel structuring logics of capitalism, patriarchy, and popularity.[64] Sure, it's shitty because it often feels downright impossible in these times to think outside the logics of the neoliberal corporate internet-military-industrial complex.[65] But think, speak, and share we can and must:

- SHiT #8: people need time to ponder so they can be truly ethical and thoughtful.
- SHiT #9: people need people.
- SHiT #10: people need art and complexity.

Like Reynolds, we, the everyday users of video technologies (some of us anti–Black racism activists, some of us peaceniks, some of us unwitting bystanders to atrocity), are the viewers and producers of the viral images of violence and death that saturate our screens. But it is critical that beyond accounting for our viewing of these images, we also ask for better accountability from the platforms that deliver and reframe these images for us.[66] Currently, the vast majority of us watch viral—and really almost all video—through platforms owned by corporate entities with for-profit mandates that have little to do with the ethical and political scrutiny that I have been suggesting is core to ethical and maybe even effective media practices in a time of viral Black death and increasing presidential media bellicosity.

318 | *Reclaiming Popular Documentary*

Those who seek peace, those who have known war and rape and bullying, understand the grotesque logic of vicious unearned force.[67] Hence, we must speak our internet truths. Our truths about patriarchal violence and those who use it to feed their greed and dominance. Our truths about human goodness that manifests in the face of anti-Black violence, war and its bombastic lead-ups, willing cheerleaders, corporate beneficiaries, and technologies of expression and destruction. Our internet truths must not move blindly from popularity to visibility, money, and mayhem. I seek truths based on more decent logics than virality or virility. "People make the internet. and bombs. and #fakenews. and poetry and song and community. Only we have the power to know and do better." This was and remains my Superhardconclusion.

Notes

1. My earlier works linked together in this piece are (1) "Trump's Alpha Male Posturing Was Made for Our Media Age"; (2) #100hardtruths-#fakenews; (3) "How Do I (Not) Look"; (4) *Learning from YouTube*.

2. Since writing this piece, my project has taken a final turn, to thinking about and engaging in Fake News Poetry Workshops as radical digital media literacy. See fakenewspoetry.com and a related podcast, *We Need Gentle Truths for Now* (https://shows.acast.com/we-need-gentle-truths-for-now).

3. See my media, writing, teaching, and scholarly work at alexandrajuhasz.com.

4. See mediapraxis.org, *Integrating Theory, Practice and Politics*, where I have written and taught about this radical integration.

5. See my discussion of my movement to the internet in "You Get the Picture."

6. See Juhasz, *Learning from YouTube*.

7. Juhasz, "Feminist Online Activism," 20–21.

8. See Juhasz and Jesse Lerner, *F Is for Phony*.

9. See Juhasz, "Increasingly UnProductive Fake."

10. See the ev-ent-anglement website, http://ev-ent-anglement.com.

11. "#89, ten (more!) superhardtruths about #100hardtruths (certainly not) needed," Juhasz, #100hardtruths-fakenews.

12. See Juhasz, "Fred Rant."

13. Fuller, "MOAB."

14. Engel Rasmussen, "US 'Mother of all Bombs.'"

15. Sciutto, "Trump Promises."

16. Baker, "Trump Threatens."

17. See B. Williams, "Trump's Immigration."

18. See de Vogue, "DACA Judge Reading Trump's Tweets Carefully."

19. See Schwarz, "Obama's Charlottesville Tweet."

20. See Watson, "Twitter Says Trump's Threat to North Korea Was 'Newsworthy.'"

21. See Ward, "Trump Just Revealed a Covert CIA program."

22. Feminist and queer scholars have a lengthy and complex body of work on virility: the psychoanalytic and political imbrications of gender, sexuality, and power. See for instance, Ahmed, *Differences That Matter*.

23. Critical internet scholars have a recent but intricate body of work about virality and its connections to power, pleasure, disease, disorder, and digital infrastructure. See, e.g., Payne, *Promiscuity of Network Culture*.

24. One body of critical internet studies links virality and the closing down of our attention to the needs, interests, and expressions of the least known and seen in our culture, e.g., the disabled. See, e.g., Treviranus, "Value of the Unpopular."

25. See Prigano, "Days after Charlottesville Violence."

26. There is a long and complicated body of thinking by feminist scholars about gender, sexuality, masculinity, and power. See for instance, Jardin and Smith, *Men in Feminism*.

27. There is a long and complicated body of theory by feminist media scholars about the male and other gazes. See, e.g., Mulvey, *Visual and Other Pleasures*.

28. See Juhasz, "Interview."

29. Juhasz, *Learning from YouTube*.

30. Ibid., "popularity" search results 1–31: http://vectors.usc.edu/projects/learningfromyoutube/search.php?sq=popularity.

31. Ibid., "TOUR #3": http://vectors.usc.edu/projects/learningfromyoutube/texteo.php?composite=84.

32. Ryan, "Short History of the End of the World."

33. There is a long and rich tradition of scholarship in critical internet studies focusing on the perils and pleasures of participation. See for instance, Barney et al., *Participatory Condition in the Digital Age*.

34. There is a robust feminist, queer body of research and scholarship about the toxic worlds of internet commenting and participation. See, e.g., FemTechNet's resources available from its Center for Solutions to Online Violence.

35. There is a lengthy and meaningful body of scholarship on the interrelations of power, looking, visibility, and control. See for instance, Sturken and Cartwright, *Practices of Looking*.

36. The ethics of seeing, showing, and representing have long concerned documentary theorists, particularly those who work with disenfranchised communities (women, people of color, the poor, Indigenous people, the disabled). See, e.g., Danto, Hashimi, and Isabel, *Think/Point/Shoot*; Rangan, *Immediations*.

37. See Jenkins, Ford, and Green, *Spreadable Media*.

38. Scholars in visual culture focus on the nexus of the look and larger systems of power and control. See for instance, Mirzoeff, *How to See the World*.

39. See, e.g., Juhasz, *AIDS TV* and *Women of Vision*.

40. The weaponized, militarized, violent dangers of being seen—such as torture, surveillance, or sexual abuse—are a significant focus of numerous essays in Juhasz and Lebow, *Companion to Contemporary Documentary Film*.

41. At the 2016 meeting of the Society for Cinema and Media Studies, I attended the panel "Black Images Matter: Contextualizing Images of Racialized Police Violence," featuring the work of critical race and media scholars Safiya Noble, LaCharles Ward, Roopali Mukherjee, and Ellen Scott. A packed room of media scholars listened to, and then discussed, the ramifications, histories of, and contexts for looking at images of Black protest, violence, and death. See, e.g., Noble, "Teaching Trayvon."

42. S. Williams, "How Does."

43. See Sontag, *On Photography*.

44. Lebow, "Unwar Film."

45. Ibid., x.

46. Zarzycka, *Gendered Tropes*, xvi.

47. Malkowski, *Dying in Full Detail*.
48. Ibid.
49. See Terry, *Attachments to War* and "Killer Entertainments."
50. See Dewey and Ohlheiser, "How Live-Streaming Has Forever Changed the Way We View Violence."
51. See Juhasz, "On Iran Verite."
52. Juhasz, "Thoughts on Teaching."
53. See my work and that of many others thinking about the role of visual culture within contemporary activist culture in Bookchin et al., *Militant Research Handbook*.
54. Many scholars theorize from and beyond the momentary pleasures of internet sociality. See Lovink and Rasch, *Un(Like) Us Reader*.
55. There is a strong and important body of scholarly work on the economic underpinnings of social media. See, e.g., Vaidhyanathan, *Googlization of Everything*.
56. Feminist theory and history has much to tell us about patriarchy. See Lerner, *Creation of Patriarchy*.
57. Feminist thinking on the role of the phallus is legion. See Nicholson, *Second Wave*.
58. Mathis-Lilley, "Trump Was Recorded in 2005."
59. Feminist and queer theorists think long and hard about the performative rather than biological nature of gender, sex, and sexuality. See, e.g., Butler, *Gender Trouble*.
60. Juhasz, "Conclusion."
61. Critical internet studies looks to the very mixed lived results of internet activism. See, e.g., Morozov, *Net Delusion*.
62. Critical internet studies links state and corporate power to digital architecture and algorithms. See, e.g., Chun, *Power and Control*; Cheney-Lippold, *We Are Data*.
63. Much recent work in media studies looks not at images but at the technological, corporate, state infrastructures that move them. See, e.g., Parks and Starosielski, *Signal Traffic*.
64. The cruelty of neoliberalism affects most of our habits. See, e.g., Berlant, *Cruel Optimism*.
65. Feminist theorists contribute to rare and much-needed conversations about what might be possible outside of neoliberalism. See, e.g., Gibson-Graham, *End of Capitalism*.
66. Manjoo, "Mark Zuckerberg Follows a Familiar Playbook."
67. See decades of work by feminist peace theorists and activists, e.g., Confortini, *Intelligent Compassion*.

References

Ahmed, Sara. *Differences That Matter: Feminist Theory and Postmodernism*. Cambridge: Cambridge University Press, 1998.
Baker, Peter, and Choe Sand-Hun. "Trump Threatens 'Fire and Fury' against North Korea If It Endangers US." *New York Times*, August 8, 2017. https://www.nytimes.com/2017/08/08/world/asia/north-korea-un-sanctions-nuclear-missile-united-nations.html?mcubz=0.
Barney, Darin, Gabriella Coleman, Christine Ross, Jonathan Sterne, and Tamar Tembeck, eds. *The Participatory Condition in the Digital Age*. Minneapolis: University of Minnesota Press, 2016.
Berlant, Lauren. *Cruel Optimism*. Durham: Duke University Press, 2011.
Bookchin, Natalie, Pamela Brown, Suzahn Ebrahimian, colectivo Enmedio, Alexandra Juhasz, Leónidas Martin, MT L, Nicholas Mirzoeff, Andrew Ross, A. Joan Saab, Marina Sitrin, eds. *The Militant Research Handbook*. New York: NYU Media, Culture and

Communication, 2015. http://www.visualculturenow.org/wp-content/uploads/2013/09/MRH_Web.pdf.
Butler, Judith. *Gender Trouble: Feminism and the Subversion of Identity*. New York: Routledge, 1990.
Chun, Wendy. *Power and Control*. Cambridge: MIT Press, 2008.
Cheney-Lippold, John. *We Are Data: Algorithms and the Making of Our Digital Selves*. New York: NYU Press, 2017.
Confortini, Catia Cecilia. *Intelligent Compassion: The Women's International League for Peace and Freedom and Feminist Peace*. Oxford Scholarship Online, 2012. http://www.oxfordscholarship.com/view/10.1093/acprof:oso/9780199845231.001.0001/acprof-9780199845231.
de Vogue, Ariane. "DACA Judge Reading Trump's Tweets Carefully." CNN, September 18, 2017. http://www.cnn.com/2017/09/18/politics/daca-trump-tweet/index.html.
Danto, Annette, Mobini Hashimi, and Lonnie Isabel, eds. *Think/Point/Shoot: Media Ethics, Technology and Global Change*. New York: Routledge, 2016.
Dewey, Caitlin, and Abby Ohlheiser. "How Live-Streaming Has Forever Changed the Way We View Violence." *Washington Post*, July 8, 2016. https://www.washingtonpost.com/news/the-intersect/wp/2016/07/08/how-live-streaming-has-forever-changed-the-way-we-view-violence/?utm_term=.94a711ed2bc9.
Engel Rasmussen, Sune. "US 'Mother of all Bombs' Killed 92 Isis Militants, Say Afghan Officials." *Guardian*, April 15, 2017, https://www.theguardian.com/world/2017/apr/15/us-mother-of-all-bombs-moab-afghanistan-donald-trump-death-toll.
FemTechNet. "Center for Solutions to Online Violence." Accessed March 1, 2018. https://femtechnet.org/csov.
Fuller, Bonnie. "MOAB: Twitter Goes Wild on Trump's Afghanistan Bomb Attack—See Memes." *Hollywood Life*, April 13, 2017. http://hollywoodlife.com/2017/04/13/moab-memes-twitter-reacts-donald-trump-bombing-isis-afghanistan.
Gibson-Graham, J. K. *The End of Capitalism (As We Knew It): A Feminist Critique of Political Economy*. Minneapolis: University of Minnesota Press, 2006.
Jardin, Alice, and Paul Smith, eds. *Men in Feminism*. New York: Routledge, 1987.
Jenkins, Henry. "Learning from YouTube: An Interview with Alex Juhasz (Part One)." *Confessions of an Aca-Fan* (blog), February 19, 2008. http://henryjenkins.org/blog/2008/02/learning_from_youtube_an_inter.html.
Jenkins, Henry, Sam Ford, and Joshua Green. *Spreadable Media: Creating Value and Meaning in a Networked Society*. New York: New York University Press, 2013.
Juhasz, Alexandra. *AIDS TV: Identity, Community and Alternative Video*. Durham, NC: Duke University Press, 1995.
———. "Conclusion: It's Our Collective, Principled Making That Matters Most." In "Queer Feminist Media Praxis," special issue, *ADA* 5 (Summer 2014). http://adanewmedia.org/2014/07/issue5-juhasz.
———. "Feminist Online Activism: As Teaching/Community/Space Making." In *Militant Research Handbook*. New York: New York University, 2013. http://www.visualculturenow.org/wp-content/uploads/2013/09/MRH_Web.pdf.
———. "Fred Rant." *Transformative Works and Culture* 9 (2012). http://journal.transformativeworks.org/index.php/twc/article/view/295/258.
———. "How Do I (Not) Look? Live Feed Video and Viral Black Death." *JSTOR Daily*, July 20, 2016. https://daily.jstor.org/how-do-i-not-look.
———. "The Increasingly UnProductive Fake." *No More Potlucks* 4 (July–August 2009). http://nomorepotlucks.org/site/the-increasingly-unproductive-fake/.

———. *Learning from YouTube*. Cambridge: MIT Press, 2011. http://vectors.usc.edu/projects/learningfromyoutube/texteo.php?composite=83.

———. *Media Praxis: Integrating Media Theory, Practice and Politics* (blog). Accessed October 2, 2020. http://aljean.wordpress.com/.

———. "On Iran Verite." *Learning from YouTube*. Accessed November 30, 2020. http://vectors.usc.edu/projects/learningfromyoutube/texteo.php?composite=6.

———. #100hardtruths-#fakenews website. Last updated October 19, 2019. http://scalar.usc.edu/nehvectors/100hardtruths-fakenews/index.

———. "What Is Media Praxis?" http://www.mediapraxis.org/?page_id=8.

———. "Thoughts on Teaching on YouTube (April 28, 2008)." *Learning from YouTube*. April 28, 2008. http://vectors.usc.edu/projects/learningfromyoutube/texteo.php?composite=164.

———. *Women of Vision: Histories in Feminist Media*. Minneapolis: University of Minnesota Press, 2001.

———. "You Get the Picture." *FRAMES Cinema Journal* 1 (July 2012). http://framescinemajournal.com/article/you-get-the-picture/.

Juhasz, Alexandra, and Alisa Lebow, eds. *A Companion to Contemporary Documentary Film* Hoboken, NJ: Blackwell Press, 2015.

Juhasz, Alexandra, and Jesse Lerner, eds. *F Is for Phony: Documentary and Truth's Undoing*. Minneapolis: University of Minnesota Press. 2006.

Lebow, Alisa. "The Unwar Film." In *A Companion to Contemporary Documentary Film*, edited by Alexandra Juhasz and Alisa Lebow, 454–474. Hoboken, NJ: John Wiley and Sons, 2015.

Lerner, Gerda. *The Creation of Patriarchy*. London: Oxford University Press, 1987.

Lovink, Geert, and Miriam Rasch, eds. *The Un(Like) Us Reader: Social Media Monopolies and their Alternatives*. Amsterdam: Institute for Network Cultures, 2013.

Malkowski, Jennifer. *Dying in Full Detail*. Durham: Duke University Press, 2016.

Mathis-Lilley, Ben. "Trump Was Recorded in 2005 Bragging about Grabbing Women 'by the Pussy.'" *Slate*, October 7, 2016. http://www.slate.com/blogs/the_slatest/2016/10/07/donald_trump_2005_tape_i_grab_women_by_the_pussy.html.

Mirzoeff, Nicholas. *How to See the World: An Introduction to Images, from Self-Portraits to Selfies, Maps to Movies, and More*. New York: Basic Books, 2016.

Morozov, Evgeny. *The Net Delusion: The Dark Side of Internet Freedom*. London: PublicAffairs, 2012.

Mulvey, Laura. *Visual and Other Pleasures*. New York: Palgrave Macmillan, 2009.

Manjoo, Farhad. "On Russian Meddling, Mark Zuckerberg Follows a Familiar Playbook." *New York Times*, September 22, 2017. https://www.nytimes.com/2017/09/22/technology/mark-zuckerberg-facebook-russian-ads.html?mcubz=0.

Nicholson, Linda. *The Second Wave: A Reader in Feminist Theory*. New York: Routledge, 1997.

Noble, Safiya Umoja. "Teaching Trayvon: Race, Media, and the Politics of Spectacle." *Black Scholar* 44, no. 1 (Spring 2014): 12–29.

Payne, Robert. *The Promiscuity of Network Culture: Queer Theory and Digital Media*. New York: Routledge, 2015.

Parks, Lisa, and Nicole Starosielski, eds. *Signal Traffic: Critical Studies of Media Infrastructures*. Chicago: University of Illinois Press, 2015.

Prigano, Christina. "Days after Charlottesville Violence, Trump Retweets Meme of 'CNN' Being Run Over." *Boston Globe*, August 15, 2017. https://www.bostonglobe.com/news/politics/2017/08/15/days-after-charlottesville-violence-trump-tweets-meme-cnn-being-run-over/WD4loKWBmmbQJhZmvigHEP/story.html.

Rangan, Pooja. *Immediations*. Durham, NC: Duke University Press, 2017.

Ryan, Erin Gloria. "A Short History of the End of the World." *Daily Beast*, August 13, 2017. http://www.thedailybeast.com/a-short-history-of-the-end-of-the-world.

Schwarz, Hunter. "Obama's Charlottesville Tweet Is Most Liked in Twitter History." CNN, August 16, 2017. http://www.cnn.com/2017/08/15/politics/obamas-charlottesville-tweet/index.html.

Sciutto, Jim, Barbara Starr, and Zachary Cohen. "Trump Promises North Korea 'Fire and Fury' over Nuke Threat." CNN, August 9, 2017. http://www.cnn.com/2017/08/08/politics/north-korea-missile-ready-nuclear-weapons/index.html.

Sontag, Susan. *On Photography*. New York: Farrar, Straus and Giroux, 1977.

Sturken, Marita, and Lisa Cartwright. *Practices of Looking: An Introduction to Visual Culture*. London: Oxford University Press, 2009.

Terry, Jennifer. *Attachments to War*. Durham, NC: Duke University Press, 2017.

———. "Killer Entertainments." *Vectors*. Accessed March 1, 2018. http://vectors.usc.edu/projects/index.php?project=86.

Treviranus, Jutta. "The Value of the Unpopular: Counteracting the Popularity Echo-Chamber on the Web." Science and Technology for Humanity Conference Proceedings, 2009.

"Trump's Alpha Male Posturing Was Made for Our Media Age." *DAME*, September 7, 2017. https://www.damemagazine.com/2017/09/07/trumps-alpha-male-posturing-was-made-our-social-media-age.

Vaidhyanathan, Siva. *The Googlization of Everything*. Berkeley: University of California Press, 2011.

Ward, Alex. "Trump Just Revealed a Covert CIA Program—Over Twitter." *Vox*, July 25, 2017. https://www.vox.com/world/2017/7/25/16025136/trump-syria-cia-twitter-program-end-covert.

Watson, Chloe. "Twitter Says Trump's Threat to North Korea Was 'Newsworthy' and Will Not Be Taken Down." *The Guardian*, September 26, 2017. https://www.theguardian.com/technology/2017/sep/26/twitter-trump-threat-north-korea-newsworthy.

Williams, Brenna. "Trump's Immigration Policy (or What We Know about It) in 13 Illuminating Tweets." CNN, August 26, 2016. http://www.cnn.com/2016/08/26/politics/donald-trump-immigration-tweets/index.html.

Williams, Sherri. "How Does a Steady Stream of Images of Black Death Affect Us?" NBC News, July 11, 2016. https://www.nbcnews.com/news/nbcblk/editorial-how-does-steady-stream-images-black-death-affect-us-n607221.

Zarzycka, Marta. *Gendered Tropes in War Photography*. New York: Routledge, 2016.

ALEXANDRA JUHASZ is Distinguished Professor of Film at Brooklyn College, CUNY. She is author of *AIDS TV: Identity, Community, and Alternative Video* and of *Women of Vision: Histories in Feminist Film and Video*. She is editor (with Jesse Lerner) of *F Is for Phony: Fake Documentary and Truth's Undoing*, (with Alisa Lebow) of *A Companion to Contemporary Documentary Film*, (with Yvonne Welbon) of *Sisters in the Life: A History of Out African American Lesbian Media-Making*, and (with Jih-Fei Cheng and Nishant Shahani) of *AIDS and the Distribution of Crises*. She is producer of feature films *The Watermelon Woman* (1996) and *The Owls* (2010).

17

POPULISM, PARTICIPATION, AND PERPETUAL INCOMPLETION
Performing an Urban History Commons

Rick Prelinger

Since 2006, I have produced twenty-six feature-length urban history "film events" in San Francisco (fifteen events during the period 2006–2020); Detroit (five events, 2010–2014); Oakland and East Bay (two events, 2009 and 2014); Los Angeles (three events, 2010, 2016, and 2019); and New York (one event, 2017).[1] Each *event*, a descriptive term chosen to consciously distinguish them from "films," brings together archival footage from home movies, studio-produced background process plates, industrial films and outtakes, newsreels, and other rarely seen or unseen film ephemera.[2] Screenings occur before an audience that is encouraged to vocalize as the event unfolds—to identify people, places, and events; to ask questions of others; and to opine, disagree, and comment freely. In most cases I also act as emcee, offering contextual information and encouraging participation. Presented pointedly as nonnostalgic projects undertaken to encourage and sustain discussion about possible urban futures, these film events are conceived as popular documentaries with physical presence and participation at their core.[3] Eschewing narrative and character-driven structures associated with contemporary mainstream documentary, they appear "underproduced" but are in fact intricately constructed, foregrounding lightly edited archival film segments as evidence and offering audiences the privilege of seeing original documentation without the interference of background music or narrated soundtracks.

The twenty-six events have awakened an intense level of interest and engagement in their audiences. Collectively, they have been performed 115 times (both in the cities on which they are based and in other venues throughout

North America and Europe) and seen live by an estimated forty-five thousand spectator-participants, plus an unknown number of viewers online and at screenings in ambient environments. In addition to urban history events, I have also produced the first iteration of a participatory documentary on the changing history of agriculture and farming, *Farms Lost and Found*, which premiered in Santa Fe, New Mexico, in 2016, and *No More Road Trips?* (2013), another interactive film event on travel and mobility in the United States, widely presented in person and online.

Unlike almost all films, these are made for noisy audiences; and unlike most "interactive" and "participatory" documentaries, they are realized through public assembly rather than algorithm. This chapter seeks to establish that the *popular* in *popular documentary* describes not simply content or intention but the circumstances governing exhibition and public reception; that we might expand our understanding of cinema to encompass works made primarily for participatory public assemblies; and further, that countertrends to forms of interactive documentary primarily realized through algorithms and digital platforms are not only possible but formative.

Antecedents

While the presence of a live narrator and the encouragement to audiences to engage in real-time vocal intervention might seem to fall outside the realm of accepted spectatorship, these attributes actually echo practices traditionally part of popular entertainment and documentary performance. A short inventory: The presence of the *benshi* (live narrator) was integral to Japanese silent cinema, evolving from similar roles in the kabuki and Noh theatrical traditions, and persists today in the Neo-Benshi and other similar artistic practices. In the West, the Elizabethan theater, whose pits were often said to be populated by rowdy "groundlings" commenting loudly on plays and performers, prefigures a highly engaged form of audience interactivity. Later the theatrical space functioned as a virtual stage onto which racially integrated audiences performed social relations. As Elizabeth Maddock Dillon describes, deterritorialized common lands were remapped into the space of the theater; eighteenth- and early nineteenth-century audience members didn't just go to the theater to see a play; they went to represent themselves, to make common space and often common cause. In 1804, a Boston writer complained that the theater didn't have bright enough lighting during the show, because people weren't there just for the performance. And when *Richard III* was performed at the Bowery Theater in New York in 1832, over three hundred audience members swarmed the stage to assist in slaying the tyrannical king.[4] Later in the nineteenth century, travel lecturers (most prominently Burton Holmes) combined first lantern slides and later moving pictures and performative commentary into touring travelogues, an entertainment genre that continues to flourish today.[5]

In the 1920s, Bertolt Brecht spoke of the sports audience, particularly those assembled to watch a boxing match, as an ideal audience for his "epic" theater. Such audiences are highly knowledgeable and aware, uninhibited, vocal, opinionated, and keen observers maintaining "eyes on the course" rather than simply "eyes on the finish."[6] One might also compare this to the performative spectatorship occurring in premultiplex urban cinemas, where the "rule of silence" never strictly applied. Finally, discussion time is built into some educational and training films, where sequences of black leader are inserted to permit stopping the projector for discussion. It has also been a routine practice for films to end with an ask, with direct questions designed to elicit postfilm discussion.[7] Other films use narration or intertitles to ask questions of viewers without necessarily giving time for questions to be heard.[8]

Production Trajectory

The Lost Landscapes series originated in 2006, when Chris Carlsson, cofounder of Shaping San Francisco, an organization foregrounding local histories excluded from triumphalist canons, asked me to put together a program of archival material. But its direct precursor was a May 1991 event in Britton, South Dakota, occasioned by my discovery of three hours of home movies shot in 1938–1939 by Ivan Besse, manager of the Strand Theater. I was asked by Britton's mayor and by a former resident-turned-publicist to bring them back to Britton for a screening. As the audience sat in the Strand watching Mr. Besse narrate scenes of themselves and their kin, the room stirred with excitement and conversation, and it suddenly became clear that spectatorial silence and moviegoing were not inextricably linked. The first *Lost Landscapes of San Francisco* event in 2006 was similarly surprising; the audience, 120 people squeezed into a 70-seat dance theater, took over the narration from the emcee, led by a chorus of experienced local historians seated in the front row. Attendance quickly grew, and in 2008, the series entered into a productive association with Long Now Foundation, a nonprofit organization focused on "long-term thinking" and perhaps best known for its sponsorship of the 10,000 Year Clock. The 2008 screening moved to Cowell Theater, a 400-seat auditorium where an estimated 250 others were unable to gain admittance, some viewing the event from a hastily installed video monitor in the lobby. Moving to Herbst Theatre in 2009–2011 permitted 900 to attend, but starting in 2012, the event had to move to the 1,400-seat Castro Theatre. The most recent event (December 2019) played to over 2,600 people on two evenings. Since 2012, events have also been repeated at the 550-seat Internet Archive theater and elsewhere, and in the fall of 2013, I made *Bay Motion*, a four-screen installation at Oakland Museum of California significantly influenced by *Lost Landscapes* that blended public and private histories of the San Francisco Bay and was seen by tens of thousands of visitors.

The Detroit series (2010–2012; 2014–2015) grew out of a deep interest in Detroit's contested history (especially its history of race relations and labor) and many visits to collect industrial films and home movies, especially in the 1980s and 1990s. (As one of the major centers of American industry, Detroit was also a locus of media production, and specialized studios, including the well-known Jam Handy Organization, produced tens of thousands of industrial films from the 1910s through the 1980s.) Without much premeditation, I proposed a Detroit urban history screening to curators at MOCAD (Museum of Contemporary Art Detroit). The story of the San Francisco screenings repeated itself on a slightly different scale: after setting out 150 chairs in MOCAD's cavernous space (once an auto parts factory), some four hundred people showed up, representing most of Detroit's distinct communities. Four more Detroit events have followed, presented at MOCAD, Salt and Cedar Workshop, Detroit Free Press's Freep Film Festival at the Detroit Institute of Arts, at Traverse City Film Festival, and many venues outside Detroit.

The intensity of these city-specific film events led me to project a broader geographical footprint. Arising out of a long-term desire to make a history of the United States in the twentieth century told completely through changes in the landscape, I made *No More Road Trips?* in 2012–2013, aided by a generous Creative Capital grant. Made completely from home movies, the film constructed a dream automobile journey from the Atlantic Ocean to the Pacific, using footage from about eighty families shot between 1924 and the late 1970s. Originally intended to provoke discussion about the changing nature of mobility in North America and the potential oncoming obsolescence of auto travel (which some speak of as "peak travel"), the film may perhaps have been more successful as a realization of geographer John Brinckerhoff Jackson's formulation that "landscape is history made visible."[9] Like the *Lost Landscapes* events, *Road Trips?* presumed the engagement of a vocal audience, even though it also manifests as a contemplative film. It played as a work in progress at South by Southwest and the San Francisco International Film Festival and premiered as a finished work at the New York Film Festival. Since that time, it has also been widely screened at festivals, universities, and community events in North America, Europe, and Australia.

As the high cost of living in San Francisco pushed much cultural and political activity toward the Eastern side of the Bay, I was frequently asked to consider producing an Oakland *Lost Landscapes*. After a one-time presentation in 2009, I made a more structured film in 2014 that played a number of venues in and around Oakland and Berkeley, including the Oakland Museum of California and the Oakland City Council chambers. But it seemed clear that the Oakland event should become a community project maintained by Oaklanders. So I "repatriated" it to Oakland writer, artist, and activist Alex Cruse, giving her the film and the raw footage, and I have updated the gift with new material as it emerges. Since 2015 she has presented events and screenings regularly in Oakland.

Aided by a small commission from the Roy and Edna Disney/CalArts Theater (REDCAT) in 2015, I began work on *Lost Landscapes of Los Angeles*, which first screened late that year as a work-in-progress at REDCAT in downtown Los Angeles. After a year of rethinking, I completed the film at the end of 2016 and screened in Rotterdam and at two Los Angeles screenings in early 2017. This film has turned out quite differently than its predecessors. While it is rich in detail, it isn't grounded in regional minutiae—myth and topography both play a role. Unlike most evocations of LA that foreground its show-business history, the mythic aspect is derived from topography and amateur cinema rather than from popular culture. As I edited it, I realized I was making something that verged on being a film-film, rather than a film-event like the other Lost Landscapes. The result is a film with a split personality—a contemplative film that works differently whether or not there is audience participation, though I have noticed that audiences tend to take cues from an emcee before rising to the occasion and speak. For the first time, I also provided explanatory lower-third titles providing dates, places, and identifications. Like other Lost Landscapes events, this one is fueled by the discovery of new source material, and there is nearly infinite coverage of Los Angeles and its environs waiting to be seen publicly for the first time. But the importance of Los Angeles as a laboratory for thought, making, and struggle demands that future events take their lead from something more than the opportunity to unveil new material. I presented a completely new iteration of *Lost Landscapes of Los Angeles* at the Los Angeles Public Library's Central Library in December 2019.

Most recently, *Lost Landscapes of New York* was commissioned by the Museum of the Moving Image and first presented at New York University's Skirball Center in November 2017. Somewhat uneasily foregrounding visually and socially striking points on a vast spectrum of time, space, race and ethnicity, this eighty-three-minute event was structured as a set of discrete sequences demarcated by intertitles, marking a move on my part towards making urban history events that are more conceptually driven. Some sequences were also built around conditions that characterize current life in New York: racially based, aggressive policing; the growth of extreme poverty; housing shortages and speculation; the poor condition of transit infrastructure; the hunger for information in a time when newspapers are eclipsed as media sources; and others. While it is certainly a sketch for future New York programs, it is also a prefiguration of an archival film on the function and structure of cities I hope to finish over the next few years. It will also serve, I hope, as a working example of interactive and participatory documentary that is not dependent on algorithms, and I hope it will constitute an intervention in current discussions on the operational attributes of documentary media. The film received great attention in New York, and further screenings occurred in 2018 and 2019.[10]

Making Events

Making these events (especially the annual San Francisco event that takes place in December) has become a ritual. Research takes far more time than production. Relevant material constantly surfaces within Prelinger Archives, the collection I control; its home movie archives are deep, comprising an estimated seventeen thousand home movies, fewer than half of them viewed. In addition to our own collection, people who know of the screenings offer material from their family collections; archivists come forward to offer the use of films in their archives; and I am often informed about material that local history organizations have collected from their constituencies. People also scout films for me in their communities; the Detroit films would be much less interesting had I not experienced the kindnesses of four Michiganders who continually provide new images for *Lost Landscapes of Detroit*. There is still much to be discovered, and I hope the existence of so much film unseen in public will encourage people to start projects like this in other cities. In 2016, for example, Baltimore moving image archivist Siobhan Hagan presented *Baltimorama* at the Cinema Ephemera festival, the first of what I hope will be many events focused on her city.[11]

Research takes a full year, but editing commences four to six weeks before each show. As usual in editing, the process is iterative, but it has also become intuitive, beginning with lengthy assemblies (as long as fifteen hours) that over time reduce to the length of a short feature film. I make some editing decisions unconsciously; their reasons for being may not even emerge until I see the film on the big screen. But in general the approach is to assemble a lot of material in rough order and then to edit down from there, for as the architect Keller Easterling, with whom I collaborated in the 1980s and 1990s, once noted: "Subtraction is growth." Each film is cut with attention to its presentation as a live event, with time allowed for audiences to read and parse complex or crowded images and to recover attention after laughter. My audiences, at least in San Francisco, are attuned to the roughhewn qualities of home movies and know how to look at outtakes and other material that might not find its way into other kinds of films. I have no problem showing glitches, flash frames, dirt, and fuzz or even reproducing repetition in the original film documents, as that makes it clearer that I'm foregrounding primary evidence and showing what it often looks like. It is likely that Lost Landscapes audiences do not realize that the editing ratio of the films is sometimes fifty to one, perhaps even greater, and that each annual San Francisco program is generally composed of over 80 percent new material. That said, thoughtful repetition creates a sense of continuity and engagement and is important to repeat audiences (there are more than a handful of people who have attended all fourteen San Francisco programs); certain favorite sequences are therefore repeated from year to year.

I have sometimes been told these are city symphonies, a suggestion I cannot fully evaluate. Most of the films balance a topographical approach (in the British sense)[12] with a focus on the visual minutiae of human social behavior—an approach that would not be out of line with the work of Walther Ruttmann or Dziga Vertov. Like Ruttmann and unlike Vertov, these films tend to focus on enigmatic evidence and strive to elicit a kind of detail-oriented viewing that never slackens. It is hard both to interpret the traces of human behavior with finality and to apprehend every bit of evidence in a moving process plate. And if these events as edited possess a structural antecedent, it would more likely be found in Straub/Huillet rather than canonical, symphonic structure. Above all, the events do not typically seek to invoke notions of a "common humanity"—they rather focus on specific communities, neighborhoods, crafts, trades, and historical moments.

Personal Documents and Process Plates

The most dramatic change in the contour of the events has been the move from depicting primarily topography and place to showing people and their behavior. The films have evolved toward a mix that primarily centers around home movies, with occasional process plates, outtakes from feature films, and television shows shot on film.

One distinctive virtue of home movies is that they help to solve the problem of overnarrativization that has become the curse of contemporary documentary, whose gatekeepers so often require narrative arcs and compelling characters. Home movies themselves provide the "storytelling" that filmmakers are strongly encouraged to impose on the images and sounds they capture, and the role of the maker using home movies might therefore resemble that of the anthologist more than that of sole author. Every home movie is *de minimis* a capsule narrative, if only as the articulation of a relationship between the shooter and who or what is being shot, and many home movies are even more complex narratives. Home movies also tempt audiences toward immediate identification with their subjects, and their intimacy and historical material counterbalance one another. Home movies are redolent with historical significance that is easily interpreted, especially if a context for doing so is created. Finally, they contain immense evidentiary value that is only beginning to be recognized.

In the beginning, I mostly used film that showed places and landscapes that had dramatically changed or were no longer in existence, and it took a long time for *Lost Landscapes of San Francisco* to shift toward majority-home movie mode. But after about 2010, I realized that footage of streets, buildings, and neighborhoods wasn't enough—I'd concentrated on the ground rather than the figure. I came to understand that footage of people doing what people do coalesced to constitute a human landscape, and that landscape wasn't just seen in long shot; landscape was the stage on which people performed social relations with one another, as home movies eloquently show.

I'm often asked whether using home movies skews the shows toward depicting wealthier families. The universe of home movie images is more inclusive than most people imagine. While it's true that the first ten years of home movies (1923–1933) mostly emanate from families of means because of the high expense of 16 mm film stock and processing (about $1,400 per hour, in today's dollars), the introduction of cheaper 8 mm movie film in 1933 enabled a much more diverse group to shoot home movies. There's a flowering of home movie expression in the 1930s—working families, families of color, rural families, and young people all shot home movies, and the breadth of documentation is extraordinary. Even some working-class families produced important 16 mm collections.

The San Francisco, Los Angeles, and New York events have also been deeply enriched through the use of background process plates, a category of footage high in evidentiary value that most people have seen but few would recognize. Process plates are moving backgrounds intended for rear projection in a shot, such as people driving a car, riding in a cab or a train, or even atop horses. In the movies, these often appear jumpy and poorly focused. But original process plates are rock-steady, sharply focused and very often dense records of the look of a street, a road or the countryside. And while they are rarely seen outside studio libraries, they offer amazing records of cityscapes, especially when shot with a moving camera whose point of view may stretch for miles.

Assembly, Not Algorithm

Today, participatory and interactive documentary has in many minds and instantiations become inextricable from technology. Most new interactive and participatory documentaries meet their viewers in the browser, through apps or social media platforms. Viewers are kept at a certain distance, and their contributions are most often mediated through algorithms and technological apparati. What viewers add to the performance of an interactive documentary might be aggregated into a composite reaction that loses the specific traces of their contribution or, conversely, treated as an exemplary reaction that when edited into place crowds out contributions considered less interesting by editorial gatekeepers. By this suggestion I do not mean to say that editorial intervention inevitably produces adverse results—but what such intervention enables happens *within* the extended production process of the film. Similarly, much "live cinema" currently being produced is built around scripted commentary and precomposed music such that projections are performances bound to makers' intentions rather than viewers' reactions. While this kind of gatekeeping may be habitual, it is not inevitable.

The urban history film events I describe find their public articulation outside the production process; they are realized only in public assembly, through the encounter between film and audience. The work of making them includes a conditional disavowal of directorial authority. Viewers take on new roles after being encouraged to vocalize, interrogate and discuss; the lowering of the lights first elicits tentative speech acts that quickly expand into more self-confident talking, joking, noisemaking. Members of the audience segment into quiet conversers whose words impact a small area of the room; others with louder and more assertive voices who aim their words at the entire theater; explainers providing historical background or details on individual segments (such as, conspicuously, transportation historians); and questioners aiming interrogatories at the emcee or at the general audience. While I have found that an audible continuum that ranges from buzz to roar violates the rule of spectatorial silence and is thus difficult for many cinephiles to accept, it is extremely popular among more community-oriented audiences. I've sometimes joked that my films are all failures, because they're contemplative films that play before vocal audiences. But in recent years I've started to understand how contemplation is not necessarily silent or solitary.

More positively, I've discovered that archival footage—critically, home movies—change character when blown up to theater-screen size. The change of scale also provokes a role change in the audience who, without necessarily expecting it, become more than simple commentators and perform new and sometimes unpredictable modes of agency. They turn into ethnographers, noticing and remarking on every visible detail of kinship, word and gesture and every interpersonal exchange. They also respond as cultural geographers, calling out streets and neighborhoods and buildings, reading signs aloud, repeating tradenames and brands and marking extinct details in the cityscape. If voices could be captured (and this would be difficult, because it is hard to intelligibly record the voices of hundreds of people in one room), the recording might constitute a kind of urban research project distributed through a crowd of investigators. Each successful identification, each naming achieved, is an emotional trigger and reinforces audience members to say more.

On the other hand, films unreel very quickly, and most audience reactions are prompted by images rather than more deliberate interventions about history, landscape, and power. While it may be too much to expect serious praxis to occur in a diffuse sea of real-time responses, I consider encounters with original and relatively unmediated archival material to be potentially more formative than viewings of highly composed documentaries that invest viewers with lower degrees of agency. The lack of conventional narrative structure, plot, and characters and the performative character of the event may, however, prevent audiences from thinking much about the event *as a film*. Compared to the abundance of commentary about specific sequences and source materials, I see or hear little critique of the films, and perceive considerable distance between my work to construct them and the audience's appreciation of the events as a whole.

Essays and Interventions

Essays take different forms: exposition, meditation, and argument, among others. And so do interventions, which might come as a surprise in the middle of a process that seems to be about something else, or as defamiliarization or reformulation of a relation that suddenly no longer seems predictable.[13] As essays, the Lost Landscapes films can take all three forms. They are easily apprehended as exposition, structured as meditative experiences (though this is sabotaged by my concurrent invitation to participate), and argue for taking a critical historical (and futurist anterior) approach to the city. They embody a strategy I call "historical intervention," which in simplest terms is reinjecting the record of the past in the present so as to affect the future. I hope to enable a jump from images to ideas. If presenting vivid historical images of familiar scenes and places triggers viewers to contemplate visible and invisible differences between past and present, I'd like to cause an analogous jump from present into future.

Yet these films are not tightly crafted essays. Each is a snapshot of what I want to make with the footage I possess at editing time, and I make each one in full realization that others will follow. They embody what filmmaker and cultural theorist Craig Baldwin calls "availableism"[14] and what architect and designer Sara Dean, speaking of *Lost Landscapes of Detroit*, calls "considered non-completion."[15] Each event draws from and capitalizes on those that have come before, and each implies a sequel.

Politics, Positionalities, and Potentials

I often describe archives as both anchorages and launchpads and as spaces for both retrospection and rehearsal. These words perfectly describe the polarities of the urban history events, which seek to move viewers in the direction of being their own historians—to come to terms with history as both feeling and process. But perhaps the most significant attribute of archives today is their relative enclosure. Most archival material is not accessible for viewing, and what is accessible for viewing is not available for reuse except by special arrangement. The wealth of the archival record is primarily available to public audiences only through distortingly contextualized commercial media products. It is rare that entertainment consumers are offered unmediated archival material, which may in part explain the online popularity of the unedited 1906 film *A Trip Down Market Street before the Fire* after it was profiled on *60 Minutes*.[16] The wide circulation of this film sensitized many people to the existence of moving image archives and the qualitative attributes of the archival moving image record. I would hope that the Lost Landscapes series works to do the same.

I see great potential in the presentation of historical moving images as evidence, and I am hopeful audiences will increasingly find means to craft whatever narrativization or contexts make sense to them. One film is not the same to all audience members. I have found that Black and white Detroiters watching *Lost Landscapes of Detroit* often see very different films. And there is one vexing contradiction around the presentation of granular evidence. The filter of local history tends to throw up highly granular detail as a defense against tough or irreconcilable questions. Many in my audiences are fascinated with historical detail. While I love that this is true, and I am in awe of the complex time and space mapping that lives in the heads of many in our local history community, I am much less interested in the minutiae of local history than I am in the process of daylighting it, in foregrounding relationships between history and contemporary life. I tend to think more about the conditions prevailing in the past than I do about the specifics of what was once located where. I see San Francisco, Detroit, Oakland, and Los Angeles as cities of extreme contestation, cities in which battles were fought to maintain racialized power and control, cities filled with zones where bodily safety was contingent on race, class, gender and age. Not everyone wants to recall how African Americans have been priced out and "redeveloped" out of San Francisco, especially since World War II, or how Chinese families were prohibited from living on the west side of the city for many years. I hypothesize that focusing on the web of granular historical detail may screen out uncomfortable issues. Or perhaps people have become too worried about the possibility of evoking anger or triggering conflict. But to me acknowledging every element in a city as the product of some sort of conflict, as the embodiment of power relations, is unavoidable, and this becomes part of my live commentary as the films roll by. It's impossible to recall urban histories without considering the urban present. I would be the last person to deny the fascination of the past, but the potential of the future interests me much more.

My positionality is also a very real issue. Who am I to speak about these cities? To interpolate oneself as a teller or reteller of histories is to construct one's own pedestal. Usually these are not my stories to tell. How do the people who inhabit the place shown in a film want to recall the events, trends and relationships the film shows? In general, I think of these events, especially those that take place outside my own city, as inputs to a process that I only assist—that I'm only involved in as a scout and presenter, not necessarily as an interpreter or authority. I tell Detroiters that the future of their city is theirs to decide and theirs to struggle for, that the images I'm showing support their discussions and that I'm not trying to express an opinion about what they ought to do. At the same time, I make the programs available online so that community members can show them as they please and remix the footage to make their own historical videos. (For the first program, I produced DVDs and gave them out at the screening.) After the first three programs in Detroit, I also realized I didn't want to use the *Lost Landscapes* title any more, and changed the title to the rather prosaic *Yesterday and Tomorrow* in Detroit. It seemed to me that it was up to Detroiters how much they wanted to engage with a discourse of loss.

The question of who is shown and who is absent in the footage also raises questions of erasure and inclusion. Though the surviving corpus of home movies depicts a more diverse group than most people imagine, it is far easier to find material that correlates with whiteness and wealth, and it can take very hard work to represent the ethnic mix of most places. Audiences readily ask why there are few people of color in older footage. Over time I have found significant holdings of Bay Area material representing many communities. But workers at the event where I first presented the completed *Lost Landscapes of Los Angeles* in early 2017 asked why there were so many more minutes (about forty) showing white people than minorities (about eight), and why I used so many landscape shots that were relatively empty of people. They suggested using news and documentary footage so as to more fully represent the life and labor of Black, Asian, and Latinx Angelenos. I accepted their critique, but it will take serious work to address that lack of inclusion. The 2019 iteration of the Los Angeles film initiates this effort by deeply foregrounding the everyday experiences of Angelenos who are Black, Indigenous, and people of color.

By contrast, I have worked hard to represent both Black and white Detroit. This is perhaps one reason why Detroit's communities have been so kind in furnishing footage to use. That said, there have been screenings in mostly white parts of Michigan during which I can hear intakes of breath when images of Black Detroit come on screen. The emotions surrounding the white diaspora from Detroit are often still raw, and many white Detroiters express discomfort with images showing Black emergence and presence. Not every use instance can be perfectly motivated and flawlessly executed; we need to take risks and engage with communities to daylight material that every generation needs to see and reinterpret through their own lenses. But ultimately communities have the strongest claim to their own history, and I take it on faith that this is where history is most effectively presented.

This leads us back to intervention in another realm. Making these urban history events is not filmmaking as usually practiced; it is a form of social practice that encompasses film research, reformatting, editing and presentation. But to reduce the process to a series of screenings in large rooms staged by a person possessing considerable archival privilege risks drastically reducing the potential of these events to address and change the future. One route that seems urgent and perhaps inevitable might be to think of the screenings not as ends but as means. What if Lost Landscapes evolved into a community project whose work happened mostly at the neighborhood level? What if younger makers connected with elders to find images, explicate them and identify people pictured, and edit presentations that would first happen locally? Later, neighborhood segments might coalesce into a longer-form event that could be shown to the entire city. But to shift the emphasis from a one-time event to enabling a process of local connection and discovery would relocate historical agency from one filmmaker to many others, and perhaps be a stimulus for media training as well.

I do not seek to bury the algorithm. But I question any retreat from public assembly, especially if such retreat occurs under the rubric of engagement, as so much interactive cinema asserts. Public assembly substitutes affective power based on presence and unpredictability for the simulative power of algorithmic media. The virtual auditorium of apps and browsers provide various senses of collectivity but at the same time accentuate the split between on-screen and off-screen engagement. Without dismissing the potential of technologically enabled interactive and participatory media, I would strenuously argue that the difficulties of realizing a participatory commons in an unequally provisioned world should not inhibit us from low-tech, person-to-person experimentation. We are not always going to be able to rely on programmers, sysadmins, code and connectivity to enable community in virtual spaces. I would also argue that restoring big-screen experience coupled with direct, dialogical participation is a route toward staging the meeting of difference without its dilution, a means to an end rather than an end in itself.

Finally, public assembly begs the question of what ends it could serve. The confluence of shared interests that lead people to gather in a room for a film signifies the commencement of a process that most films never seek to take further. What more could we do with an assembly of people gathered in a room than simply screen a movie? Could we stimulate audiences to take on greater agency and new responsibilities? Could a screening be a model for deeper participation, for collective efforts to remediate conditions that resist individualized labors and concerns? Could we try to make theater-in-the-round within a rectangular box? Could we model a new commons?

Acknowledgment

My archival work and writing takes place upon the occupied traditional lands of the Yelamu Ohlone people, including the villages known as Petlenuc, Sitlintac, Chutchui, Amuctac, Tubsinte, and Ompuromo, whose sites are within the boundaries of today's city of San Francisco. The Ohlone people are still present throughout the city and Peninsula of San Francisco, and we live among them today.

Notes

1. Most of my films are available for free viewing and downloading at http://www.prelinger.com. The 2020 San Francisco event was presented live online because of COVID-19.
2. Throughout this chapter, I will use the terms *films* and *events* interchangeably, choosing particular alternatives depending on context.
3. A distinction should be recognized here between the types of participation and interactivity of digital tools against which these events' vital attributes of liveness, synchrony, performance, and community engagement are specifically contrasted.
4. Dillon, *New World Drama*, 4–5.
5. See Ruoff, "Around the World in Eighty Minutes."
6. Brecht, *Brecht on Theatre*, 6, 37.
7. See the Discussion Problems in Group Living series.
8. See *You and Your Friends*.
9. Jackson, "Forum 1," quoted in Jackson and Horowitz, *Landscape in Sight*, x.
10. Despite certain surface similarities, the ethos of these film events is deliberately conceived in opposition to the computational and algorithm affordances of interactive documentary and participatory media.
11. See MacDonald, "Cinema Ephemera."
12. See Backhaus and Murungi, *Lived Topographies*, xxi.
13. I have previously articulated this argument in a deep interview whose text I prepared via email. See Schiller, "Essayistic Interventions.
14. See de Bruyn, "Evening on Baldwin's Mountain."
15. Prelinger and Dean, "Considered Non-completion," 272–279.
16. A query on YouTube returns 3,950 hits relating to this original film, totaling over 7 million views.

References

Backhaus, Gary, and John Murungi. *Lived Topographies and Their Mediational Forces*. Oxford: Lexington, 2005.

Brecht, Bertolt. *Brecht on Theatre: The Development of an Aesthetic*. Translated and edited by John Willett. New York: Hill and Wang, 1964.
de Bruyn, Dirk. "An Evening on Baldwin's Mountain." *Senses of Cinema*, April 2001. http://sensesofcinema.com/2001/craig-baldwin/baldwin-mountain/.
Dillon, Elizabeth Maddock. *New World Drama: The Performative Commons in the Atlantic World, 1649–1849*. Durham, NC: Duke University Press, 2014.
Discussion Problems in Group Living series. Produced by Centron Productions for Young America Films. Four films in the series may be seen at Internet Archive, https://archive.org/search.php?query=centron%20%22discussion%20problems%20in%20group%20living%22.
Jackson, J. B. "Forum 1: Landscape Reflects Culture, History." *Centre Daily Times* (State College, PA), October 2, 1975.
Jackson, J. B., and Helen Lefkowitz Horowitz, eds. *Landscape in Sight: Looking at America*. New Haven, CT: Yale University Press, 1997.
MacDonald, Jonathan. "Cinema Ephemera: The Festival of Useful Film." *Sound and Vision*, July 5, 2016. https://aboutsoundandvision.wordpress.com/2016/07/05/cinema-ephemera-the-festival-of-useful-film/.
Prelinger, Rick, and Sara Dean. "Considered Non-completion: A Correspondence between Rick Prelinger and Sara Dean." *Scapegoat* 5 (2013). http://www.scapegoatjournal.org/docs/05/SG_Excess_272-279_P_PRELINGER.pdf.
Ruoff, Jeffrey. "Around the World in Eighty Minutes: The Travel Lecture Film." *Visual Anthropology* 15, no. 1, (2002): 91–114.
Schiller, Lucy. "Essayistic Interventions: Taking the City into the Theater." *Essay Review*, 2017. http://theessayreview.org/essayistic-interventions-taking-the-city-into-the-theater.
You and Your Friends. Produced by B. K. Blake for Association Films, 1946. https://archive.org/details/0763_You and_Your_Friends,_E0175602375514. Page no longer available.

RICK PRELINGER is Professor of Film and Digital Media at the University of California, Santa Cruz. His films include the archival feature *Panorama Ephemera* (2004), *No More Road Trips?* (2013), and various urban history film projects.

18

THE ARMCHAIR JUROR

Audience Engagement in True Crime Documentaries

George S. Larke-Walsh

The social media interest in the Netflix documentary series *Making a Murderer* (2015 and 2018) is no surprise when you consider that true crime narratives have long been one of the most popular genres in US fiction and nonfiction. From novels, magazines, and newspaper accounts of court cases to TV legal and crime-stopper series and televised criminal trials, audiences have been encouraged to act as participatory viewers in the judgment of crimes by bearing witness to presented evidence and helping to assign guilt. It is generally understood that an important aspect of true crime narratives is the eventual reestablishment of law and order through the successful identification of the criminal. Audiences may be subjected to the gory details of criminal activities, but in the end justice is—or will be—served and society's moral compass restored. The current popularity of true crime documentaries has developed within that long-established tradition.

Alongside acknowledgment of that tradition, this chapter considers the popularity of true crime narratives that question or directly indict the impartiality and neutrality of the justice system. Specifically, it will focus on *Making a Murderer* and how this series appeals to its audience's sense of justice through emotional and critical engagement. By employing a narrative that incorporates the traditional crime format in order to critique the judicial system, *Making a Murderer* offers a particular framework of audience engagement that questions the moral compass of the very system that is supposed to protect people as citizens. This chapter asks the following two questions: Does narrative manipulation and the promotion of either/or solutions to complex legal processes deny the possibility for audience critical engagement? And how do the emotional responses encouraged in the audience make this type of true crime narrative so compelling? To answer these questions, this chapter will draw on affect theory as it has been applied to film studies and to crime narratives more specifically. Affect is connected to emotion insofar as it lies behind it—affect is a response, emergence, or a measure of intensity that can then result in emotion. However, Brian Massumi contends that affect can help explain the contradictory, or unsettling experience of emotions (or the inability to explain them).[1] Therefore, affect is a useful framework to explain the sometimes incomprehensible and contradictory emotional engagement encouraged by true crime narratives and is especially pertinent to the disruption caused by narratives of injustice.

Criminal injustice narratives disrupt the traditional true crime format of clearly defined goodness in law and order versus evil in the criminal character. *Making a Murderer* not only investigates the accused (Steven Avery and Brendan Dassey) but also questions the Manitowoc County Police and the District Attorney's Office involved in the prosecution. This disruption places the audience in the privileged position of, say, an armchair juror who judges not only the accused but also the police and the legal system as a whole. While we may consider that jury role as a dispassionate or objective one, it is evident that the details of crimes encourage sympathies, compassion, and even outrage and frustration. Furthermore, the series also exaggerates and manipulates these emotions to enhance audience engagement. As an example of the contemporary convergence of documentary and fictional techniques, *Making a Murderer* utilizes a format that manipulates audience responses while also distancing them from the reality of the topic; they are simultaneously swamped with emotions and facts. In consequence, a real-life tragedy is transformed into both an entertaining and frustrating puzzle for viewers to explore, debate, and solve. As Kathryn Schulz of the *New Yorker* reported in her response to *Making a Murderer*, such true crime documentaries "turn private tragedies into public entertainment."[2]

Both series have been both applauded and derided in equal measure for their attention to the minutiae of the crimes, investigations, and legal processes involved. The initial documentary project was in production for ten years and details the criminal cases against Steven Avery in Manitowoc County, Wisconsin. It begins with his release from prison in 2003 after serving eighteen years of a life sentence for sexual assault: The case has been overturned with the help of the Innocence Project after DNA evidence proved his innocence, and Avery has subsequently filed a $36 million civil lawsuit against the Manitowoc County Sheriff's Office, which convicted him. In 2005, Avery is arrested for the murder of Teresa Halbach and is eventually convicted and sentenced to life imprisonment in 2007. The implicit premise of the series is that the Manitowoc County Sheriff's Office should not have had any involvement in the Halbach murder case. Furthermore, the actions of the police officers, the court system, and some court-appointed lawyers were at the very least injudicious in their case against Avery or, at worst, downright corrupt. Evidence presented in the series suggests not only that the Manitowoc County Sheriff's Office rushed to convict him of the sexual assault in 1985 but also that it tampered with evidence and neglected to pursue alternative leads during his arrest and trial for murder in 2007. The series does not insist Avery is innocent of the charge of murder, but it does ask questions about systemic bias, collusion, and unprofessionalism in the criminal system. A second season (2018) involves a further ten episodes that continue to investigate the crime and documents the legal processes involved in filing numerous appeals for retrials. Thus, as a true crime text, *Making a Murderer* is about much more than just whodunit.

Criminal Injustice Narratives and the History of True Crime Genre

Much has been written about the popularity and format of the traditional whodunit true crime genre in recent years.[3] Most literature focuses on the genre's obsession with certainty and closure and its supportive and uncritical view of law enforcement. True crime narratives in the United States can be traced back to the early days of European settlement in the seventeenth century. From newspaper reports and reprints of execution sermons to modern case study books, TV series, and documentaries, true crime narratives have been used to try to explain everything from the spiritual journeys of killers, the gory details of murder cases, the psychological or sociological motivations behind criminal acts, and the intricacies of detection and the judicial process. The true crime genre presents itself as a fact-based genre whose basic purpose is to educate audiences about the various realities involved in criminal activity and society's attempts to contain it. However, as Murley notes, "true crime always fictionalizes, emphasizes, exaggerates, interprets, constructs, and creates 'truth', any relationship to the facts is mediated and compromised."[4] She suggests that true crime narratives in the twentieth century have gradually moved away from spiritual, psychological, or sociological exploration in favor of a focus on the maintenance of preconceived ideas of law and order.

In essence, though, the modern true crime narrative still tends to favor law enforcement and the successful capture and containment of criminals all represented through "a symbolic reassurance of closure, capture and the reestablishment of order."[5] Such a predictable format allows audiences to revel in the alarming spectacle of criminal activities while anticipating the restoration of morality and security by story's end.

The gory details of criminal acts are described within stable and secure reassurances that justice will prevail, even when a crime remains unsolved. Murley argues that the mix of "satisfying formula and tantalizing ambiguity"[6] is the hook that keeps viewers engaged; we are firmly on the side of law and order in the hope of bringing all criminals to justice. The most obvious influences on modern true crime documentaries are the television series *Cops* (1989–), *America's Most Wanted* (1988–), and *Unsolved Mysteries* (1988–2002 and 2020–). These series all focus on the desire to solve a case and arrest a suspect. *America's Most Wanted* and *Unsolved Mysteries* involve direct appeals to viewers for help in this process. John Walsh's famous tagline from *America's Most Wanted*, "Remember: you can make a difference," is a constant reminder that the police require the public's support in order to keep them safe. Such TV serializations favor a formalized, nondiscursive, and noncritical approach to crime. The TV schedule has various channels at least partially devoted to true crime programming, such as Tru TV (formerly Court TV), Investigation Discovery (a subsidiary of the Discovery channel), and A&E. Shows tend to be a mix of reenactments and interviews that describe criminal events in shocking and brutal detail, but they also have interviews with the police and other law enforcement to provide reassurance that justice will prevail. Gary Cavender writes that the genre is "defined by repetitious, often formulaic plots and characterizations that yield predictability and stability in cultural production."[7] Murley describes this formula as a cathartic format that encourages "viewers to ignore the murky root causes of crime and instead concentrate on those who have transgressed."[8] Similarly, Pamela Donovan notes how such "reality programming offers a way for the viewers to meld their skepticism and their necessary trust of public servants in an increasingly privatized world."[9] It is evident from all of these studies that traditional formats of true crime on television operate within a particular formalized structure of crime and punishment.

Feature-length (or long-form) documentaries, specifically those made for cinema release or streaming, are not bound by the same format constraints as television series. Therefore, while many feature-length true crime documentaries and docuseries are influenced by television formats, it is not surprising that we find more varied and complex themes and structures in their narratives. It is fair to say the basic structure of reenactment and interview that typifies the television format remains a staple foundation, but what does change is the clear distinction between the law and criminality. Longer narratives allow for more discussion of the possible motivations for crime, including the spiritual, psychological, and sociological contexts often ignored by television formats. For instance, *Making a Murderer* dedicates as much of its first ten episodes to the contexts for the crime as it does to the investigation and court procedures. Hence, the longer narrative and the resultant discussion of the motivations for crime may be the simplest reason why the series appears critical, rather than blindly supportive, of the legal system. It directs audiences to debate the evidence at hand while allowing ample time for emotional engagement with the accused and their families. While it should be noted that not all longer narratives result in a critique of the justice system, *Making a Murderer* is a high-profile example of one that certainly does that. It is also not unique, for injustice narratives have become an increasingly popular subgenre of true crime over the last three decades in US documentary, a trend that arguably emerged after the huge success of Errol Morris's *The Thin Blue Line* (1988). Criminal injustice narratives combine the formal aesthetics of fiction and true crime television, such as *America's Most Wanted* and the conspiratorial tone of *Unsolved Mysteries*. They appeal to audiences through both intellect and emotions by asking them to take a second look, question the official verdict of a crime that has previously been investigated, and consider the plight of the accused as well as the victims. Criminal injustice narratives most often rely on the benefit of hindsight to reimagine the crime and its investigation. Audiences get to review events from a seemingly objective viewpoint outside of institutional bias or the confines of investigative procedure; thus, documentaries appeal to audiences as amateur sleuths and ask them to help solve the crime or correct the injustice.

Within this subgenre of criminal injustice, there are two types of narrative: those that shed light on a possible miscarriage of justice where the convicted person remains in prison, such as *Making a Murderer*, and those that explore the institutional or social prejudices and inadequacies that have caused and may continue to cause injustice in a more general sense. For instance, *Capturing the Friedmans* (2003), *The Trials of Darryl Hunt* (2006), *The Central Park Five* (2012), *Into the Abyss* (2011), *Crime after Crime* (2011), and *West of Memphis* (2012)[10] are all stories of past crimes and legal injustices where it is too late for audiences to change the verdicts or fates of the accused. *Death on the Staircase* (2004) and *The Jinx* (2015) focus on police investigations and court cases that fail to solve crimes. Both of these examples also focus on the influence extreme wealth has on the criminal process and variously inspire curiosity, disgust, outrage, and frustration at a system susceptible to such manipulation. *Gideon's Army* (2013) focuses on the gross inadequacies in the legal system for public defenders and their clients and should inspire audiences to demand changes. However, its failure to solicit viewer identification through individualized case studies may be a hindrance to the documentary's affective impact. Regardless, all of these diverse examples focus on true crime and the plight of both victims and the accused caught up in a system that seems to have lost a sense of proportion or justice. They may include reenactments of crime and interviews about the search for justice, but the ambiguities of their findings cannot inspire concrete action from an audience to change events. In contrast, the possibility that a documentary film or series may have an effect on a criminal case is not only a moral motivator for production; it is also a financial incentive. *Making a Murderer* capitalizes on these incentives within a structural format that has been so effective in true crime narratives in magazine, novel and previous television forms and adapts them for its own end. As a documentary that sheds light on a crime and conviction where those involved are still in prison, it is evident the narrative structure allows for a similar appeal to the "remember: you can make a difference" statement encouraged by *America's Most Wanted*. Only this time, instead of identifying law enforcement as the moral center of the narrative, the documentary appeals to the viewers' sense of right and wrong. Alongside *Making a Murderer*, two other influential examples of this style are *Dear Zachary* (2008), which criticizes the Canadian legal process, and the TV series *The Case of Adnan Syed* (2019, a follow-up to the radio podcast, *Serial*, 2014). All of these focus on the criminal justice system in ways that question the processes and outcomes for the accused as well as victims and their families. For instance, both *Making a Murderer* and *The Case of Adnan Syed* feature convicted criminals who may—or may not—be innocent yet are serving life sentences. *Dear Zachary* is the useful crossover example here, because it does not feature a convicted prisoner, but it does appeal to audiences to help change a law.[11] Thus, it is a criminal injustice narrative that appeals for concrete action.

Armchair Jurors

Documentaries that encourage audiences to engage in the topic as amateur sleuths or pseudo-jury members often result in cultural discourses beyond the text and expand the relevance and consequent profitable life span of the series. The transmedia impact of *Making a Murderer* is an excellent example of adapting the traditional true crime format to appeal to an audience's sense of justice as well as encouraging a plethora of news reports, online discussions, and political campaigns that keep the story, and thus the documentary, in the media spotlight. It should be noted that the percentage of viewers who go beyond passive activism to actual activism is small, but even the continual reading and sharing of opinions, memes, and news stories helps keep the topic in the popular consciousness. Since the first series was aired, Brendan Dassey, Avery's nephew who was sentenced alongside him, had his conviction overturned (August 12, 2016), but as of this writing, he is yet to be released. The lawyers must take credit for that court decision, but we should also recognize the series and associated online interest in the case bolstered by viewer-led activism as a significant factor in producing this outcome. The online response to Dassey's continued incarceration has focused on the "obvious injustice" involved in his conviction. Discussions are centered primarily on the coercion used by the sheriff's office during his initial arrest interviews and makes much of Brendan's young age, low intelligence, and subsequent vulnerability at the time. In the series, the sheriff's office is portrayed as predatory in its eagerness to secure evidence against Steven Avery, while Dassey's own defense team colludes with the prosecution to ensure a conviction. This aspect of the injustice narrative is rooted in the traditional style of television true crime in that it encourages audience engagement based on simple either/or questions. The binary structure of something as either right or wrong, legal or illegal, is the foundation of the true crime narrative format and acts as a reassurance to audiences that answers can be found. Injustice narratives aim the questions not at the accused but back at the legal system that is supposed to know and protect right from wrong. Placing the legal system under scrutiny in such a way empowers audiences, because it suggests the following: if the police or courts cannot be trusted to enact justice, then the public has a duty to intervene and restore notions of fairness, security, and common sense in society.

The fact that true crime documentary uses fictional techniques to portray the effects of crime and the justice system on real people's lives can raise many ethical questions about the exploitation of personal tragedy for public consumption. This difficult area of discussion is even harder to define in the case of criminal injustice narratives wherein the accused or convicted criminal is aiming for an appeal against their conviction. The distinction between victims and perpetrators is confused and contested to the point that all participants are fair game to accusations of guilt. In fact, *game* is a useful word to describe their structure, because, as Kristen Fuhs insightfully argues, "documentaries about trials become, in a sense, meta-trials."[12] Audiences are encouraged to view and critique the entire judicial process as a competition between various actors as much as, if not more than, a personal tragedy. *Making a Murderer* utilizes specific observational, interview, and fictional styles to focus on the flaws in the judicial system in order to elicit strong feelings in viewers. However, these strong feelings may not necessarily include sympathy for the victims, their families, or law and order officials. They may only include strong feelings toward the principles of justice, without any real connection to the people involved. This is because the format, argument, fictional and emotional qualities encourage viewers to respond both emotionally and intellectually but not in any unified manner. Injustice narratives rely on audiences experiencing contradictory, but intense feelings that evolve into a belief that they can see the logic in a case where the system could not. As armchair jurors, viewers witness the flaws and feel indignation at the fallibility of the judicial system without having to bear any responsibility for the decisions made. Thus, armchair jurors are able to feel pity for the victims as well as the accused but avoid a strong personal identification with either.

While the *Making a Murderer* series has been enormously popular and garnered praise on social media and general news sites, it has also received plenty of criticism. For instance, Michael Qazvini and James Barrett from the *Daily Wire* describe the series as manipulative entertainment: "in an attempt to sensationalize an open-and-shut murder case, filmmakers Laura Ricciardi and Moira Demos infused uncertainty and suspense into their carefully crafted narrative to titillate audiences."[13] This review is obviously suspicious of the filmmakers' motivations. Its reference to "titillation" also highlights the writers' own scorn at a project (and possibly even an entire genre) that, in their eyes, is manipulative and has no function beyond voyeuristic sensationalism. In contrast, June Thomas in *Slate* believes the series encourages audiences to think for themselves: "the lack of voiceover makes the show's indictment of the legal and law enforcement system around Avery even more effective; it lets Ricciardi and Demos communicate their message more subtly—without the willful instructiveness of . . . narration—while still allowing viewers to feel as though we are weighing the evidence and deciding guilty or not guilty for ourselves."[14]

In direct response to Thomas's review, Bronwen Dickey, also in *Slate*, disagreed: "viewers only *feel* as though they are deciding for themselves. In truth, the conclusions were set up for them long ago."[15] Here, Dickey assumes Thomas's positive review is naive to the influence of prime-time television formats and the requirements for taut storytelling in the true crime genre. Therefore, like Barrett in the *Daily Wire*, Dickey implies the commercially driven true crime format is unable to function beyond the level of factual entertainment. The resultant conclusion is that any audience member who believes they have the ability to respond to the series in an intellectual manner must be ignorant of that manipulation and therefore their response is naive and untrustworthy.

The study of documentary has traditionally valued those films that encourage distanced and alienated spectator responses. This is mainly due to the form's connections to "truth" and the associated expectations of intellectual or educational objectivity. This would explain why the true crime genre is acknowledged as a popular documentary form but not necessarily one that is critically praised. Just as Carl Plantinga states melodrama in fiction film is maligned for its sentimentality,[16] the true crime genre disturbs the intellectual or educational thrust of documentary through its connections to emotions such as the thrill of curiosity or the disgust at human behavior. Alison Young notes how "crime compels as much as it repels,"[17] while Anita Biressi suggests "discourses of true crime help to produce the modern social subject who is both fearful and vigilant, but also intrigued by crime."[18] We should extend these emotional responses to acknowledge how true crime documentaries, especially those dealing with injustice, also encourage viewers to question the bases for those feelings of fear, vigilance, or intrigue. The true crime injustice narrative is a prime example of how a documentary can encourage incongruent emotions. For example, *The Wrap* suggests memes of *Making a Murderer* will make you laugh while you seethe.[19]

The meme shown suggests that an audience will have emotional responses to the scenario portrayed, but those responses will require an intellectual understanding of the social and political context of the subject in order to have full effect. Thus, the meme photograph of the car key behind a pair of shoes reminds viewers of the ridiculous argument in the prosecution's case, shown in episode six, that such an item lying in plain view could not be found in eight days of police searching a house. However, the laughter that this allusion encourages is mixed with anger and outrage that such an event was accepted in a court of law and helped convict the accused. In consequence, the laughter is mixed with anger that necessarily encourages a reflection on the political and social circumstances that could allow such injustice to prevail. This one small example from beyond the media text, one that does not even allude to the more gratuitous details of the crime or the conviction, reveals the importance of intensity and emotion in encouraging audiences'

Fig. 18.1 This meme photograph from *The Wrap* exemplifies audience engagement with *Making a Murderer* (2015).

active engagement with the series and extending that engagement beyond the viewing experience.

Emotional and Intellectual Engagement

Alison Young's work on affect in audience responses to images of crime in fiction helps explain the continued popularity of the true crime genre as well as the congruent emotions encouraged in *Making a Murderer*. Her book, *The Scene of Violence: Cinema, Crime, Affect*, focuses mainly on fictional images of violence that produce responses of shock or horror. However, her discussion of the image as an "encountered sign" is useful for a discussion of true crime documentary because it provides a vocabulary for understanding the emotional connections between a spectator and images on screen. As stated, crime is a fascinating topic because "bound up with disapprobation and distaste for crime is an intense interest in its forms, its motivations and impacts."[20] Young draws on the work of Gilles Deleuze to explain how "spectatorship is not a distanced or impersonal activity, but rather works through processes of identification in and through the cinematic image."[21] She recognizes the importance of "feeling" alongside "seeing" in an audience's responses to an image, proposing that "we regard the cinematic image as an encountered sign. In this encounter, *seeing* is only one dimension of the spectator's relationship to the image: just as important are hearing, feeling, remembering."[22] Young theorizes about the notion of haptic vision, wherein the eyes fulfill the nonoptical function of touch or smell. In response to a cinematic image, a viewer's emotional reaction may include feelings that conjure other senses, such as the smell of grass or becoming physically uncomfortable. This is very similar to Massumi's argument that affect is the moment *before* emotion takes place, an impulse or intensity that arises from the encounter with such as an image or sound. The coming-to-emotion can be interpreted as a result of affect, but it is not a simple cause and effect. Thus, Young's argument of affect is the process of understanding how the viewer is implicated in the image through the haptic nature of spectatorship. The formulaic structure of most crime narratives produce uncomfortable yet exciting responses of shock or horror but then provide a resolution that reinstates the calm surety of justice. She suggests that crime narratives that do not provide such resolutions violate "the border that separates community from criminality, law from disorder, body from violence."[23] Injustice narratives disrupt that border between community and criminality because they suggest crime affects everyone and is not always resolved. The story is simultaneously not about us, and yet it is. Such narratives implicate audiences in multiple ways; they provide intriguing mysteries, but they also question the processes by which justice is served and so the experience of watching an injustice narrative encourages the contradictory impulses of intrigue and discomfort. In consequence, the intense pleasure or excitement of watching an injustice narrative is bound up in the anxieties and frisson of disorder or chaos. Justice does not prevail, and we cannot be sure exactly where criminality begins and ends. Thus, watching an injustice narrative is an intense but freeing experience because we feel we have a role beyond spectatorship—to actively search for clues about guilt and innocence.

The act of watching *Making a Murderer* feels like a game or puzzle. The series has a manipulative narrative aesthetic that intends to promote the possibility of Avery and Dassey's innocence while simultaneously suggesting systemic inadequacies in the Wisconsin judicial system. However, the evidence is contradictory and the effect of those contradictions on the audience arouses intrigue and contradictory emotions; as the internet meme website suggests, we may laugh as we seethe. If we accept Avery and Dassey as the series' co-victims alongside Teresa Halbach, then it is safe to say that the Special Prosecutor Ken Kratz is presented as one of the series' villains (alongside the Manitowoc detective James Lenk) and appears in the most contradictory moments of the series. For instance, the first day of Avery's trial includes a short montage sequence of the various parties arriving in court. The sequence begins with a shot of Avery's nervous face framed by indistinct people who surround him. We then see his slow-moving frail mother entering the court and being subjected to a metal detector search. In contrast, shots of eager journalists include Special Prosecutor Ken Kratz shaking hands and laughing with a reporter. The next edit shows Kratz striding down the same corridor in which we earlier saw Avery's mother and entering the court, only Kratz of course avoids the metal detector and associated security by walking around and straight past the guards. This sequence does more than introduce the main characters for the courtroom, it is visual evidence of the unequal treatment of these characters, and thus, American citizens in general. Avery and—by proxy—his mother should be innocent until proven guilty, yet they are either imprisoned or subject to security searches. In contrast, Kratz is shown as above the law, for he is allowed to avoid all security checks. Furthermore, his buddy connections to the media might also suggest his ability to control how justice is explained to wider society. In consequence, some of the main characters of the first day of court are presented within a clear hierarchy of power and societal imbalance. Viewers are implicated in these montages because of the way the images encourage feelings of sympathy, bias, or unease.

The sensational news conference where Kratz details the horrific crimes against Teresa Halbach before the trial even begins is expertly positioned in the series to undermine the credibility of Kratz's conduct. In fact, that scene has a dual role of implicating the audience in the horror of the crime while simultaneously questioning its veracity. On the one hand, it is an example of the lurid attraction of the true crime genre, where details of brutality are explicitly recounted, but on the other hand, it critiques such attraction by encouraging repulsion of those details and questioning the appropriateness of their revelation on an early evening newscast. Kratz is framed as an example of the distasteful voyeurism and opportunism that surrounds true crime. His eagerness to share such an exaggerated narrative of Halbach's final hours is disrespectful to the victim, her family, and the criminal process. However, the inclusion of the broadcast allows the audience to participate in that voyeurism while also distancing itself and critiquing the cultural processes that encourage such a broadcast to exist. The scene then is a striking example of the incongruent emotions of intrigue *and* repulsion—or the underlying role of affect in creating an emotional response. The moment encourages contradictory emotions as well as an intellectual reflection on the social and political impact of such media sensationalism. An audience's emotional response may battle variously between intrigue and horror at the details, outrage at the blatant manipulation of the media and the justice system by a district attorney, and indignation that such an event would occur without anyone addressing its impact on the case. The emotional response is not just a knee-jerk, adrenergic one that titillates audiences, it is a more complex emotion that, as Young and Plantinga observe, implicates the audience in the sounds and images. It is an example of affect that can be explained through the uneasy feelings of both an emotional and intellectual response. It makes an audience "sit up and engage"—it enhances the desire to engage with the text by providing an incentive to do so. While *Making a Murderer* employs many voices of reason to represent its moral and intellectual center, it mainly relies on empowering audiences to believe in their own sense of fairness and justice in order to identify the guilty and solve the crime.

To paraphrase Biressi, true crime remains a popular genre because it constantly replays a society's fear of crime, the need to stay vigilant against the possible spread of crime alongside a natural curiosity about transgressive behaviors of others. Injustice narratives take these same emotions and add an extra basis for fear; fear of the justice system, the need for vigilance, and a curiosity for its structural mechanics. The intrigue in *Making a Murderer* is the implicit suggestion that US law enforcement would, at best, collude with a neighboring county district attorney's office to wrongly convict a young man in order to prove the guilt of another or, at worst, plant evidence and target an innocent man as retaliation for his civil action against them. The vigilance is presented in the understanding that crime needs to be successfully prosecuted in order for society to remain stable and secure, but those employed in enacting justice must be trustworthy and above accusations of bias or corruption. The natural curiosity emanates from the first two suggestions and leads to a desire for answers to be found in order to restore the moral compass. This can either be concrete evidence that proves Avery's guilt, evidence that proves guilt in law enforcement, or a combination of the two.

In conclusion, it is evident injustice documentaries are a popular subgenre of true crime, but the question of narrative manipulation does not split audiences into simple categories of naive or informed, as some reviewers suggest. Narrative manipulation provides the emotional impetus to engage with the text in an intellectual manner. The eventual response will be based as much on an individual's own cultural prejudices and beliefs as any manipulation—or narrative mechanics—in the text. The popularity of injustice narratives, like true crime in general, lies in the invitation from texts to participate in the mystery in an emotional *and* intellectual manner as amateur sleuths or armchair jurors. Viewers feel they have made their own mind up about events and this activity alone can make audiences feel that they have participated constructively in the promotion of justice. Such passive activism that exists in the attraction to true crime narratives is described by Pamela Donovan as the encouragement of a strong emotional response to the information without the demand for concrete action: "Since violent crimes present a recurrent challenge to the outer limits of social consensus (no one, including criminals, advocates them), they are of natural interest to the polity. . . . One may stand up and be counted, uncontroversially and without much effort, by watching reality crime programming."[24]

While some viewers may be encouraged to create petitions, participate in advocacy groups, or simply post blogs, create memes, and make other statements through social media, more passive viewers are still emotionally and intellectually engaged enough to feel that their participation as a viewer alone operates as an act of civic responsibility. Hence, the true crime genre has a complex and varied social function. It is not one that can be reduced to simple ideas of right and wrong, even though the structural format often presents its information in such a binary. The right and wrong presented in the genre has a function in engaging its audiences through a topic that not only concerns everybody, but in a way that anybody can understand. How much a viewer recognizes or questions the bias in each text will differ in every individual, but the emotional and intellectual responses encouraged are substantial and a key to understanding the popularity of true crime across a wide variety of audiences.

Notes

1. Massumi, *Parables for the Virtual*.
2. Schulz, "Dead Certainty."
3. Fishman and Cavender, *Entertaining Crime*; Nasheri, *Crime and Justice*; Jewkes, *Media and Crime*; Murley, *Rise of True Crime*; Fuhrman, *Murder Business*.

4. Murley, *Rise of True Crime*, 13.
5. Ibid., 119.
6. Ibid., 118.
7. Cavender, "In the Shadows of Shadows," 81.
8. Murley, *Rise of True Crime*, 121.
9. Donovan, "Armed with the Power of Television," 123.
10. *West of Memphis* (2012, Amy Berg) is a companion film to Joe Berlinger and Bruce Sinofsky's *Paradise Lost* films (1996, 2000, 2011) that first shed light on this story. Also, *The Trials of Darryl Hunt*, *West of Memphis*, and *Crime after Crime* catalog the appeals process and eventual release of the main protagonists.
11. Zachary's bill was successfully entered into Canadian law in 2010.
12. Fuhs, "Legal Trial," 804.
13. Qazvini and Barrett, "Don't Believe the Press."
14. Thomas, "What Really Makes Making a Murderer so Good?"
15. Dickey, "Emotional Manipulations."
16. Plantinga, "Notes on Spectator Emotion," 373.
17. Young, *Scene of Violence*, 3.
18. Biressi, *Crime, Fear*, 2.
19. Nakamura, "9 'Making a Murderer' Memes."
20. Young, *Scene of Violence*, 3.
21. Ibid., 7.
22. Ibid., 11.
23. Ibid., 153.
24. Donovan, "Armed with the Power of Television," 132.

References

Biressi, Anita. *Crime, Fear and the Law in True Crime Stories*. Basingstoke, UK: Palgrave MacMillan, 2001.

Cavender, Gray. "In the Shadows of Shadows: Television Reality Crime Programming." In *Entertaining Crime: Television Reality Programs*, edited by Mark Fishman and Gray Cavender, 79–94. New York: Aldine De Gruyter, 1998.

Dickey, Bronwen. "The Emotional Manipulations of Making a Murderer." *Slate*, January 15, 2016. http://www.slate.com/articles/arts/culturebox/2016/01/making_a_murderer_is_so_emotionally_manipulative_it_left_me_angry.html.

Donovan, Pamela. "Armed with the Power of Television: Reality Crime Programming and the Reconstruction of Law and Order in the United States." In *Entertaining Crime: Television Reality Programs*, edited by Mark Fishman and Gray Cavender, 117–140. New York, Aldine De Gruyter, 1998.

Fishman, Mark, and Gray Cavender. *Entertaining Crime: Television Reality Programs*. New York, Aldine De Gruyter, 1998.

Fuhrman, Mark. *The Murder Business: How the Media Turns Crime into Entertainment and Subverts Justice*. Washington, DC: Regnery, 2009.

Fuhs, Kristen. "The Legal Trial And/In Documentary Film." In *Cultural Studies* 28, nos. 5–6 (2014): 781–808.

Jewkes, Yvonne. *Media and Crime*. London: Sage, 2008.

Massumi, Brian. *Parables for the Virtual: Movement, Affect, Sensation*. Durham, NC: Duke University Press, 2002.
Murley, Jean. *The Rise of True Crime: Twentieth Century Murder and American Popular Culture*. Westport: Praeger, 2008.
Nakamura, Reid. "9 'Making a Murderer' Memes That Will Make You Laugh While You Seethe." *The Wrap*, August 12, 2016. http://www.thewrap.com/9-making-a-murderer-memes-that-will-make-you-laugh-while-you-seethe/.
Nasheri, Heieh. *Crime and Justice in the Age of Court TV*. New York: LFB Scholarly Publishing, 2002.
Qazvini, Michael, and James Barrett. "Don't Believe the Press: Steven Avery Is Guilty of Murder." *Daily Wire*, January 5, 2016. http://www.dailywire.com/news/2363/dont-believe-press-steven-avery-guilty-murder-michael-qazvini. Page no longer available.
Plantinga, Carl. "Notes on Spectator Emotion and Ideological Film Criticism." In *Film Theory and Philosophy*, edited by Richard Allen and Murray Smith, 372–393. Oxford: Clarendon, 1997.
Schulz, Kathryn. "Dead Certainty: How *Making a Murderer* Goes Wrong." *New Yorker*, January 25, 2016. https://www.newyorker.com/magazine/2016/01/25/dead-certainty.
Thomas, June. "What Really Makes Making a Murderer so Good? There's No Narrator." *Slate*, December 30, 2015. http://www.slate.com/blogs/browbeat/2015/12/30/what_really_makes_making_a_murderer_so_good_unlike_serial_and_the_jinx_there.html.
Young, Alison. *The Scene of Violence: Cinema, Crime, Affect*. New York: Routledge, 2010.

GEORGE S. LARKE-WALSH teaches Film and Media Studies at the University of Sunderland. She is author of *Screening the Mafia: Masculinity, Ethnicity and Mobsters from The Godfather to The Sopranos* and editor of *A Companion to the Gangster Film*.

NEW (OLD) ONTOLOGIES OF DOCUMENTARY

Steve F. Anderson

It has been more than a quarter-century since Bill Nichols posited his influential taxonomy of documentary modes. In this time, numerous innovations in media technologies and theorizations of the affective potentials of documentary have occurred, and there now exists an extensive body of work that unites a documentary ethos with various affordances of emerging media. While the first generation of digital documentary—sometimes called "database documentaries" distributed online or via physical media formats such as CD- or DVD-ROM—occupied a rarefied position on the fringes of the academy, recent innovations have brought such processor-intensive technologies as 360-degree video and navigable 3D environments within reach for ordinary consumers. Virtual reality (VR) documentaries invert the logic of interactive documentaries in which filmmakers provide access to large collections of media, allowing viewers to choose their own adventure. At present, however, VR documentaries are generally too data-, processor-, and time-intensive to indulge in a profusion of content. The need to create short experiences is reinforced by most viewers' inability to tolerate extended periods in the head-mounted display (HMD) without experiencing discomfort. Rather than abundance, then, the VR documentary relies on subjective experiences of intensity and immediacy, in many cases, making an appeal directly to the body through emotion and affect rather than intellect or reason. In the context of "popular documentary," these features contribute significantly to defining the relation between VR documentary and the elusive and ill-defined goals of social impact.

The recent proliferation of consumer-grade technologies capable of capturing and displaying 360-degree video has been accompanied by the anachronistic return of visual positivism—an unproblematic association between seeing and believing—as a privileged mode of documentary filmmaking. The unbounded frame—it would be more accurate to say the *movable* frame—of 360-degree video viewed in an HMD provides viewers with the luster of agency, affording the freedom to look in any direction in order to view pixels that have been mapped onto the interior of an imaginary sphere or cylinder.[1] Sounds that have been computed to be perceived as if they originated from precise locations in space add depth and richness to the experience, such that it simulates sensorial immersion. Somewhat unexpectedly, these features, in combination, have revitalized the historical tradition of social issue documentary through a generation of 360-degree videos devoted to issues of social justice, environmentalism, political engagement, and the like. In tandem with the proliferation of social issue 360-degree documentaries comes a series of pernicious claims, namely that the sense of immersion or "telepresence"—a viewer's perception that their body occupies a space different from its actual location—inherently amplifies the viewer's capacity to empathize with the plight of human figures seen there.[2] The combination of social-issue-driven subject matter and the supposedly enlightening experiences they engender form the foundation of a remarkable profusion of promotional rhetoric espousing the transformative potentials of VR. The result has been widespread notoriety of these videos, which, in turn, has been orchestrated into a campaign to extend the market for virtual reality headsets beyond gaming to include viewing 360-degree video. While "social issue VR" has effectively served to legitimize the technology, I will argue that the ideals of empathy, immersion, experience, and presence that dominated the cultural discourse of virtual reality in the 2010s should not be exempted from long-established critiques of documentary representation.

The resurgence of VR in marketing contexts spawned a predictable hype-cycle describing consumer-grade, PC-based HMDs and lower-cost, stand-alone, or mobile-phone-based viewers. As the market for VR continues to expand, evangelists for the technology intently promote this-time-things-will-be-different narratives, hoping to overwrite memories of the medium's previous commercial disappointment in the 1990s. A persistent lack—or perhaps a conscious suppression—of historical context related to VR allows a rising generation of 360-degree video makers to understand their work in terms of novelty and exception rather than as an extension of a decades old documentary project. Meanwhile, VR's market capitalization is estimated at over $20 billion by 2020, and the number of consumer headsets predicted to be in circulation ranges into the tens of millions.[3] A key strategy for marketers is to normalize VR headsets as an everyday component of domestic entertainment and computing, coextensive with everyday technologies such as personal computers or mobile phones.

At the time of this writing, the most prominent hardware manufacturers operate in a tight orbit around the digital gaming and software industries, with a North American market dominated by tech industry giants such as Facebook, Google, HTC (High Tech Computer), Valve, Samsung, Sony, Microsoft, and Apple. It comes as something of a surprise, then, that some of the most widely seen content to be produced for these platforms has emerged from socially engaged documentary or "immersive journalism" rather than—as many expected—the world of first-person shooter video games. In 2017, the Facebook-owned hardware manufacture Oculus announced that it was offering $1 million to support an initiative called "VR for Good"; this was followed shortly by media distributor Valve and hardware manufacturer HTC (comakers of the Vive HMD) announcing their investment of $10 million in a project termed "VR for Impact."[4] Notable documentary VR experiences featured in the Sundance Film Festival's New Frontier section since 2013 have engaged topics such as the Syrian refugee crisis (multiple projects), campus rape, solitary confinement, antiabortion activism, domestic violence, the Chilean military coup, and the Ebola epidemic in West Africa.[5] Likewise, fully half of the projects featured in the Tribeca Film Festival's VR showcase in 2017 were documentary-related, with a majority that were simultaneously invested in issues of social justice or environmental advocacy. The single largest expansion of VR viewership came in November 2015, when the *New York Times* distributed more than a million low-cost cardboard viewers to its subscribers in anticipation of rolling out regular 360-degree news content. The *Times* describes its VR offerings in sensational terms: "Stand alongside Iraqi forces during a battle with ISIS. Walk on a planet three billion miles from the sun."[6] *Forbes* quotes Dean Baquet, executive editor of the *New York Times* on the launch of NYTVR in 2016: "Whether *The Times* is on the campaign trail, the front lines of Aleppo, or in the front row at Fashion Week, 'The Daily 360' brings you there to bear witness with us."[7]

While new ways to witness continue to proliferate, the time is ripe to reexamine the impact of technological shifts on the documentary project. It is axiomatic to my argument that the technological innovation of computational, procedural, and interactive media poses a greater challenge to documentary than the crisis of representation that accompanied the rise of digital imaging in the previous century.[8] Specifically, what is at stake in these emerging modes of documentary is not simply the ontological status of documentary images in relation to the optically perceived world. These days, nearly all images either originate in digital form or are digitized for purposes of editing or distribution. Merely concerning ourselves with "digital" rather than "computational" media deflects attention from broader questions about how meaning is created through interactive, generative, or responsive systems and information architectures and haptic simulation. This chapter considers the transformation of popular documentary through the lens of consumer-grade, immersive technologies, while challenging the conventional wisdom that VR is an "empathy machine" producing direct emotional responses in viewers.[9]

Interestingly, and with notable exceptions, many documentary makers who have gravitated to the 360-degree format do not come from backgrounds in traditional documentary film or video making. We may speculate on why this is the case, but the most likely reasons are the format's disruption of numerous core skills of traditional documentary making. The truth claim immanent in the 360-degree video format—which offers literally nowhere for filmmakers or their apparatus of production to hide—favors long takes with a static camera in a visually rich environment. Many of the conventions of documentary cinema—handheld camera work, montage editing, even talking head interviews—are thus rendered anathema to the 360-degree video format. Among the conventions resurrected from Nichols's "Expository Mode" is the frequent use of omniscient voice-over narration, another anachronism in documentary VR. In addition, the wide-angle lenses used in virtually all 360-degree rigs result in a field of view in which nearly everything is in focus. The spherical images that are stitched together from multiple camera viewpoints necessitate avoiding action that takes place too close or too far from the camera rig. Accepted wisdom in the field dictates that subjects maintain a minimum distance from the camera of no less than two meters in order to avoid stitching artifacts or "seams" marking the border where one camera viewpoint transitions to another.[10] So, 360-degree documentary brings with it a return to classical Hollywood's early devotion to long takes and deep focus as if the interceding half century of theoretical reconsiderations of these features of realist representation simply never happened.

A thorough interrogation of viewing practices arising from 360-degree video is beyond the scope of this chapter; however, the context of 360-degree documentaries intended for popular audiences provides an illuminating case study. What is it about moving images viewed radially from the center of an imaginary sphere that suggests authenticity of experience for viewers? In spite of being promoted as "360-degree video," the visual field that is available via the current generation of VR headsets is actually considerably more restricted than much conventional screen viewing. Typical consumer HMDs deliver no more than a 90- to 110-degree horizontal field of view, a noticeable reduction from the 180 degrees or more available to the naked eye. True, VR viewers can rotate their heads or bodies to focus on any part of a theoretical, spherical viewing surface, but the angle of view available at any given time still represents a significantly reduced visual field.

We should also remember that a vast majority of 360-degree video is not viewed inside an HMD. By far the widest distribution for this media takes place via web browsers or mobile applications, where viewers have the option of clicking or tapping and dragging to explore different areas of the image. The online distribution of 360-degree video reaches its largest audience on Facebook with over 1 billion users worldwide via a dedicated 360-degree media viewer built into the platform. On Facebook, 360-degree video can also be used as the background imagery for the company's social VR platform known as Spaces. Users of the Spaces application wear an HMD in order to interact with other users in real time. Individual users are represented in Spaces as cartoonlike 2D avatars superimposed on a selected 360-degree image or video. Emotion and gesture recognition allow a Spaces avatar to approximate the bodily movements and facial expressions of the user wearing the HMD, such that it is possible for two or more avatars to communicate with voice, approximated facial expressions and preanimated gestures while perceptually occupying a shared virtual space. During this communication, Spaces also allows users to select video orbs to activate as background imagery, inviting users to experiment with effects akin to teleporting from one 360-degree video environment to another.

An early example of the Spaces application illustrates the problematics of this capacity for remote experience. On October 10, 2017, Facebook founder Mark Zuckerberg and the company's head of social VR Rachel Franklin posted a live-streamed video conversation in which they illustrated the platform's capacity for virtual travel, using PBS video of the aftermath of Hurricane Maria that destroyed much of Puerto Rico in September 2017. Zuckerberg and Franklin appear in the video as cartoonlike avatars operated from two different locations within Facebook headquarters in Menlo Park, California. The point of the live broadcast was twofold: to publicize the functioning of Facebook's still new Spaces platform and to promote the fact that Facebook was actively contributing to relief efforts in Puerto Rico to the tune of $1.4 million. An underlying factor in Facebook's connection to the destruction in Puerto Rico is its feature allowing disaster victims or those in geographic proximity

Fig. 19.1 Facebook founder Mark Zuckerberg demonstrates the ability of avatars to exchange a high five on a virtual visit to posthurricane Puerto Rico (2017).

to an emergency situation to mark themselves as "safe" as a gesture of reassurance aimed at members of their social network. At one point in the video, Zuckerberg points out that, because Puerto Ricans have been without power for days, in addition to being without basic necessities of food and health care, they had also been prevented from logging in to their Facebook accounts to update friends and family about their posthurricane status.

In the course of their virtual tour of the devastation in Puerto Rico, Zuckerberg and Franklin demonstrate the ability of their avatars to execute a virtual high five, against the backdrop of a 360-degree video of a street in Puerto Rico where houses are submerged under several feet of floodwater.[11] In another part of the video, Zuckerberg effuses about the experience of the 360-degree video, "One of the things that's really magical about virtual reality is you can get the feeling that you're really in a place . . . we're looking around and it feels like we're really here in Puerto Rico where it's obviously a tough place to get to now and a lot of people are really suffering with the aftermath of the hurricanes." Such moments ignited a wave of criticism directed at Zuckerberg for the perceived insensitivity of the livestream and prompted the company to issue an official apology on his behalf.[12] The relevant part of this anecdote is the facility with which VR proponent Zuckerberg equated the use of spherical video as the background of a Spaces session with the experience of "really" being on site and witnessing the devastation in Puerto Rico.

Fig. 19.2 Zohar Kfir's interactive VR experience *Testimony* (2017) utilizes a 360-degree viewing environment for video vignettes.

If realism—"the feeling that you're really in a place"—has reemerged as the ideal for 360-degree documentary, then what alternatives exist? Projects such as Zohar Kfir's *Testimony* (2017) make use of the medium's spherical viewing environment to deliver elements of content that are not, themselves, immersive. In *Testimony*, viewers are invited to interactively explore a collection of video interviews with survivors of sexual abuse. The viewing environment of *Testimony* is an amorphous, dark space, where gently pulsing lines link video interviews presented in circular vignettes on all sides of the viewer. A gaze-based selection mechanic allows viewers to choose a particular video testimony to watch simply by looking at it; to end a testimony, the viewer simply shifts their gaze away from the speaker. When activated by the viewer's gaze, the circular video window grows larger and the video begins to play, occasionally accompanied by background visuals that resonate with the content of the individual's testimony. There is nothing about the presentation of *Testimony* to suggest that its goal is to elicit a uniquely empathetic response from viewers. In fact, most of the basic affordances of the 360-degree format could have been achieved through other strategies of interactive documentary presentation, suggesting that the attention marshaled by *Testimony* with regard to the sensitive and difficult subject of sexual abuse was partially due to the novelty of its association with the VR format. The power of Kfir's project lies not in some special claim to elicit empathy from viewers but, rather, in the creation of a uniquely intimate viewing environment where viewers can engage with a difficult subject on their own terms. The activation of the viewer's gaze as the mechanic for triggering each video sequence underscores the fact that testimony is not simply the rendering of a story but requires a listener to bear witness. *Testimony* thus defies the logics of both immersion and realism as the primary affordances of documentary VR, favoring instead an updated variant on the choice mechanic of interactive cinema, and a uniquely intimate mode of viewership.

Historically, the social issue film has epitomized documentary's "sober discourses," featuring a strong, ethically motivated point of view and a rhetorical approach that couples rational argumentation with an evidentiary truth claim. With many documentary VR "experiences," however, the burden of argumentation is shifted from a filmmaker's direct analytical address to the presumed production of empathy toward documentary subjects who are often in a state of crisis or distress. The work of VR producer Nonny de la Peña is exemplary in this regard.[13] Calling her work "immersive journalism," de la Peña has created a series of social issue VR projects engaging issues such as hunger, domestic violence, police brutality, the Syrian refugee crisis, antichoice activism, solitary confinement, and more. In each case, viewers are invited to serve as witnesses to events that are re-created as computer generated environments combined with documentary audio. While much current VR documentary favors high-resolution visuals, the majority of de la Peña's work relies, in contrast, on comparatively low-resolution graphics as well as animated figures that belie the presumed need for realistic visuals to deliver the experience of witnessing. The truth claim implicit in much of de la Peña's work derives instead from documentary sound captured during an event that is then visually re-created using a game engine. The gap between documentary audio and graphical re-creation opens a space for viewers to consider their own relationship to the events depicted.

Resistance to naive realism is also available through nonnormative viewing practices. For documentary VR experiences that are time-based rather than interactive or procedurally generated, "agency" is limited to selecting one's field of view. For 360-degree video, viewers are further constrained to a single viewing position that does not allow for movement in space. Thus, where experienced game players might seek to deliberately test the limits of agency and control in a playable world, viewers of 360-degree video have limited opportunities to perform a resistant or even negotiated reading of a VR experience. An illuminating exception was described by Kathryn Hamilton in a February 2017 article for *New Inquiry* titled "Voyeur Reality."[14] Hamilton poses a postcolonial critique of *CLOUDS over Sidra* (2015) directed by Chris Milk and Gabo Arora. *CLOUDS* was the first of several acclaimed VR films commissioned by the United Nations SDG (Sustainable Development Goals)

Action Campaign under the title UNVR with the stated goal "to bring the world's most pressing challenges home to decision-makers and global citizens around the world, pushing the bounds of empathy."[15]

UNVR quickly produced more than a dozen films, nearly all under ten minutes in length and distributed free online. Actual viewing numbers are difficult to document, but the real audience for this project is not just viewers with access to the required viewing technology but decision-makers in organizations in a position to take action on the issues represented. The series' historical connection to a documentary tradition—as well as its investment in affective experience—is explicitly referenced in the title of a 2016 project *You Are There* (2016),[16] which tells the story of the last child in Kenya to have been infected with the polio virus. Similar rhetorical gestures accompany projects such as Marshmallow Laser Feast's *In the Eyes of the Animal* (2015), which offers an experience of occupying a forest setting perceived through different virtual lenses. De la Peña's Emblematic Group tagline, "Step into the Story," makes a similar promise of virtual teleportation for viewers to become witnesses to distant events that are often violent or tragic.

The focus on empathy in these works presumes, in unusually stark terms, the need for generating understanding toward victims of disaster, misfortune, or violence. The "empathy" that viewers are invited to experience serves to restore the humanity of those who have suffered or are in the process of suffering before the viewer's eyes. The subjects of these documentaries, in turn, are invited to perform their humanity for the camera, in effect playing their part in what Pooja Rangan has criticized as "humanitarian rescue missions in which documentary serves as a humanizing prosthesis for dehumanized subjects."[17] Although Rangan's book *Immediations: The Humanitarian Impulse in Documentary* (2017) offers focused case studies on four adjacent areas of documentary representation (the child, the refugee, the autistic, the animal), the methods of humanitarian representation that she charts map readily onto the practices of 360-degree documentary, especially those produced by and for organizations such as the United Nations.

Rangan's central conceit of "immediation" provides a lens through which to observe the conjunction of multiple characteristics of the humanitarian documentary: the constituents of the term's portmanteau—immediacy and mediation—but also easily idealized characteristics such as urgency, liveness, and presence. Rangan poses an especially incisive critique of a practice that was once offered as the solution to the appropriative tendencies of humanitarian documentaries. As critiqued by Trinh T. Minh-ha and Fatima Tobing Rony, among others, the practice of distributing cameras to documentary subjects in order to catalyze self-representation is seen not as the antidote to Western voyeurism but rather an extension of it. Unlike the compact, portable video camcorders that originally inspired the practice of seeded self-representation, the complexity of the apparatus required to produce 360-degree video—both in terms of capture and postproduction—makes it impractical to invite documentary subjects to record themselves. However, because there is "nowhere to hide" from the gaze of a 360-degree camera, the process of shooting often involves filmmakers simply setting up a camera in a strategic location and allowing it to record while they scurry out of sight. Under these circumstances, it is not uncommon for human subjects to curiously scrutinize the unfamiliar apparatus, resulting in images which, on playback, afford a uniquely voyeuristic experience to viewers who watch from the disembodied position of the camera.

Unlike traditional documentaries in which observed subjects can and do "look back" at the camera—a dynamic that has been central to feminist and postcolonial critiques of the power dynamics inscribed in seeing and being seen—the presence of a human operator invariably inflects the nature of this visual exchange. Furthermore, a traditionally edited documentary can easily remove such looks at the camera, only leaving them in the final film if a diegetic rupture is desired by the filmmakers. By contrast, an unaccompanied 360-degree camera rig may be regarded with less apparent self-awareness by the subjects being documented—in other words, there is no evident "exchange of looks" between documentarian and subject, only the curious gaze of an "other" confronted with an elaborate piece of high-tech equipment. I would argue that this dynamic resembles in important ways the mode of self-representation critiqued by Rangan. People who are seemingly left alone in the presence of a 360-degree camera, after expressing initial curiosity, may not even realize the camera is recording and simply go about their business. Others may pause to investigate the apparatus more closely. The current generation of cameras most commonly used for documentary field work ranges from oversized spheres resembling a communication satellite with up to twenty-four lenses pointed in all directions to more compact spherical, cubical, or cylindrical apparatuses, though rarely with fewer than six cameras in the array. Regardless of the specific physical apparatus, accepted practices of 360-degree video capture (in which filmmakers and technicians are hidden from view) uniquely efface the human element of documentary recording, even compared with the conventions of observational documentary.

Even the most rigorously observational documentaries did not invest exclusively in delivering a sense of omniscient presence to viewers. The strategy of filmmakers to be as innocuous and all-seeing as a "fly on the wall" remained an elusive and dubious goal as observational documentarians made frequent use of conventions drawn from narrative cinema, including genres, character arcs, and didactic editing, to sharpen points of argumentation. In VR documentaries, conventions of 360-degree recording allow filmmakers to choose the location and height of the camera, but other typical, cinematographic variables, such as focal length and framing, remain entirely fixed, while the unforgiving omnidirectionality of the camera's gaze deters the use of extradiegetic lighting and camera movement. Cameras may be started and stopped by remote and some systems allow low-resolution previews of the scene to be wirelessly transmitted so that filmmakers have an approximate sense of what is being captured. Documentary subjects, then, are often presented without any visible evidence of a film crew or the capture apparatus. Under these circumstances, human subjects may or may not consciously perform "for the camera," but they are almost always presented as the sole inhabitants of the space, while viewers occupy the role of an invisible—and literally centered—observer.

The centrality of the viewer—coupled with the omniscient, disembodied presence characteristic of 360-degree video—throws certain problematic aspects of the medium into sharp relief. In a fascinating exercise in the deliberate misuse of the VR viewing apparatus, theater director Kathryn Hamilton viewed the entirety of *CLOUDS over Sidra* while looking straight down, refusing the ostensible pleasures and voyeuristic epistephilia (Nichols's term) of the 360-degree format and instead focusing on parts of the viewing plane that are intended to go unnoticed, specifically the footprints left by otherwise invisible camera operators. Hamilton notes: "VR practitioners make a claim, as the early proponents of photography did, that it is a 'slice of life,' 'really being there,' 'unmediated,' a 'transparent communication.' But the footprints in *Clouds Over Sidra* suggest something else: a dense meeting point of different agendas above which the user is positioned, and through which the user views the world."[18]

The expectation of normative viewing—aligned with the observational practices associated with tourism—is provocatively disrupted by Hamilton when she insists on aiming the HMD straight down for the duration of the project. In addition to avoiding the intended viewing position, Hamilton's chosen angle of view offers a reminder of the absence of both the viewer's body and that of the filmmakers themselves. From this viewpoint, the perspective of *CLOUDS* appears to be that of a floating and disembodied eye, albeit one that is positioned at approximately "eye-level" according to conventions of

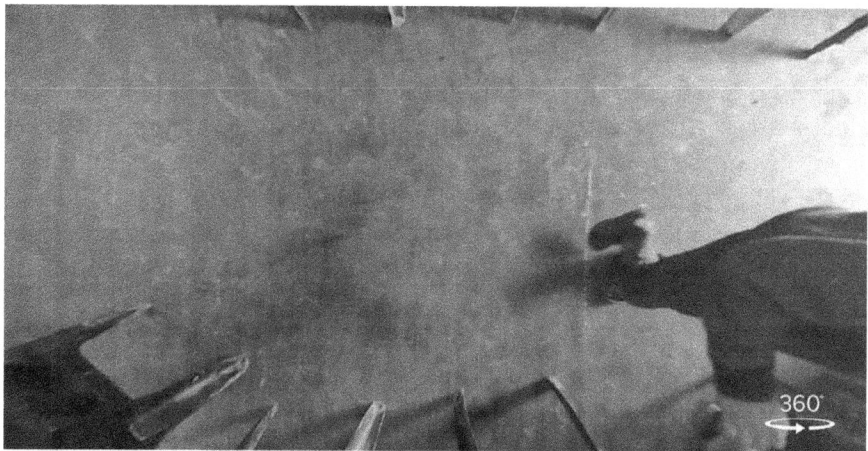

Fig. 19.3 A resistant viewing of *CLOUDS over Sidra* (2015) refuses the epistephilic pleasures of immersive cinema.

VR shooting. An additional factor that is observable from this perspective is that the area directly below a 360-degree camera is also the least likely to be optically represented. Instead, most 360-degree video stitching software algorithmically "fills in" those parts of the image where the camera's support apparatus such as a monopod is typically located. This process resembles that of the "content aware fill" feature found in image editing software that allows users to delete unwanted objects from the foreground of an image and to extend the visual logic of the surrounding areas to cover the resulting gap. The effect, in some cases, is an impression that pixels or colors in the image have been stretched or duplicated around the nadir point of the sphere, creating a vaguely uncanny hybrid of lens-based and algorithmically generated imagery. The "truth claim" inherent in this part of the spherical image is at its weakest, and it is here that Hamilton focuses attention.

The very features most enthusiastically celebrated by Zuckerberg in the Facebook tour of Puerto Rico are the most damning for Hamilton. "To the degree that VR offers the illusion of greater proximity to the real than film or photography, it also increases the problematics of the medium. VR invites the user into a visual and aural immersion, without the user facing any of the consequences of being immersed in that space." The strategy of resistant viewing offered by Hamilton is further inspired by an explicit critique by Edward Said of the Orientalism of the European documentary viewer toward the Eastern other: "The 'essential relationship' that Europe has toward the 'orient' is a relationship of strong toward weak, one common manifestation of which is the portrayal of the 'oriental' as a child, or childlike, and the European as the mature adult. In *CLOUDS Over Sidra* the user, substituting for the camera, is placed into a literal enactment of that metaphorical relationship."[19] While a normative, or "correct," viewing of *CLOUDS* indeed enacts an eerily literal expression of the power relationships critiqued by Said, Hamilton's strategy of refusal offers a provocative alternative. Unlike presumed ideals of viewer "empathy" or "immersion," I would argue that the type of resistant viewing promoted by Hamilton deserves to be considered a defining—and potentially redeeming—feature of the VR documentary.

My hope is that, as the novelty of the technology wears off and the fetishized wholeness of VR "immersion" becomes increasingly fragmented, remixable, reconfigurable, and open to more resistant modes of reception, flimsy assertions about viewer empathy may be productively replaced by more complex models of viewer experience and response. At the same time, we should recognize the success with which VR documentary makers have created an audience for a vital and otherwise easily neglected range of documentary subjects. This must be regarded as a positive if problematic development, even if it is motivated by the desire of hardware manufacturers to incite consumers to justify the purchase of an entirely new display apparatus for the home. The emphasis of a disproportionate number of VR documentaries on socially relevant and otherwise "difficult" issues represents an interesting but probably transient phenomenon. Just as it is up to VR documentary makers to make the most of this emergent moment of possibility, it is equally incumbent on viewers to develop increasingly complex strategies for viewing, responding and creatively substituting the allure of empathy and immersion for critical thinking and engaged action in the world outside the HMD.

Notes

1. Especially in light of the imprecision with which these terms are used in trade publications and popular discourse, a brief disambiguation is in order. This chapter adopts the term *360-degree video* to signify spherical or cylindrical viewing environments in which primarily lens-based live action or animated sequences are viewed. This is distinct from the umbrella terms *virtual reality* or *VR*, which include computationally generated, interactive 3D environments. Because 360-degree video may also be integrated with computer generated animations or environments, a better distinction is the extent to which the two forms are prerendered on a fixed timeline or procedurally generated to support temporally elastic and interactive experiences.

2. Examples from trade publications and public talks abound. Among the most widely cited instances are two 2015 TED Talks by With.in cofounder Chris Milk and Emblematic CEO Nonny de la Peña.

3. Other estimates range as high as $40 billion (see Orbis Research, "Global Virtual Reality Market").

4. See Oculus, "VR for Good"; HTC Vive, "VR for Impact."

5. For example: *Assent* (dir. Oscar Raby, 2014), *Project Syria* (dir. Nonny de la Peña, 2015), *Clouds over Sidra* (UNVR and VRSE, 2015), *Kiya* (dir. Nonny de la Peña, 2015), *Waves of Grace* (UNVR and VRSE, 2015), *Perspective* (dir. Rose Troche and Morris May, 2015), *Across the Line* (dir. Nonny de la Peña, 2016), *6x9* (NFB, 2016).

6. *New York Times*, "NYTVR."

7. Hanlon, "*New York Times* Launches."

8. A more thorough articulation of this distinction may be found in Anderson, *Technologies of Vision*.

9. For an earlier effort to counter this conventional wisdom, see Sutherland, "Limits of Virtual Reality."

10. See Wohl, *360-Degree Video Handbook*, 27.

11. The image of Zuckerberg's avatar giving a virtual "high five" to Facebook's head of social VR Rachel Franklin served as the featured image in McGoogan, "Mark Zuckerberg."

12. Zuckerberg later responded to critical comments on the video: "One of the most powerful features of VR is empathy. My goal here was to show how VR can raise awareness and help us see what's happening in different parts of the world" (Mark Zuckerberg's Facebook page, October 11, 2017).

13. De la Peña's documentary VR work was directly influenced by Mel Slater, whose Event Lab at the University of Barcelona has been operating at the forefront of cognitive science research using virtual reality since the 1990s. De la Peña and others have also used biofeedback for measuring viewers' responses to the emotional content of virtual reality experiences. See de la Peña, "Embodied Digital Rhetoric." Generally speaking, however, the efficacy of empathy in VR is rarely subjected to rigorous evaluation and/or direct comparison with nonimmersive formats.

14. Hamilton, "Voyeur Reality."

15. UNVR, "About."

16. *You Are There* was the title of a CBS radio and television series that ran from 1950 to 1957, in which historical events were reported as contemporary news stories.

17. Rangan, *Immediations*, 2.

18. Hamilton, "Voyeur Reality."

19. Ibid.

References

Anderson, Steve F. *Technologies of Vision: The War between Data and Images*. Cambridge: MIT Press, 2017.

de la Peña, Nonny. "Embodied Digital Rhetoric: Soft Selves, Plastic Presence, and the Nonfiction Narrative." In *Digital Rhetoric and Global Literacies: Communication Modes and Digital Practices in the Networked World*, edited by Gustav Verhulsdonck and Marohang Limbu, 312–327. Hershey, PA: IGI Global, 2014.

———. "The Future of News? Virtual Reality." TED Women, May 28, 2015, 09:18. Monterey, CA. https://www.ted.com/talks/nonny_de_la_pena_the_future_of_news_virtual_reality.

Hamilton, Kathryn. "Voyeur Reality." *New Inquiry*, February 23, 2017. https://thenewinquiry.com/voyeur-reality.

Hanlon, Patrick. "*The New York Times* Launches Daily 360 VR News." *Forbes*, November 1, 2016. https://www.forbes.com/sites/patrickhanlon/2016/11/01/the-new-york-times-launches-daily-360-vr-news.

HTC Vive. "VR for Impact." Accessed November 22, 2019. https://vrforimpact.com.

McGoogan, Cara. "Mark Zuckerberg Apologises for 'Tasteless' Puerto Rico VR Video." *Telegraph*, October 11, 2017.

Milk, Chris. "How Virtual Reality Can Create the Ultimate Empathy Machine." TED Talk, March 18, 2015, 10:18. Vancouver, Canada. https://www.ted.com/talks/chris_milk_how_virtual_reality_can_create_the_ultimate_empathy_machine?language=vi.

New York Times. "NYTVR." Accessed November 22, 23019. http://www.nytimes.com/marketing/nytvr.

Oculus. "VR for Good." Accessed April 24, 2017. https://www.oculus.com/vr-for-good.

Orbis Research. "Global Virtual Reality Market Forecast 2020." Reuters, April 24, 2017. https://www.reuters.com/brandfeatures/venture-capital/article?id=4975. Page no longer available.

Rangan, Pooja. *Immediations: The Humanitarian Impulse in Documentary*. Durham, NC: Duke University Press, 2017.

Said, Edward W. *Orientalism*. New York: Vintage, 1979.

Sutherland, Ainsley. "The Limits of Virtual Reality: Debugging the Empathy Machine." MIT Open Documentary Lab Docubase, 2015. https://docubase.mit.edu/lab/case-studies/the-limits-of-virtual-reality-debugging-the-empathy-machine.

UNVR: United Nations Virtual Reality. "About." Accessed November 22, 2019. http://unvr.sdgactioncampaign.org/home/about.

Wohl, Michael. *The 360-Degree Video Handbook*. Los Angeles: Vrrrynice.com, 2017.

STEVE F. ANDERSON is Professor of Digital Media in the UCLA School of Theater, Film and Television and in the Department of Design Media Arts. He is author of *Technologies of History: Visual Media and the Eccentricity of the Past* and of *Technologies of Vision: The War between Data and Images*.

INDEX

Numbers in italics refer to illustrations.

Abric, Christopher, 146
absolutist terms, 291
Abu Ghraib scandal, 121, 128, 181, 189–96; "Gilligan" incident, 194–95
academia, 114–15
Academy Awards, 37, 184, 228, 239; for Best Documentary Feature, 243, 259
acceleration, 28–29; attention span and, 75, 77; benefits of to representation, 80, 89; of climate change, 86–88; of deceleration, 56, 88–89; desire for speed nurtured by capitalism, 68; as "nonplace"/space destroyed by, 79; reduction of warning time, 79–80, 89; in technological development, 87; as violence, 75, 79. *See also* deceleration; slow violence
An Accented Cinema: Exilic and Diasporic Filmmaking (Naficy), 234
accented film, 234
accountability, social media and, 317–18
activist media, 303–4. *See also* social action
Adams, Randall, 120, 185, 188
advocacy, 2, 5, 6, 9, 229, 241–42, 255, 358
Aerial America (Smithsonian Channel), 57
aerial documentaries, 7, 57–74; drone technology, 45, 55, 57–60; fly-over, 55, 57–59, 65, 68. *See also* global documentary
affect and emotion, 245, 300; affect defined, 341; true crime genre and, 341, 345, 347–48, 349–53. *See also* empathy
African American singers, 267–70
Agha-Soltan, Neda, 313–15
"agrarian paradox," 93
agribusiness (Big Food), 91–92; abject status, 93, 95–96, 100; meat industry, 97–98; monocultural agriculture, 94; monstrosities of, 95–96; pastoral marketing, 92, 94, 95, 97, 107; scale and image of plenitude, 96, 97. *See also* food documentaries

agriculture: elegiac and Edenic visions, 93–94, 97; sustainable, 91–93
Akerman, Chantal, 161
algorithms: "film events" as counter to, 325, 329, 332–33, 337, 338n10; internet/social media control and, 316; VR editing and, 367
All You Need Is Love (Palmer), 262
Alter, Nora M., 159, 174n3
amateur filmmakers, 139, 141, 153, 157, 300
Ambuhl, Megan, 194
American Dharma (Morris), 133–34
American Dream, 200, 201, 205, 209
American Experience (PBS), 39
American Express, 114, 150, 151
America's Most Wanted (television series), 343, 344, 345
Amy (Kapadia), 259
Andersen, Thom, 114–15, 165–67
Anderson, Steve F., 6, 300–301
animation, 99–100, 106, 220; in *Citizenfour*, 231–34, *232*; ISOTYPE, 103, *103*, 105; in music documentary, 149; of newspapers, 123
Anstey, Edgar, 104–5
Anthropocene, 63, 67, 69, 92, 99
anticognitive mapping, 67–70
antihero, filmmaker as, 222–23
antirepresentational turn, 8, 180, 220–37; aesthetics of failure and, 221–23; dramatization of representational failures, 220, 224; four approaches, 224–25; ironic forms of pedagogy, 225, 226–27; missing/disappeared/invisible subjects, focus on, 224–26, 230, 234; obfuscation, 220, 224, 225, 236; surveillance regimes, critique of, 220, 224; withdrawal from representation, 224, 225, 227. *See also Citizenfour* (Poitras); post 9/11 documentaries
Arcade Fire, 150
"archival anxieties," 282

371

archival images, 5, 240, 277; access to, 282, 334; China Film Archives, 284; enclosure of, 334; films as, 287–88; "identification," 280; "pastness," bringing audience into contact with, 282, 285; responsibilities of filmmakers, 283; unrepresentability and, 281; "unruliness" of, 282, 289, 292; use of incites doubt, 280; without narration and soundtracks, 324, 332. *See also* "film events"; Nanking (Guttentag and Sturman)

Arora, Gabo, 363, 366–68

Arriflex, 161

Arthur, Paul, 10n5, 222–23, 224

Arthus-Bertrand, Yann: *7 Billion Others*, 62; *Earth from Above*, 62; *Home*, 55, 58, 62–64, 63, 67, 69

Askew, David, 279

Association of Independent Video and Filmmakers, 41–42

Astruc, Alexandre, 161

Ata Kak: Time Bomb (Corbin and Lowe, RBMA), 152

Atlas Unfolded (Barbosa, RBMA), 152

Attenborough, David, 61

attention spans, 75, 77

audience, 15–19, 278, 299–301; appreciation, 16–17; as armchair jurors, 340–41, 345–49; calls to action, 88, 91; "citizen food consumer," 95; collaboration with, 88–89, 300, 324–39; "contract" with, 185; documentary's ability to influence, 222; fly-over evokes sense of power in, 58–59, 64; interactive technology and, 87; justice, sense of, 340–41; local historians, 326, 333, 334, 335; as omniscient, 60–61; popular culture and, 17–19; at premultiplex urban cinemas, 326; roles of in film events, 332–33; self-awareness, 27–28; self-reflection, 62, 92, 95; as shopper, 92–93; spectatorial embodiment, 55; sports, 326; voyeurism, participation in, 350–51. *See also* "film events"

Audiovisualcy, 171

audiovisual essay. *See* video essay

Aufderheide, Patricia, 7, 13–14, 21

Auschwitz, 281

Auslander, Philip, 154n18

Austin, J. L., 182

Austin, Patti, 267

auteurs, 2, 5, 179; American, 20; "buying in" to corporate interests, 26; city symphonies and, 160–61; private interest documentary auteurism, 13; video essay and, 163–64, *164*. *See also individual auteurs*

authenticity, 9, 66, 169, 193, 222–24, 282

"The Author as Producer" (Benjamin), 124

autobiography, 188, 191, 194, 222

availableism, 334

Avant, Clarence, 264, 265–66

Avery, Steven, 341, 346, 351

awards, 135n20; Academy, 37, 184, 228, 239; Academy, for Best Documentary Feature, 243, 259; Cannes Film Festival's *Palme d'Or*, 277; Emmy, 37, 292; Human Rights Watch Nestor Almendros Prize for Courage in Filmmaking, 243; Oscars, 36; Peabody, 37, 43, 292; People's Voice Award in Animation, 149; Webby Awards, 149

B-29 bomber, 185

Baby Mama High (Ross), 44

Bad Day at Black Rock (Sturges), 168

Baker, Michael Brendan, 6, 114

Baker, Peter, 308

Baldwin, Craig, 334

Balk, Harry, 266

Balog, James, 82–83, 84

Balsom, Erika, 223

Baltimorama (Hagan), 329

A Band Called Death (Covino and Howlett), 240, 260, 270–73

Bank, Mirra, 214

Banks and the Poor (NET), 38

Banksy, 225

Bannon, Steve, 133–34

Baquet, Dean, 358

Baraka (Reggio), 64, 65

Barber, Brad, 46

Barbosa, João, 152

Baril, Céline, 20

Barker, Jennifer, 94

Barnouw, Erik, 39

Baron, Jaimie, 282, 287, 289, 292

Barrett, James, 347, 348

Bateman, Conor, 159–60, 163

Bathrolomew-Strydom, Craig, 263–64
The Battle of China (US Signal Corps), 285–88, 286, 294n53
Bay Motion (Prelinger), 327
Bazin, André, 93
BBC (British Broadcasting Corporation), 39
"beautiful soul," 94
Beck, Richard, 61
Believing Is Seeing: Observations on the Mysteries of Photography (Morris), 121
Bendjelloul, Malik, 264
Benjamin, Walter, 124
benshi (live narrator), 325
Bentler, R. J., 149
Berg, Maggie, 28–29
Berlinale (2016), 163, 171
Besse, Ivan, 326
beyond-objectivity journalism, 45
Billionaires for Bush, 226
biological warfare, 128, 130–32, *131*
Biressi, Anita, 348, 352
Blackfish (Cowperthwaite), 252
Black people, violence against, on social media, 312–13, *313*, 317
Blackside (production house), 40
La Blogothèque, 146
Blue Planet (BBC), 67
body: fast-moving camera's effect on, 58; physiological reactions, 59; "telepresence," 357; VR documentaries and, 301, 356–57
body genre, 55, 58–59, 71n11, 241. *See also* aerial documentaries
Bolter, Jay David, 142, 151
Bonnefoy, Mathilde, 228–29
borders, 126, 169, 230
Bordwell, David, 142, 145, 151
born-digital news sources, 37
Born into Brothels (Briski and Kauffman), 239, 242–49, 252; Calcutta Zoo scenes, *248*, 248–49; documentary modes in, 242–43; increased speed in, 247–48; racist colonial legacy of extracting children, 253; scholarly criticism of, 241, 243–44; sex workers, stigmatization of, 246–48, 254
"both sides" narrative, 39–40
Bowery Theater (New York), 325–26
box office figures, 2, 22, 24, 26, 184, 190, 200, 249, 277

branded documentary, 24–26, 30n36, 37–38
Brecht, Bertolt, 326
"A Brief History of Goth" (Cull), 141, 148, 149, *150*
A Brief History of Time (Morris), 189
Briski, Zana, 242–49, *248*
British documentaries, 103
British invasion groups, 267
broadcasting and cablecasting, 37–38
Brooks, Peter, 244
Brows Held High (YouTube video essay channel), 168
Buck, Pearl S., 286
Buñuel, Luis, 187–88, 195
Burnett, Colin, 142
Burns, Ken, 7, 39–40; stylistic imitation of, 36–37
Bush, George W., 196, 226–27
Butler, Judith, 197n6

cable outlets, 37–38, 203–4
calls to action, 88, 91, 100
Canada, austerity measures, 23
capitalism, 17–18, 23–25, 28, 61–70; anxieties about destruction of planet, 61–62, 65, 67–68; body genre of, 55, 58; capitalist realism, 25; cognitive mapping and, 63, 68–70; culture of excess, 211; desire for speed nurtured by, 68; divided subjectivity in, 63–64; embodied subjectivity in, 59; financial crisis of 2008, 205, 211; influence of, 209; insecurities preyed upon, 202; representation of, 69; vernacular sublime, 55, 68, 69. *See also* neoliberalism
Capitalism and Communication (Garnham), 23
Capra, Frank, 285–87
Carbon for Water (infomercial), 30n41
Carlson, Tucker, 43
Carlsson, Chris, 326
Carnegie Commission, 41
Carr, David, 124–25
Carson, Rachel, 93
Cartographies of the Absolute (Toscano and Kinkle), 68–69, 70
Castile, Philando, *313*, 314
cause-and-effect logic, 168
Cavender, Gary, 343

Center for Investigative Reporting, 37
Center for Media & Social Impact, 46
Center for Social Media, 278
Central Intelligence Agency (CIA), 117–21, 197n9
Channel 4 (United Kingdom), 49n11
character-driven narratives, 45–46
Chasing Coral (Orlowski), 56, 76, 82, 85–88
Chasing Ice (Orlowski), 56, 76, 82, 83–85
children, 34, 45, 66; as moral referents, 246–47; at risk, Calcutta, 239, 246–49, *248*; as victims, 105. See also *Born into Brothels* (Briski and Kauffman)
Chile, 226
China, 278–79
Chomsky, Noam, 24
Chopra, Joyce, 214, 215
Christopherson, Scott, 46
Chronique d'un été (Rouch and Morin), 214
Cineaste, 195
cinema: persistence of, 141–42; postclassical, 145
Cinema Ephemera festival, 329
cinematic techniques, military technologies linked with, 76, 78, 80
cinema vérité, 3, 45, 201; French tradition, 214. See also feminist vérité
cinephilia, 162
Cisco Systems, 139
Citizenfour (Poitras), 8, 180, 220, 227–37; animation in, 231–34, *232*; as documentary thriller, 8, 227–28; as epistolary film, 234; landscapes and documentation, *233*, 234; nationalisms and citizenship in, 230–31; Poitras as character in, 229; public privacy and private publics, 231–34; as queer film, 235. See also antirepresentational turn
citizenship, 28, 62, 230–31
city symphonies, 159–61, 174n3, 330
civil rights movement, 40, 43
Clayton, Merry, 267, 268, 270
climate change: acceleration of, 86–88; agriculture's role in, 91–92, 101; glacier recession, 82–85; time-lapse cinematography as technique for visualizing, 76, 81. See also environmental documentary; slow violence
CLOUDS over Sidra (Milk and Arora), 363–64, 366–68, *367*

clown time, 305, 306
Coffey, Dennis, 263, 264–65, *265*
cognitive mapping, 55, 63; anticognitive mapping, 67–70
Cold Fact (Rodriguez), 263, 264
Cold War, 66, 131–32, 185
collaboration, with audience, 8–89, 300, 324–39
Collecting Visible Evidence (Gaines and Renov), 124
colonial humanism, 62, 63, 66, 68–70
colonialism, 34, 61–66, 68, 70, 253, 282
Columbia glacier, 85
Columbus (Kogonada), 164
Comic-Con (2012), 26
Coming from Reality (Rodriguez), 264
commercial-populist opener, 20
"committed" documentaries, 220, 241, 246, 255n4
commodification, 22–26, 26, 30n36, 37–38
commons, 15, 337–38; commodification of, 22–24; deterritorialized, 325; tragedy of, 25
A Companion to Popular Culture (Burns, Gary, ed./Wiley Blackwell), 4
compositional and editorial techniques, 142–43
compression and doublespeak, 306
computational media, 359
The Concert for Bangladesh (Swimmer), 267
Conde Nast, 148
confession, 193, 194, 195
Congress, public television and, 41–42
"considered non-completion," 334
consumer-grade VR, 356–59
consumerism, 28, 200, 209, 211; environmentalism haunted by, 95, 99, 107
consumption, 18–19, 240, 315
Containment (Galison and Moss), 43
Cook, Pam, 253
Cool Capitalism (McGuigan), 17
Cops (television series), 343
copyright laws, 157, 158, 166–67, 170, 266
coral bleaching, 86–88
corporate interests: internet/social media and, 304, 305, 311, 316–18; music documentary and, 148, 150; online music documentaries and, 141. See also capitalism; neoliberalism
corporate sponsorship, 16; "buying in" to, 22, 24, 26; in-film commercials, 24–25; of online music videos, 114

Corporation for Public Broadcasting (CPB), 38, 40–42
Corrigan, Timothy, 158, 169
Costa Rica, 250
countercinema, feminist, 215
counterpedagogy, 226
counterperformative, 7, 182–83, 190–91, 194
counterpublic, 182–83
counter-visuality, 100, 107
Coutts, Devon, 7, 55, 56
The Cove (Psihoyos), 252
Covino, Mark, 260
Cowperthwaite, Gabriela, 252
Crazy Horse (Wiseman), 20
creativity in documentary, 278, 283, 292, 293n9
Crimean War photographs, 128
criminal injustice narratives, 8, 300, 341; history of true crime genre and, 342–45. *See also* true crime documentaries
crisis: public broadcasting and, 47; of representation, 301, 358–59; slow violence and, 81
Criterion Collection, 114, 161–65, *163*, 168
critical internet studies, 303, 319n23, 319n24
critical political possibilities, 99–100
critical race scholarship, 312, 319n41
Cruse, Alex, 328
Cubbit, Sean, 80–82, 251
Cull, Joren, 149
cultural minoritarianism, 48
cultural populism, 17–19
Cultural Populism (McGuigan), 17–18
Cutler, R. J., 203

Daily Wire, 347–48
Dargis, Manohla, 189–90
dark ecology, 56, 96
Darrow, Chris, 270
Dassey, Brendan, 341, 346, 351
database documentaries, 256
data visualization, 76, 80–84, 82, 87
Davis, Clive, 271
Davis, Don, 271
Day, James, 41
Dean, James, 265
Dean, Jodi, 97
Dean, Sara, 334

de Antonio, Emile, 187
Dear Zachary (Keunne), 345, 354n11
Death (band), 240, 260, 270–73, 274n16
death, internet images of, 312–14, *313*, *314*
deceleration, 75–76; acceleration of, 56, 88–89
declarative mode of address, 166
The Decline of Western Civilization (Spheeris), 153
Deep Blue (Harlin), 249
de Fren, Allison, 5, 114–15
de la Peña, Nonny, 364, 369n13
de Man, Paul, 179, 182, 189, 193, 195, 197n12
De Mare, Anne, 45
Demme, Jonathan, 267
democracy, 21, 25, 46–47
Demon in the Freezer (Morris), 128, 130–32, *131*
Demos, Moira, 347
Dewey, John, 46
Dickey, Bronwen, 347–48
Didi-Hubermann, Georges, 281
difference, orchestration of, 66–67
Diggin' in the Carts (RBMA), 152
digital documentary, 6, 113, 123; database documentaries, 256
Dillon, Elizabeth Maddock, 325
Direct Cinema, 3, 214–15
discernible reality, 196, 198n42
discourses of sobriety, 119
Disney Studios, 101
distribution, 26; on public television, 38
diversity: public television and, 42–48
DNA evidence, 341
docbusters, 20, 21, 26, 30n19; components of, 28
Docmedia, 122–24
DOC NYC film festival, 27
docudrama, 4, 117. *See also* Morris, Errol; Op-Docs (*New York Times*)
documentaries: affect and emotion in, 245; blurred boundaries, 124; branded, 24–26, 30n36, 37–38; convergence of newspaper with, 124; creativity in, 278, 283, 292, 293n9; hybridization, 223, 236; language philosophy of, 182–83; "mainstream," maligned, 245; melodrama, relationship to, 245–46, 252–55; radical history in, 193; surveillant gaze of, 243; television as traditional venue for, 23. *See also* online documentary

documentary community, 14
"documentary contract," 4
documentary ecologies, 55. *See also* environmental documentary
documentary studies, 1–3; anticapitalist and antirealist commitments of, 200–201; popular documentary undertheorized, 2
Donovan, Pamela, 343, 352
Dovey, Jon, 123
Drag City Records, 272–73
drone technology, 45, 55, 57–60
Druick, Zoë, 7, 28, 31n55, 55
Duffy, Enda, 68
Dugan, Tim, 181, *190*, 191
Dulles, Allen, *120*
Dunye, Cheryl, 304
Duvernay, Ava, 226
DVDs, 60, 161–62, 174; as "Auteur Machines," 164
Dying in Full Detail (Malkowski), 313
Dylan, Bob, 264
dystopian allegory, 229

Earth from Above (Arthus-Bertrand), 62
Easterling, Keller, 330
eating disorders, 201–5, *202*
Eclair 35mm Cameflex, 161
ecocinema, 71n14, 92
ecodocumentary, 7–8; food documentaries, 56
eco-kitsch, 56
ecological consciousness, 56, 92
The Economist, 16
Edgar Wright-How to Do Visual Comedy (Zhou and Ramos), 166
education, 31n55; discussion time built into films, 326; film in classrooms, 28; ironic forms of pedagogy, 225, 226–27; public television and, 38; radical digital media literacy, 303–4
educational documentaries, 203–4
elegy, 93–94, 97, 100
Elfman, Danny, 189
elitism, 17–18
Elizabethan theater, 325
Ellroy, James, 166
Elsaesser, Thomas, 242, 245, 247, 248
Else, Jon, 283, 285
Emblematic Group, 364

eminent enrollment, 28, 29
emotion. *See* affect and emotion
empathy: entangled, 252; VR as "empathy machine," 301, 359; VR as intimate viewing environment, 363–64. *See also* affect and emotion
encoding-decoding thesis, 18
Enough to Eat? The Nutrition Film (Anstey, 1936), 104–7, *105*, *106*
entertainment, 1, 5, 6, 240, 278; lack of self-awareness, 28; manipulative, 347, 350–51, 353; private tragedies as, 341; privatization of, 23; social change said to be inspired by, 19–20
environment, contradictory views of, 93–94
environmental documentary, 2, 55–111; aerial fly-over, 57–74; "dark ecology," 56, 96; data visualization and, 80–82; ice core science, 84; "Man" in, 63, 67; soundtracks, 59, 61, 66–67; tie-ins with tour companies, 59. *See also Chasing Coral; Chasing Ice*; climate change; nature documentary; time-lapse cinematography
environmentalism, consumerism linked with, 95, 99, 107
epistephilia, spectacle of, 56, 99, 366
Eshun, Kodwo, 173
essay films, 114, 157–63, 165–67; auteurism and, 161; city symphonies, 159–61, 174n3, 330; critical aims, 159; dialogic relationships, 158; fractured vision and perceptual distortion, 158–59; perceptual anomalies of, 158–59; as refractive, 158, 169–70, 172–74. *See also* video essay
The Essay Film-Some Thoughts of Discontent (Lee), 172–73
essays, 333–34
ethics, 283–85; archival, 283; audience walkouts, 20; "do no harm," 278, 280, 284; melodramatic documentary and, 243, 251; social media viewing and, 316–18, *317*; visceral form of, 99
event, as concept, 324
Every Frame a Painting (Ramon, Zhou), 165–68
evidence, 127–28, 134, 159, 165, 221–22; archival documents incite doubt, 280; DNA, 341; in environmental documentaries, 83, 86–88,

94; historical moving images as, 335; lightly edited archival film segments as, 324
excuses, 7, 189–96, 198n36
Exit through the Gift Shop (Banksy), 180, 220
expedition film conventions, 66
"expertise," 168–69, 215
expository mode, 144, 149, 283, 359
extinction, human, 92
Extreme Ice Survey (EIS), 82, 84
Eyes on the Prize (Blackside production), 40
Eyes on the Prize II (Blackside production), 40

Facebook, 360-degree video on, 360–61, *361*
Faces Places (Varda, JR), 180, 220
Fahrenheit 9/11 (Moore), 226–27, 277
failure: aesthetics of, 221–23; invisibility and aesthetics of, 235–36; queer art of, 99; of representation, 220
fake documentary, 304
fake Fred, 306, *307*
"fake news"/"alternate facts," 4, 132
The Family of Man exhibit and publication, 66, 70
Fandor streaming site, 170–71
Fanning, David, 42
Farm Security Administration photographs, 128
Farms Lost and Found (Prelinger), 325
Farnel, Sean, 27–28
Fassin, Didier, 191–92
feature-length format, 3, 114, 243, 259; music documentaries, 139–41, 145, 148, 151–52; true crime documentaries, 343–44
Federal Communications Commission (FCC), 39
The Feminine Mystique (Friedan), 212
feminism, 1970s, 211–15
Feminism and Documentary (Waldman and Walker), 213
feminist studies, 179–80, 253, 365; anticapitalist and antirealist commitments of, 200–201; antirealist feminist film scholars, 215; applied to internet and social media, 301–23
feminist vérité, 8, 179–80, 200–219; everyday lives, focus on, 206, 210, 214–15; reparative reading and, 213–17
Fenton, George, 61

Ferrante, Anthony, 249
festivals, documentary, 8, 13, 15–35, 23, 328; Australian, 159; commercialization and audience attendance, 8; DOC NYC film festival, 27; keystone films, 15, 17; New York Film Festival, 328; as niche market, 23; opening-night film form, 17, 19–20; Planet in Focus film festival, 30n41; populist commitment and, 15; San Francisco International Film Festival, 328; VR documentary at, 358. *See also* Hot Docs Canadian International Documentary Festival (Toronto)
festival studies, 8, 13
F for Fake (Welles), 161, 167–68, 173–74
F for Fake and the Death of the Author (Kallgren), 168–69
F for Fake: How to Structure a Video Essay (Zhou and Ramos), 167–68
Field of Vision, 37
Fifer, Sally Jo, 43
Fillion, Mitch, 147–48
"film events," 300, 324–39; antecedents, 325–26; assembly, not algorithms, 325, 329, 332–33, 337, 338n10; essays and interventions, 333–34; home movies in, 324, 326–27, 329–31, 332–33, 336; human landscape, 331; local historians at, 326, 333, 334, 335; *Lost Landscapes of San Francisco* event (Prelinger), 326–27; making, 329–30; new iterations, 328; as nonnostalgic projects, 324; politics, positionalities, and potentials, 334–38; production trajectory, 326–29; 16 mm collections, 331; as social practice, 337; white material predominates, 335–36. *See also* populism
Filmmaker Magazine, 228–29
Films Beget Films (Leyda), 282
film studies, 2, 122, 163, 244, 261, 341; feminist, 201, 216
film style, problem-solution model of, 142–43
financial crisis of 2008, 125, 205, 211, 212
First Person (Morris), 129
Fischer, Lisa, 267, 268
F Is for Phony: Fake Documentary and Truth's Undoing (ed. Juhasz and Lerner), 304
Fisher, Mark, 25
Fitch, George, 283–84, *284*, 290, 292

5 Broken Cameras (2011), 220, 225
Flaherty, Robert, 3
fly-over, 55, 57–59, *58*, 65, 68
Fogel, Joshua, 279
The Fog of War: Eleven Lessons from the Life of Robert S. McNamara (Morris), 7, 120, 131, 179, 183–86, *186*; "Believing and Seeing Are Both Often Wrong," 186
Food (Kenner), 56
Food and Magic (Negulesco, 1943), 101–2, *102*
food documentaries, 91–111; early, 104–7, *105*, *106*; "good" vs. "bad" food, 94, 95–96, 100; grocery store scenes, 92–93; infographics, 92, 97; magic and, 101–2, *102*; World War II–era, 92, 101, *101*. *See also* agribusiness (Big Food); agriculture
Food Inc. (2008), 91–111; banality of, 94–95; "dark ecology" approached in, 56, 96; as elegiac, 93–94, 97, 100; end titles, 94, 97; epistephilia, spectacle of, 56, 99; "good" vs. "bad" food, 94, 95–96, 100; guilt, phenomenology of, 95, 99; individual action focused on, 93, 94, 96–97; infographics in, 56, 92, 97–100, *98*; kitsch style, 100, 106; as melodrama, 96–97; *New York Times* review of, 94, 95, 99; opening credit sequence, 92; pastoralism not dismissed in, 94, 107; pathos alternated with frenetic action, 98–99; structural factors not addressed in, 96–97; Takepart survey, 91, 94–95, 97; voice-over, 92–93, 107
Food Will Win the War (Disney), 101, *101*
Ford, Gerald, 117
Ford, Phil, 273
Formenti, Cristina, 100
The 4th Dimension, 271
Franklin, Rachel, 360–61, *361*, 369n11
freedom, to participate in culture, 28
French documentary traditions, 62
French New Wave, 161
Fricke, Ron, 64–66, 67
Friedan, Betty, 212
Friedberg, Anne, 78
Friedman, Robert, 22
FRONTLINE (PBS), 39, 43
Fuhs, Kristen, 347
funding, 16, 22–26, 37

Gaines, Jane M., 124, 222, 241, 246
Galison, Peter, 43, 45
Garnham, Nicholas, 23
Gas, Light, and Coke Company of Great Britain, 104
Gaspay, Marissa, 207
Gates, Ruth, 87
gaze, militarized, 59, 64, 65, 67, 70
general-interest documentaries, 46
Generation Wealth (Greenfield), 179, 200, 208–13, *210*, 217n11
geographic displacement and exile, 234
Getz, John, 283–84, *284*, 290
Gibney, Alex, 43, 45
Ginling Women's College (Nanking), 284–85
Girl Culture (Greenfield), 203–4
glacier recession, 82–85
Glass, Philip, 66, 129
Gledhill, Christine, 244–45
global digital communication landscape, 1990s, 263
global documentary: colonial humanism in, 62, 63, 66; fly-over evokes sense of power, 58–59, 64, 67–70; militarized gaze in, 59, 64, 65, 67, 70; proprioceptive aesthetics and anticognitive mapping in, 67–70. *See also* aerial documentaries
God's-eye view, 60, 65, 78–79
Gombrich, E. H., 142–43
The Good Earth (Buck, movie adaptation), 286
government interests, social media and, 304
Grainge, Lucian, 259
Grant, Catherine, 164, 171
Great Britain interwar era, 104
The Greatest Movie Ever Sold. *See POM Wonderful Presents: The Greatest Movie Ever Sold* (*PWPTGMES*; Spurlock)
Green Documentary: Environmental Documentary in the 21st Century (Hughes), 186–87
Greenfield, Lauren, 8, 179–80, 200–219; editing choices, 212; *Generation Wealth*, 179, 200, 208–13, *210*, 217n11; *Girl Culture*, 203–4; interviews, 203–4, 206–15; *The Kingmaker*, 179; *Queen of Versailles*, 179, 200, 205–8, *208*, 212, 214, 226; slick televisual style, 180, 205, 210; in tension with anticapitalist and antirealist

commitments, 200–201; *Thin*, 179, 200, 201–5, *202*, 214
Greenpeace, 250
Green Revolution, 101
Greenwald, Glenn, 231, 234, 235
Groovesville Records, 271
"groundlings," 325
Gruen, Lori, 252
Grusin, Richard, 142, 151
Guggenheim, Davis, 93
Gulf of Tonkin Resolution, 185–86
Gulf War, 78
Guthman, Julie, 93, 94, 99
Guttentag, Bill, 240, 278. See *Nanking* (Guttentag and Sturman)
Guzman, Patricio, 226

Hackney, Bobby, 270, 271–72
Hackney, Dannis, 270, 271–72
Hackney, David, 270, 271
Hackney, Julian, 272
Hackney brothers, 270–73
Hagan, Siobhan, 329
Haiven, Max, 22, 23
Halbach, Teresa, 342, 351
Halberstam, Jack, 99, 223–25, 235
Hall, Stuart, 18
Hamer, Dean, 44
Hamilton, Kathryn, 363, 366–68
Hampton, Henry, 40
Hands of Bresson (Kogonada), 163, *164*
Happy Mother's Day (Leacock and Chopra), 215
Hardin, Garrett, 25
Harlan County USA (Kopple), 215
Harlin, Renny, 249
Harman, Sabrina, 128, 194
Harrelson, Woody, 284
Harris, Andy, 44, 48
Harris, David, 120, 188
Harun Farocki Institut (Berlin), 171
Haver, Ronald, 162
HBO, 203–4
head-mounted display (HMD), 356–57, 360, 366
Heavy Metal Parking Lot (Heyn, Krulik), 153
Hedges, Chris, 211
Helfand, Judith, 43

Helms, Jesse, 42, 44
Hemingway, Mariel, 284–85
Henderson, D. A., 130–31, 132
Hendrie, Brett, 27, 31n52
Hensley, Lisa, 132
Hersh, Seymour, 117–21, *118*, 135n3, 135n7, 135n9
Herzog, Werner, 2
heterodiegetic narrator, 61
Heumann, Joseph K., 93
"A Hierarchy of Innocence" (Moeller), 246–47
Hill, Judith, 267
historical documentaries, 5, 43, 45, 240. See also *Nanking* (Guttentag and Sturman)
historical intervention, 334
history format, 39
Hoberman, J., 189
Hogarth, David, 122
Hollywood film industry, 160; "historical pictures," 286; VR documentary's affinities with, 359, 365–66
Hollywood Reporter, 205
Holocaust, 280–81, 293n19
Home (Arthus-Bertrand), 55, 58, 62–64, *63*, 67, 69
Home Is Where the Heart Is (Gledhill), 244–45
home movies, 324, 326–27, 329–31, 332–33, 336
Homestretch (De Mare and Kelly), 45, 46–47
home theaters, 59
Homm, Florian, 211–12
"Honest Truths: Documentary Filmmakers on Ethical Challenges in Their Work" (Center for Social Media), 278
hope, 97
Hot Docs Canadian International Documentary Festival (Toronto), 8, 13.15, 16–17; cultural populism and, 17–19; efficiency trumps engagement, 19; list of opening-night films, *34–35*; programming, 19–21; success of, 8, 13, 18–19
Howlett, Jeff, 260
How Not to Be Seen: A Fucking Didactic Educational .Mov File (Steyrl), 221
HTC (High Tech Computer), 358
Huber, Alison, 262
Hughes, Helen, 186–87, 251, 256n31
humanitarian documentaries, 59, 62, 246
humanitarian representation, 364
human-nature relations, 56

Hurricane Maria (Puerto Rico), Spaces application and, 360–61, *361*, 367
Huston, John, 194
Huxley, Julian, 105
hypernarration, 165, *173*

identity, shaped by capitalism, 202
identity politics, 220
illustrated lecture genre, 104
illustration, vs. representation, 287–89, *289*
image, as "encountered sign," 349–50
imagination, images and, 281
IMAX, 57–58, 68, 70
"immediation," 364
Immediations: The Humanitarian Impulse in Documentary (Rangan), 364
immersive documentary, 6, 259, 300–301, 363–64
"immersive journalism," 363–64
Inception, 153
An Inconvenient Truth (Guggenheim), 93
Independent Lens (PBS), 37, 42, 43, 44, 48
independent music distribution, 266
Independent Television Service (ITVS), 37, 40, 42–43, 43–44; character-driven narratives, 45–46; historical documentaries, 45; selection process, 44
indexicality, 221, 285, 287–88
industrial and amateur film, 300, 327, 329–31
Industrial Revolution, 78
influence, theory of, 142
infographics, 7, 55; in *Food, Inc.*, 56, 92, 97–100, *98*; hyperbole, 101, *101*; World War II-era food films, *101*
innocence, 246–47
Innocence Project, 341
"In Reference to Visual Essays" (2016 Berlinale), 163, 171
interactive documentaries, 123, 140, 145, 325, 332, 356
interactive technologies, 87
international documentaries, 226
internet/social media, 5; accountability and, 317–18; compression and doublespeak on, 306; corporate interests and, 304, 305, 311, 316–18; death, images of, 312–13, *313*, *314*; hidden costs of "free," 316; popularity-driven, corporate-dominated online communities, 299; quick voting silences other points of view, 311; #SayHerName campaign, 317; streaming services, 37, 139, 151; video traffic, 139; violence against Black people on, 312–13, *313*, 317; virality is virility, 305, 306–12; weaponization of viral media, 309, *309*, 316. *See also* music documentary; SHiTsticle
intersectional scholarship, 1–2, 180, 240
interventions, 333–34
interviews: in *Citizenfour*, 227; by Greenfield, 203–4, 206–15; interviewee hidden from camera, 225; in ITVS films, 22, 24; by Morris, 7, 117–19, 127, 129, 131–32, 135n28, 179, 181–88, 191–96; in music documentaries, 143–44, 152; Nanking Massacre and, 279, 292; by Spurlock, 22, 24; in true crime documentaries, 343–47; virtual reality (VR) and, 359, 362
Interviews with My Lai Veterans (Strick), 193
In the Eyes of the Animal (Marshmallow Laser Feast), 364
[In]Transition, 158
investigative audiovisual journalism, 37
Iraq War, 227
Iron Man franchise, 22, 30n26
irony, 7, 179, 197n12, 223; antirepresentational ethos, 180; declared dead, 183, 196; ironic forms of pedagogy, 225, 226–27; as performative, 181–83, 189; political, 185; reenactment, 181, 184–85; on social media, 299; vocal, 186–87; in works of Morris, 181–99
isolation and indifference, 1
ISOTYPES (International System of Typographic Picture Education), 103, *103*, 105
ITVS, 13

Jackie Chan-How to Do Action Comedy (Zhou and Ramos), 166
Jagger, Mick, 269
Jahrling, Peter, 131
Jameson, Fredric, 68
Jam Handy Organization, 327
Japan, 278–79. *See also Nanking* (Guttentag and Sturman); Nanking Massacre (Rape of Nanking, 1937)

Japanese denialist TV program, 292
Japanese silent cinema, 325
Japanese video game music, 152
"Jargons of Authenticity" (Arthur), 222
Jaws (Spielberg), 249
Jazz on a Summer's Day (Stern), 143
Jefferson, Tony, 18
John, Mable, 270, 274
John Legend and the Roots, 150
Johnston, Claire, 215
Jones, Gloria, 268
journalism, 14, 117–38; electronic, 113–14, 121; immersive, 363–64; right-wing attacks on, 132–33
Joyce at 34 (Chopra and Weill), 214
judicial system, critique of. See *Making a Murderer* (Netflix); true crime documentaries
Juhasz, Alexandra, 5, 215, 299
Jump Cut, 192

Kahana, Jonathan, 7, 179, 220
Karpinski, Janis, 195
Kauffman, Ross, 241, 247
Keathley, Christian, 161, 163
Kelly, Kristen, 45
"Ken Burns effect," 36–37
Kennebeck, Sonia, 45
Kennedy, John F., 128–30, *130*
Kenner, Robert, 56
Kerry, John, 227
Keyframe (Fandor), 171
keystone films, 15, 17, 28–29
Keywords (Williams), 4
Kfir, Zohar, *362*, 362–63
Khan, Sabiha Ahmad, 7, 55, 56
King, Encke, 166
King, Rodney, 222
King Kong (laserdisc), 162, *163*
Kinik, Anthony, 7, 113–14
Kinkle, Jeff, 68–69, 70
kinoglaz (cinema eye), 160
kitsch, 100, 106
Klein, Melanie, 216
Knight of Cups (Malick), 160
Koch, David, 43, 45
Kogonada, 114, 162–65, *164*, 171, 174n15, 175n21, 175n30

Kōgo Noda, 174n15
Kopple, Barbara, 215
Koyaanisqatsi (Reggio), 58, 64
Kozloff, Sarah, 61
Kratz, Ken, 351–52
Kuma Hina (Hamer and Wilson), 44

L.A. Confidential (Hanson), 166
Lambsbread, 271–72
Lamm, Kimberly, 208
Landberg, S. Topiary, 8, 180
Land without Bread (Buñuel), 187–88, 195
language philosophy, 182–83
Lanham, Richard A., 17
Lanzmann, Claude, 280–81, 293n19
Larke-Walsh, George S., 8, 300
laserdiscs, 161–63, *163*
Last Hijack (2014), 225
Laudan, Rachel, 96
Learning from YouTube (Juhasz), 304, 305, 309–10, 314–15
Lebow, Alisa, 312–13
Lee, Kevin B., 114, 169–74, *173*; *The Essay Film-Some Thoughts of Discontent*, 172–73; *Shooting Down Pictures*, 170; *The Spielberg Face*, 170–71, 172; *What Makes a Video Essay Great*, 173
Lee, Spike, 150
Left, 18, 226
legibility: bureaucratic, 224, 230; moral, 96, 245, 247; obfuscation as counter to, 224, 230, 235, 236
Lenk, James, 351
Leonsis, Ted, 291
Lesage, Julia, 192
Let There Be Light (Huston), 194
Leyda, Jay, 282, 285, 287, 289
"Liar, Liar, Pants on Fire" (Morris), *127*, 127–28
Life series, 56
Liner Notes, 148, 149
Lingo, Kathleen, 125–26, 135n22
listicles, 301, 305–6
liveness, 145–46, 151, 154n18
Livingston, Jennie, 181
Lodge, Guy, 209
Long Now Foundation, 326
look, 319n35, 319n36, 319n41; looking askance, 312–13; looking awry, 312–13; subject "look back," 365

Lorentz, Pare, 286
Los Angeles, 211
Los Angeles Plays Itself (Andersen), 115, 165–67
Lost Landscapes series (Prelinger), 300, 324–39; *Lost Landscapes of Detroit*, 327, 329, 334, 335–36; *Lost Landscapes of Los Angeles*, 328, 336; *Lost Landscapes of New York*, 329; *Lost Landscapes of San Francisco*, 326–27, 330
Love, Darlene (Wright), 267–68, 269
Love, Heather, 216

MacDonald, Scott, 71n14
Mackenzie, Midge, 215
Magee, John, 290–91
"Magee Film," 281, 290–91, 294n59, 295n61
Magnolia Pictures, 205
mainstream documentaries, 2, 8, 13–14, 16, 69, 203–4
Making a Murderer (Netflix series), 8, 300, 340–55; critique of justice system in, 344; fictionalized aspects of, 346–47; as game or puzzle, 350–51; lack of narration, 347; manipulative narrative aesthetic, 347, 350–51, 353; meme underscores criticism of judicial system, 348, *349*; reviews of, 347–48; transmedia impact of, 346; villains, 351–52
Malcolm X test, 283, 285
Malick, Terrence, 160
Malkowski, Jennifer, 313
Manhatta (Sheeler and Strand), 160
Manitowoc County Police, Wisconsin, 341–42, *349*, 351
Mansome (Spurlock), 24
Man with a Movie Camera (Vertov), 161
March of the Penguins (Jacquet), 277
Marker, Chris, 161
marketing: exposé documentary on, 20; global, 23; pastoral, 92, 94, 95, 97, 107; as untrustworthy, 107; of VR technologies, 357–58
Marks, Laura, 256n31
Marshmallow Laser Feast, 364
masculinist video violence, 312–16
masking techniques, 225
Mask of Nippon (National Film Board of Canada, 1942), 294n52
Massumi, Brian, 300, 341

materialist culture, 200
McDonald, Chris, 27, 31n52
McGuigan, Jim, 17, 18
McNamara, Robert, 179, 185–86, *186*
meaning: audience/consumer as source of, 18; breakdown of, 96
media industries studies, 261
media object, 6, 143
media praxis, 303–4
mediapraxis.org, 303, 304, 305, 318n4
media studies, 4, 122
medical-industrial complex, 202, 204
medium, remediation of, 142
melodrama, 348; as cross-cultural form, 244–45; documentary, relationship to, 245–46, 252–55; public discourse and, 245; victim, tradition of, 241–42, 246–49, 251; villains, 246
melodramatic documentary, 8, 96–97, 241–58; conventions of, 239; ethical questions, 243, 251; moral polarization in, 239, 242, 245–48, 251, 253–54; pathos in, 239, 242–48, *247*, *248*, 251, 253, 255; social uplift messages, 243; strategies of, 242, 244. See also *Born into Brothels* (Briski and Kauffman); *Sharkwater* (Stewart)
melodramatic imagination, 244
Michel, Frann, 243, 253
microalgae, 87
militarized gaze, 59, 64, 65, 67, 70
military technologies, 75–80; cinematic techniques linked with, 76, 78, 80; domination of space by visual technology, 79; smallpox stocks, 128, 130–32, *131*; visual production as violent, 78–79
Milk, Chris, 363, 366–68
Milliken, Christie, 8, 239
Milton, John, 134
Minh-ha, Trinh T., 364
miniseries, documentary, 40
minority consortia, public television, 41–42, 48
Minority Report (Spielberg), 123
Mirzoeff, Nicholas, 92, 100
misogyny: eating disorders and, 204; in reviews of *Generation Wealth*, 209–10; in white relationships, 206–7
Miss America Foundation, 206

missionaries, Western, 282–83
MK-Ultra program (CIA), 117–21
MOCAD (Museum of Contemporary Art Detroit), 327
modernity, "structure of feeling" of, 58
Moeller, Susan, 246–47
monetization, 151
Moon, Vincent (Mathieu Saura), 145–48
Moore, Michael, 2; on audience, 277–78, 292; *Fahrenheit 9/11*, 226–27, 277; *Roger and Me*, 3, 222; on secret of successful documentary, 277–78
moral formalism, 189
moral legibility, 96, 245, 247
Morin, Edgar, 214
Morris, Errol, 2, 5, 100, 113–38, 179; *American Dharma*, 133–34; *Believing Is Seeing: Observations on the Mysteries of Photography*, 121; blog posts, 126; *A Brief History of Time*, 189; "The Case of the Inappropriate Alarm Clock," 128; critical and popular failures, 183, 184; *Demon in the Freezer*, 128, 130–32, *131*; excuses, use of, 189–96; *First Person* episodes, 129; *The Fog of War*, 7, 120, 131, 179, 183–186, *186*; *Gates of Heaven*, 186; "Interrotron," 129, 188; irony in works of, 181–99; "Liar, Liar, Pants on Fire," *127*, 127–28; "The Most Curious Thing," 128; *Mr. Death: The Rise and Fall of Fred A. Leuchter, Jr.*, 189; *New York Times* Op-Docs series, 7, 113, 121–22, 124–26, 128–32; "Not Every Picture Tells a Story," 126; *November 22, 1963* (Morris), 128–30, *130*, 135n28; "pariah" figures, interest in, 133–34; photography, interest in, 121, 124, 127–28; reenactment in works of, 181, 184–85, *186*, 188–89, 192–96; "simulation microfiche reader" technique, 131, 134; *Standard Operating Procedure*, 7, 121, 131, 179, 181, 183, 189–96, 220; *Tabloid*, 131, 188; television commercials, 183, 188; *The Thin Blue Line*, 3, 118, 120, 184, 187, 188, 190, 222, 344; *The Umbrella Man*, 128–29, 135n28; *The Unknown Known*, 7, 179, 183, 196, 220; *Vernon, Florida*, 186; "visual storytelling," 188; War Trilogy, 7, 179, 183–84; "Will the Real Hooded Man Please Stand Up?," 128;

Wormwood, 117–21, *118*, 126, 131, 132, 182–83, 196, 197n9
Morton, Timothy, 56, 93, 94, 95–96, 107
Moss, Robb, 43
motion picture technology, 76
mourning, work of, 292
movable frame, 357
Moyers, Bill, 41
Mr. Death: The Rise and Fall of Fred A. Leuchter, Jr. (Morris), 189
Mulvey, Laura, 162, 215, 216, 253, 256n21
Murley, Jean, 342–43
Murray, Robin L., 93
Museum of the Moving Image, 329
music documentary, 6, 46, 139–56; animation in, 149; audiovisual aesthetics, 145; biographies, 143; broad currents and trends, 143; compilation format/archival project, 144; concert documentary, 143–44; conservative style, 143–44, 150–51; creativity and, 139–40; ethnographic studies, 144; as extension of recording industry, 262; feature-length productions, 139–41, 145, 148, 151–52; impressionistic strategy, 144–45; industrial structure of, 260; journalistic visual representation strategy, 144–45; liveness of popular music, 145–46, 151, 154n18; long-form music video format, 146; made-for-television, 144; non-Western artists, 152, 153; nostalgia in, 239–40; postclassical, 145; recording industry and, 259, 260, 262; recovery mode, 239–40, 259–76; rockumentary, 143, 145; small-gauge motion picture photography, 152–53; *Southern Souls*, 114, 141, 145–48; structure and mode of address, 144; *The Take Away Show*, 114, 141, 145–47, *147*, 153; tour/"making of" film, 143–44; vernacular style, 141, 145, 154; virtual reality (VR), 153–54; web as distribution and exhibition space, 140–41, 145. *See also* internet/social media
musicologist-detectives, 264

Nader, Ralph, 24, 30n36
Naficy, Hamid, 234
Nanking (1938 Japanese propaganda film), 288–90, *289*

Nanking (Guttentag and Sturman), 277–97; China screening of, 292; controversy over, 291–92; editing decisions, 286–88; ethics in decision making, 278, 280, 284–85; illustration vs. representation in, 287–89, 289; interviews with survivors, 292; Nelson as producer, 240, 277; "Pathé News Reel #4," 286–88, 288, 294n50; primary source approach, 279–86; truth, problem of, 283

Nanking (Nelson, producer, 2007), 5

Nanking Massacre (Rape of Nanking, 1937), 240, 278–79; appropriated as ideological tool, 279; "Magee film," 281, 290–91, 294n59, 295n61; "Magee Film," 281, 290–91, 294n59, 295n61; "Safety Zone," 279; Western documentation of, 279

National Bird (Kennebeck), 45

National Educational Television (NET), 38

National Film Board of Canada, 294n52

National Geographic, 62, 64, 65

nationalisms, 230–31

National Multicultural Alliance, 42, 44

National Security Agency (NSA), 180, 229

The National: Something Out of Nothing (*New York Times*), 153

National WWII Museum (New Orleans), 294n53

"native"/indigenous subjects, 66

nature documentary: humans kept out of picture, 60, 61; narration, 60, 61; urgent problems kept off screen, 59, 61, 65–67. *See also* environmental documentary

near-future hope, 91, 94–95, 97

Nebab, Virginia, 207–8, 208

negative speech acts, 7

Negulesco, Jean, 101–2, 102

Nelson, Dylan, 5, 240

Nelson, Stanley, 283

Neo-Benshi, 325

neoliberalism, 17, 211–12, 222; anti-politics of, 94; audience growth, focus on, 19; cruelty of, 320n64; cultural populism and, 18; failures of state, 223–24; "free trade fantasy," 97. *See also* capitalism

Neurath, Marie L., 103

Nevins, Sheila, 203–4

The New Black (Richen), 44

new documentary, 222–23

New Inquiry, 364

"New Platforms for Docmedia: 'Variant of a Manifesto,'" (Wintonick), 122–23

News from Home (Akerman), 161

newspapers, 7, 113–14, 123–26; videos in, 123–24, 125–26. *See also* Op-Docs (*New York Times*)

news sources, traditional, 37

New Yorker, 129, 205

New York Film Festival, 328

New York Times, 94, 95; blog posts, 126; NYTVR, 358; Opinionator column, 7, 126–27; tablet-friendly version, 124–25; VR technology and, 358. *See also* Op-Docs (*New York Times*)

Nichols, Bill, 196, 198n36, 221–22; expository mode, 359; on expressivity of documentary, 278; fiction vs. nonfiction, 236n5, 256n22; on irony, 197n12, 197n19; on popular memory, 277; sobriety, discourses of, 119, 196, 205, 256n21; "spectacles of epistephilia," 99, 366; taxonomy of documentary modes, 356, 359; on "voice," 186, 187

Nielsen ratings, 37

Nixon, Richard, 38, 41, 79, 81

Nixon, Rob, 75–79, 81, 89

No More Road Trips? (Prelinger), 325, 327–28

nonrealist modes of representation, 220

non-Western musics, 152, 153

nostalgia, 239–40; environmental, 93, 100; imperial, 62

Nostalgia for the Light (Guzman), 226

NOVA (science series), 37, 39

November 22, 1963 (Morris), 128–30, 130, 135n28

"Now Media" era, 122–23

NPR (National Public Radio), 95

NYTimes.com, 113

Oakland Museum of California, 327

Obama, Barack, 234

obfuscation, 220, 224, 225, 236

Oculus, 358

Olson, Eric, 117–21, 132

Olson, Frank, 117–21, 132, 197n9

Once (Carney), 147

One Direction: This Is Us (Spurlock), 31n44

online documentary, as news journalism, 7, 121–22
Op-Docs (*New York Times*), 7, 113, 121–22, 124–26, 128–32, 135n20; attacks on journalism and, 133. *See also* Morris, Errol
opening-night film form, 19–20; keystone films, 15, 17, 28–29; list of films, *34–35*; politically safe social action, 27–28
ordinary people, 17–18, 188
Orientalism, 185, 367–68
Orlowski, Jeff, 76, 82–89; *Chasing Coral*, 82, 85–88; *Chasing Ice*, 82, 83–85
Otolith Group, 173
Our Capital (China Film Archives), 284
outrage, production of, 241
OVEE (online viewing platform), 46–47
overnarrativization, 331
Ozu, Yasujirō, 174n5

Page One: Inside the New York Times (Rossi), 124–25
Palestine, Israeli occupation of, 225
Palmer, Landon, 6, 239–40
Palmer, Tony, 262
parachute filmmaking, 29
Paradise Lost (Milton), 134
paranoid readings, 216–17
Paris Is Burning (Livingston), 181–82
Park Avenue (Gibney), 43, 45
Parker, Mark, 162
Parker, Trey, 168
Pärt, Arvo, 129
Participant Media, 91
participatory commons, 337
participatory documentaries, 332
pastoral marketing, 56, 92, 97, 107
Pathé newsreels, *286*, 286–88, *288*, 294n50
pathos, 98; in melodramatic documentary, 239, 242–48, *247*, *248*, 251, 253, 255
patriarchy, violent behaviors of, 309, 315–16
PBS, 13–14
Peace Officer (Barber and Christopherson), 46
Peeping Tom (Powell), 162
Peleg, Hela, 223
perception, co-opted by image-capture technology, 78–79
"Performative Utterances" (Austin), 182
performativity, 181–83, 189

Persepolis (Satrapit, Paronnaud), 180, 220, 225
personal, critique of, 187–88
personal documentary, 209–10
personal memoir documentary, 44–45
petishism/anthropomorphism, 251, 256n31
Pfeffer, Tad, 84
phallus, 309, 315
phantom ride, 58, 68, 78
photogenie, 190
photography, 121, 124, 127–28
Pinochet, Augusto, 226
Pitchfork Classic, 148, 149
Pitchfork Classic: The Flaming Lips' "The Soft Bulletin" (Bentler), 148
Pitchfork Media, 114, 141, 148–50
Pivot (social action entertainment channel), 19
Pixar films, 99
Pixarvolt, 99
planetary wildlife documentaries, 59–62
Planet Earth II (BBC), 56
Planet Earth series (BBC), 56, 58, 59–62, 69, 71n18; God's-eye view in, 60
Plantinga, Carl, 348, 352
pleasure, vernacular sublime, 55, 68, 69
The Plow That Broke the Plains (Lorentz), 93
point-of-view documentaries, 7, 42; POV (PBS), 37, 42–44
Poitras, Laura, 5, 179; as character in *Citizenfour*, 229; *Citizenfour*, 180, 220–37; *My Country, My Country*, 229; *The Oath*, 229; political exile and, 231; post-9/11 trilogy, 229
political action, 7
political documentaries, 180, 193
political mimesis, 222
politics, 179
politics, emotion and, 245
Pollan, Michael, 99
POM Wonderful company, 24, 26, 30n20, 31n45
POM Wonderful Presents: The Greatest Movie Ever Sold (*PWPTGMES*; Spurlock), 13, 15, 19–21; as branded documentary, 24–25; earnings, 31n44; false sense of public interest in, 22–24; not radical, 21–22; positioned as socially conscious, 20–21; technical aspects, 24

386 | Index

Popov, Serguei, 132
popular, as term, 4–5, 16
popular, the, 5–6, 9, 15; in popular documentary, 325
popular culture, 1–3; academia and, 114–15
popular documentary, 2–6, 9, 10n5, 13, 356; critical attention to, 2; definitions, 4, 16–17; digital documentary, 6; the popular in, 325. *See also* digital documentary; music documentary
popularity, 179; contests, rooted in optics, 311; dastardly functions of, 303; of fake news, 305–6; measurement of, 16; middle-of-the-road sensibility of, 310; as patriarchal, 308–9; violence inherent in, 308–10, *309*; as YouTube's organizing structure, 309–10
popularity-function, 6
populism, 15, 324–39; cultural, 17–19. *See also* "film events"
Porter, Dawn, 43
possibility, 97, 99–100, 281
post 9/11 documentaries, 8, 179–80, 220; materiality and lived consequence in, 224. *See also* antirepresentational turn
postclassical cinema, 145
postmodernism, 2, 183
post-traumatic stress disorder, 192
POV (PBS), 37, 42–44
poverty, stereotypes about, 247
Powaqqatsi (Reggio), 64
Powell, Michael, 162
power, fly-over evokes sense of, 58–59, 64, 67–70
Prelinger, Rick, 5; *Bay Motion*, 327; *Lost Landscapes of Detroit (Yesterday and Tomorrow)*, 327, 329, 334, 335–36; *Lost Landscapes of Los Angeles*, 328, 336; *Lost Landscapes of New York*, 329; *Lost Landscapes of San Francisco*, 326–27, 330; *Lost Landscapes* series, 300, 325; *No More Road Trips?*, 325, 327–28; Oakland project "repatriated," 328. *See also* "film events"
Prelinger Archives, 329
primary sources, 279–86; US Signal Corps propaganda films, 285–88, *286*, *288*
prime-time television formats, 347–48
privacy, 220, 224; public privacy and private publics, 231–34

private interest documentary auteurism, 13, 20; antipublic interests and, 21–22
problem-solution model of film style, 142–43
process plates, 331, 332
production-curation cycles, 29
propaganda films, 3, 78, 101, *101*, 251, 281, 294n52; US Signal Corps "Why We Fight" series, 285–88, *286*, *288*
proprioceptive aesthetics, 55, 58–59, 62, 67–70
proximal alternate reality, 91, 95
Psihoyos, Louie, 252
public, shaped by documentaries, 46–48
public affairs, 14, 38–39
Public Broadcasting Act of 1967, 36, 38
Public Broadcasting Service (PBS), 37–38; POV (PBS), 37, 42–44
public interest, false sense of, 22–24
public privacy, 231–34
public television, 7, 13–14, 36–53; conservative backlash against, 42–44; conservative programming, 43; defense of by documentarians, 38; digital-era experiments, 49; diverse styles and perspectives, 44–46; diversity in theory and practice, 42–44; documentaries as shaping force, 46–48; in-house genres, 39–40; minority consortia, 41–42, 48; prime-time controversies, 43, 47–48; reach of, 36, 38; storytelling strategy, 39. *See also* Corporation for Public Broadcasting (CPB); Public Broadcasting Service (PBS)
punk movement, 153
punk rock, 272–73
The Punk Rock Movie (Letts), 153

Qazvini, Michael, 347
Quatsi trilogy (Reggio), 56, 64–67
Queen of Versailles (Greenfield), 179, 200, 205–8, *208*, 212, 214, 226
queer art of failure, 99, 224, 235
The Queer Art of Failure (Halberstam), 223–25, 226, 235
Questlove, 273
"quota films," 174n3

Rabinowitz, Paula, 222
racism, 47, 222, 317
radical digital media literacy, 303–4

RadicalMedia, 21–22
Rago, Zack, 88
The Ramones, 273
Ramos, Taylor, 115, 165
Rangan, Pooja, 364
Reagan, Ronald, 41
Realer Than Reel: Global Directions in Documentary (Hogarth), 122
realism, 215–16; capitalist, 25; melodrama and, 244–45; withdrawal from representation, 224, 225, 227. *See also* antirepresentational turn
"realist debates," 216
reality TV, 8, 23, 36, 180, 204, 205. *See also* true crime documentaries
Realscreen magazine, 26
Rechtman, Richard, 191–92
recording industry, 259–73; exploitation of persons of color, 260, 266, 267; music documentary as extension of, 262
recovery documentary, 6, 239–40, 259–76; on arbitrary nature of fame, 269–70; authority of canon in, 261, 264–65, *265*, 269–70, 273; cultural reinvestment due to, 266; gatekeeping practices challenged in, 261, 267–68, 273; "greatness" as frame of reference, 261, 262, 265–66; media industries and, 261–73; record hunting, 272; recording industry's exploitation of persons of color, 260, 266, 267; structural barriers to going solo, 268–69; subject matter of, 259–60. *See also 20 Feet from Stardom* (Neville)
Red Bull Music Academy (RBMA), 114, 141, 151–53
reenactment, 283; in Morris's work, 181, 184–85, *186*, 188–90, 192–96, 197n9; in true crime documentaries, 343, 345
referentiality, 5
Reggio, Godfrey, 56, 58, 64–67
remediation, 114, 142–43
Remnick, David, 135n9
Rencontres internationales du documentaire de Montréal, 20
Renov, Michael, 4, 114, 255, 282, 283–84, 292, 293n9
reparative reading, 213–17
representation, 7; benefits of acceleration to, 80, 89; crisis of, 301, 358–59; failures of, 220; illustration vs., 287–89, *289*; in music documentaries, 139–47, 149, 151–54; nonrealist modes, 220; politics of, 180; self-representation, 364–65; of slow violence, 75–78, 80; technologies of, 223; time-lapse as technique of, 80–82; virtual reality (VR) and, 357
Republican Party, 132–33
republican pedagogical tradition, 62
resistance, 6; of audience to truth, 291; to enclosures on documentary culture, 25; Pixarvolt, 99; readings of VR, 363, 366–68, *367*; through rituals, 18; VR technology and, 301
Retro Report, 113
revision, 142–43
revisionist programs, 292
Reynolds, Diamond, 314, 317
Ricciardi, Laura, 347
Rich, Ruby, 2
Richard III (Shakespeare), 325–26
Richen, Yoruba, 44
Riggs, Marlon, 42–43
The River (Lorentz), 286
Roberts, Martin, 65–66
rockumentary, 143, 145
Rodowick, David, 141–42
Rodriguez, Eva, 264
Rodriguez, Sixto, 262–66, 272
Roe, Annabelle Honess, 99–100
Roger and Me (Moore), 3, 222
Rony, Fatima Tobing, 364
Rose, Mandy, 123
Rosenbaum, Jonathan, 169
Ross, Heather, 44
Rossi, Andrew, 124–25
Rostock, Susanne, 43
Roth, Michael S., 280–81
Rotha, Paul, 102–4, *103*
Rouch, Jean, 214
Rowland, Steve, 264–65
Roy and Edna Disney/CalArts Theater (REDCAT), 328
Rumsfeld, Donald, 13, 179, 196, 197n9
Run Lola Run (Tykwer), 228, 229
Ruttman, Walther, 330

Sachs, Leon, 62
"safe" films, 27–28

Said, Edward, 367–68
Salatin, Joel, 94
Samsara (Reggio), 55, 58, 64–67, *65*
San Francisco Bay area, 327
San Francisco International Film Festival, 328
San Francisco Newsreel, 214
Sang-Hun, Choe, 308
Sans Soleil (Marker), 161
Satoru Mizushima, 291
Saura, Mathieu. *See* Moon, Vincent (Mathieu Saura)
Saxton, Libby, 281
The Scene of Violence: Cinema, Crime, Affect (Young), 349–50, 352–53
schema, 142–43
Schickel, Richard, 189, 246
Schlosser, Eric, 107
Schmerberg, Ralf, 152
Schulz, Kathryn, 341
scientific theater, 194
Scott, A. O., 126, 228, 243
Scott, James C., 223–24
Searching for Sugar Man (Bendjelloul), 239, 259, 260, 263–66
Sea Shepherd Conservation Society, 250–51, 256n28
Sedgwick, Eve, 216
Seeber, Barbara K., 28–29
Seeing Like a State: How Certain Schemes to Improve the Human Condition Have Failed (Scott), 223–24
Segerman, Stephen "Sugar," 263–66
Seitz, Matt, 251
self-knowledge, 119
sensational nonfiction documentaries, 204
September 11, 2001, 183, 190, 192. *See also* post 9/11 documentaries
7 Billion Others (Arthus-Bertrand), 62
sex workers, stigmatization of, 246–48, 254
Seymour, Nicole, 92
Shaping San Francisco, 326
Shapiro, Evan, 19
"Shark Fin Mafia," 250
shark finning/fishing, 239, 241, 249–51, 254, 256n27
Sharknado (Ferrante), 249
Sharkwater (Stewart), 239, 249–54, 252; slavery, evocation of, 251; Stewart's embrace of shark in, 250, 251–52, 252

Sheeler, Charles, 160
Sherman's March (McElwee), 222
SHiTsticle (superhardtruths, SHiTs), 305–312; 317–318
Shoah (Lanzmann), 280
Shooting Down Pictures (Lee), 170
short forms, 113–14; monetization and, 151; online, 139–40, 146–47. *See also* music documentary; Op-Docs (*New York Times*)
shot length, diminishing, 28
Siegel, David, 206, 214
Siegel, Jackie, 205–8, 212, 214
Silent Spring (Carson), 93
Six Seconds in Dallas: A Micro-Study of the Kennedy Assassination (Thompson), 128–29
Sklar, Robert, 195
Slate, 347–48
Slow movement, 13, 28–29
slow violence, 55, 56, 75–90; acknowledging, 77; aftereffects of, 75, 78; as attritional, 76–77; as centuries-old phenomenon, 77–78; definition of, 76–77; imperative to act on, 81–82; representational problem of, 75–78, 80, 89; rethinking, 76–77; time to react as imperative, 79–80, 89. *See also* climate change; environmental documentary
Slow Violence and the Environmentalism of the Poor (Nixon), 75, 76–78
Smaill, Belinda, 95, 96, 244, 245
smallpox stocks, 128, 130–32, *131*
Smithsonian Channel, 57
Snowden, Edward, 8, 227–36, *232*; antirepresentational position of, 230
Sobchack, Vivian, 100
sobriety, discourses of, 119, 196, 205, 256n21, 363
social action, 171–72, 255n4; "doing good" films, 27–28; entertainment said to inspire, 19–20; films positioned as, 20–21; imperative to act on climate change, 81–82; politically safe, 27–28; victim tradition, 241–42; visual activism, 56, 92
social documentary, 93, 208
social justice: UNVR films, 363–64; VR documentary and, 357, 358, 363–68
social problem film, 106
Solheim glacier, 83
Sonagachi, Calcutta, 242–49
Sontag, Susan, 312

soundtracks: archival images without, 324, 332; authentic sound recreated, 293n29; for environmental documentary, 59, 61, 66–67; improvised by audience, 300; "melody of the world," 67; Op-Docs, 129; virtual reality (VR) documentary, 356–57
South Africa, fan base for Rodriguez, 263, 265–66
South by Southwest, 328
Southern Souls, 114, 141, 145–48
South Park (Parker, Stone et al), 168
space, destroyed by acceleration, 79
Spaces application, 360–61, *361*
"The Spam of the Earth: Withdrawal from Representation," 221
Spears, Brian, 271
Spector, Phil, 267–68
speed, desire for, 68
Speed and Politics (Virilio), 79
Spielberg, Steven, 123, 170–71, *172*, 249
The Spielberg Face (Lee), 170–71, *172*
sports audience, 326
sports documentary, 10n6
Springsteen, Bruce, 269
Spurlock, Morgan, 2; action figure, 26; antipublic interests and, 21–22; on documentary as "last bastion of free speech," 21, 25, 30n21; *Mansome*, 24; *One Direction: This Is Us*, 31n44; *POM Wonderful: The Greatest Movie Ever Sold*, 13, 15, 19–25; *Super Size Me*, 21, 25, 31n43, 94
Standard Operating Procedure (Morris), 7, 121, 131, 179, 180, 183, 189–96; 220; counterperformative in, 190–91; entertainment and punishment integrated in, 196; politics of radical distrust in, 195; self-enclosed economy of, 192–93
state, failures of, 223–24
Steams, Michael, 66
Stelter, Brian, 124–25
Stern, Burt, 143
Stewart, Rob, 249–54, 252, 256n35
Steyerl, Hito, 221
Sting, 269–70
Stone, Roger, 133
Stoney, George, 43
Stop Making Sense (Demme), 267, 268
Storycast (PBS YouTube channel), 49
storytelling format, 39

Strand, Paul, 160
Strand Theater (Britton, South Dakota), 326
streaming services, 37, 139, 151, 170
street theater, 226
Strick, Joseph, 193
Sturges, John, 168
Sturman, Dan, 240, 278, 284. See also *Nanking* (Guttentag and Sturman)
subjective statements, 187
subjectivity, 172, 216, 224, 278; in capitalism, 63–64; embodied, 59
success, as theme in history films, 40
Sundance Film Festival, 29, *34*, 114; New Frontier section, 358; US Documentary Competition, 205; VR documentary at, 358
Super Size Me (Spurlock), 21, 25, 31n43, 94
surveillance, 220–21, 224, 243, 319n40; government, *34*, 45, 67, 228, 231, 234–36
suspicion: climate of, 195; hermeneutics of, 215–16
Sussex Records, 264
Swami, Praveen, 243
Swimmer, Saul, 267

Tabloid (Morris), 131, 188
The Take Away Show (WNYC Studios), 114, 141, 145–48, *147*, 153
Takepart survey, 91, 94–95, 97
"Tales of Sound and Fury" (Elsaesser), 242, 245
Talking Heads, 267, *268*
"Talk of the Town" (*New Yorker*), 129
Tarkovsky, Andrei, 167
technologies, 141, 145; acceleration of developments in, 87; algorithms, 332–33, 337; body aligned with cinematic apparatus, 35, 58; choice mechanic, 363–64; consumer-grade VR, 356–59; interactive, 87; laserdiscs, 161–63, *163*; military, 75, 78; motion picture, 76; music documentaries and, 152–53; portable cameras, 161; representational, 76; sight machines, 78–79; of war, 75–76
television: concerns about demise of, 122; globalization of market, 59; as traditional venue for documentaries, 23. See also public television
televisual documentary, 203–4
temporality, double, 97

Terrence Malick's City Symphony (Bateman), 159–60
Terry, Jennifer, 313–14
testimony, 187–88
Testimony (Kfir), 362, 362–63
text-based provocations, 299
theatrical distribution, 37
theatrical documentary, 143
Theodore, Mike, 263
They Shoot Pictures Don't They? website, 170
Thin (Greenfield), 179, 200, 201–5, 202, 214
The Thin Blue Line (Morris), 3, 118, 120, 184, 187, 188, 190, 222
13th (Duvernay), 226
Thomas, June, 347–48
Thompson, Josiah "Tink," 128–30, 135n28
360-degree video, 356–57, 368n1; visual field of, 359–60, 363, 365–66. *See also* virtual reality (VR); virtual reality (VR) documentary
thriller format, documentary, 8, 227–28, 250–51
Thurston, Matilda Calder, 285
time: double temporality of elegy, 97; needed to react, 79–80, 89
time-lapse cinematography, 7, 55, 56; in action, 82–85; camera equipment, 88; emotional impact of, 81–82, 84–85, 89; as representational technique, 80–82; slow violence and, 75–90; as technique for visualizing climate change, 76, 81. *See also* environmental documentary
Time magazine, 183
Titicut Follies (Wiseman), 40
Tongues Untied (Riggs), 42–43
topographical approach, 330
Toronto. *See* Hot Docs Canadian International Documentary Festival (Toronto)
Toronto Film Festival, 167
torture documentaries, 192
"Torture Documentaries" (Lesange), 192
Toscano, Alberto, 68–69, 70
"Trailblazers 2012" list (*Realscreen*), 27
trauma, 190–94, 204
travel, virtual, 55, 57–58
Trembling Before G-d (DuBowski), 225

Tribeca Film Festival, 358
A Trip Down Market Street before the Fire (Miles), 334
true crime documentaries, 8, 300, 340–55; activism of audience, 346, 353; affect/emotion and, 341, 345, 347–48; armchair jurors, 341, 345–49; complexity of vs. either/or solutions, 340–41, 352–53; contexts for crime in, 344; contradictory impulses of intrigue and discomfort, 350–52; critique of judicial system through, 340–41, 348–49, 349; docuseries, 343; emotional and intellectual engagement in, 349–53; example films, 344–45, 354n10; failed police investigations, 344–45; feature-length films, 343–44; fictionalized aspects of, 342, 346–47; history of true crime genre, 342–45; influence of extreme wealth on criminal process, 345; real-world impacts of, 346; reenactment in, 343, 345; reestablishment of surety of justice, 340, 350; replay's society's fear of crime, 352; television series, 343; tradition of genre, 340. *See also* criminal *in*justice
true crime genre: cathartic format, 343; fictionalized aspects of, 342; gory details described, with reassurances, 343, 350–51; law and order focus, 342–43; reenactments and interviews, 343, 345; television channels, 343
Trump, Donald, 43, 133, 299; "mother of all bombs" on YouTube, 309
Trump administration, 303; first one hundred days, 299, 305
trustworthiness, 4, 20–21, 186–88, 278, 284, 348, 352
truth, 4, 9, 104, 160; archival images and, 283; audience resistance to, 291; creativeness and, 278; government attacks on, 196; irony and, 187–88; mimetic-based claims, 303, 305; true crime genre and, 348
The Truth about Nanjing (Mizushima), 291
20 Feet from Stardom (Neville), 239, 259, 260, 267–70, 268
24 Davids (Baril), 20

The Umbrella Man (Morris), 128–29, 135n28
uncanny, 100

Underground (Wexler), 225
United Nations SDG (Sustainable Development Goals) Action Campaign, 363–64
United States: American Dream, 200, 201, 205, 209; decentralized public television, 38; disappearance/incarceration of African American men, 226; melodrama as dominant cultural mode in, 96, 106; testimony and confession in political documentary, 193; trauma era, 192
universalism, discourse of, 60, 62, 68
Universal Music Group, 259, 260
"unknown knowns," 119
The Unknown Known (Morris), 7, 179, 183, 196, 220
unpopularity, 7
unrepresentability, 281
Unsolved Mysteries (television series), 343, 344
Unstaged, 150, 153
unveiling, rhetoric of, 103–4, 106–7
UNVR, 363–64
"unwar film," 312–13
Uprising of '34 (Stoney, Helfand, and Rostock), 43
urban history, 324–25; city symphonies, 159–61, 174n3, 330; local histories, 326; process plates, 332; triumphalist canons, 326. *See also* "film events"
Urban History Commons project, 300
US Agency for Global Media, 43
USA Today, 123
US Library of Congress, 300
US Signal Corps films, 285–88, *286*
USS *Maddox*, 186

values, commodification of, 22–24
Valve, 358
Vancouver Never Plays Itself (Zhou and Ramos), 115, 165–68
Vautrin, Minnie, 284–85
Vector Institute (Soviet Union), 132
Venice Film Festival, 133
Veradero (illegal fishing boat), 250
vérité. *See* cinema vérité; feminist vérité
vernacular style, 141, 145, 154

vernacular sublime, 55, 68, 69
Vernallis, Carol, 145, 151
Vertov, Dziga, 122–23, 160, 330; *Man with a Movie Camera*, 161
Vevers, Richard, 86
Vevo, 114, 141, 150, 151
victim, tradition of, 241–42, 246–49, 251
video, internet, 139
videocassette recorders, 153
video compression, 141, 145
video essay, 157–77; auteurs and, 163–64, *164*; competition for viewership, 167, 170, 174; Criterion Collection, 114, 161–65, *163*; explanatory mode, 163; film as topic of, 165; poetic register, 163; supercuts and formal dissections, 158, 159, 162–63, *164*; videographic criticism, 114–15, 158–59. *See also* essay films
"Videographic Film Studies" (Grant, Vimeo channel), 171
video-on-demand venues, 37
videos, in newspapers, 123–24, 125–26
"video slogans," 314–15
Vietnam: A Television History (WGBH), 40
Vietnam War, 185–86, 190, 193
Vietnam War series (Burns), 39, 185–86
The Village Voice, 189
Vimeo, 114, 148
violence: acceleration as, 75, 79; against Black people, on social media, 312–13, *313*, 317; ethical looks at masculinist videos, 312–16; risk of reinscription, 280; virality as virility, 306–12; of vision, 78–79. *See also* slow violence
virality: critical internet studies on, 319n23, 319n24; as virility, 305, 306–12
Virilio, Paul, 75–76; *Speed and Politics*, 79; *War and Cinema*, 78–79
virtual reality (VR): "content aware fill" feature software, 367; expectation of normative viewing, 366–68; gaming and software industries, 358; head-mounted display (HMD), 356–57, 360, 366; human element effaced, 365–66; marketing of, 357–58; ontological status of images, 358–59. *See also* 360-degree video; virtual reality (VR) documentary

virtual reality (VR) documentary, 6, 153–54, 300–301, 356–69, 368; core skills of traditional documentary disrupted, 359; empathy and, 363–64; as "empathy machine," 301, 359; historical context lacking or suppressed, 357; social justice, 357, 358, 363–68; traditional documentary conventions in, 366; wide-angle lenses used, 359

visibility, 16, 56, 197n6, 221, 224; data visualization, 76, 80–84, 87; invisibility and aesthetics of failure, 235–36; maximum, 60; politics of, 312

Visible Evidence, 2

vision, technologies of, 57

visual activism, 56, 92

visual positivism, 357

voice, 186–88, 190

"The Voice of Documentary" (Nichols), 187

voice-of-God narrator, 149

voice-overs, 92–93, 103–4, 107, 209–11, 359; in *Citizenfour*, 234; irony and, 186–87; VR documentary and, 359

voyeurism, 247, 347, 352, 363–66; cameras handed to subjects as extension of, 364–65

"Voyeur Reality" (Hamilton), 363–64

VR for Good (Oculus), 358

Wajcman, Gérard, 280

Waldman, Diane, 213

Walker, Janet, 213

Wal-Mart, 94, 97

Walsh, John, 343

Waltz with Bashir (Folman), 180, 220, 225

war: aftereffects of, 78; first-person shooter logic of war footage, 313–14; food propaganda during, 101; images of as irresistible, 312–13; stages of, 132; technologies of, 75–76. *See also* World War II

War and Cinema (Virilio), 78–69

War on Terror, 196, 227

Warpaint (commercial production company), 26

Warren, Shilyh, 8, 179–80

War Trilogy (Morris), 7, 179, 183–84

Watergate scandal, 135n9

The Watermelon Woman (Dunye), 304

Watson, Paul, 250, 256n28

Waugh, Thomas, 220, 255n4

Waxman, Henry, 42

Weather Underground, 225

Web 2.0, 122, 126

Weill, Claudia, 214

Weitz, Chris, 175n21

Welles, Orson, 161, 167–68, 173–74

Western point of view, 65, 65–66

WGBH, 40

What Difference Does It Make? A Film about Making Music (Schmerberg), 152

What Makes a Video Essay Great (Lee), 173

Wheatley, Helen, 59

white femininity, 206–8

"white paper" documentary form, 36

white saviors, 243, 247, 253–54

The Who, 270

"Why We Fight" series (US Signal Corps), 285–88, *286*, *288*

Wiegman, Robyn, 215, 216

wildlife documentary, 251

Williams, Linda, 58, 60, 96, 97, 99, 106, 122, 245

Williams, Raymond, 4, 17, 18

Williams, Sherri, 312

Wilson, Joe, 44

Wilson, Robert, 284

Wilutzky, Dirk, 229

Winehouse, Amy, 259

Winter Soldier (Winterfilm Collective), 193

Winton, Ezra, 8, 13

Wintonick, Peter, 122–23

Wiseman, Frederick (Fred), 7, 20, 39, 40, 229; *Crazy Horse*, 20; *Titicut Follies*, 40

WNET, 47

The Woman's Film (San Francisco Newsreel), 214

women, success in documentary field, 201

Women Talking (Mackenzie), 215

Wonder, Stevie, 269

Wood, Robert, 120

Word Is Out (Adair, Phenix, et al), 225

World of Plenty (Rotha, 1947), 102–4, *103*

World War II, 3, 101, *101*; Holocaust, 280–81, 293n19. *See also* Nanking Massacre (Rape of Nanking, 1937)

Wormwood (Morris, Netflix Original docudrama), 117–21, *118*, 126, 131, 132, 182–83, 196, 197n9

The Wrap, 348, 349

XL Catlin Seaview Survey, 86, 88

Yale University Divinity School Library, 282
Yes Men, 226
The Yes Men Are Revolting (Vamos, Servin, Nix), 226
The Yes Men Fix the World (Vamos, Servin, Engfehr), 226
The Yes Men (Ollman, Price, Smith), 226
You Are There (UNVR), 364
Young, Alison, 300, 348, 349–50, 352–53
YouTube, 37; activist media on, 304; *Brows Held High*, 168; copyright policy, 166–67, 170; *Every Frame a Painting*, 165–66; first-person shooter logic of war footage, 313–14; *Home*, 55, 58, 62–64, *63*, 67, 69; "mother of all bombs" videos, *309*; PBS, 49; Philando Castile videos, *313*; popularity as organizing structure, 309–10; Russian-funded sites, *308*; supercuts and formal dissections, 158, *159*; *Vancouver Never Plays Itself* (Zhou and Ramos), 115, 165–68; Vevo, 150; "video slogans," 314–15
Yudie (Bank), 214

Zarzycka, Marta, 313
Zero Days (Gibney), 220, 225
Zhou, Tony, 115, 165, *173*
Zuckerberg, Mark, 360–61, *361*, 367, 369n11, 369n12

www.ingramcontent.com/pod-product-compliance
Lightning Source LLC
Chambersburg PA
CBHW020827160426
43192CB00007B/552